CARDANO'S COSMOS

CARDANO'S COSMOS

The Worlds and Works of a Renaissance Astrologer

Anthony GRAFTON

HARVARD UNIVERSITY PRESS
CAMBRIDGE, MASSACHUSETTS
LONDON, ENGLAND

Printed in the United States of America
Second printing, 2001

First Harvard University Press paperback edition, 2001

A version of this book was published in German
in 1999 by Berlin Verlag as *Cardanos Kosmos: Die Welten und Werke eines Renaissance-Astrologen*

Library of Congress Cataloging-in-Publication Data

Grafton, Anthony,
Cardano's cosmos : the worlds and works of a Renaissance astrologer / Anthony Grafton.
p. cm.
Includes bibliographical references (p.) and index.
ISBN 0-674-09555-3 (cloth)
ISBN 0-674-00670-4 (pbk.)
1. Cardano, Girolamo, 1501-1576—Contributions in astrology.
2. Astrology—History. I. Title.
B785.C34G73 1999
133.5'092—dc21 99-30238

Designed by Gwen Nefsky Frankfeldt

To the memory of Charles Schmitt

CONTENTS

ILLUSTRATIONS

PREFACE

THIS BOOK represents the end of a long and immensely challenging journey. My interest in astrology was first kindled by Noel Swerdlow while I was still an undergraduate at the University of Chicago. He also first put a copy of Cardano's *100 Genitures* into my hands, collaborated with me on a series of studies in ancient beliefs about dates and calendars, and has taught me a vast amount. Peter Brown and Glenn Most, the original pied pipers of Princeton's Group for the Study of Late Antiquity, induced me to return to the classical tradition in divination and gave me invaluable materials as a reward. Throughout the later 1980s and early 1990s, I collected material about Renaissance astrology in general, and Cardano in particular, whenever my researches on chronology allowed.

The Wissenschaftskolleg zu Berlin, which invited me to devote the year 1993–94 to research, made it possible at last for me to spend several months of uninterrupted study on Cardano. This book rests chiefly on the close reading of his major works that I carried out in Berlin. Support from the Ecole des Hautes Etudes en Sciences Sociales, in Paris; the Internationales Forschungszentrum Kulturwissenschaften, in Vienna; the Dibner Institute, which invited me to spend most of summer 1997 in Cambridge, Massachusetts; and the Institute for Advanced Studies of the Hebrew University, in Jerusalem, enabled me to devote short periods to further research. My thanks go to the directors and staffs of these humane institutions; also to the authorities of the libraries in which I worked: the Firestone Library of Princeton University; the Huntington Library and Art Gallery; the Biblioteca Apostolica Vaticana; the Folger Shakespeare Library; the libraries of the Free University of Berlin and the Preussische Staatsbibliothek zu Berlin; the Niedersächsische Staats- und Universitätsbibliothek, Göttingen;

the Bibliothèque Nationale de France; the Warburg Institute; the National and University Library, Jerusalem; the Staats- und Universitätsbibliothek Carl von Ossietzky, Hamburg; the Herzog August Bibliothek, Wolfenbüttel; the Bayerische Staatsbibliothek, Munich; and, above all, the Bodleian Library.

My warmest thanks of all go to those of my fellow scholars who gave me their advice, encouragement, and criticism—especially my colleagues at the Wissenschaftskolleg, David Güggerli and François Hartog; my fellow students of Renaissance astrology, Paola Zambelli and the late Pierre Brind'Amour; and the late Thomas Kuhn. Audiences at the Wissenschaftskolleg, the Free University of Berlin, Harvard University, Princeton University, the University of Delaware, and the University of Frankfurt listened and responded to early presentations of my theses. My friend Thomas Kaufmann and several generations of undergraduate students in the European Cultural Studies Program at Princeton University helped to shape many of the arguments put forth here. So did the remarkable class of graduate students in art history with whom I had the good fortune to work at Columbia University in fall 1996. Many individual Princeton students have taught me an immense amount about one or more of the subjects touched on here, but I owe a special debt to Claudia Brosseder, Cynthia Cupples, Katharine Gill, Bill North, Grant Parker, and Megan Williams.

Ian Maclean not only set a new standard with his own work on Cardano, but also chastened some of my wilder theories. Nancy Siraisi allowed me to read her own exemplary book on Cardano as a medical man, *The Clock and the Mirror,* long in advance of publication. More generously still, she read and castigated every page of this work in an early draft. I owe her more than I can say. Jorge Cañízares and Lauren Tamar Kassell provided immensely useful commentaries on the whole text. So did the two anonymous referees consulted by Harvard University Press, who produced trenchant and helpful readings. My fellow historians of the emotions in Jerusalem—especially Gadi Algazi, Natalie Zemon Davis, and Rudolf Dekker—offered bracing last-minute criticism. Larry Kim, Peter Knecht, Annette Wunschel, Lindsay Waters, and Nancy Clemente performed the final alchemy that made a manuscript into a book. My thanks to all.

CARDANO'S COSMOS

chapter one

THE MASTER OF TIME

At some point in the mid-1570s, François d'Amboise came to Rome to see ruins and celebrities. Among the men that he visited was Girolamo Cardano—a world-famous natural philosopher, doctor, and mathematician, who had come to Rome after being tried, and condemned for a time to house arrest, by the Inquisition. Though forbidden to teach publicly, Cardano worked hard: he spent time with the leading doctors in the city and wrote a lurid, meticulously detailed autobiography, a strikingly unrepentant apology for his own life. The room he lived in was as characteristic of him as the texts he wrote. Instead of pictures, the walls bore banners with the phrase TEMPVS MEA POSSESSIO—"Time is my possession." The old man who raked his fingers through the embers of a life's hot fires saw himself as the master of time itself.[1]

In one sense, the autobiographer is always the master of time, the recorder who imposes shape and direction on events that, as experienced, usually lacked both. But sixteenth-century writers more often depicted time as a threatening, autonomous figure than as a plastic body of material awaiting the artist who could give it form. Embodied in myth as Cronos, the threatening ancient god who had devoured his own children, time leveled magnificent buildings and destroyed great reputations, changing Rome itself—as another French traveler, the philosopher Michel de Montaigne, mused a few years later—so much that its original inhabitants could not have recognized it.[2] Analyzed in pragmatic terms as an endless series of momentary opportunities for action, promising occasions for investments, voyages, and lawsuits, time called for continual attentiveness. In its seeming triviality, it escaped the control of the dilettante who missed his appointments and deadlines. But it rewarded the continual attention of the mature man who began each day by working out a list of necessary appointments and actions in his diary, and ended it by checking that he had carried out each task on time. "My sons, you must observe the time"—so the old practical merchant, Giannozzo degli Alberti, warned his young relatives in Leon Battista Alberti's dialogues *On the Family,* telling them at Polonian length that hurry was a sure sign of incompetence and levity.[3] No one showed more sensitivity than Cardano to time in both its formidable aspects: "But what is time?" he asked in his massive work *On Subtlety.* "While nothing ever belongs to it, everything is still in it, and it is omnipresent. It both generates everything and kills everything. It is the author of life and death. As the expectation of it is very long, so the memory of it is very short. Though it always accompanies us, we never recognize it. And though there is so much of it, it can never be repaired. Hence its loss is more serious and more trivial than that of any other thing."[4] Cardano knew, if anyone did, how hard time was to understand and control.

Cardano, moreover, had had a taxing, and sometimes a bruising, passage through the time of his own life—a life which combined professional success with personal disasters. He was born in Pavia on 24 September 1501 and grew up in and around Milan. In the later fifteenth century, Milan had been a wealthy, economically expanding, and powerful state. It was ruled by one of Italy's great families, the Sforza, whose patronage Leonardo da Vinci and many other artists and intellectuals actively sought. But by the time of Cardano's adulthood, in the 1520s, Milan and its Lombard hinterland had become a battleground fought over by vast French and Imperial armies, repeatedly struck by plague and other disasters, poorer and less powerful than it had once been. After a period of French rule the city passed into the hands of the Holy Roman Emperor Charles V, who appointed a viceroy to administer it. Unlike Florence and Venice in the same period, accordingly, Milan had ceased to be an intellectual center: the once-flourishing Milanese publishing industry, for example, though it still functioned, no longer produced many products ambitious enough to compete with those of the Roman and Venetian presses.[5]

Cardano—who even as an adolescent had shuddered at the prospect of dying unknown—did his best to move into the professional and intellectual elite.[6] He studied in Pavia and Padua: after a very difficult early career, he taught with some success and considerable notoriety, first at Pavia and later at Bologna. He became one of the creators of modern algebra and even of modern technology, devising what Europeans still call "le cardan" or "das Kardangelenk," the universal joint. Eventually these achievements—as well as the many bitter public quarrels in which Cardano became involved—

won attention not only in Lombardy, but across Europe. Cardano's books sold well. Some, like his encyclopedic *De subtilitate,* not only became best-sellers but also received the highest literary compliments of the period, ferocious attack and shameless plagiarism. The most prominent natural philosophers of the sixteenth and early seventeenth centuries mentioned and cited him regularly. He even received and accepted an invitation to travel to far-off Paris—and later, to distant and barbarous Edinburgh—to provide medical advice for John Hamilton, the last Catholic archbishop of St. Andrews. Cardano saved the archbishop's life, receiving an enormous honorarium and giving his lucky client fifteen more years to enjoy before Protestants executed him.[7]

Cardano's life could supply material for several kinds of imaginative writing. In his youth he played the role of the protagonist of a historical novel in the gaudiest purple style of the nineteenth century. One day—as he told the story, much later, in his autobiography—Cardano gambled with a Venetian. Realizing that his opponent was cheating, he forced his way out of the house, recovering his money on the way. Cardano then wandered the streets for some hours, frightened of discovery. Trying to board a ship, he stumbled on the gangway and fell into a canal—while wearing the full armor he had donned in case of trouble. The relief he felt when the crew of a boat pulled him out of the water turned to horror when he recognized the ship's captain as his opponent of the morning. But the captain decided to help him, presumably since he too wanted no trouble with the notoriously strict Venetian authorities.[8] By contrast, as an old man, Cardano played the part of the hero of a tragedy or opera—perhaps a Lear. He raged and mourned when his older son, Giambattista, a gifted doctor in his own right, was arrested, tried, convicted, and executed for murdering his wife with a focaccia laced with arsenic, and when his younger son, Aldo, turned out to be a ne'er-do-well and petty thief.

But Cardano found his best part as a middle-aged man, when he became the hero of a university novel in the style of David Lodge. As an important professor, Cardano devised many of the customs and practices of modern academic life. He drew up, for example, a list of the seventy-three important writers who had cited him or mentioned him with praise.[9] Cardano's list became in its turn a model for many later scholars' autobiographies and biographies, which followed him in documenting their subjects' reception in detail. He thus deserves the credit (or blame) for inventing a device usually regarded as a creation of modern sociology of science, the citation index. Cardano even anticipated many of the new scientific and literary possibilities offered by the computer. To readers of *On Subtlety,* he offered an easy recipe for editing a piece of writing. Simply take two copies of the written text, cut them up into sections, and try them in new sequences until satisfied. Glue the results into a stout notebook made of cardboard and give it to the publisher.[10] Anyone who reads two texts, or two versions of one text, by Cardano will see at once how seriously he took his own advice—and how well he would have used the merge function of a personal computer.

Cardano regularly revealed the vanity that marks all great professors. He wrote not one, but four versions of his autobiography, as well as four analyses of his own horoscope. He interpreted the myth of Narcissus in a novel way: the youth who fell in love with his own reflection in the water stood for the scholar who lost himself in pleasure reading his own work. Cardano prided himself on the fact that beautiful women regularly loved and stroked him—at least in the virtual form of his own books ("women read too," he reminded his imagined, presumably male, gentle reader).[11] Like all good heroes of satirical novels, Cardano paid the price, and more than the price, for his posturing. In 1557 he became the object of the most savage book review in the bitter annals of literary invective. Julius Caesar Scaliger, another vain and articulate natural philosopher of Italian origins, devoted more than nine hundred quarto pages to refuting one of Cardano's books, *On Subtlety*, and promised to return to the subject at still greater length. Though Scaliger died without producing more than a fragment of this promised polemic, his *Exercitationes* became a standard work in university curriculums—perhaps the only book review ever known to undergo transformation into a textbook.[12]

In his last years, finally, Cardano faced the Inquisition. Having already ceased to teach in the vain hope of propitiating the Inquisitor of Bologna, he found himself first imprisoned, then held under house arrest, and finally condemned, in 1571, to abjure his heretical views. He promised to refrain from publishing or teaching in the Papal States, and though he dedicated himself, in his last years, to producing a set of corrections to his earlier works, he never received permission to print his self-castigations.[13] Cardano's *Autobiography* itself—the most widely read of his writings—may well represent a further effort to purge himself of suspicion. If so, this detailed and sometimes lurid account of his supernatural gifts and his dealings with spirits can hardly have had its intended effect.[14]

As Cardano faced the task of setting all of this experience into order, however, he applied the tools of a discipline expressly designed to describe the sinuous course of time past and foretell the bumps and swerves of time yet to come: astrology. Astrologers used the movements of the sun, the moon, and the five known planets, Mercury, Venus, Mars, Jupiter, and Saturn, to predict and explicate both the collective history of the human race and myriad individual histories of health and disease. Cardano was a master astrologer who performed all the normal services astrologers offered and contributed to all the normal genres of astrological writing. In this book I will examine Cardano's own lifelong efforts to use the stars to find the order in the apparent chaos of his own life and the world in which he lived it.

No study of Cardano—or of any astrologer in premodern Europe—can limit itself to examining what he wrote. In practicing astrology, as Cardano regularly said, he did not create a new discipline but drew on and tried to reform a very old one—one of the oldest disciplines still in widespread use today. For two and a half millennia, in fact, astrologers have worked in ways that clearly reveal deep continuities in assumptions and methods. The oldest individual horoscopes now extant were created in Mesopotamia in the fifth century B.C.E. and after, probably by the very same Babylonians who devised the first known form of mathematical astronomy. The most recent horoscopes drawn up by scientists were the work of the most technically advanced natural philosophers in seventeenth-century Rome and London.[15] Though no modern university in Europe or the United States has a department of astrology, the art still flourishes across the Western world. Elegant occult bookshops from Geneva to Pasadena purvey astrology in all of its varied flavors, while the readers of tabloid newspapers around the world enjoy the very primitive form of it that appears, along with much practical advice, in the so-called daily horoscope.[16]

Any historian who attempts to study an individual segment of this long history must repeatedly risk mistaking traditional, and even ancient, ideas and methods for new ones. For the historian of classical astrology confronts a tradition that lasted many centuries, one that combined remarkable flexibility in application with a durable commitment to a recognizably uniform set of ideas and techniques, which reached their canonical form as early as the Hellenistic age. The astrologers of Rome in the time of Cicero, the astrologers of Baghdad in the age of Harun ar-Rashid, and the astrologers of Nuremberg in the generation of Albrecht Dürer worked from the same cosmological premises, projected the same beneficent and threatening images into the heavens, and used for the most part the same mathematical techniques. But they worked for radically different societies and clients, and in radically different institutional and professional settings.[17] The historian must somehow do justice to both the durability and the flexibility of the tradition: must combine an appreciation of astrology's long life as a single, identifiable enterprise with an awareness of the continual transformation of the social worlds it served and the techniques and ideas of which it consisted.[18]

The continuity of the astrological tradition is, perhaps, unmatched in the intellectual history of the West. All astrologers—whether in ancient Babylon or Hitler's Munich—assume that they understand the language of the stars, that they possess a set of rules which enable them to decipher the book of the heavens. This analogy may sound very modern, even modish. Current intellectual fashion dictates the comparison of events to texts. Efforts to interpret all systems of symbols as languages flourish wildly: original recent books have shed new light on the languages of politics, of flowers, and of clothing.[19] But in the case of astrology, the analogy itself forms part of a long-established tradition. Giovanni Gioviano Pontano, who published his treatise *On Celestial Things* in 1512, argued explicitly that the language of the stars conformed in all essential ways to the language of humans. The letters of the Roman alphabet, he pointed out, elegantly adapting an ancient metaphor, could be combined in thousands of ways to form new words. Very simple alterations in spelling caused major changes in sense. The adjective *avidus,* for example, readily becomes the more intense *avidior, avidior* becomes the still more intensive *avidissimus,* and *avidissimus,* in its turn, sinks down to become *avidulus* after only minor surgery. Every transformation of the sign transforms its meaning.[20]

Stars and planets, Pontano argued, formed the letters of a cosmic alphabet. Clear, simple attributes—color, external appearance, speed and direction of motion—expressed the character and revealed the influence of the individual planets. The red color that supposedly characterized Mars, for example, revealed its hot, dry, warlike nature. Every planet had not only its own qualities, moreover, but also its allies and opponents among the other planets, the stars, and the degrees and signs of the Zodiac. A taxonomic grid that took both qualities and relationships into account enabled the astrologer to establish a full set of qualities for each celestial body and place. Venus, as Mars's chief opponent, necessarily had the opposed qualities, cold and wetness.

Every planet, in other words, played the role of a letter with defined qualities. Every astrologically significant configuration of two or more planets—for example, when two of them met, or came into conjunction—resembled a word or a phrase, the sense of which the astrologer could determine. The conjunction of Venus and Mars, a beneficent and a maleficent planet, offers a relatively simple case in point. Every astrologer knew that in this case Venus would overcome her brother, since love is stronger than anger. This

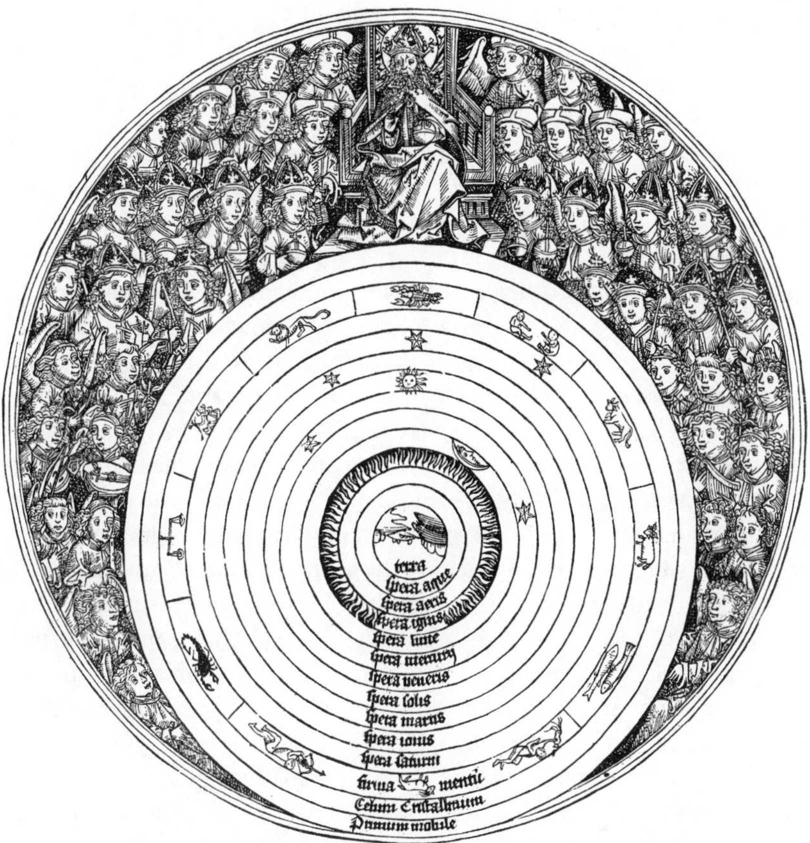

Figure 1 The astrologer's cosmos. At the center are the four elements—earth, air, water, and fire—which form the habitable world and all its minerals, vegetables, and animals. Outside the imperfect and changeable realm of the elements, which reaches up to the sphere of the moon, revolve the planets, embedded in crystalline spheres: the moon, Mercury, Venus, the sun, Mars, Jupiter, and Saturn. Outside the sphere of Saturn, the most distant of the planets, appear the signs of the Zodiac. And outside the celestial spheres appear the nine orders of angels and the Heavenly Father.

apparently simple principle inspired both the philosopher Marsilio Ficino, who discussed it in a splendid set-piece in his commentary on Plato's *Symposium,* and the artist Sandro Botticelli, who embodied it, in a spectacularly erotic form, in his panel painting *Mars and Venus,* now in the National Gallery, London.[21]

European astrologers made use not only of this celestial hermeneutics, which came originally from Mesopotamia, but also of a cosmology, which came originally from Greece. According to the scheme first laid out by Plato and then elaborately developed by Aristotle and others, often in ways that Plato would have found unacceptable, the universe has two main parts: the upper realm of the celestial spheres, which revolve around the earth, and the lower realm of the four elements. In the upper realm, "tout n'est qu'ordre et beauté, luxe, calme et volupté." The stars and the planets, embedded in crystalline spheres, make the unchanging music of eternity. In the lower realm, by contrast, things and creatures composed of the four elements—earth, air, fire, and water—are born and grow, become old and die. Down here, things change incessantly; the elements play an unending drama, which seems to have no clear script. But that which is complete, does not change, and moves in a uniform way is higher than that which changes. And the higher rightly rules the lower. Accordingly, the music of the spheres in the upper realm extends its influence to the living creatures in the lower realm. They dance to it—at least to the limited and imperfect extent allowed by the messy and changeable matter of which they consist. The cosmology justified the hermeneutics. It explained, as dozens of manuals and lecture courses patiently made clear, why the astrologer could infer from the smooth and predictable movements of the planets the jerky and uneven future movements of plants, animals, and humans on earth.[22]

The astrologer, finally, also relied on a set of mathematical data and techniques, which combined the methods and discoveries of Mesopotamian and Greek astronomers and astrologers with those of some of their successors. Astronomical tables enabled astronomers and astrologers to predict the future movements of the planets and their astrologically significant positions with reasonable accuracy. Astronomical instruments—above all the astrolabe—made it possible to fix the times of births and other vital events with precision. Astrologers used these techniques to lay out the positions of the signs of the Zodiac and the planets at a significant moment: that of the birth or conception of a client, for example. They also used them to identify the ascendant, or degree of the Zodiac which was rising over the horizon at the moment of birth, and to divide the Zodiac, locating the four cardinal points and delimiting the twelve segments, called houses, which defined the effects of planetary influence. The positions of the planets in these determined, in succession, how long clients would live, what talents they would possess, and how much they would prosper. Most frequently of all, at least in early modern times, astrologers used a simplified set of computations to determine what influence the planets would exercise at a particularly important moment in a client's life, or to help the client choose a course of action. Short-term predictions about marriage, investment, prescriptions of drugs, and proscriptions from politics could thus rest on a sound quantitative basis.[23]

Astrologers' tasks varied widely. The most intellectually ambitious practitioners of the art used astrological principles to investigate world history. The simple fact that Saturn and Jupiter reach conjunction every twenty years, for example, could become a sort of ground bass for world history as a whole. Persian, Jewish, Arabic, and European astrologers in turn used it to fix and account for the great turning points in world history, like the rise of new religions, and to predict history's end.[24] Pierre D'Ailly, a Frenchman, set this quite correctly—in a special, French sense—in C.E. 1789.[25] Ordinary astrologers erected figures—drew up charts of the heavens for a given instant—by the thousands, working out the prospects for an immediate cure for any ailment from lovesickness to housemaid's knee.[26] The most central and challenging task of the skilled astrologer remained the same, however, over the centuries and millennia: to draw up the genitures—charts of the heavens at the moment of an individual's birth—that would explain how celestial influences formed the character of individual people, cities, and countries, as the hot seal stamps the wax.

The long-term similarities between ancient and early modern astrology extend beyond the realm of theory and technique. Any historian who wants to study the social history of astrology in the Renaissance should begin with a marvelous book about Hellenistic Egypt: Franz Cumont's *L'Egypte des astrologues.* Here, "stripped of all astrology," appears a world of clients appealing to the astrologer for advice and help in a wide range of personal and public situations—one that matches, with surprising precision, the range of situations in which Renaissance astrologers also carried out their jobs.[27] In Egypt and other lands around the ancient Mediterranean, as in Italy and other lands around the same sea fifteen hundred years later, astrologers counseled all orders of society. Emperors and princes, merchants and housewives took advice from them. In Egypt as in Italy, a cosmic religion became intermingled with the older official cult. The proud Leonora of Aragon refused to pray until the Ferrarese court astrologer Pellegrino Prisciani explained to her that she should imitate the kings of Greece (whom he did not identify further). They prayed, Prisciani told her, when the moon reached conjunction with Jupiter and other necessary conditions were fulfilled, which explained why they always obtained their wishes.[28] In Egypt as in Italy, finally, the astrologer determined codes of conduct for situations ranging from great public events to individual decisions about careers and marriages. The government of the Florentine Republic, a bastion of early political rationality, whenever possible gave its generals their batons of command at astrologically sanctioned moments.[29] Leonello d'Este, a tasteful and erudite prince, the prize pupil of Guarino of Verona, made his wardrobe decisions astrologically. Every day he wore clothes of a color chosen to draw down favorable planetary influences.[30]

In Renaissance Europe as in Hellenistic Egypt, the omnipresence of astrology refutes any efforts to draw firm distinctions between high and low, elite and popular culture. Dürer drew on astrological images and ideas in his subtle and erudite *Melencolia I,* a mysterious engraving which he aimed at a small, refined public of humanists. But he also did so in his simple broadsides, which he produced for the ordinary men and women in the marketplace (where, indeed, his wife sold them).[31] The preserved horoscopes and textbooks of astrology mirror the hopes and expectations, anxieties and terrors of a whole society—as Dürer's particular images mirrored his own dreams, which were permeated in their turn with astrological images.

At the most abstract level, astrologers ancient and early modern carried out the tasks that twentieth-century society assigns to the economist. Like the economist, the astrologer tried to bring the chaotic phenomena of everyday life into order by fitting them to sharply defined quantitative models. Like the economist, the astrologer insisted, when teaching or writing for professional peers, that astrology had only a limited ability to predict the future. Formally speaking, after all, astrology concerned itself with the interplay of general forces rather than the outcome of a single configuration of them. The very number of questions that could be posed about any given horoscope ran into the thousands, ensuring that any given prediction had a tentative character.[32] Like the economist, the astrologer proved willing in practice, when powerful clients demanded it, to predict individual outcomes anyhow. Like the economist, the astrologer generally found that the events did not match the prediction; and like the economist, the astrologer normally received as a reward for this confirmation of the powers of his art a better job and a higher salary.

Like the economist, finally, the astrologer became the butt of universal criticism—and still proved indispensable. Even the sharpest critics of astrology did not escape the pull of this ubiquitous science. The shrewd, pragmatic historian Francesco Guicciardini ridiculed astrologers, as he did his friend Machiavelli, since he held that the human intellect could not possibly predict the tangled future course of social and political life, whether it relied on astrological or on political forms of analysis. He pointed out, as another hard-bitten Florentine political figure, Coluccio Salutati, had pointed out before him, that the astrologers flourished because of a psychological condition, a confirmation bias, that they shared with their clients. Both remembered only the astrologers' successes, the predictions that came out correctly. Their far more frequent errors were simply forgotten. Guicciardini took the popularity of the astrologers as clear proof of the fallibility of the human intellect (something he never hesitated to assert).[33] For centuries, Guicciardini, like Luther, enjoyed the reputation of having seen through the most widespread delusion of his culture. Recently, however, Raffaella Castagnola has published Guicciardini's own geniture, using a wide range of other documents to set it into context. The historian, like the contemporaries he mocked, consulted a specialist astrologer. He had his horoscope drawn up by Ramberto Malatesta, a nobleman who retired to Florence after murdering his wife and losing his possessions to a popular revolt. Guicciardini and Malatesta evidently knew one another well, to judge from the details of his character that Malatesta described, and he seems to have studied Malatesta's predictions with some care.[34] The cleareyed cynic was no more rigorous in his rejection of astrology than the fools born every minute around him. Nowadays no one escapes the terrestrial economy; in the sixteenth century, as in the Hellenistic and Roman world, no one escaped the celestial economy.

For all these similarities, however, the astrology of the Renaissance was more than a simple revival of its classical forerunner. The astrological tradition does not form a seamless whole. The social context within which astrologers work changed radically between antiquity and the Renaissance, and their own activities changed with the times, especially as their art grew in popularity and sophistication from the twelfth century onward. The astrologers of the Renaissance and their enemies could use new media, for example, which no ancient writer could have imagined. As astrology became the object of new forms of publication, as these in turn reached new strata of partly educated and uneducated readers, the ancient art became the object of a strikingly modern form of public debate.

The content, as well as the context, of astrology underwent major changes in the course of time. Astrology resembles a glacier. It consists of several different strata and forms of material; it moves constantly, if imperceptibly; it rubs continually, and noisily, against other materials of very different kinds; and it reveals many fissures and crevasses on close inspection. Central doctrines of Renaissance astrology—like that of the great conjunctions of Saturn and Jupiter—did not have classical origins. Central relationships between astrology and other predictive disciplines took on new forms in the early modern world. In antiquity, astrologers and medical men competed, as representatives of separate arts. Ptolemy, who wrote the one technically informed and systematic handbook of astrology that survives from the ancient world, compared medicine and astrology, admitting that they served somewhat similar ends. But he also emphasized the differences between the kinds of specialized knowledge they had to offer.[35] Even in antiquity, as one would expect, astrologers and doctors borrowed ideas and techniques from one another (Ptolemy himself praised the Egyptians for unifying medicine and astrology). In the Middle Ages, in both the Islamic and the European worlds, many tried to combine the two arts. Italian universities "of arts and medicine" offered formal courses in astrology, as one of the liberal arts most likely to be useful to a medical man. Doctors often competed with astrologers to draw up horoscopes, since they had learned to do so at university, and clients sometimes asked for astrological as well as medical counsel. Some medical men even tried to apply the precise, quantitative methods of astrology in medical practice.[36] Medical practitioners played a prominent role in Symon de Phares' late-fifteenth-century list of astrologers who had attained worldly success.[37] At the same time, however, debate ranged over whether particular illnesses were best accounted for on medical or astrological grounds. Both the Black Death of 1348 and the supposed advent of syphilis just before 1500 stimulated astrologers and doctors to direct polemical treatises against one another's explanatory claims.[38]

Sometimes the development of astrological doctrines and practices followed directions that ancient thinkers would never have expected. Some medical men—like Ficino and Paracelsus—went so far as to treat astrology as the core of medical doctrine, a central source of reliable therapies and dietetic advice.[39] Some philosophers—like Pietro Pomponazzi—went so far as to treat astrology as a universal causal explanation for all physical processes in the universe—including the effects of prayers.[40] Meanwhile, others tried to expose astrology as a tissue of fraud and error. Giovanni Pico della Mirandola, for example, framed a brilliant, systematic critique of astrology, which rested on a set of assumptions and methods radically different from those of the older anti-astrological polemics of Cicero and some Fathers of the Church. As professionalized medicine based on university study came to play a larger and larger role in the everyday life of the social elite, assessments of the power and value of astrology were urgently needed—for example, by the royal relatives and counselors who had to treat rulers and princes whom they had come to see as mentally ill, rather than demonically possessed.[41] The nature and level of the Renaissance debate about astrology, in short, were as novel as the public it reached and the media that fostered its development.

Distinguished cultural historians have devised some powerful models with which to explain the nature and impact of early modern astrology. The cultural historian Aby Warburg saw astrology as a vital, but also a dangerous, part of the classical tradition. It embodied in his eyes something like a perpetual Dionysiac temptation to throw off the burden of personal responsibility, to ascribe control over one's emotions and actions to superior, malevolent forces. Every thinker of the Renaissance had to struggle with this dark power in order to win the space for free thought that creative activities require. Ernst Cassirer took this last point further, showing that the systematic character of astrology in fact created room for innovative thinking. Pomponazzi used astrology to develop a radically new vision of the universe, one in which the same powers pervaded and ruled the celestial and the physical world, continuously and without interference—an absolutist astrological cosmology quite alien to the astrological tradition itself.[42] Michel Foucault, by contrast, portrayed Renaissance astrology as a revealing example of the ways in which a particular "épistémé"—a system of rules as grandiose, dark, and subterranean as a Piranesi prison—controlled the thought and writing of a whole epoch. No philosopher or scientist could escape the cage of assumptions that confined them, compelling them to see themselves, and all other natural beings, as controlled by a network of higher and lower forces, as prisoners writhing in a sticky web of influences.[43] Keith Thomas, finally, emphasized the social role, rather than the technical content, of astrology. In his view, the fragile environmental and social situation of early modern people largely explained their fascination with astrology and other nonrational forms of predictive magic. Fire, flood and famine, human and animal infertility threatened everyone, the rich as well as the poor. No rational means of predicting or preventing such events existed. Yet their effects pervaded society, making it difficult to preserve families and their property over the generations and turning cities into so many demographic black holes, into which endless numbers of poor immigrants were sucked, often with lethal results. Insurance, which rested on statistical, rather than celestial, measurements, came into being only in the seventeenth century—and only after astrology and the other occult arts had lost their cultural value. In earlier periods, only the astrologer could use the best quantitative methods of the time to predict the future and offer useful counsels for averting risk and exploiting opportunities.[44]

Each of these models emphasizes a vital aspect of astrology. Each of them also complements the others. But if all are necessary, none is sufficient. Warburg never accepted that astrology was, in its own way, a great achievement of classical reason: that it, like geography and medicine, represented one of the great taxonomic disciplines of the Hellenistic and early Imperial periods.[45] Cassirer, who did understand Renaissance astrology in this way, intensively studied the discipline's theoretical foundations but took little interest in its practice. Foucault never admitted, though he certainly knew, that the astrology and natural philosophy of the early modern period contained basic assumptions and procedures taken directly from earlier sources—an admission that has radical consequences for his method. Thomas, who for the first time shed real light on the social background of early modern astrology, could not do full justice at the same time to the richness and complexity of early modern astrology as an intellectual system, especially as this reached its fullest development outside England.

Where cultural and social historians have emphasized the relations between astrology and its wider environment, historians of the exact sciences have traced the internal history of the field. Otto Neugebauer, David Pingree, Bernard Goldstein, Francesca Rochberg-Halton, Alexander Jones, and others have reconstructed the long-term history of astrological doctrines and practices in depth and detail. They have separated the historical layers of the astrological tradition. They have identified the techniques to be found in particular horoscopes, treatises, and commentaries. And they have published and analyzed a vast number of astrological documents.[46] By applying similar techniques to the astrological histories and horoscope collections of the later Middle Ages and the Renaissance, John North has laid the technical foundations on which any study of Renaissance astrology must rest.[47] These studies have brought out, as less technical ones could not, the intellectual seriousness, internal consistency, and richness of much astrological thought. But they have tended to say less about the social and cultural uses of astrology. Cardano, as we will see, was continually attentive to such issues, and his own work rewards attention at least as much for what it reveals of his context as for its own technical content. A sort of triangulation, accordingly, is needed—a form of analysis that moves between the internal and the contextual, losing neither from view and letting neither dominate.

Happily, a number of scholars have provided models for this kind of study as well. Valerie Flint's magisterial investigation of magic and religion in the early Middle Ages shows in detail how church authorities both condemned and accommodated the ancient art of divination from the heavens.[48] Paola Zambelli has carried out precise case studies, enriched by archival material of great interest, in astrological practice in Renaissance Italy and Germany—studies which pay due heed both to the astrological techniques used by their protagonists and to the larger surroundings in which they employed them.[49] C. H. Josten and Ann Geneva have traced in crisp detail, drawn from the incomparably rich astrological manuscripts of the Bodleian Library, the lives and worlds of seventeenth-century English astrologers.[50] Germana Ernst has expertly analyzed the astrological theories of Tommaso Campanella, whose stormy career as public prophet involved the use of astrology both to foment a revolution in south Italy, which failed, and to imagine a perfect society, which many readers still find provocative.[51] Jean Dupèbe and the late Pierre Brind'Amour have reconstructed with deep erudition and pitiless clarity the practices, economic and technical, of the most notorious of all Renaissance astrologers, Nostradamus himself—who emerges as a brilliant charlatan, in the terms of his own time as well as ours.[52] Their work—like that of the other scholars I have mentioned—informs many pages of the present study.

Each encounter with an earlier scholar has left its impress on this work. Warburg's interpretation of astrology revealed gaps on close inspection, but his work remains the fullest and most insightful recreation of the ways in which Renaissance intellectuals exchanged and discussed astrological information. The early Foucault of *Les mots et les choses* provided poor guidance into the mind of the Renaissance astrologer, but the later Foucault of *Le souci de soi* afforded remarkable insights into the aims of his everyday practice.[53] Keith Thomas' work shaped this study of an astrologer and astrology very different from those whom he analyzed.

I wanted to do justice to both the rationalism and the irrationality of Renaissance astrology, to both its traditional and its novel contents, to both its ancient sources and its modern social role. I wanted to ask if the astrologers of the Renaissance, who occupied themselves in part with reading and commenting on ancient texts, might have something to contribute to the interpretation of ancient astrology—if they might help us set the seemingly dry works of Ptolemy and Firmicus into a more fully articulated social and cultural context, which could help to restore their human interest. Above all, I wanted to be surprised. I wanted to develop my specific analytical questions not in advance, but as I worked through primary sources: to put them to raw data assembled not in accordance with a modern archivist's or historian's choices, but by an early modern scholar.

In July 1572, Hugo Blotius, an intellectual from the Netherlands who would soon become court librarian to the Holy Roman Emperor Maximilian II, finished an account of his travels in Italy during the previous year and a half. He meant this pocket-sized manuscript to serve as both a guide and a notebook for a young friend, Ludwig von Hutten. Hence he cast many of his

Figure 2 Portrait of Cardano from the title page of his *Libelli duo* (Nuremberg, 1543).

experiences in the form of instructions. Though Blotius had a sharp eye for all of Italy's pleasures and dangers, from spectacular landscapes to bad inns, he took particular interest in Bologna, a splendid city with a splendid university. Here, he remarked, most foreigners visited four scholars: the historian Carlo Sigonio, the jurisconsult Angelus Papius, the doctor and philosopher Ulisse Aldrovandi, and Giovanni—he meant Girolamo—Cardano, to whom he prudently did not assign a single profession. Blotius gave the addresses of all four men, praising Aldrovandi's hospitality with special warmth: "Others are very amiable, and the most accessible of all is Ulisse Aldrovandi, who has in his charge the garden of medicinal plants in Bologna, at the palace of the legate or governor. At home he also has a spectacular museum, stuffed with every kind of flowering herb, and all the other natural things that are to be seen."[54] Aldrovandi, in other words, offered northern callers open access to his fantastic museum of the natural world, with its thousands of exhibits and hundreds of drawings of exotic plants and animals, and did so with great grace and warmth.[55] By contrast, Blotius warned, those wishing to visit Cardano must take extreme care: "They must not praise him to his face, they must be brief, and they must ask whether they can expect any more of his books to appear in the near future."[56] Otherwise, his tone suggested, Cardano might explode, showing his guests the door rather than the secrets of nature. Yet Blotius clearly thought this dangerous voyage worthwhile.

Like Blotius, I have decided to visit this difficult but intriguing figure, who makes an ideal informant. For Cardano wrote at fantastic length, and in a fantastic style, about every topic in the astrological tradition (and many others).[57] His *Complete Works,* published long after his death, fill ten folio volumes and some seven thousand pages. Every column offers a striking observation, anecdote, or reference. Cardano drew up horoscopes for the living and the dead, wrote technical treatises, and commented in a uniquely frank way on his discoveries, his experiences, and his relations with his clients. But this vast intellectual territory, for all its richness and fertility, has remained largely unexplored. The length, variety, and technical density of Cardano's books have deterred scholars from approaching him. Though good monographs describe his work on the mathematics of games of chance, his natural philosophy, and his medicine, only Germana Ernst has analyzed his astrological work in any detail.[58] A projected critical edition of Cardano's works has reached only a preliminary stage. For years to come, all students of his work will be condemned to play the role of caterpillars exploring tiny portions of an enormous flowering garden. Riddles outnumber solutions, and dark areas surround every light one. Even now, in short, the road to Cardano has its share of dangers.

Yet Cardano makes a good witness nonetheless. Consider just one of the many passages in which he laid down the law for his fellow astrologers, telling them not only how to do their jobs but how to behave and even what to wear:

> The astrologer must observe nine conditions, to avoid making a wrong use of this art and bringing upon himself not glory and profit, but great loss and danger . . . In the past astrology yielded me no profit, and some of my rivals used the bad reputation of my art to argue that I was also wholly vain. But after I learned to observe the following rules, it brought me no small profit, and caused basically no harm to my reputation. Anyone who observes these will practice the art in an inoffensive manner, and with no less glory and utility than the doctors of our time earn with their medical art. For the predictions of astrologers—if they carry out their divinations on the basis of this book, and observing these conditions—are far more secure than the level of knowledge

> about disease which the doctors of our time have attained, given the diligence with which astrology is taught here, and the carelessness with which medicine is pursued. Therefore, first of all, do not set out to make a prediction until you have completely mastered the instructions given here, and everything which is required, as detailed above. For example, you must know at once when the planets are moving rapidly in their courses, because they are in the upper parts of their epicycles, or when they are moving slowly, in the lower parts—except for the moon. And you must make many trial predictions about your own case. Second, you must strip yourself of all fear, hatred, and affection when predicting, for they will cause involuntary errors. Third, you must not apply this art in practice before all the city, or in public, or publish anything. For those who do so make themselves infamous even when their predictions are true. And they are all the more laughable when they turn out to have been wrong. Fourth, do not make predictions for someone who is testing you [trying it on?], or has a problematic time of birth, or for no fee, or for a very small fee, or for someone who makes fun of the art. For in such cases the art is brought into disrepute, and it becomes an occasion for error when we try to predict things that are important and hard to find out with only a small effort. I rejected a fee of two hundred crowns for making a single horoscope: think about whether you are more practiced in this art than I am. Fifth, do not make a prediction unless you have carefully examined and worked through every point, down to the smallest details, while taking account of the client's condition, family, country, law, age, and so on. Sixth, on no account make any prediction for a wicked man; and, accordingly, for anyone you do not know, or for a harsh tyrant. Seventh, when making a prediction, communicate it only to your client, do not publish your predictions widely. And do not give answers about insignificant things, but only about very important and clear ones, and do it briefly, not trying to fill up whole pages, and do not give them in ambiguous or contradictory form. But do it purely, neatly, chastely, cleanly, briefly, clearly, following the example of the tenth geniture discussed above [in Cardano's *Liber xii geniturarum*]. Eighth, never make a firm prediction to a prince of a great evil, but only of the danger of one. Ninth, in every prediction add: "If he does not rashly expose himself to the risks posed by common disasters" . . . But let the astrologer himself be prudent, gentle, of few words, elegant, well-dressed, grave, faithful, and honest, and exemplary in every way. For often the artist can adorn the art.[59]

This passage describes an ideal astrologer—the sage, grave, austere, rich but uncommercial, who refuses to practice his art until he has fully mastered its mathematical and astronomical bases and who accepts only affluent and serious customers. It also refers to many kinds of astrological practice, only some of which Cardano viewed with approval. The astrologer, by Cardano's account, could predict about serious or trivial matters, taking account of the client's birth horoscope or failing to do so, in secret or in public, prudently or imprudently. The good astrologer, evidently, knew enough to pick the first alternative in each case, and by doing so showed himself worthy to carry on his ancient and honorable art. The bad astrologer, by contrast, chose in each case the second alternative, and by doing so made himself and his discipline into laughing-stocks. Yet Cardano—as he confessed—had not always confined himself to the practices he recommended to others.

Firmicus Maternus, an author Cardano knew and disliked, offered a similarly "idealized portrait" of the good astrologer, complete with recommendations on everything from diet to delivery of judgments:

> Study and pursue all the distinguishing marks of virtue . . . Be modest, upright, sober, eat little, be content with few goods, so that the shameful love of money may not defile the glory of this divine science . . . See that you give your responses publicly in a clear voice, so that nothing may be asked of you which is not allowed either to ask or to answer . . . Have a wife, a home, many sincere friends; be constantly available to the public . . . avoid plots . . . In drawing up a chart, do not show up the bad things about men too clearly, but whenever you come to such a point, delay your responses with a certain reticence, in case you seem not only to explain but also to approve what the evil course of the stars decrees for the man.[60]

When Cardano emphasized the astrologer's need for dignity and the importance of predicting for higher motives than mere gain, he repeated the teachings of the ancients.

But Cardano's precepts ranged still more widely than those of his astrological sources. Here and elsewhere he laid out not only ethical rules for the astrologer's conduct, but technical standards for the interpretation of horoscopes—criteria which would make it possible to identify and interpret in a rigorous way the full range of astral facts relevant to a single individual's fate. Such instructions for use did not figure among the abstract rules that filled Ptolemy's *Tetrabiblos.* In formulating them, Cardano very likely drew on other arts besides astrology—for example, on the detailed manual of dream interpretation by Artemidorus of Daldis (second century B.C.E.), a text which he knew well.[61] Unlike Ptolemy, Artemidorus described not only the rules of his art, but also the ways in which a dream interpreter should apply them in practice:

> To interpret a dream, the expert must sometimes move from the end to the beginning, sometimes from the beginning to the end . . . When the dreams are incomplete and offer insufficient clues, so to speak, the interpreter must add something on his own, especially in dreams where one sees letters which have no coherent meaning or a word unrelated to the thing. The interpreter must then transpose or change or add letters or syllables . . . The interpreter,

> accordingly, must be well equipped with his own stock of methods, and not confine himself to what is found in books. Anyone who thinks he can be a perfect interpreter of dreams on the basis of the art alone, without natural aptitude, will turn out to be only partly competent, and will never arrive at his goal . . . Try to identify the causes for everything and to attach an interpretation, and reasonable proofs, to each dream, for fear that even if you say things that are entirely true, you may seem less expert if you indicate only the results, without a demonstration.[62]

Cardano's work, in short, forms a great, constantly changing screen, on which the reader can watch an expert in several ancient divinatory arts blending their surviving texts in order to recreate what the textual record did not reveal.

The surviving materials, finally, make it possible to construct a richer setting for Cardano's work than for any other ancient or medieval astrologer. His astrological works, which took many forms, complement one another, offering detailed information on both his theories and his practices. Since many of these texts evolved as Cardano revised them, they document the evolution of his thought, providing a partial replacement for the correspondence which he burned. The forms they took, as objects designed for particular publics, and the information they provide about how Cardano worked his way into the discipline of astrology, reveal much about the strategies that guided his career—not always successfully. Germana Ernst, to whose work I owe much, has already demonstrated that an approach like this can bring to light vital material not to be found in the seventeenth-century edition of Cardano's works, where they appear stripped of prefatory matter and in a single, frozen form.[63]

Many annotated copies of Cardano's books survive, as well as manuscript notebooks in which contemporary readers recorded their responses to Cardano's work and that of his rivals, underlining, summarizing, discussing, and sometimes criticizing his precepts. Finished texts by Cardano's contemporaries also discuss his work, often polemically and at length. By joining to the methods normally applied in intellectual history those used in the new discipline known as the history of books and readers, as Ann Blair has shown in detail, we can follow the development and the reception of the work of an early modern natural philosopher, identifying those features of it which touched off powerful reactions in his own environment.[64] This approach makes it possible to reconstruct Cardano's thought not only systematically, as one must do for his ancient predecessors, but chronologically, investigating the ways in which particular situations in his life modified, or did not modify, the astrological tools he used to understand them. For classical astrologers, as for classical medical writers, we must construct from shards and fragments an imaginary mosaic representing the lost marketplace in which they advertised, competed for clients, and proffered advice and treatments for their problems. Cardano brings us into the markets in which he actually worked, letting us hear the cries of the experts trying to attract attention and those of the customers who received and tried to use what they had to offer—at least as he himself perceived, recorded, and responded to them.[65]

In the course of this book we will see that Cardano often addressed a larger public as well as an individual client. He often ignored the cautions which, he argued, the wise astrologer would always observe. And he never ceased to incur some of the very risks against which he cautioned his readers and clients. But we will also see that his violations of his own rules were as typical of the astrological milieu—and thus as historically revealing—as his efforts to observe them. And we will repeatedly hear him confessing, with apparent frankness, to his repeated errors of technique and even of professional ethics.

Cardano combined wide astrological interests with obsessively detailed self-revelation. This makes him the ideal object for the inquiry mounted here—an inquiry which seeks to combine the irreconcilable perspectives of the parachutist and the truffle-hunter, to show that a single case study can yield both a detailed, even microscopic investigation of an individual's mind and environment and a wide-angled survey of the millennial intellectual traditions which shaped both.

chapter two

THE ASTROLOGER'S PRACTICE

LIKE THE PATIENT who visits the office of a modern dentist or ophthalmologist, the client who stepped across the threshold of an astrologer's chambers in the fifteenth or sixteenth century entered a realm that seemed both strange and familiar, both laden with powerful symbols and equipped with impressive tools. Contemporary images, though always stylized, still suggest plausibly enough that the consulting rooms contained both reference works and instruments. Like the books and machines in the doctor's office, those in the astrologer's consulting room served two purposes: they established his professional authority, creating an impressive atmosphere, and they provided his chief technical tools, offering him the data and techniques he needed. The astrologer might well have a globe of the heavens, which would serve to decorate his chambers and to remind him and his client of the beauty of the stars, as traditionally mapped into constellations—a quality easily forgotten by one caught up in the gritty quantitative details of drawing up and explaining a geniture or an interrogation. But the astrologer would also certainly have technical reference works: the open book on the reading stand in Figure 3, for example, seems to be an almanac offering both diagrams of some sort, on the left-hand page, and tables on the right. The almanac was the astrologer's essential desk reference: a work largely consisting of tables, which would provide him with all the data he was likely to need to construct and interpret genitures and interrogations. But he might also have astronomical instruments: for example, an astrolabe, which he could use for making precise measurement of the time at which he cast a nativity or made an observation, or an armillary sphere (see Figure 8).

Like the modern doctor, the astrologer would record the technical data on a form divided into categories, which enabled him to select, organize,

Figure 3 The astrologer and his client. The sun, at the upper right, is shining brilliantly, but the new moon is also visible nearby, apparently causing a solar eclipse and allowing the stars to appear in the daytime sky. The astrologer is presumably computing the results of these celestial events.

and record the significant facts. Unlike the modern doctor, he drew the form up himself, following a scheme which had been developed over the millennia: even though the form was hand-written, its construction and use could hardly have been more precisely regulated, and it provided a speedy and effective way to reduce the complex and multiple signals sent by the moving bodies in the heavens to a single, readable message. The Zodiac—the path that the sun traces through the sphere of the stars—had been divided since antiquity into twelve signs, each 30 degrees long and each represented by an animal or other symbol. The motions of the moon, the sun, and the planets were measured against these, as seen by an observer looking outward from the earth—just as they are still tabulated for purposes of navigation to this

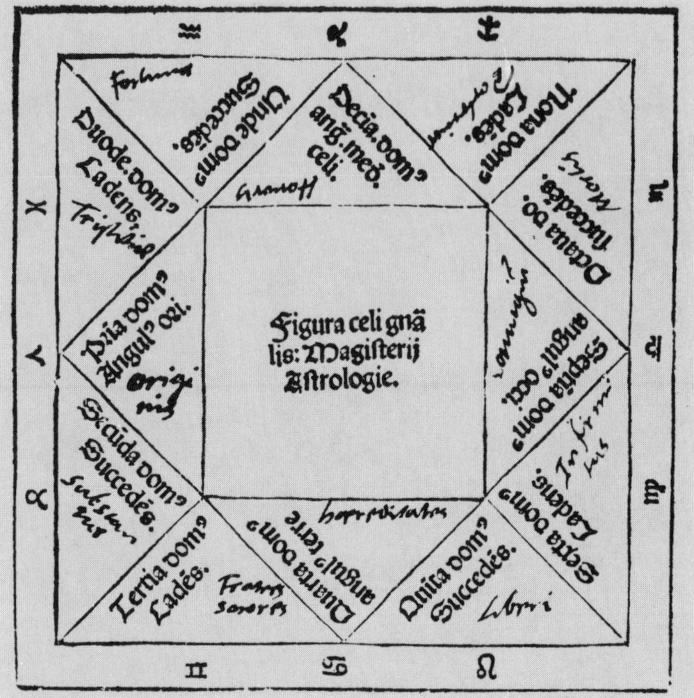

Figure 4 The standard form of a geniture, from Stoeffler and Pflaum's *Almanach nova,* showing the first of the twelve houses at nine o'clock with the other eleven following in a counterclockwise direction. The owner of the book has written in each house the sphere of life on which it had the most influence.

day. Though genitures took many forms, all of them were seen as two-dimensional, schematic renderings of the three-dimensional configuration assumed by the planets before this backdrop.[1]

The standard form used in the Renaissance was the one shown in Figure 4, from the textbook of astrology which Johannes Stoeffler and Jacob Pflaum included with their almanac *Almanach nova* (Venice, 1504). Their diagram represented the Zodiac as flattened out onto the page. The traditional symbols for its twelve signs appear in the outer margin, starting with Aries at nine o'clock and moving counter-clockwise: Aries, Taurus, Gemini, Cancer, Leo, Virgo, Libra, Scorpio, Sagittarius, Capricorn, Aquarius, and Pisces. Each of these signs had its own character and influence, which an astrologer had to learn.

To determine the impact of the planets at a given moment, however, the astrologer could not simply establish their positions on the Zodiac—a process to which I will return below. He first had to divide the Zodiac up, for the moment in which he was interested, into the twelve houses of the geniture. These divisions—which began at nine o'clock, at the point where the sun's path, or ecliptic, crossed the horizon of an observer at the point in question, and continued counter-clockwise from one to twelve—were numbered and referred to by technical terms rather than names: for example, the first, fourth, seventh, and tenth were called the "angles." In a geniture, each of them theoretically assumed control over a particular part of the client's life, following a scheme which the astrologer also had to grasp. An anonymous reader of Stoeffler and Pflaum's book who compared their diagram to the explanatory text has actually written the functions of the houses onto the printed page shown in Figure 4. He notes that the first one determines "origin," the second "wealth," the third "brothers and sisters," and so on, down to the last two, which are responsible for "fortunes" and "sorrows" respectively. At the very start of a practitioner's astrological training, in other words, came the first challenge. Like a soldier mastering the parts of a gun until it becomes second nature to disassemble it, check and clean all its parts, and return them to usability, the astrologer had to know all the parts of the standard diagrams which he imposed on the cosmos, and their functions, so well that he did not have to think before applying them.

This process was not simple. The ecliptic crosses the celestial equator at an angle of about 23½ degrees. The twelve houses normally do not coincide with the twelve signs of the Zodiac, but cut across them. And the lengths of the twelve houses that divide it differ, depending on the standpoint from which the observer looks at it. So the astrologer had to begin laying out a geniture by working out, either by observation or from tables, exactly which point of the Zodiac was rising at any given time and exactly where the borders of the twelve houses fell. A variety of more or less schematic systems for doing this existed: almanacs, for example, offered tables of houses, drawn up for particular latitudes, which could be used to lay out the houses of a geniture for the place in question relatively quickly (see Figure 6). As we will see, the choice of methods for dividing the Zodiac into houses provoked both technical debates and personal quarrels.

Modern newspaper horoscopes—which are far more primitive than ancient or Renaissance genitures—are composed as if it were simple to determine which celestial influences would dominate the life and activities of a client at a given moment. The reader's "sign"—the sign of the Zodiac in

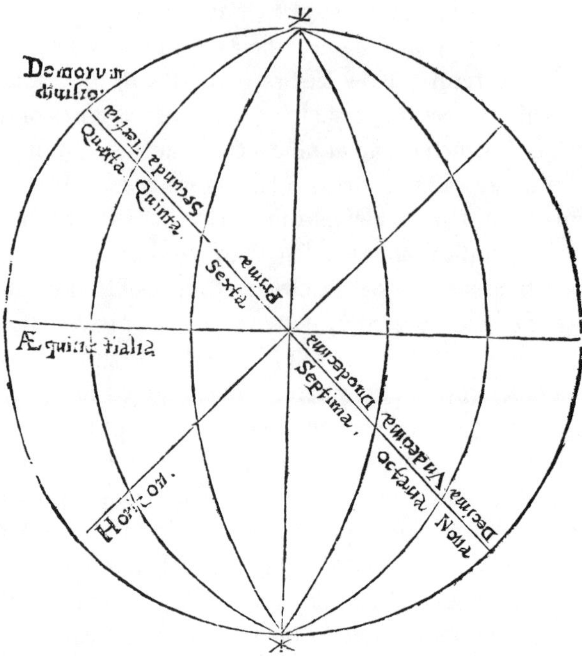

Figure 5 The twelve houses laid out on the Zodiac, from Robert Fludd's *Utriusque cosmi historia* (London, 1618). The houses were thought of as dividing the Zodiac—the band of the heavens through which the sun and the planets passed—into twelve parts.

which the sun was on the date of his or her birth—supposedly determines everything from moods to market share. In the Renaissance, however, everyone—informed laypeople as well as astrologers—knew that the astrologer could not simply choose one house and call it dominant. Instead, he had to plot the positions of the sun, the moon, the five planets, and the head and tail of the dragon (the points where the moon's path, projected out onto the heavens, intersected that of the sun) for the time in question. Each planet, like each house of the geniture, had a character, associated more or less closely with the ancient god for whom it was named. Each, accordingly, also had properties that set it apart from the rest, being hot or cold, dry or wet, and exercised a particular influence on the mutable creatures on the earth below it. The astrologer had to commit these properties and influences, as well as the qualities of the twelve houses, to memory. And even then he could only begin the most technical part of his job.

Tabula domorum ad.42.Gradus latitudinis

♈

Tps a		10	11	12	1	2	3 Do
meridie		♈	♉	♊	♋	♌	♍ m°
h	m	g	g	g	g	g	g
0	0	0	9	20	20	12	3
0	4	1	10	21	21	12	4
0	7	2	11	22	21	13	5
0	11	3	12	23	22	14	5
0	15	4	13	24	23	14	6
0	18	5	14	25	24	15	7
0	22	6	16	26	24	16	8
0	26	7	17	26	25	17	9
0	29	8	18	27	26	18	9
0	33	9	19	28	26	18	10
0	37	10	20	29	27	19	11
0	40	11	21	♋	28	20	12
0	44	12	22	1	29	21	13
0	48	13	23	2	29	21	14
0	51	14	24	3	♌	22	14
0	55	15	25	3	1	23	15
0	59	16	26	4	2	23	16
1	3	17	27	5	2	24	17
1	6	18	28	6	3	25	18
1	10	19	29	7	4	26	19
1	14	20	♊	8	4	27	20
1	18	21	1	8	5	27	21
1	21	22	2	9	6	28	21
1	25	23	3	10	6	29	22
1	29	24	4	11	7	29	23
1	33	25	5	12	8	♍	24
1	36	26	6	12	9	1	25
1	40	27	7	13	9	2	26
1	44	28	8	14	10	2	26
1	48	29	9	15	11	3	27
1	52	30	10	16	12	4	28

♉

Tps a		10	11	12	1	2	3 Do
meridie		♉	♊	♋	♌	♍	♍ m°
h	m	g	g	g	g	g	g
1	52	0	10	16	12	4	28
1	55	1	11	17	13	5	29
1	59	2	12	17	13	6	♎
2	3	3	13	18	14	7	1
2	7	4	14	19	15	7	2
2	11	5	15	19	15	8	3
2	15	6	16	20	16	9	4
2	19	7	17	21	17	10	4
2	22	8	18	22	18	10	5
2	26	9	19	23	19	11	6
2	30	10	20	24	19	12	7
2	34	11	21	25	20	13	8
2	38	12	22	25	21	13	9
2	42	13	23	26	22	14	10
2	46	14	23	27	22	15	11
2	50	15	24	28	23	16	12
2	54	16	25	29	24	16	12
2	58	17	26	29	25	17	13
3	2	18	27	♌	26	18	14
3	6	19	28	1	26	19	15
3	10	20	29	2	27	20	16
3	14	21	♋	3	28	21	17
3	18	22	1	3	29	22	18
3	22	23	2	4	29	23	19
3	27	24	3	5	♍	23	20
3	31	25	4	6	1	24	21
3	35	26	5	7	2	25	22
3	39	27	5	8	3	26	23
3	43	28	6	8	3	26	23
3	47	29	7	9	4	27	24
3	51	30	8	10	5	28	25

☉ ♑ 3

Figure 6 A table of houses from Stoeffler and Pflaum's *Almanach nova.*

In the first place, the astrologer had to locate the planets on the Zodiac and in the twelve houses of the chart in question. To do so, he could sometimes consult the heavens at the moment in question—but of course, some or all of the planets could be below the horizon, in the first six houses, at the moment of birth, even if one could be certain of carrying out an observation then in good weather conditions. Usually, the astrologer found his

1524	Motus Solis et Lune et Planetarum Capitisque in Zodiaco															
Februarius					M	A	M	A	M	A	M	D	M	D		
	☉ ♒		☽ ♑		♄ ♓		♃ ♓		♂ ♓		♀ ♓		☿ ♒		☊ ♒	
	g	m	g	m	g	m	g	m	g	m	g	m	g	m	g	m
Brigide v. 1	21	58	17	52	9	58	9	59	7	40	0	14	8	28	29	15
Purificatio 2	22	58	29 ♒	51	10	5	10	13	8	26	1	30	10	18	29	12
Blasij 3	23	59	11	48	10	12	10	27	9	12	2	45	12	9	29	8
4	24	59	23 ♓	44	10	19	10	41	9	59	4	1	14	1	29	5
Agathe v. 5	26	0	5	37	10	27	10	55	10	45	5	16	15 ♓	53	29	2
Dorothee v. 6	27	0	17	23	10	34	11	9	11	32	6	32	17	45	28	59
c 7	28	1	29 ♈	6	10	42	11	23	12	18	7	47	19	39	28	56
8	29 ♓	1	10	49	10	49	11	37	13	5	9	3	21	33	28	53
Appollonie v. 9	0	1	22 ♉	40	10	57	11	51	13	51	10	18	23	28	28	49
Scholastice 10	1	1	4	52	11	4	12	6	14	38	11	33	25	22	28	46
11	2	2	17 ♊	30	11	12	12	20	15	24	12	48	27	16	28	43
12	3	2	0	32	11	19	12	35	16	11	14	3	29 ♓	9	28	40
13	4	2	13	48	11	27	12	49	16	57	15	18	1	3	28	37
c Valentini 14	5	2	27 ♋	21	11	34	13	4	17	43	16	33	2	57	28	34
15	6	2	11	22	11	42	13	18	18	29	17	48	4	51	28	30
Juliane 16	7	2	25 ♌	46	11	50	13	33	19	15	19	3	6	44	28	27
17	8	3	10	22	11	57	13	47	20	1	20	18	8	38	28	24
18	9	3	25 ♍	6	12	5	14	2	20	47	21	33	10	31	28	21
19	10	3	9	50	12	13	14	16	21	33	22	47	12	24	28	18
20	11	3	24 ♎	36	12	20	14	31	22	19	24 ♓	2	14	16	28	14
c 21	12	3	9	20	12	28	14	45	23	5	25	16	16	8	28	11
Petri cathe. 22	13	3	24 ♏	2	12	36	14	59	23	51	26	31	18	0	28	8
23	14	2	8	32	12	44	15	14	24	37	27	45	19	51	28	5
Matthie ap. 24	15	2	22 ♐	37	12	51	15	28	25	23	29 ♈	0	21	41	28	2
25	16	2	6	19	12	59	15	42	26	9	0	15	23	31	27	59
26	17	1	19 ♑	38	13	7	15	57	26	55	1	29	25	19	27	55
27	18	1	2	33	13	15	16	11	27	41	2	44	27	7	27	52
b 28	19	1	15	8	13	23	16	25	28	27	3	59	28 ♈	55	27	49
29	20	0	27	18	13	31	16	39	29	13	5	13	0	40	27	46
Latitudo planetarum ad diem				1	1	32	0	58	0	7	0	56	1	58		
				10	1	32	0	57	0	6	1	1	1	58	Mensis	
				20	1	31	0	57	0	5	1	4	1	21		

Figure 7 The movements of the planets in February 1524, from Stoeffler and Pflaum's *Almanach nova.*

basic data in the almanac. A typical one—like that of Stoeffler and Pflaum—traced the motion of the planets, sun, moon, and dragon's head through the Zodiac, day by day, for years in advance. Thus the astrologer who needed to draw up a chart for a date in February 1524 could look up—in a work published as early as 1506—the planets' general positions in the

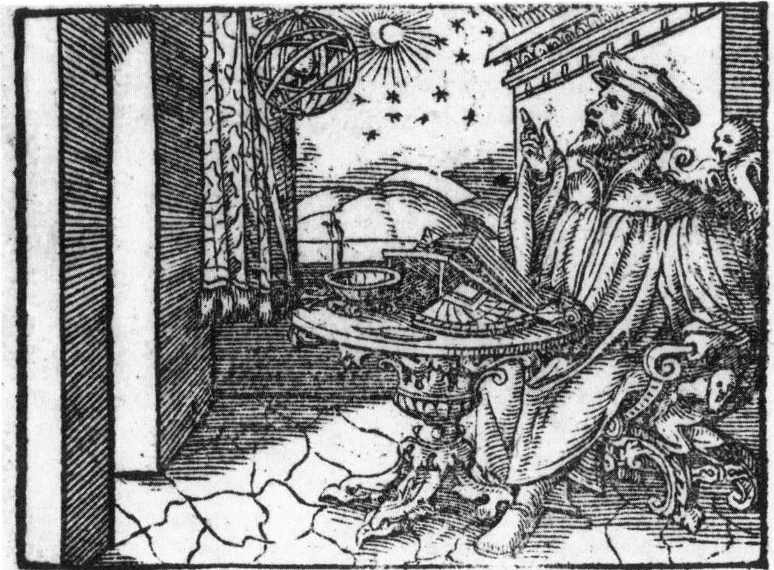

Figure 8 An astrologer, surrounded by his tools, watching a solar eclipse: the moon appears directly in front of the sun, enabling the stars to become visible. Note the armillary sphere and the book—perhaps an almanac—on the stand before him.

Zodiac, and their latitudes, at any given time (Figure 7). He had enough data to make it possible to compute a very rough geniture very rapidly indeed. True, almanacs were notoriously inaccurate, since they rested in considerable part on very old data and parameters. Astronomers and astrologers who used almanacs to predict such dramatic events as solar eclipses and conjunctions of the planets sometimes found themselves forced to admit that the positions predicted in their almanacs were considerably in advance of or behind the true ones, though on other occasions the planets closely bore out predictions. A certain amount of worry about the stability and value of almanacs was spreading among astronomers in the late fifteenth and early sixteenth centuries, and more than one—like Johannes Regiomontanus—called for a radical reform. For the most part, however, astrologers found that they could use their tables to draw up charts that met the needs of most customers in a rapid and efficient way.

Even the locating of exact planetary positions, however, did not exhaust the astrologer's responsibilities. Once the astrologer had established the principal data, he still had to interpret them. And as everyone knew, that required more than a simple listing of the planets and their properties. In Leon Battista Alberti's dialogues *On the Family,* written in the 1430s, the young scholar Lionardo set out to derive from classical texts a set of rules for the creation and maintenance of friendships. He explained that physical beauty won the affection of Solon for Pisistratus and of Socrates for Alcibiades, while Sulla made his soldiers love him by leaving them in Asia, where they could engage in sexual lives more varied and rowdy than Roman tradition had permitted. And Lionardo promised that the study of history could provide many similar "very useful instructions on how to win friends."

The older and more experienced Adovardo retorted at once that such rules grossly oversimplified the complex, ever-changing webs of relations that connect—and separate—men at court. As evidence he cited the example of astrology:

> Ah! Anyone who wants to give a really full account would have to have a lot more precepts than this. Imagine someone whom the astronomers have taught that Mars inspires the force of armies and the rage of battle, Mercury teaches many sciences and subtlety of intellect and marvelous arts, Jupiter governs ceremonies and religious minds, the sun grants rank and sovereignty, the moon stimulates voyages and female and plebeian movements, Saturn hinders and delays our thoughts and efforts. Imagine that he knew all of their natures and powers, but had no idea in which part of the sky, or at what elevation, each of them has more or less power in itself, and with which rays each of them forges friendship or enmity with the others, and what effect they can have, in conjunction, toward causing good or bad fortune. Certainly he would be no astrologer.

Knowing the general nature of the planets, Adovardo concluded—like knowing only the general nature of the great men whose influence radiated downward on the ordinary men and women at a court—was only "the basic introduction to knowing the infinite number of other ways of predicting and discerning the effects which the heavens tend to produce."[2]

Once the astrologer had mastered each element of his art, in other words, he also had to master the even more complex rules for determining how each of them affected the others. The position of a planet in a given sign of the Zodiac or a given house of a geniture would affect its powers, enhancing or diminishing them by a complex set of rules. So would its relation to the brighter stars on the Zodiac, each of which also had set astrological meanings and functions. So might the decans—the strange demonic beings, ultimately derived from Egypt, three of which ruled each sign of the Zodiac, each of them being responsible for 10 degrees; or the paranatellonta, the stars which rose alongside a given degree of the Zodiac; or the degrees of the

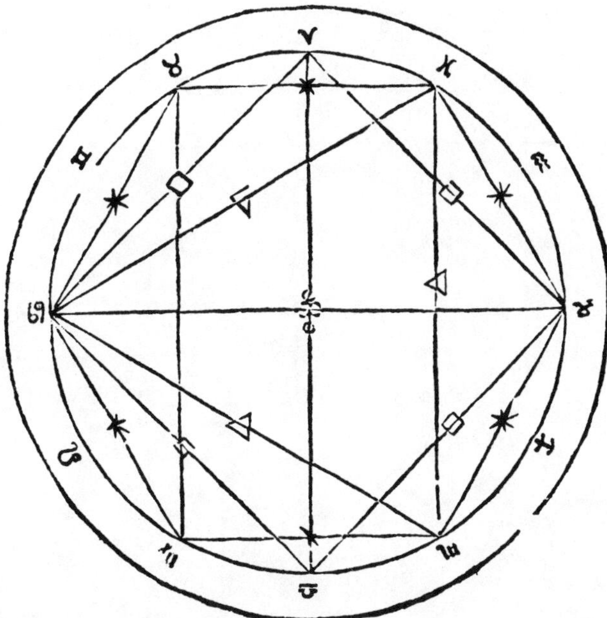

Figure 9 The aspects, from Stoeffler and Pflaum's *Almanach nova:* opposition (180 degrees), trine (120 degrees), quartile (90 degrees), and sextile (60 degrees apart).

Zodiac themselves, which had effects of their own, distributed and tabulated by complex numerological rules.[3]

So, above all, would the relation in which the planet stood to the other planets in a given chart. If one imagines oneself looking down from the pole of the Zodiac on the signs and planets, all of them stand at particular angular distances from one another, known as "aspects." The most significant of these had been established since antiquity:

Opposition (180 degrees)
Trine (120 degrees)
Quadrature (90 degrees)
Sextile (60 degrees)
Conjunction

Opposition and quadrature were hostile relations, trine and sextile positive. Conjunction was particularly important, especially when it took place

1524	Aspectus Lune ad Solem & Planetas						Solis & plaꝫ inter se.
Febr	☉	♄ oc	♃ oc	♂ oc	♀ oc	☿ or	
1							☌ ♄ ♃
2							
3						☌ 1	
4	☌ 2 47				☌ 23		☽ ☊
5		☌ 10	☌ 11	☌ 10 32			☌ ♄ ♂ ☌ ♃ ♂
6							
7							
8							
9	⚹ 16					⚹ 2	
10		⚹ 12	⚹ 14	⚹ 20	⚹ 14		☌ ♄ ♀
11						□ 23	☌ ♃ ♀
12	□ 4 55	□ 20	□ 22				
13				□ 6	□ 3		
14	△ 14					△ 11	
15		△ 1	△ 4	△ 12	△ 12		
16							☌ ♂ ♀
17							☌ ☉ ☿
18							☽ ☋
19	☍ 0 25	☍ 4	☍ 7	☍ 21	☍ 23	☍ 5	☌ ♄ ☿
20							☌ ♃ ☿
21							☌ ♄ ☉
22							
23	△ 10	△ 7	△ 12			△ 22	
24				△ 5	△ 12		
25	□ 18 58	□ 12	□ 17				☌ ♃ ☉
26				□ 14		□ 13	
27		⚹ 21 34			□ 0		
28	⚹ 8		⚹ 2 32				☌ ♂ ☿
29				⚹ 4	⚹ 18	⚹ 8	

Figure 10 Shown above are the aspects of the sun, moon, and planets, day by day, through February 1524, from Stoeffler and Pflaum's *Almanach nova.* The column on the far right of the page above lists conjunctions of the sun and planets. On the facing page is Stoeffler and Pflaum's notorious prediction that these signs would be followed by terrible events on earth.

rarely, as did the conjunctions of Saturn and Jupiter, which fell every twenty years.

Obviously, the astrologer had to identify and calculate the effects of all the significant aspects in a given geniture. Once again, the almanac helped: it listed not only the positions of the planets, but their aspects to one another, day by day. Like graphs, such lists revealed unexpected connections

Anno Chriſti domini		1524			Ephemerides
		Biſextilis			
Aureus numerus	5		Quadrageſima	14	Februarij
Cyclus ſolaris	21		Paſca	27	Martij
Littere dominicales	c	b	Rogationes	1	Maij
Inditio	12		Aſcenſio domini	5	Maij
Interuallum	6	hepdo. 2 dies	Pentecoſte	15	Maij
Septuageſima	24	Januarij	Aduentus dñi	27	Nouembris

Hoc anno nec Solis nec Lune eclipſim cõſpicabimur. Sed preſenti anno errantiũ ſiderũ habitudines miratu digniſſime accidẽt: In menſe eñ Febru-ario 20 coniunctõnes cũ minime mediocres tum magne accident. quarum 16 ſignum aqueum poſſidebũt. que vniuerſo fere orbi climatibꝰ regnis pro-uincijs ſtatibus dignitatibus brutis beluis marinis cunctiſq; terre naſcen-tibus indubitatã mutationem variationẽ ac alterationẽ ſignificabunt. talẽ profecto qualem a pluribꝰ ſeculis ab hiſtoriographis. aut natu maioribꝰ vix percepimus Leuate igitur viri chriſtianiſſimi capita veſtra.

Saturnus a 23 Junij ad 9 Nouembris retrogradus
Jupiter a 18 Julij ad 14 Nouembris regreſſu vexabitur
Mars hoc anno progredietur
Venus a 21 Septembris ad 1 Nouembris contra ſignorum ſeriem deferetur
Mercurius a penultimo Martij ad 22 Aprilis Item a 24 Julij ad 16 Auguſti Et a 17 Nouembris in 10 Decembris regreſſiones perficiet.

among numerical data, which might otherwise have escaped attention. Stoeffler and Pflaum's table of aspects for February 1524, for example, revealed that what they took to be a portentously large number of conjunctions would take place in a short period. This led them to predict changes to nature and society more radical than any recorded by historians for centuries, or remembered by the oldest of the old (Figure 10). Obviously, such phenomena could also show up in an individual's geniture—or could be made to do so, as they were when Cardano's rival Luca Gaurico set the birth of Martin Luther in 1484, so that it would coincide with, among other phenomena, a massive planetary conjunction in Scorpio. As we will see in watching Cardano and others practice their art, a system of rules for applying

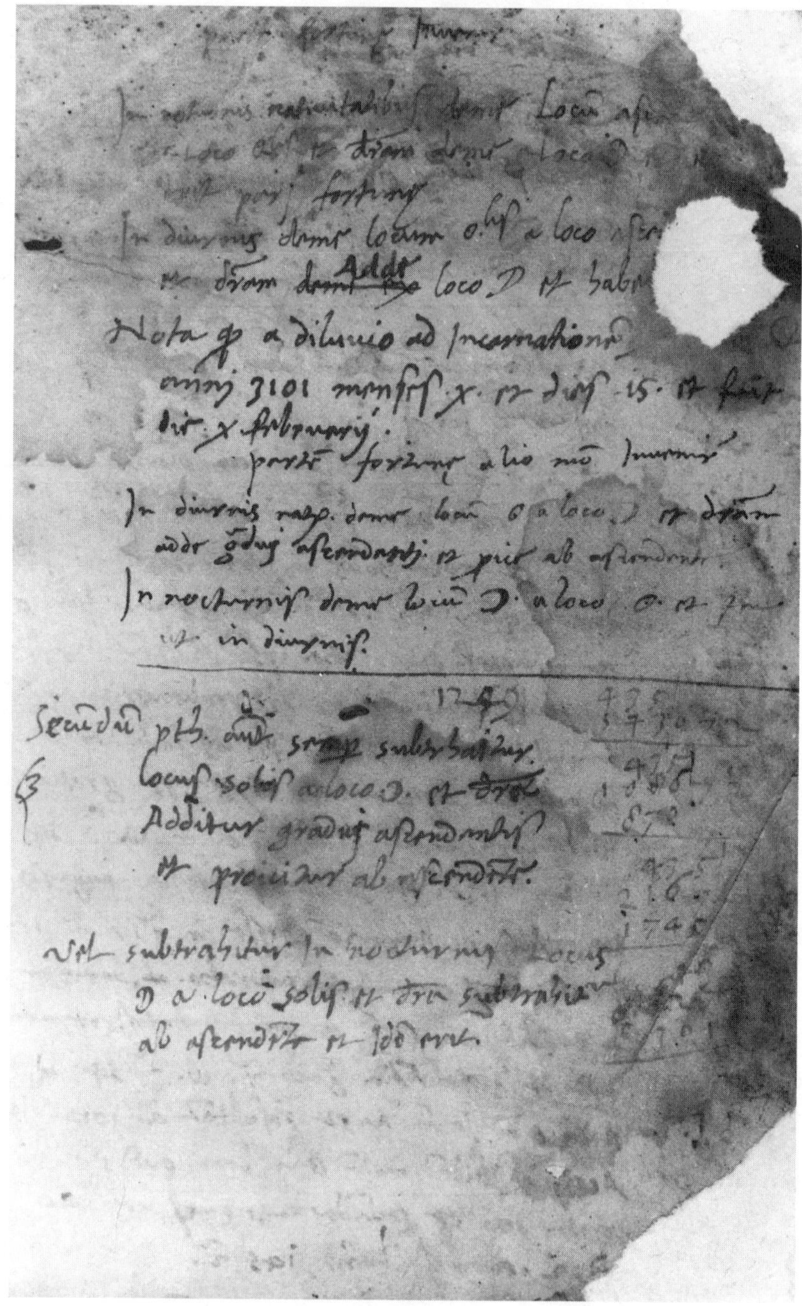

Figure 11 A reader's notes on the information and techniques needed to use Stoeffler and Pflaum's *Almanach nova,* written in a copy of a 1522 edition of the book.

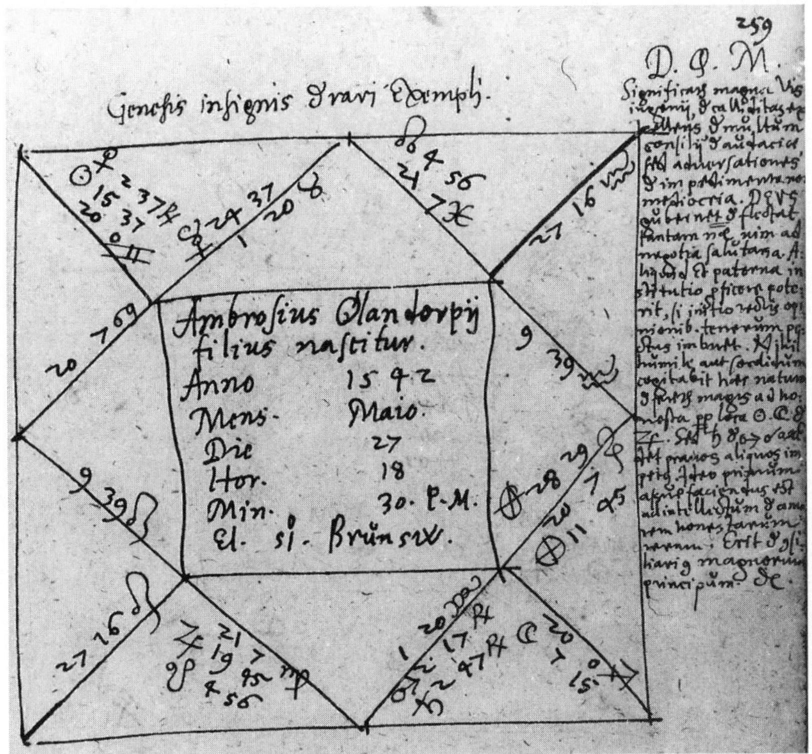

Figure 12 The geniture of Ambrosius Glandorp, from a manuscript collection bound with a copy of Luca Gaurico's *Tractatus astrologicus* (Venice, 1552). The text at right interprets the geniture, entitled "A Truly Remarkable Birth" by the maker of this collection, as showing that Glandorp has extraordinary abilities but will need careful parental oversight.

what the astrologer knew about the effects of any given planet and the qualities of any given star or sign enabled him to read the heavens with extraordinary freedom.

Simply reading manuals and almanacs could not enable most students of astrology to attain a full mastery of the art. Some attended formal lectures—for example, those held in schools of medicine. Others worked their way with pen in hand through the forests of tables and aphorisms, doing and redoing computations and learning the many different ways in which one could solve almost any given technical problem. The page of manuscript shown in Figure 11, for example, was written by a student who used the blank leaves in a copy of a later edition of Stoeffler and Pflaum's almanac,

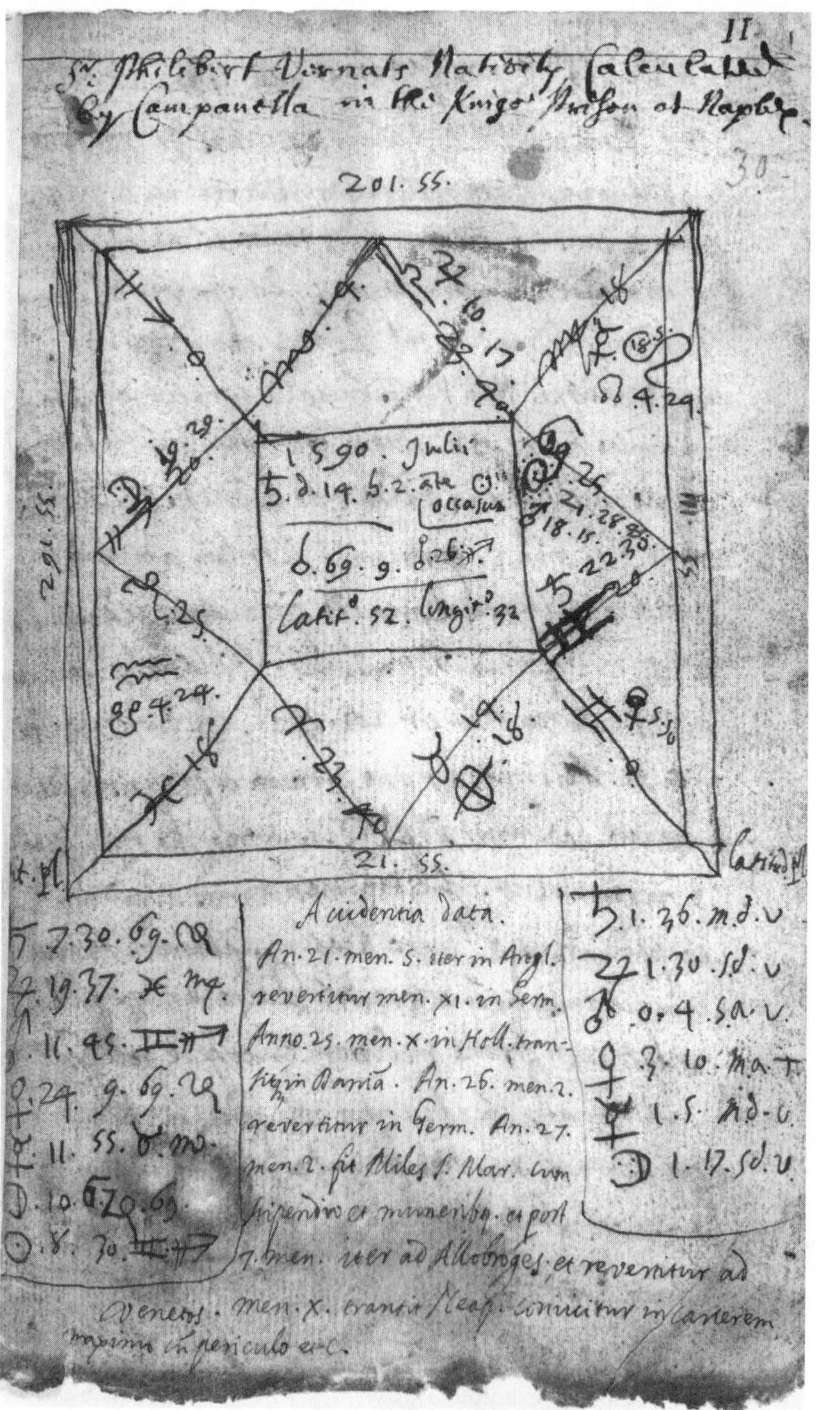

Figure 13 Tommaso Campanella's luxury geniture for Philibert Vernat.

published at Venice in 1522, to record two different kinds of information (Figure 11). On the one hand, he sets down in years, months, and days the interval—a standard one in astronomical tables deriving from the Alphonsine Tables—from the Flood to the Incarnation. On the other hand, he also notes different procedures for determining the Lot of Fortune (a place in the geniture which could have significant impact on the effects of solar, lunar, and planetary influences). Ptolemy, for example, held that one should establish this by finding the distance from the sun to the moon and counting it off from the ascendant, while Manilius and others offered different procedures for daytime and nighttime nativities.

In the end, the astrologer produced a chart: for example, a geniture, in which he laid out the twelve houses at the moment in question, recorded his client's name, dated his birth, and identified, in a commentary, the most significant features of the chart. These could be succinct: that of the young Ambrosius Glandorp, born at Braunschweig in May 1542, emphasizes that the positions of the sun and moon, which are in opposition to each other, and that of Jupiter in the third house will ensure that his character is basically sound—though the conjunction of Mars and Saturn in the fifth house will cause some countervailing evil influence, against which his parents will have to guard (Figure 12). This brief document presented only the main features of the geniture of one who would—according to the anonymous commentator—become a spectacularly brilliant young man. Like many of its kind, it offered assertions rather than proving its points.

Other genitures—like the very long one which the prophet and astrologer Tommaso Campanella drew up, while in prison in Naples, for Philibert Vernat—went into far greater depth, discussing each planet's influence on the others, the effects of each house of the Zodiac, and the changing impact of the positions of the planets at the yearly "revolutions" of the client's birth (Figure 13). Such luxury products, naturally drawn up in most cases for clients who enjoyed wealth and position, became a vehicle for political and ethical advice as well as an application of astrological principles.

Armed with the geniture—his own, perhaps, or that of a newborn son—the client went his way, prepared to avert evil influences and capitalize on favorable ones, warned in advance of potential threats to his career, his fortune, and his health—and even alerted to the likeliest dates for his own death. No single formula encapsulates, no single career embodies the experiences of all astrologers and their clients: individual variations, as we will repeatedly see, were enormous. But Cardano's astrological career, and the experiences and impressions of those who used his work, unfolded in this general context.

chapter three

THE PROGNOSTICATOR

CARDANO entered the world of astrology in 1534, by publishing a *pronostico*—a pamphlet, stuffed with predictions about the short and the long term. Cardano's contribution to this popular genre, which appeared in Milan and Venice, was written in Italian, with an admixture of Latin. Only a few pages long, it offered its readers what looks at first like a wild, even contradictory, mix of contents. Claims to predict the future development of world religions and politics flanked efforts to hedge such bold bets, while both made curious neighbors for Cardano's list of predictions about the weather. Starting as he meant to go on, Cardano offered his readers an attractive combination of cries of doom and warnings not to exaggerate their precision: "DO not expect this to take place within 20 or 50 years. But I have true knowledge that the world must soon undergo a complete renewal. Therefore pay attention. Sacred Scripture and astrology have shown us, without doubt, that our insatiable rapacity must soon come to an end. If evil is prophesied, do not feel sad, for as the Psalmist writes, 'Many are the whips of the sinner, but mercy will surround him who hopes in the Lord.'"[1]

Even in this maiden voyage into print, Cardano portrayed himself as a pure astrologer surrounded, like the virtuous patriarch in Paolo Uccello's fresco of the Deluge, by evil competitors shrieking at the top of their lungs. Cardano insisted that he made no claims to omniscience, and tried to avoid even the appearance of bias in his predictions. His competitors, by contrast, failed every test, both ethical and technical. They told princes not the truth but what they wanted to hear. Their predictions rested on weak foundations, because most of them were "defiling this noble science of astrology, since they barely know how to use the Alphonsine Tables"—the standard astronomical tables, created under the patronage of Alfonso X el Sabio of

PRONOSTICO
O VERO IVDICIO GENERALE COM
POSTO PER LO ECCELLENTE MES-
SER HIERONYMO CARDANO
PHISICO MILANESE, DAL
1534. INSINO AL .1550.
CON MOLTI CAPI
TOLI ECCEL-
LENTI.

Licentia data, dalli Magnifici Signori, a chi ſtampara, ouer
fara ſtampare, queſto Pronoſtico, caſca in pena
de ſoldi duoi, per ogni iuditio,
di queſto Auttore.

Figure 14 The title page of Cardano's *Pronostico,* showing a bearded seer predicting the downfall of the city behind him.

Castile around 1272 and popularized, in a later, Latin form, in the fourteenth century.[2] Yet these charlatans profited by their incompetence and the gullibility of their patrons: "the men of real value and learning are not rewarded by, or even known to, the lords: the more someone knows how to say things that please, the more he is thought to know."[3]

In order to make clear the scientific basis of his work, Cardano began by showing that he had a firm astrological reason for predicting that the church must soon undergo radical change. To support his claim he referred to one of the many long-period motions of the stars long used as the basis of astrological prediction. At the origins of Christianity, Cardano argued, the first degree of the constellation of Aries in the sphere of the fixed stars—the eighth of the nine celestial spheres, counting outward from the earth—had been in conjunction with the first degree of the sign of Aries in the ninth sphere, which held the signs of the Zodiac.

This additional crystalline sphere, offset in its axis from the eighth, was posited by medieval Arabic astronomers, who had used its motion to account for the precession of the equinoxes—the fact that the sun did not return at the end of each tropical year, the period that intervened between two occurrences of a given solstice or equinox, to the same point on the sphere of the fixed stars. The perfect original correlation of the two spheres, Cardano argued, "was a sign of a great equality, which in truth produced our faith." At present, however, the first degree of the Zodiacal sign of Aries was almost 50 degrees away from its original place, at 20 degrees of Taurus. The loss of equality in heaven produced a loss of faith on earth. Only when the first degree of Aries reached the sign of Sagittarius in the ninth sphere, "which is still a long time away, around 1300 years," would the situation begin to improve, "and therefore I say in general that men must become worse than they are now, so far as the faith is concerned." Even the slight improvement that the influence of Jupiter would cause could not reverse the general downward course of religion. The church would not undergo substantial change for the better until 1764, and no major improvement would take place until C.E. 1800—a goal perhaps too distant to provoke strong hopes or calm deep fears.[4]

Cardano flanked this long-term prediction, based on the slow movement of the equinoxes and solstices through the celestial sphere, with others that rested on more immediate celestial portents. The planetary conjunctions of 1524 and 1525 in the signs of Pisces and Aries, he argued, also indicated destruction for the church. That of 1564 "denoted the renovation of all the religions, the Christian and the Muslim."[5] Similarly, a whole series of omens had recently appeared in the sky and the atmosphere, all of which made the short-term future look very dark. The strange new race of birds which appeared in Alessandria, the thunderbolt which toppled the battlement of a tower in Milan, and the star which appeared over the Broletto there ("which one of my fellow citizens, a man distinguished for his remarkable learning, says was Venus: I neither deny this nor affirm it")—all offered evidence about things to come, even if Cardano also felt compelled to denounce "the falsity of the men who tell these tales," the *cantastorie,* or public singers of tales, who spread in the marketplaces the rumors to which prognosticators like Cardano gave more permanent form in print.[6]

As yet, Cardano did not feel able to draw all the consequences that these data could reasonably yield. He refused to offer precise predictions about all upcoming wars and their outcomes, since, as he said, "there is no part of astrology harder than this one, and yet the bulk of these crazy diviners speak more boldly about it, in their bestiality, than about anything else."[7] He also insisted, against Martin Luther, that not all dramatic celestial events caused or symbolized radical changes on earth. Luther was wrong, for example, to hold that a series of recent eclipses "signify the approach of the end of the world."[8] Eclipses were natural, not supernatural; if they really showed that the end was coming, anyone with a good astronomical table could work out the exact date. Eclipses, moreover, were not general signifiers: any given solar eclipse, after all, must remain invisible to many of the earth's inhabitants. When the end finally did come, Cardano argued, "there will be supernatural signs and miracles in the Christian and Mosaic law, designated by the sun and moon. There would be much to say about this—but it is enough for now to understand that we are still far from that time."[9] Anticipating the disasters to come, in Cardano's case, did not mean proclaiming Apocalypse Now. His predictions, for all their threatening tone, postponed the date of the Messiah's return and Armageddon to long after his own time. This relatively conservative form of eschatology has never been unusual, of course; and it makes especially good sense in a work with which, Germana Ernst has suggested, Cardano hoped to appeal to Pope Paul III himself.[10]

Predictions on the grand scale gave way, from time to time, to much more modest bulletins about the local and the near term. Cardano foresaw problems ahead for Charles V, the Holy Roman Emperor who had defeated the French in Italy in 1525 and seemed to control the political and religious fate of Europe. The *Pronostico* spoke less of his future triumphs than of the comets and other omens that would accompany his death, like that of Julius Caesar. Cardano also worried about the duke of Milan, Francesco II Sforza. Cardano still believed, in 1534, that his overlord could continue to rule his state independently (in fact, this puppet ruler died in 1535, just after

Cardano wrote, whereupon Imperial governors took over, backed up by Spanish troops).[11] Less sweepingly still, Cardano gave his readers very precise weather predictions, warning them in advance of a drought between 6 July and 9 August 1536, and foggy and tempestuous weather on the twenty-fifth of August 1537.

The *Pronostico,* in short, mingled discussion of the predictable motions of the sun, moon, and planets with interpretation of unique, unpredictable portents, not all of which took place in the heavens. It combined gloomy prophecies of the transformation of the church with expressions of partial optimism. It provided both practical advice for farmers, doctors, and others concerned with short-term futures and theoretical advice for the rulers of church and state. It all amounted to a heap of incoherencies—as well as a bold first publication for a scholar with no reputation. To make sense of Cardano's moves, we need to know the rules of the game he meant to practice and to have a sense of the personal and historical situations in which he began to play it.

The prognostication or *practica*—the kind of short predictive work that Cardano issued—was not a new genre. Since the twelfth century, when Islamic scientific texts and methods began to be made available in the West, astrology had been widely practiced. As in antiquity, specialist astronomers saw astrology as a way of applying their theoretical and mathematical work to practical concerns. A much larger number of medical men held—in theory at least—that the prudent doctor would not prescribe a remedy or perform a surgical operation except at an astrologically determined propitious time. Both groups contributed to what gradually grew into a profuse, even sprawling body of ephemeral literature. In the middle of the fourteenth century, for example, as the threatening planetary conjunction due to take place on 14 March 1345 came closer, both Jewish and Christian thinkers predicted terrible wars and an outbreak of disease. Papal patronage, as well as independent speculation, seems to have inspired the production of at least some of the short predictions that began to circulate then in manuscript form.[12] But members of the mercantile and professional elites also eagerly read these works, responding to them with emotions that ran the gamut from skepticism to panic.[13]

In the fourteenth and fifteenth centuries, astrology became a standard part of the curriculum in universities with medical schools. Issuing short predictions for the year to come formed part of professors' assigned tasks at Bologna and elsewhere. Court astrologers in France and elsewhere produced similar short-term bulletins. The political uncertainty of the later Middle Ages and two great outbreaks of disease, the Black Death in the 1340s and syphilis in the 1490s, both seem to have made readers even more eager to have brief, accessible news of things to come. Over time, the subjects of astrological predictions became grander and grander, as did their scale.

The doctrine of the great conjunctions offered a simple, easily applied astrological template for the interpretation of current events and the prediction of future ones. Its availability did much to turn "astrology into a hermeneutics of the end of the world." Gradually, despite reservations on both sides, more and more authors of prophecies began to use astrological doctrines to give their works technical authority, and more and more astrologers began to include prophecies of doom and glory with their computations.[14] The invention of printing, finally, made it easier for such texts to reach a wide public, not only because each work existed from the start in multiple copies, but also because printers could seize on, excerpt, or simply plagiarize attractive specimens of the genre once a single copy reached them.[15]

Prognostications differed as widely in details of argument and execution as their authors differed in local culture and technical preparation, but they had some common characteristics nonetheless. They usually took the form of short booklets, in Latin or the vernacular. Cardano's *Pronostico* had a title-page woodcut of a prophet, sitting before a city in which a tower has fallen and a fire has broken out, applying a pair of dividers to an image of the heavens that also bears a scale—no doubt a symbol of the judgment to come. It offered only five leaves, or ten pages, of roughly printed text broken up into short paragraphs. Both the woodcut and the short, segmented text that followed it made clear that the booklet was meant to be accessible to a large public—one not equipped to decipher large, demanding texts wreathed with learned commentary. Visually, it was more appealing than the usual Italian prognostication, in which the six or eight pages of text came unaccompanied by a vivid illustration like Cardano's. In its mingling of a traditional vision of the prophet—and of the destruction he forecast being visited on the world—with the quantitative and symbolic paraphernalia of astrology, it resembled many of the German prognostications that announced a flood in 1524. In other respects, it followed convention even more closely.

Typically, Italian prognosticators concerned themselves, as Cardano did, with a combination of large-scale astronomical events which would affect the entire world and short-term, local conditions which would be of immediate practical interest to a specific group of readers. Their use of astrology rarely required detailed computation. Often they cited the great conjunctions of Jupiter and Saturn, with their simple, twenty-year rhythm and their powerful associations, or more dramatic configurations of the planets, to explain such important events as the rise of syphilis. A famous broadside of

1496 by Theodoricus Ulsenius depicts a man covered with gross lesions on his face and legs, the manifest signs of his disease, under a Zodiac in which the planets have come together in conjunction in the sign of Scorpio. Simple, memorable causal explanations of this kind—rather than precise, fine-grained examinations of the natal horoscopes of individuals—made up the staple material for such texts.[16] So did precise, easily falsifiable weather predictions of the sort offered not only by Cardano, but by most prognosticators down to Johannes Kepler—who continued to take a serious interest in devising techniques for scientific meteorology long after he had lost faith in many other aspects of traditional astrology.[17]

The sweeping generalizations, sonorous, deliberately frightening language, and banal details about rain and snow that filled Cardano's text found echoes in the work of his forerunners and competitors, especially in northern Europe but also in Italy. The ambitious and prominent astrologer Luca Gaurico and his followers issued Latin and Italian *prognostica* which matched Cardano's topic for topic, offering predictions about the fortunes of royal houses and the vicissitudes of the weather with equal confidence. Gaurico's pupil Joannes de Rogeriis announced, in a *prognosticon* dedicated to Francis I in 1537, that "at the end of A.D. 1537, the king of the Turks will not attack the Christians in Italy with his army, and no bloody war will take place"—though he immediately qualified this bold statement.[18] He predicted that Cosimo de' Medici would not long rule in Florence, if his information about Cosimo's horoscope held good; that Paul III would prepare a general council; and that "before the end of the year 1538, the empire of [the Turk] will be destroyed, and his wicked soul will go to the horrid swamps of the underworld, not to return"—two bad guesses out of three.[19] De Rogeriis did not always soar in the fleecy realms of high politics. He was just as happy when deploying the gravest and most pompous prose to predict the obvious: "there will be great heat throughout the summer, and in the autumn great winds will blow."[20]

Readers cowered in the middle of a whirlpool of predictive print, bewildered by "the continual circulation of prophecies, predictions, and horoscopes of every kind."[21] Humorists soon appeared to mock the fashionable pursuit of foreknowledge. The same ill-assorted themes that filled Cardano's booklet and those of his rivals reappeared in a number of parodies and satires, like Rabelais's *Pantegrueline Prognostication* and the *Practica for the Year 1565* issued by Hans Wyermann from Bern, "doctor of the seven lazy arts," who predicted that more snow would fall on the mountains in January than on the lake of Geneva, and more ice would appear in winter than in August.[22]

Prognostications by the dozen came off presses across Europe. Neither the clichés with which they were laden nor the bent nibs with which their parodists tried to prick them seem to have slowed their circulation. Matthew Parker, the erudite Elizabethan archbishop of Canterbury, dismissed the "prognostication of Mr Michael Nostre Damus" as a "fantastical hotch-potch." But most people were not self-assured and highly educated Protestant intellectuals like Parker. From the sailors in the Spanish fleet to the French king and his courtiers, ordinary men and women read the pamphlets of Nostradamus with absorbed fascination and tried to act on their predictions. Copies of Nostradamus' leaflets, accompanied by detailed covering letters, filled the official pouches of both Catholic and Protestant diplomats.[23]

Cardano's little book followed convention in most respects. He agreed that well-known planetary conjunctions—notably the great conjunctions of Saturn and Jupiter which had occurred in 1524 and would recur in 1564—predicted changes in the universal church—indeed, in all known religions. More ambitiously, he also tried, as we saw, to use the precession of the equinoxes to predict the long-term evolution of Catholicism. But his astrological interpretation of the way the eighth and ninth spheres interacted to shape world history, in both its technical detail and its wider explanatory claims, harked back to well-established and widely known traditions. The authors of the Alphonsine Tables had set the era, or baseline date, when the two spheres actually coincided—the date, as Cardano put it, when the first degree of the sign of Aries in the Zodiac corresponded precisely to the first degree of the constellation of Aries in the eighth sphere—as 17 May C.E. 15—a date which fell suspiciously near the midpoint between the incarnation of Jesus, at the beginning of the Christian era, and his crucifixion in the early thirties. They had also posited a larger mystical chronology, which determined the change in the precession over time, making the two spheres oscillate over a period of 7,000 years and suggesting that 7 × 7,000 years, or 49,000 years, would constitute a Great Year.[24]

Cardano very likely picked at a thread that Alfonso's astronomers had woven into the fabric of their work themselves when he argued that precession shaped religion.[25] This general mixture of long- and short-term prediction, conjunctionist astrology and political prophecy, closely resembled that to be found in a prognostication also published in Milan, five years after Cardano's, by Ottavio Cane Gaurico—who gloomily held that the conjunction of Saturn and Mars "threatens cruel wars and the deaths of many men," but optimistically predicted that the Grand Turk would suffer "the ruin of his state and life" before the end of 1572.[26]

More generally, Cardano confined himself, in the *Pronostico*, to citing and exploring relatively well-known sources. To give his work the proper, dramatic tone of dire prophecy, he laced it with biblical quotations from the Psalms and elsewhere. Classical support for the idea that portents preceded all great events came, Cardano claimed, from Caesar, who described fiery omens and rains of stones. Cardano recognized that readers had a taste for such wares: describing the condition of Milan, he remarked that many "await, in vain, a certain pronouncement of fra Amadio, on the Angelic Pope." This was a reference to the prophecy known as the *Apocalypsis Nova*, a work ascribed to a repentant knight named Amadeus, which circulated widely in manuscript, and which predicted, among other events, the transformation of state and church in Italy.[27] Like other prognosticators, Cardano read astrology as well as prophecy. The older sources he drew on included Ptolemy and the twelfth-century Jewish philosopher and astrologer Abraham ibn Ezra, whom he cited to support his view that even the Roman church, "so far as temporal matters are concerned, is subject to the stars, though so far as the faith is concerned it is not."[28] He even quoted one illustrious modern writer—the Bolognese astrologer and chiromancer Bartolomeo Cocles, whose prophetic powers were famous—to support his attack on efforts to draw up horoscopes for cities.[29] Like other prognosticators, in sum, Cardano drew on ancient and modern, published and unpublished, technical and prophetic texts. His work, like theirs, became a natural locus for the encounter of high and low, in content as in readership.

In listing and interpreting the most prominent astronomical events of the years he dealt with, Cardano also followed the norms of prognostication. Great conjunctions and eclipses normally dominated the astronomical sections of Italian and northern almanacs.[30] Achilles Pirmin Gasser, issuing a similar work for 1544 in Germany a few years later, used the four eclipses that he knew would take place between 10 January and 29 December, three lunar and one solar, to predict the appearance of sea monsters, serpents, thunder, lightning, floods, eruptions of blood, and a great transformation of human conduct. This would, in turn, have terrible results for the Christian religion, diminishing both "the worthiness of priests" and "royal revenues." Like Cardano, Gasser paid due heed to the great conjunction of Saturn and Jupiter which would take place in Scorpio on 5 September—and which may well have provided the chief astronomical motivation for writing his little book in the first place. Similar conjunctions, he recalled—perhaps drawing on the work of Pierre d'Ailly, who had already lined up great conjunctions with historical events—had announced the Flood, the promulgation of the Mosaic law, and the rise of Islam.[31] This one would take place in the ill-omened sign of Scorpio, "a place which deserves to be called that of ill fortune, and is particularly assigned to ills of the human body and illnesses." It portended war, tribulation, and the spread of a new "hypocrisy" of "pseudo-prophets."[32] Gasser also predicted such localized phenomena as the weather, the success or failure of crops, and even the quality of minerals that would be mined. Like Cardano, finally, Gasser hedged all his predictions with repeated remarks that the influence of any given celestial event might well be altered or canceled by others. Thus the eclipses of the year in question would "produce results largely contrary to," and far worse than, those portended by the movements of the planets.[33] Though Cardano was a Catholic living in Italy and Gasser a Protestant living in a free city of the Holy Roman Empire, the similarities between their pamphlets seem far more striking than the differences. In general terms, accordingly, Cardano did nothing out of the ordinary when he compounded an almanac with an exhortatory astrological pamphlet about life, the universe, and everything.

Cardano composed and published the *Pronostico* at a difficult point in his career. Born illegitimate, though his father later married his mother, Cardano completed his studies in his mid-twenties, only to find that his birth barred him from entrance into the College of Physicians in Milan. Cardano's bastardy may well have been nothing more than a pretext for refusing him entrance to this professional organization, the real reason being Cardano's own character and conduct. Always contentious, always sharp-tongued, he subjected his colleagues to sharp criticism both in conversation and in one of his earliest medical works. This was an unusual—not to say suicidal—step in a period when most medical men insisted on the merits of the school they had emerged from. At all events, Cardano found himself excluded from the medical elite in Milan and forced to work as a country doctor in small towns: Sacco (Saccolongo) outside Padua, and Gallarate near Milan. Not until 1535 did he receive an appointment to give public lectures in mathematics on feast days at Milan, in a position once held by his father. He did not begin to publish works in mathematics and medicine until 1536.[34]

Cardano's little astrological brochure evidently represented, in part, a simple effort to make some money. Many years later, he recalled the difficulties that he had survived as a poor young man. Cardano asked himself how he had survived as an outsider, rejected by the College of Physicians, victimized by thieves, and subject to his own bad habit of spending enormous amounts of money on books: "Did you give private lessons? No. Did you borrow? No. Did you ask someone for a gift? I doubt I could have found anyone, and I would have been ashamed. Did you go on an austere diet? Not even that. What then? I wrote astronomical tables"[35]—a description that could apply almost as easily to the *Pronostico* of 1534 as to the astrological works he produced, as we will see, a few years later.

The prognosticator could profit from his work in several ways. At the most basic level, he could hope to make money from the sale of the book itself. Cardano, as Ian Maclean has shown, took the clever step of obtaining a legal privilege for his pamphlet, which he issued with a Milanese specialist in such works, Gotardo da Ponta, as well as with the Venetian printer Vincenzo de Bindonis.[36] He could thus claim for himself the income the book generated. The actual revenues from the sale were probably small. But such volumes could have potential value of other kinds. Cardano—like Gasser and many other prognosticators—had medical training and wished to make a career as a doctor. Though not yet a member of the Milanese College, he described himself on the title page of his *Pronostico* as "a doctor from Milan." Like Gasser—who confessed that his *Prognosticum* was the first publication of someone who had previously done his computations for private use only—Cardano probably hoped to gain customers and repute for his medical services even if he failed to earn large sums of money as an author.

It is less certain how Cardano hoped to deal with the vast range of technical and political problems that he and other prognosticators confronted. When he added his own trickle to the vast spate of prophetic pamphlets that roared through the European market squares of the late fifteenth and early sixteenth centuries, he needed to find a way to mark it, to make it stand out. But he failed to do so, as we have seen, and apparently realized that he had. Some evidence suggests that he tried to suppress the memory of his first little book. Certainly Cardano never included the *Pronostico* in his own lists of his writings. The image that he had printed on the title page of his next astrological work, which appeared in 1538—a portrait with the device "No prophet is accepted in his own country"—speaks volumes.[37] And Cardano's failure was hardly surprising. Since the late fifteenth century, influential writers like the Germans Johannes Lichtenberger and Joseph Grünpeck had mingled astrology with eschatology. Cardano's prophecies of starry doom cannot have rung too loudly in ears that cries of impending calamity had battered for decades.[38]

Italy and the Holy Roman Empire were undergoing a political, military, and religious crisis in the years when Cardano began to write. The small states of Italy, for a century the school of politics and diplomacy for the rest of Europe, had become the battleground for French and Spanish armies far larger than any Italian power could hope to match. Once-great powers like Cardano's Duchy of Milan faced the loss of political independence for

PRONOSTI-
CVM DOCTORIS IOSEPHI
Gruenpeck, Ab Anno trigeſimo ſecun
do uſq; ad Annū quadrageſimum
Imperatoris Caroli quinti, plæ-
raſq; futuras Hiſtorias
continens.

Figure 15 The title page of Joseph Grünpeck's *Pronosticum.* The fierce imperial eagle provides a good parallel to the title page of Cardano's *Pronostico.* So does Grünpeck's text, which predicts "terrors to be awaited from the heavens, which can be caused by both the planets and the fixed stars."

which they had struggled for centuries. The Empire, long the object of political struggle between the emperors and local princely and city governments, had also produced the first successful challenge in centuries to the universal authority of the Catholic church, the Protestant Reformation. Social, political, and religious controversies raged—and flared up into the raw violence of the German Peasants' Revolt of 1525 and the Anabaptist movement that formed in its wake. In these years of political and military crisis, Italy and the Empire had become the stage for a continuing vaudeville theater of predictors. Some were erudite, like Giovanni Mercurio, the Platonizing prophet who stalked the streets of Rome in 1484 bearing on his hat the words "This is my son Pimander, in whom I am well pleased." Some were charismatic, like Girolamo Savonarola. Genuine works by him and forgeries, printed in pamphlet form and equipped with striking woodcut illustrations in the style of Ghirlandaio, made the Catholic world resound with their message of hope and transformation long after Savonarola met his death in Florence.[39] Bearded prophets and hawkers of lurid, tattered pamphlets stalked the marketplaces of Italian cities, where intellectuals and shopkeepers alike eagerly collected and discussed their prophecies. Holy women, some of whom even bore the stigmata, adorned the convents and courts of sophisticated cities like Ferrara, whose rulers vied for their presence—and for the political support and comfort provided by their divinely inspired prophecies.[40] Cardano—who firmly believed that his lifetime had fallen in an age of wonders—knew that his pamphlet had to capture a niche in a sharply competitive prophetic ecology.[41]

Cardano tried to achieve this, as we have seen, by asserting his proficiency as a technical astrologer. In doing so, however, he managed less to show what was special in his own method of prognostication than to acknowledge that the whole enterprise faced an internal technical crisis. Astrology had always had its critics. In the ancient world, Cicero, Augustine, and others had drawn up a litany of complaints about the determinist folly of the astrologers. Some argued, for example, that astrologers could not account for the different characters of twins, like Jacob and Esau. Such criticisms rarely applied in any direct way to the practices of real astrologers—most of whom, far from claiming access to a single, universal causal system, regularly acknowledged the role of upbringing and environment and insisted that they could not predict even the life of a single individual from the positions of the planets at his or her birth alone. Ptolemy, who laid out in his *Tetrabiblos* an early, systematic account of astrology, explained far more effectively than any of astrology's opponents the necessary limitations of his approximate predictive art.[42]

In the fourteenth century and after, however, critics of astrology began to wield new, sharp tools along with the older, blunt ones bequeathed them by Cicero and Augustine. Nicole Oresme observed that it took millennia for celestial phenomena to recur even once; some never did. The astrologers, who had been working for only the few thousand years since Noah's Flood, could not possibly have derived their rules for interpreting the effects of conjunctions and oppositions from observation. They simply had not had enough time.

At the end of the fifteenth century, finally, Pico della Mirandola mounted a scathing, deeply informed attack on the pretensions of the astrologers in his *Disputationes adversus astrologiam divinatricem.* Close reading of astrological literature in many languages, western and near eastern, classical and modern, enabled him to reveal the enormous amount of sand that astrologers had used when pouring the very foundations of their art. Basic doctrines like that of the historical impact of the great conjunctions, Pico revealed, rested not on an empirical effort to tease out the correspondences between planetary motions and historical events, but on the reverse: Astrological writers like Abu Ma'sar and Pierre d'Ailly, convinced that the great conjunctions determined all important events, had imposed this pattern on the historical data even when they contradicted it.

Astrology stood revealed, in Pico's work, as a mass of logical leaps and technical errors, devoid of scientific foundation—the natural product of the superstitious Chaldeans who had brought it into being in the first place. Worst of all, Pico exposed astrology as a fundamentally irreligious art—one whose practitioners had wrongly claimed that the immortal souls of individual men and the larger religions which they practiced were subject to the rule of the stars, themselves mere bodies without immortal souls.[43]

Pico's arguments won the enthusiastic approval of Savonarola, who summarized part of them in Italian. They also provoked the fury of astrologers like Luca Bellanti, who refuted Pico at length, making—not for the last time—the nice point that Pico had died in the very year foretold him by an astrologer.[44] More important for present purposes, they became common coin for anyone interested in astrology from any point of view. Authors of short texts like Cardano's regularly invoked Pico, positively or negatively, in the course of the polemics that broke out around the supposedly new disease of syphilis. As early as 1496, Grünpeck, following the lead of an "Egyptian" who whispered in his ear of "Hippocrates, Galen, Avicenna, Plato, Aristotle, and almost innumerable other astrologers who discussed the interpretation of natural and celestial things," described syphilis as brought about "by the configurations of the stars."[45] Others weighed in to different effect.

The debate reached a sharp key when the Leipzig professor Simon Pistoris argued at length that "even though astrology may not be said to be a part of medicine, it can be shown to be very useful, indeed necessary, to the doctor." Citing the Conciliator, the influential early fourteenth-century Paduan scholar Pietro d'Abano, as his authority, Pistoris insisted that "doctors can prognosticate the future from illnesses; similarly the astrologer can predict the future from the stars."[46]

An opponent from Nuremberg—the one-time astrologer Polich de Mellerstadt—replied in even more detail. Pico, he argued, had left astrology in such tatters "that nothing remains to be hoped for from it." He reviewed Pico's technical and historical critique of astrology in detail and with lavish praise. Pistoris he dismissed as a doctor rather than an astrologer, who owed his knowledge of the field to the ephemerides of Regiomontanus and other trivial works: "the *practicae* which they produce from year to year, [which] are more useful for latrines than in medical schools." Mellerstadt claimed to have seen one such book which, when treating the influence of Saturn for the current year 1499, advised "the brothers in religious orders, dressed in their sorrowful black habits, to take wives and marry them"—and thus, as he explained with shock, subjected the religion of Christ itself to the stars.[47] Even in the context of pamphlet literature aimed at a Latin-reading but nonspecialist public, in other words, Pico's sweeping criticism of astrology found diffusion.

Pistoris came back with an equally sweeping rebuttal, insisting that Pico had been ignorant of medicine. But Mellerstadt replied with undiminished confidence. Failing to observe the moon's motion when carrying out a surgical procedure, he observed, was every bit as dangerous as failing to do so when putting on a new garment. Pistoris' obstinacy showed only that "because astrological judgements are sold at higher prices in Leipzig than in Nuremberg, astrologers are esteemed more highly there than here"—a nice way of contrasting the hard-headed merchant public in Nuremberg with the credulous academics in the Saxon university town.[48] By the beginning of the sixteenth century, in short, any well-informed astrologer or medical man who issued a *Practica* had to be aware that he practiced a craft with a highly questionable reputation.

The philosopher, medical man, and astrologer Agostino Nifo, for example, fervently believed that doctors needed to take the effects of the heavens into account. He provided astrological counsel about the weather and other aspects of the year to come when important patrons like Gonzalo Fernández de Córdoba, whose physician he was, asked him to do so. Córdoba's whole army, Nifo told his medical students in Naples, could attest to his success at predicting the unexpected political and military events of 1504–1505 for his master.[49] But Nifo agreed with Pico that the astrology of his time badly needed reform. The "conjunctionists," who followed not the classic authority of Ptolemy but the more recent Arabic writer Abu Maʿsar, attributed too much power to the planets and their positions, too little to the eclipses of the sun and moon. Pico, for all his exaggerations, had been right to insist that the sun and moon were the preeminent celestial bodies.[50]

The Flemish mathematician and theologian Albertus Pighius agreed. He deplored the spread of "a certain breed of ignorant men, who put out for popular consumption every year ridiculous annual *Prognostica,* and ascribe all their lies, their conjurings, and their superstitions to astrology."[51] This fashion had done immense harm to the art of medicine, at Antwerp at least, "where nobody nowadays dares to profess it unless he divines with the rest of them," taking the astrologers' bad advice and performing phlebotomies and prescribing drugs at the wrong times they assigned.[52] Pighius bravely went to work to show that the astrologers' practices were rife with error of all the forms Nifo had identified and others as well. Cardano's pamphlet—with its sharp critique of the incompetence of prognosticators—merely echoed what had become a widespread view within the discipline of astrology itself.[53]

In the second and third decades of the sixteenth century, moreover, the debate spilled outward from the lively but Latinate world of the astrological writers to the shriller vernacular and public realm of the pulpit and the public square. As early as 1499, Johannes Stoeffler and Jacob Pflaum announced in their *Almanach nova* that in 1524,

> we will not witness an eclipse of the sun or of the moon. But in the course of this year, some extraordinary configurations of the planets will take place. In February, for example, there will be twenty conjunctions, of small, medium, and great importance. Sixteen of them will take place in a watery sign. These will portend certain changes and transformations for the whole world, for all regions, kingdoms, provinces, states, ranks, beasts, marine animals, and everything that is born of the earth—changes such as we have hardly heard of for centuries before our time, either from historians, or from our elders. Raise your heads, accordingly, Christian men.[54]

Gradually the idea spread that these changes would take the form of a vast new flood, a repetition of the biblical Deluge of Noah. Nifo and others tried to calm their fellow citizens, who, terrified by these predictions, built arks and climbed mountains. In the end, Nifo wrote an elaborate refutation of the Flood prediction, insisting that though heavy rain might fall in some locales, the conjunction in question could not possibly be the sign of a new

Deluge. Eclipses affected the earth far more strongly than conjunctions, and the solar eclipse of 23 August 1523 would have strongly beneficial effects. Jupiter, the beneficent planet, would dominate the maleficent Saturn. Nifo hoped that his "little book" would "render so many peoples free of this great terror."[55] It failed, of course. Arguments and counter-arguments were printed, copied, reprinted, refuted, and reasserted, in a dizzyingly complex series of debates. Paola Zambelli, the leading expert on this first media event of modern times, has found that the astrologers' theses echoed through courts and universities across Europe.

In parts of Italy where deforestation had caused severe flooding in recent years, the threat of inundation seemed very real. The astrologers and street preachers who reiterated the original prediction made it a topic of conversation throughout the peninsula. In some quarters, as Ottavia Niccoli has shown, panic spread. The rich fled to high ground in the country, as they had fled the plague in the time of Boccaccio and after, while the poor stayed put. Penitential processions and civic rites were staged to ward off disaster. Prophecies of all sorts mingled with the original astrological prediction of disaster.[56]

Not everyone shared the general panic or took part in the rituals it called forth. In the carnival of 1525 at Venice, Florence, and Rome, the flood became the object of the obscene humor appropriate to the season. In Venice, well-known public story-tellers made obscene fun of it. And when the promised rains did not fall, informal ridicule turned, at least in some quarters, into formal rituals of inversion. These were directed both at the Flood and at those figures of political and intellectual authority who had given it credence (as the church had, for example, by appropriating and stage-managing the rituals designed to turn away God's wrath). Many began to distinguish, at least in the short term, between the still venerable figure of the prophet and the more problematic one of the astrologer, at once deceptive and gullible. Niccoli, who has reconstructed these events with great learning and imagination, concludes that they had "an enormous negative effect on the figure of the astrologer."[57]

In some circles, they certainly did. Martin Luther, whose closest friend Philipp Melanchthon was a convinced believer in astrology, never missed a chance to make fun of these supposedly scientific prophets, who had conjured up a flood that did not take place in 1524, but never said a word about the Peasants' Revolt that did take place in 1525 (in doing so, he ignored the inconvenient fact that at least one pamphleteer had predicted such a rising).[58]

Niccoli, however, exaggerates somewhat when she says that after 1525, "urban populations" simply mocked astrology as something associated with illegitimate political and religious power.[59] Astrology and other forms of prediction—some with considerably less scientific basis—flourished even at the peak of the mercantile food chain (the great merchant Anton Fugger, for example, used a scryer with a crystal ball to keep an eye on what his partners in cities far from Augsburg were up to).[60] Astrological rules and codes pervaded Italian society at every level. Believers like Alessandro Farnese, who became Pope Paul III in 1534 and brought Luca Gaurico, his favorite astrologer, with him to Rome, retained their faith.[61] Even sceptics like Guicciardini, as we have seen, studied the products of the art they mocked. In some cases, indeed—as in the hands of Tommaso Campanella, at the end of the century—astrology could serve a revolutionary function, helping to give a critique of the existing order the dramatic force that could win it active followers.[62] Prophecy—as one of its greatest students, Marjorie Reeves, has pointed out—is virtually immortal, or at least virtually invulnerable to the shocks experienced by the members of a particular group when events contradict any given prediction.[63] So was—and is—astrology.

Cardano confronted a mass of professional and intellectual difficulties as he started to make his astrological career. He knew as much. In later years, he remembered that he himself had been a fierce critic and opponent of the Flood, boldly denying the truth of Johannes Stoeffler's prediction, and to the highest authority:

> Thinking that the stars portended a flood at a time when the weather was perfectly calm, he announced a great disaster to mortals. Many fled to the mountains. But I, in my twentieth year, predicted to our ruler, Francesco Sforza, that there was nothing to fear. In fact it announced the plague, which was very rare, for our city in that year.[64]

This late tale of early prudence may not deserve much credence: like most astrologers, Cardano loved, as we have seen, to predict impending doom, and disliked recalling earlier errors. But it does show that he was aware, from very early in his life, that the astrologer had to live down the highly visible errors of his colleagues. No single text—much less the little brochure he issued in 1534—could have overcome so many obstacles. And Cardano, illegitimate, poor, and confined to provincial Milan, evidently lacked the immense resources and widely cast patronage net which enabled Gaurico to make himself famous with a long series of such works, each of which he could use to qualify, supplement, and correct its predecessors.[65] Cardano would have to go another way.

chapter four

THE ASTROLOGER

Achilles Gasser's *Prognosticum* of 1544 affords, as we have seen, an informative parallel to Cardano's early *Pronostico.* It also suggests some of the Lamarckian techniques that Cardano could have adopted to give his first book a better chance of survival. Unlike Cardano, who sent his little work out into the world at his own expense, Gasser dedicated his pamphlet to another scholar, Thomas Venatorius, who in turn supplied it with laudatory verses and may well have given the author some money in return for the honor done him.[1] Like many other writers of the period, Gasser used the dedicatory letter not only as a fund-raising device, but also as a literary free space. Thus he devoted less to discussing technical matters than to describing the personal and intellectual contexts in which his work belonged. Gasser portrayed himself affectingly as a committed mathematician who had selflessly dedicated himself, in his spare time and without thought of gain or publication, to the "mathematical disciplines." Only the urging of a close friend, Georg Joachim Rheticus, "forced me to publish this prognostication, just as the elephant is said to have the power to make snakes emerge from their hiding places with its breath."[2]

Rheticus, Gasser explained, "used the authority that I accord him to persuade me to abandon the shadows and the speculative thought known as theory and to descend at last into the arena and the forum. I could thus publicly make clear to scholars what astronomy can achieve toward setting out in advance the effects of the stars when it is put to use (this, I think, is why annual judgments have come to be called 'practicae')."[3] Gasser thus made a number of points clear. In the first place, he stated, as Cardano had, that his work represented more than a crude little series of predictions based on astrological rules of thumb. Rather, it showed how to apply basic principles of astronomy to vital, pragmatic problems, and in a rigorous way. In the second place, Gasser showed that his way of doing so enjoyed the approval of a figure renowned for his prowess as an astronomer. Georg Joachim Rheticus, whose advice Gasser invoked, had written only a few years before the *Narratio prima,* the first account of Copernicus' new planetary theory. This lucid, compact piece of exposition established both his competence in the technical details of astronomy and his position as Copernicus' disciple. In 1543, he helped put Copernicus' own work through the press. The Nuremberg publisher Johannes Petreius, who brought out *De revolutionibus orbium coelestium,* also printed Gasser's *Prognosticum.* The existence of this loose network of personal and intellectual connections suggests that Gasser meant his booklet to be something more than a run-of-the-mill addition to the ever-growing pile of almanacs and tables.[4] A modest astrological publication, in other words, could draw on the prestige of eminent dedicatees and connect its author with the creators of mathematical astronomy. But to achieve this, the author had to demonstrate a level of technical competence higher than that revealed by Cardano's first publication, to ally himself with patrons who would take some interest in furthering his work, and to venture to write in Latin, for a wider than local audience.

Fazio Cardano—Girolamo's father—had known as much. Beginning his own career in the 1480s, he prepared the first printed edition of the treatise on perspective by the late thirteenth-century archbishop of Canterbury John Peckham. Doing so cost Fazio time and trouble, as he grumbled in his preface, since the highly corrupt text needed much correction and the many diagrams had to be aligned with the relevant sections of the text. But it also gave him a chance to publicize his own erudition—as well as his contacts with the publisher of the edition, Bonus Accursius, and the other Milanese printers who, he said, besieged him with requests for advice on what new works to bring out. This same project enabled him to solidify his connections with an influential cleric, Ambrosio Griffo, to whom he addressed his dedicatory letter. In the Milan of the late fifteenth century—a prosperous city and a center of publication, especially in the law, which Fazio had studied—such tactics came naturally to the aspiring intellectual. Half a century later, Girolamo evidently had to learn them again on his own—and to execute them with much less technical help.[5]

Cardano achieved both ends, and more, with his second astrological publication, the *Libelli duo,* which came out in 1538.[6] In fact, these two short texts, which Cardano described as an abridgment of a much longer set of treatises entitled *Iudicia astronomica (Astronomical Judgments),* set him on the path to some of his first literary and professional successes. The first of his works, dramatically entitled *Supplement to the Almanach,* began rather as the *Pronostico* had, with an assertion of the author's superior command of astronomy. But this time Cardano did not portray himself as a mysterious sage who drew on unstated rules to make unshakeable predictions. Rather, he played the role of an erudite, reassuring teacher, out to equip his readers with the tools needed to write predictions of their own.

"One who wishes to attain knowledge of the stars," Cardano explained, "must begin with knowledge of the planets."[7] These he described at some length, in terms of both their physical properties and their movements, in a way clearly designed to help the beginning observer or astrologer learn how to observe the skies. Like a sixteenth-century counterpart to Patrick Moore or Carl Sagan, he led the reader patiently through the mazes of the heavens, offering helpful practical comments at every turn and making clear just how the novice should study the skies, almanac in hand, moving back and forth between the tables that stated where a given planet or star should appear and the actual dots in the night sky.

> The planets are quite different from one another. For only a madman or a blind man is unaware of the sun and the moon. Venus, however, is the brightest star in the sky, very white and very large, so that it alone of the stars casts a shadow. In conjunction with the moon it seems, far from disappearing or becoming weaker, to become even more brilliant. Of all the other stars, Jupiter resembles this one most closely, but it is a little smaller and less brilliant, and unlike Venus, it does not always stick close to the sun. For Venus never departs more than 48 degrees from the sun, in advance or behind it. You can also use their positions to tell them apart, for once you have looked up in the Almanac which of them is the more easterly, it is easy to tell the one from the other. Once you know Venus, then, you know Jupiter, which outshines all the other stars except Venus. Mars shines with a reddish glow and is rather dark. Hence it seems, as it were, to twinkle a great deal. It differs from Jupiter and Venus in its small size, redness, and obscurity. Saturn matches Mars in aspect, but differs from it since it is leaden in color and less bright . . . The Almanac distinguishes the one from the other. For Saturn appears higher than Mars to the eye when they are close to each other. Mercury is always near the sun, from which it does not depart more than 28 degrees. It is rather small and bright, but not white.[8]

Cardano continued in this empirical, instructive vein for some time. He explained in even more vivid detail how to find the pole ("Turn your face toward the north, putting the East to your right and the West to your left, and you will see seven stars in Ursa Major").[9] He laid out the constellations and bright stars which the astronomer should be able to find in the Zodiac, suggesting that the reader should "have a picture of the Zodiac with the stars located as they are in the sky, or the illustrations of Hyginus or Aratus"—the poetic descriptions of the stars, which, with their illustrations, had preserved knowledge of the ancient constellations through the Middle Ages.[10] More than once he made clear to the reader how to use the data given in an almanac, in conjunction with direct observation of the sky, to work out exactly when, for example, a given planet came into conjunction with a given fixed star. Cardano emphasized the practicality of the information and methods he offered. Many clues, he assured the reader, could serve to fix a given star in the memory: magnitude, color, brightness, geometrical figures formed with other stars, and position could all help. "And once you have used all these methods to commit a given star to memory, you cannot possibly forget it unless you are a complete ass." Indeed, it should take only a short time "to attain perfect knowledge of all the stars and heavenly figures, since all the stars visible to us can certainly be seen within fifteen days."[11]

Cardano not only drew up a how-to book for amateur astronomers, but also made clear that he himself had used these techniques in practice. On the twenty-ninth of November 1537, for example, not long before sunrise, he had observed Venus in near conjunction in longitude with the brighter star in the southern *lanx* (scale), at 6 degrees and 57 minutes of Scorpio. Venus' position, which he could establish with precision from the almanac, confirmed that of the star and its constellation. Eleven further observations, he declared, served as the basis for the positions given in his list of the stars in the Zodiac.[12]

The observations and instructions Cardano laid out in *De supplemento almanach* proved his practical, rather than theoretical, expertise. He did not explain the geometrical planetary theory that had been used, for centuries, to account for some of the phenomena he mentioned—for example, why Mercury and Venus never departed more than a set amount from the sun. This fact, explained in modern astronomy by the consideration that both planets revolve around the sun on orbits considerably smaller than that of the earth, was accounted for in classical planetary theory by geometrical models which simply kept both planets, as seen from the earth, relatively close to the sun.

The second of Cardano's two texts, *De temporum et motuum erraticarum restitutione,* gave him the chance to show that he could also attend to planetary theory. He explicated in detail the problems that attended the establishment of correct lengths for the different forms of the solar year, the tropical year (the time it takes the sun to return to either equinox or solstice), and the sidereal year (the time it takes the sun to return to any given point on the sphere of the fixed stars). In this text, unlike the *Supplementum,* Cardano liberally cited the technical literature—like the book on the solar year ascribed in his period to the ninth-century Islamic astronomer Thabit ibn Qura.[13] He rehearsed the technical data on such well-established problems as the precession of the equinoxes.

Cardano set out, with a self-confidence that was not always justified, to correct errors in standard modern sources—for example, the conversions from Egyptian to Julian dates of astronomical eras and observations from Ptolemy which he found in the world chronicle of Johannes Lucidus Samotheus and the astronomical writings of Johannes Stoeffler. And he did correctly note, for example, that some astronomers had confused the era of the death of Alexander the Great, 324 B.C.E., with the Seleucid era of 312 B.C.E.—which Islamic astronomers and the authors of the Alphonsine Tables called, confusingly, the era of Alexander. This mistake led Johannes Werner, for example, to misdate the star catalogue of Ptolemy from its true era of around C.E. 138 to C.E. 150, an error that had serious consequences for any effort to establish the rate of precession, and which Copernicus himself sorted out in a short treatise.[14] Cardano even peered through the cloudy night skies on 8 June 1538, when a conjunction of Saturn and Mars took place—and noted that according to the tables, they should have been a little more than 2 degrees apart.[15] From his study of the texts and his observations, he concluded that the planetary theory of his day needed major reform.

In these two short texts Cardano went beyond what was normally expected of an astrologer writing a short, compendious textbook. Instead of taking the standard astronomical tables as givens and using the positions they yielded even when they clearly did not correspond with the real motions of the planets, he showed that he had all the skills, observational and quantitative, expected of an astronomer in the first half of the sixteenth century. Nothing that he said showed immense originality. The detailed instructions that Cardano provided for using the stars to tell time at night, for example, drew on a tradition of practical mathematics already well established in Italy. Leon Battista Alberti had described a similar way of telling time by the stars, making no claims to originality, almost a century before.[16] Many medieval and early Renaissance astronomers had corrected, or tried to correct, standard tables. The astronomer Petrus Pitatus, editing the *Ephemerides* of Johannes Stöffler, noted that he had observed on 22 May 1536 a conjunction of Saturn and Mars—one which should have taken place, according to the "diaries" of Stöffler, three days later. One of the most common ways to use almanacs and tables must have been to predict such conjunctions, and observations like Cardano's and Pitatus' were not uncommon.[17] Still, Cardano proved that like Copernicus, he had read Ptolemy's *Almagest* and later astronomical works with care; that he knew that the astronomical methods of his time needed reform; and that he had done observations of his own in the hope of establishing new parameters. When Cardano praised his own technical mastery or denied that of others after 1538, he spoke with some authority. Thus, even two generations later, Tycho Brahe read Cardano's little treatises with serious interest and cited them with some respect, even if he made fun of Cardano's proposal to fix the positions of fixed stars by reference to that of Venus, since the planetary positions as determined in Cardano's time hardly offered a flawless basis for measurement.[18]

The contrast between Cardano's practices and normal ones was sharp. Most astrologers used their tables as social scientists sometimes apply software packages: they treated these paper devices as black boxes, understanding little or nothing of the principles on which they rested and having little or no ability to compensate for their defects. Their nasty remarks about their competitors rarely rested on a demonstrated mastery of astronomical materials and methods. Marsilio Ficino, for example, enjoyed fame as an expert in medical astrology thanks to his *De vita coelitus comparanda,* a spectacularly detailed treatise on the most effective ways of using talismans and music, among other means, to draw upon the powers of the benevolent planets and avert the influence of the malevolent ones.[19] When Ficino composed his life of Plato, accordingly, he wanted to begin from the philosopher's horoscope. Though he had already discussed one version in his *De amore,* he rejected it in favor of another, taken from the late antique astrological treatise of Firmicus Maternus, which he reproduced. Apparently he did not notice that it, like the other sample horoscopes Firmicus provided for the heroes of the Trojan War and other worthies, was completely imaginary, unconnected to the planetary positions on the date of Plato's birth or any other date in real time.[20]

Georg Helmstetter of Heidelberg—the historical Faustus—omitted both the precise borders of the houses and all the planetary positions from a geniture which he drew up and interpreted for a client, to the derision of at least one reader.[21] Nostradamus' horoscopes swarmed with similarly gross errors and omissions, which evoked astonishment from his customers and ridicule from his rivals.[22] In the kingdom of astrologers without much quantitative skill, one who could read tables and find stars could reasonably claim the throne.

Though Cardano emphasized the formally astronomical component of his own work, he by no means abandoned the sort of astrology he had practiced in the *Pronostico.* After he explained how to tell the individual stars and planets apart visually, he devoted far more space to explaining how to interpret their individual effects astrologically. Cardano analyzed the characters of both the planets and the fixed stars at considerable length. He distilled tight little "aphorisms for help in judgment" from his experience: "Mars and the seventh house [mean] disagreements, quarrels, and open enemies. The Sun and the tenth, glory. Both unfortunate planets and the sixth house, diseases. The Moon and Venus and the seventh house, wives and concubines."[23] He offered not weather predictions for a given year, but rules for making them, which he drew from Ptolemy and confirmed, so he claimed, by his own observation.[24] And he still spiced his work with threatening references to long-term astrological phenomena and their historical consequences.

One chapter of Cardano's *De supplemento almanach* laid out at length an astrological explanation for history itself. If a star passed once a day through the zenith of a given place on earth—the point on the celestial sphere directly above it—it would continue to do so for a considerable period, until it moved onward because of precession. Such a star, Cardano argued, would have a "great power" over the place—a power which he conjured up with appropriately dramatic language: "When the head of Algol passed through Asia Minor and Greece, in around 400 years it utterly destroyed those provinces, and made them deserted and subject to Muslim oppression. But it has now invaded Italy, for it is directly above Apulia and the kingdom of Naples; may it bring us no harm."[25] Cardano insisted that this theory, applied retrospectively, could explain the past as well as predict the future. The last star in the tail of Ursa Major, a star of the second magnitude, passed over Rome at the time of the city's foundation, "and therefore [the Romans'] fortitude enabled them to rule the world." The same star brought the Byzantine and German empires into being in their turn. Astrology, in other words, underpinned the ancient theory of *translatio imperii*.[26]

Theories about the stellar origins of religion had notoriously proved dangerous to their own authors in the later Middle Ages. Nonetheless, Cardano could not resist them here any more than he had in the *Pronostico*—though he tried to offer genteel qualifications which might divert the wrath of theological authority:

> The Christian and Jewish religions are from God, but the fortunes of the churches militant are governed by the superior bodies. The Jewish religion is controlled by Saturn, or its star, or rather both; the Christian, by Jupiter and Mercury. The Muslims are governed by the Sun and Mars, dominating equally; hence their church maintains justice, but with great impiety and cruelty. Idolatry is ruled by the Moon and Mars. But each law is dissolved by its

> contrary. Jupiter overcomes Saturn with authority, and Mercury with reason. Mars overcomes Jupiter and Mercury, paying no heed to their arguments and raging against their authority. Saturn and Venus overcome Mars and the Sun, she with lasciviousness and he with subterfuges. The Sun and Jupiter use authority, dignity, and truth to destroy Mars and the Moon. Therefore, Christians, raise up your heads. Let him who can understand, understand.[27]

Once again—as in the *Pronostico*—Cardano followed ibn Ezra in subjecting all the peoples of the earth to the stars, so far as their practical and political affairs were concerned. Cardano's new, upmarket astrological publication in cosmopolitan Latin yielded nothing to his pamphlet in Italian, in other words, for generality of scope or ominousness of tone. Astrology still retained its stylistic link with more popular, and less technical, forms of prophecy. In fact, Cardano developed the grandiose themes of historical astrology at some length in another work which he drafted in this period, but did not manage to complete, *The Secrets of Eternity*.[28]

Cardano's theories were not so obviously superior to rival ones as he would have liked. Accordingly, he buttressed them with replies to potential objections. To the argument that a given star should affect not a single city or state but everyone living anywhere on the parallel over which it passed perpendicularly, for example, Cardano replied with qualifications. The star would have such effects only if it had reached that position on the day when the city or state in question was founded, at noon, and in conjunction with the sun.[29] What technical arguments could not achieve, the language of somber threat and mystification might. Cardano gave his readers not only clear, easily applied rules of prediction which anyone could easily grasp and use, but also rules of interpretation as rich in predictive force and slippery in practical application as any master of astrology could hope to provide:

> In every geniture there is a best position, which controls all good fortune, and a worst one, which controls all misfortune. The best place is the tenth house, or the first one, or a luminary, if there is joined with these fortune, or a propitious ray, or that of the other luminary, or a fortunate star, so that the good fortune is doubled. Thus the place of misfortune is misfortune multiplied twice.[30]

Anyone who could grasp the method laid out here—and work out exactly which planetary and stellar positions must be taken into account in applying it—obviously had access to a powerful tool for determining the effects of a given configuration of the planets unequivocally.

Equally obviously—or so it seems now—no one could hope to use rules like these as rigorously as one could apply Cardano's instructions for determining the time at night or the position of Venus. The doctrine itself was complex: the multiple possible ways of applying it ensured that the results could turn out as seemed best, in a given situation, to the astrologer. Ancient manuals of astrology, as Tamsyn Barton has shown, offered a far wider range of rules for interpretation than any practitioner could hope to apply in a single case: much less could one readily work out in advance how each of them modified the others. The very complexity of the system ensured that only a trained astrologer, an initiate, could use it. Written treatises served less as manuals to be applied than as advertisements for their authors.[31] Cardano, not for the last time, replicated ancient precedent as he too produced an astrological manual which left all the real decisions in the hands of the expert reader, not the ordinary one. Rather like Ignatius Loyola's *Spiritual Exercises,* Cardano's book offered guidance to the guide, not to the client.

Cardano, moreover, put even more devices—both social and technical—into play. To claim the financial and personal support that the *Pronostico* had not brought him, he signed his astrological work "Girolamo Castiglione Cardano"—thus insisting on his family's connection to the large and very influential clan of the Castiglione.[32] He also dedicated the little book to a particular patron: Filippo Archinto, an influential Milanese diplomat now established in Rome, as governor of the city.[33] In the dedicatory letter in which Cardano offered his thanks, he complained bitterly once again of the incompetence of the astrologers of his time. Cardano was now playing the games of scholarship with all the energy he could muster. He hoped that his little work, with its ambitious claims, would not only bring him support from Archinto, but also win him the attention of a still higher sponsor, Paul III Farnese. The pope's passion for astronomy made him the natural object of grant proposals from every prognosticator in Italy and beyond, and thanks to his connection with Archinto, Cardano did manage to meet him.[34] And though this contact proved ephemeral, the dedication at least gave Cardano another opportunity to emphasize the high technical quality and public-spirited character of his own astrology—even as he presumably received a present from Archinto for doing so. Cardano evidently found Archinto a consistently generous benefactor. Almost ten years after the first publication of the *Libelli duo,* in 1546, Cardano reiterated that only Archinto's interest had led him to publish his work in this field, which was not as lucrative as medicine and could bring its practitioners into discredit.[35]

Cardano also added a further technical element to the *Libelli*—one which seems to have done more than anything else to win attention for his little book. In the *De supplemento almanach,* discussing the technical equipment that an astrologer needed, Cardano pointed out that

> one must have as many genitures as possible, and examinations of the timing: and similarly in any given event one must observe the meetings of the planets with one another and with regard to the fixed stars in directions and revolutions. For since the same configuration produces the same effect, one must repeatedly make judgments about a given conjunction or the nature of the fixed stars, in accordance with the properties of the events in question, so that we may also make predictions in other cases.[36]

Suiting his action to his word, Cardano appended to the *Libelli* a group of ten genitures, laid out in the standard square diagrammatic form and analyzed at some length.

In principle, this little collection hardly represented a startling innovation. The astrologers of the ancient world had also assembled horoscopes for systematic study, though the one surviving specimen of this genre, the *Anthologies* of Vettius Valens, had not yet been translated into Latin, much less printed, when Cardano wrote.[37] Dorotheus of Sidon's *Pentateuch* also contained horoscopes, some of which were preserved by Abu Ali, Masha'allah, and other medieval astrologers, and circulated fairly widely in both manuscripts and printed texts—even if their data sometimes became muddled in transmission, and later writers sometimes took personal credit for the work of their predecessors.[38]

Cardano, moreover, certainly knew at least a few precedents for his enterprise. The medieval commentary on Ptolemy's *Tetrabiblos* by Haly ibn Rodoan, for example, contained its author's geniture and a number of others, variously mangled in the course of transmission and translation.[39] The English astrologers of the later Middle Ages, who taught the kings and high nobility they served to appreciate the uses of astrology, also collected the results of their work in notebooks of royal nativities, drawn up and analyzed in full technical detail.[40] Cardano's collection drew, as we will see, on similar notebooks, of Italian origin. Like the English collections, his consisted in large part of celebrity genitures: he offered the horoscopes of five intellectuals, Petrarch, George of Trebizond, Francesco Filelfo, Fazio Cardano (his own father), and Gualtiero Corbetta, and five rulers, Pope Paul III, the Holy Roman Emperor Charles V, Francis I, Süleyman I the Magnificent, and Ludovico Sforza.

Technically speaking, the horoscopes revealed no secrets that a reader could not find elsewhere. Like all other astrologers of his time, Cardano produced his genitures by computing a number of positions for the day, time, and place where the individual in question was born: those of the moon, the sun, the five planets, and the so-called head of the dragon.[41] He also established which degree of the Zodiac was the ascendant—the point rising over the horizon at the moment of birth. And he used this information to lay out the ascendant and twelve houses of each horoscope, superimposing these points and divisions on the Zodiac. This last step was crucial to the whole enterprise. The effects of the moon, sun, and planets were determined not only by their angular relations to one another, but also by the nature of the houses in which they fell, since each house determined a different aspect of the client's life. But this step also posed difficult technical choices. Astrologers could use any one of several methods to determine the location of the twelve houses, ranging from the simple and schematic to the geometrically demanding.

Cardano, however, adopted the simplest of them all. After finding the ascendant, he simply added constant intervals of 30 degrees to locate the borders of each of the twelve houses of the Zodiac, even though doing so was completely arbitrary, since the houses, as laid out for any given latitude, differ considerably in length. Cardano explicitly defended his choice of house systems, citing the authority of the well-known astrologer Paris Ceresarius, the astrological adviser to Isabella d'Este, in his defense and insisting that the equal house system was more logical, and more generally applicable, than any of its competitors, none of which could work for every latitude.[42] But any informed reader would have known that Cardano had chosen the easy way out, astronomically speaking. Just as the first printed anatomical illustrations were far cruder than contemporary anatomical drawings, so the first printed horoscope collection was carried out on a far less sophisticated technical level than its manuscript forerunners.[43] In the case of the horoscope, printing not only failed to enhance, but actually diminished, the rigor of the methods most widely employed.

This primitive version of what would become a very elaborate horoscope collection already revealed the elements of a personal style. Cardano introduced it with an elaborate series of flourishes, emphasizing that each horoscope would both inform and amaze the reader. In fact, he claimed to have chosen the horoscopes as much to stimulate the wonder that sixteenth-century readers so prized as to confirm astrological arguments with well-established facts:

> I did not add any of these genitures without due consideration or a significant cause, since each of them had some remarkable property or other. The celebrated virtues and remarkable successes of these princes illuminated the world, as the testimony of several centuries, corroborated by history, will show. True, the last came to his end in great misfortune, seeing his sons go into exile, being deprived of his state, betrayed, and put into prison, where he died in great misery. But all of them have in common the fact that I had a solid knowledge of their deeds and virtues.[44]

The scholars also deserved fame and admiration: "Petrarch's many excellent volumes," for example, "like his life, attest to his great worth and erudition."[45] Cardano, in other words, offered his readers biographical sketches of the great men of the age. He did so, moreover, on the basis of information mysteriously acquired but multiply confirmed. Cardano insisted that he had checked each geniture in two ways. He had obtained as many copies of each of them as he could from different sources. And he had carefully established that "the actions" of their subjects, "which resemble their genitures fairly closely, attest to their credibility."[46]

In the case of private individuals, Cardano held, "it will not be hard to describe the entire course of their lives and to persuade readers of the truth of my account."[47] He devoted large segments of his genitures of scholars to accounting for such noncontroversial qualities as the "sweetness" of Petrarch's poetry ("Jupiter provides this, in the house of Mercury, in quadrature with Venus") and the polyglot erudition of George of Trebizond. But he also explained Francesco Filelfo's tendency to debauch both boys and girls.[48] More remarkably, Cardano showed his willingness to analyze the discreditable side of his subject's life even in the case of his own father. Girolamo's geniture for Fazio accounted not only for the latter's long life, love of study, and loss of all his teeth at the age of fifty-eight, but also for his "knowledge of occult learning." Cardano did not stop here; he explicitly described Fazio's skill in the forbidden art of necromancy as "so great that he had no rivals in our time."[49] The lack of an inner check that enabled Cardano to reveal such facts in print no doubt contributed much to the entertainment value of all of his astrological books.

In the case of princes, Cardano knew that he was treading on dangerous ground. In the first place, he admitted, the fortunes of a prince depended to a great extent on those of his kingdom as a whole, and the individual's horoscope did not reveal the larger community's prospects. In the second place, "I cannot speak evil of them without running some risk or praise them without suspicion of flattery." Even if a prince's horoscope lacked any evidence of misfortune to come, Cardano pointed out, a prudent reader would scent flattery rather than honest analysis in a positive commentary.[50] More seriously still, since late antiquity the astrological tradition had found one simple, radical way of dealing with the conundrums posed by the special problem of princely genitures: it ignored them. In the third and fourth centuries, as Marie Theres Fögen has argued, both the Christian church and the Roman emperors began to claim absolute power in the cosmos and on earth—and to reject the claim that other bodies, like the stars, exercised influence over them. The prudent astrologer, accordingly, abandoned at least part of the authority that his predecessors would have claimed in the early years of the Roman Empire. He acknowledged—as Firmicus Maternus did in his *Mathesis*—that the emperors were gods, and as such not subject to the power of the stars.[51]

Cardano met this self-denying ordinance with scorn. "Some authorities," he wrote,

> like Firmicus, release princes' bodies and minds from all celestial causes. They could do this because, in their empty superstition, they called the princes themselves gods. We, however, may not, since we, who cultivate true piety, observe nothing superstitious in the stars, but natural causes. All men alike are tormented by heat, cold, and pain. Similarly, we cannot deny that the bodies and minds of princes are bent to good and evil effect, violently and gently, [by the stars].[52]

The pious astrologer, in short, knew that the one true god had enveloped all humans, the highest as well as the lowest, in a web of natural causes, one both written in and generated by the stars. He was duty-bound, accordingly, to reveal the conclusions of his art, at whatever personal risk or cost that might entail—as well as to confess that the stars left humans considerable room for free decision-making.

By claiming that the duty to interpret rulers' horoscopes outweighed any right to silence, Cardano cast himself in a very engaging character, that of the incorruptible political journalist who undertakes all the difficult research needed to uncover hidden facts, speaks truth to those in power, and reveals the uncomfortable realities that sensible authorities would like to have kept concealed. At the same time, however, he managed to flatter authorities of all sorts—even those most fiercely opposed to one another—and to suggest that celestial causes might explain away tragedies that might otherwise be blamed on the failings of powerful individuals. Charles V, the imperial overlord of his own city of Milan, Cardano praised fiercely, as one born to turn back the tide of "fiendish Turkish madness" from the bounds of Europe. The age of Charles V, in fact, represented a sort of climacteric for European society as a whole: "intellects have reached a final level of development, as have arts, crafts, knowledge of the earth and numbers of books, and the prince's own fortune and virtue: it is to be feared that nature has now attained its highest capacity."[53]

But Francis I, who had been Charles's ferocious enemy in the Italian wars of the 1520s, also came in for his share of praise, as a king of great intelligence and courage whose defeat by Charles had been an unavoidable blow of fortune. From this, moreover, he had fully recovered, leading a life "worthy of a king." After all, Cardano reflected, Francis' horoscope showed the planets lined up in direct opposition to Charles's horoscope: "with the planets in opposition and conflict, it is not surprising that they troubled all Italy, and almost all of Europe, to the point where the infidels became dangerous." The same great conjunctions of Jupiter and Saturn which determined the rise of Christianity and Islam, he explained, also governed the situation now; that explained why the king had lost so consistently to the emperor.[54] In these cases at least, the truth-telling astrologer revealed himself as an adroit flatterer.

Similarly, Cardano's horoscope of the unfortunate Ludovico Sforza concerned itself not with compromising revelations but with explaining how a sagacious ruler of Milan born under such favorable stars had ended his life in prison, and—so the gossip had it—poisoned. In these cases, Cardano's collection offered much the same gossipy satisfactions and warm reassurances about the future that prognosticators had long offered the good and great whom they hoped to please.[55]

Two other genitures of the powerful, however, illustrated the potential of astrology to yield politically provocative findings. Discussing the geniture of Süleyman I, Cardano began by confessing that he did not have absolutely certain knowledge of the details, and therefore would say less than he otherwise might have. But he then went on to say a good deal about this enemy of Christendom, promising him a long life and good health, and even praising his character with faint damns: "Even in the case of an enemy, virtue should have its due praise. Thanks either to dissimulation or to his true nature, he is better than all his predecessors, having kept faith absolutely with his enemies, and showing less barbarousness and cruelty."[56] More important still, the same great conjunctions of Jupiter and Saturn that gave Charles supremacy in Europe promised Islam many successes in the years to come:

> One must bear in mind the conjunction that took place in Pisces in 1524 and the one that will take place in Scorpio in 1544; they greatly favor that religion, since Cancer is the fourth sign from Aries and Scorpio from Leo and Pisces from Sagittarius. Raise up your heads, therefore, o men, and resist the danger that is about to befall you with virtue and piety. For he who rules the heavens is above the heavens. And only virtue, which ignores danger and fear, knows neither death nor burial.[57]

The most technically sophisticated astrology, in other words, still yielded some of the same brooding general prophecies as cruder techniques.

Paradoxically, however, the astrologer could also offer chirpy praise to a potential patron, without regard to the future dangers that it conjured up.

Discussing the character of Paul III, for whose eyes the whole book was evidently destined, Cardano unfolded a coruscating rhetoric of praise:

> he has largely restored the church, which was trembling on account of many heresies and had fallen into ill repute because of its excesses of luxury. He has repressed heresies, and not stirred them up. He helped Charles V to fight the Turks. He reconciled the king of France, who was stirring up great and long-lasting quarrels, with Charles, thanks to his industry, effort, gentleness, and fairness.[58]

In this passage—as elsewhere—Cardano departed from astrological analysis entirely, turning his comments on the genitures into chatty analyses of character and achievement rather like the columns on celebrities in modern news magazines. The crusading muckraker had become a spin doctor—at least when he maintained, in the wake of the Lutheran and Radical Reformations, that one pope had begun to turn the religious tide. Cardano, as we will see, viewed critics of the existing order in the church, like Erasmus, with some sympathy; his patron Archinto, who later actively supported the Jesuits in their early, difficult years, certainly held that radical changes were needed.[59] It seems impossible to read this horoscope, accordingly, except as an advertisement for its author.

Cardano's little book ended even more enticingly than it began, with a short passage in which he stated that he had so far given only a few specimens of the astrological materials already compiled and analyzed in his study:

> I have explained these genitures as examples. After this, once I have published my books in medicine, I will publish genitures of other famous men: the Emperors Julius Caesar and Octavian, with their deaths; Cicero, Nero, and many other remarkable men famous either for their virtue or their fortunes or their deeds. A whole series of these has been set down in books 7 and 10 of my "Astronomical Judgments."[60]

Nothing like Cardano's savory combination of technical astronomy, elementary astrology, political comment, and advertisements for himself had reached print before 1538. And his promise of more horoscopes to come must have whetted many appetites. No wonder that his *Libelli* drew more attention than their modest title would lead one to expect in those eventful years. In fact, as we will see, Cardano's little book brought him from local obscurity to international fame, making him a member of an international community and a participant in international discussions and debates.

chapter five

BECOMING AN AUTHOR

CARDANO did not claim that the small collection of horoscopes he published in 1538 was in itself a literary first. In fact, he made clear, at least in passing, that other astrologers had also compiled such notebooks. When Cardano emphasized, for example, that he had obtained copies of each royal horoscope "from a good many places," he indicated that his study formed only one node on an astrological communications network.[1] But no full-scale collection of horoscopes reached print before Cardano's. The highly schematic collections that formed small parts of larger technical works offered no precedent for his panel of living and recently deceased celebrities—and few of the gossipy satisfactions an eager reader could find in Cardano's vivid and personal accounts of contemporaries. Fifteenth- and early sixteenth-century astrologers normally exchanged their materials not through the new medium of print, which they used for their almanacs and tables, but through the older ones of manuscript letters and conversation. Such methods enabled the fifteenth-century astrologers Johannes Regiomontanus and Giovanni Bianchini to discuss the details of horoscopes, including those of Jesus and Leon Battista Alberti, at some length, as well as the problems of contemporary planetary theory.[2] Cardano's collection of horoscopes—which grew and changed, as we will see, in the course of time—affords glimpses backward into an earlier information economy. It also shows how an adept intellectual could make a career by bringing into the realm of print materials previously excluded from it. And it suggests some of the ways in which the experience of being printed in different places and by different publishers turned Cardano's career in new directions.[3]

Cardano seems to have begun erecting and interpreting astrological figures for clients by the early 1530s. How he learned the technical methods of the art we do not know in detail. His father, Fazio, who taught mathematics in Milan, introduced him to mathematics and astrology.[4] In the *Pronostico,* Cardano cited Fazio's opinion that the horoscope of Milan had its ascendant in Gemini.[5] Astrology, like charity, often began at home: Nostradamus, whose career offers many parallels to Cardano's, claimed to have learned special techniques from his father and grandfather.[6] But Cardano may also have attained further mastery of astronomy and astrology as a medical student. At all events, the evidence of his early horoscopes shows that he began collecting and interpreting genitures in the early years of his career in and near Milan. A number of those whose genitures Cardano inspected were identifiable, even prominent, figures in Milanese circles—for example, the humanist writer Gualtiero Corbetta, who gave Cardano his own geniture, and the historian Galeazzo Capella.[7]

In this early stage of Cardano's career he worked closely with older men who were expert in astrology, and some of whom had specialized in it. In his treatise *On Judging Genitures* Cardano analyzed the nativity of a man "born from very humbly-born parents, who was called Niccolò; but when he left his fatherland, he changed his name to Costanzo, and at Milan he was called Costanzo. At Bologna, however, he was called Niccolò, from the Symi family." This Costanzo, Cardano remarked with unusual enthusiasm, had the good fortune to have Mercury as the lord of the ascendant in his nativity. Accordingly, "though because of poverty he had not studied letters until his twenty-eighth year, he was so brilliant that he gained a modest knowledge of the humanities. He became a geometer, a mathematician, but above all a famous astrologer, so that he taught those arts publicly at Milan for several years."[8]

Costanzo or Niccolò de Symis left a number of astronomical and astrological works—including an unpublished prognostication for the same year as Cardano's first publication, 1534.[9] With characteristic verve, Cardano described a consultation which the two men held in the next year, for a patient of considerable social eminence, Paolo Sforza, the younger brother of the last Sforza ruler of Milan, Francesco II: "Weakened by loss of blood from his lungs and more or less wasting away, he had consulted Costanzo de Symis of Bologna as to whether the emperor would make him ruler of Milan in place of his brother. When he showed me the figure, I said that he would die in that year. For the moon was among the Pleiades in the sixth house, in quartile to Mars and Jupiter, which were moving through the fixed house of Saturn. And accordingly he died suddenly of suffocation while traveling."[10] Cardano also discussed the horoscope of one of his sons with

Costanzo.[11] Very likely he had some access to such men's collections of materials.

Cardano, moreover, explicitly identified one of his astrological informants. In commenting on the geniture of a boy born in 1506, he remarked that "Giovanni Antonio Castiglione, my fellow citizen, and a royal physician, and a man of distinction, said after seeing this geniture that this boy would not be able to accept nourishment, because the moon was beneath the earth."[12] Giovanni Antonio, who ended his life as a royal physician in France, was one of the most successful members of his large and well-known family.[13] Cardano celebrated his good judgment more than once—for example, in his horoscope of Galeazzo Capella, whose death "without a wife and children" Castiglione had predicted thirty years before it took place.[14] Another of the Castiglione, Bonaventura, gave Cardano the genitures of four prominent cardinals "from his notebook."[15] Still other genitures of members of the family, which appear in Cardano's *Astronomical Aphorisms* of 1547 but date from the fifteenth century, very likely came from the same source.[16] It seems all but certain, then, that Cardano began his collecting activity in the company of Milanese physicians, as well as astrologers, and that his first published collections depended in large part on what they were willing to share with him.

Manuscript circulation remained normal for texts of many kinds long after the invention of printing. Sometimes censorship, or the fear of it, played a part in determining a text's reception. A highly controversial work of natural philosophy like Pietro Pomponazzi's *De incantationibus,* for example, attracted a number of readers and critics well before any publisher proved willing to bring out the text as a whole.[17] Certain genres simply seem to have been well adapted to hand copying—for example, the Latin translations from the *Greek Anthology* produced by dozens of scholars and poets in Renaissance France and the Low countries, which migrated from one margin of a printed text to another, and the Latin and English lyric poems which reached a wide readership in Tudor and Stuart England, gravitating into and out of larger manuscript collections.[18] Short texts with potentially explosive content—like political satires and news-sheets—were particularly likely to circulate only in manuscript, from those posted on the speaking statues of Pasquino and Marforio in Rome to those exchanged by branches of the great merchant house of Anton Fugger to those sent out from specialized London scriptoria to gentlemen in the English provinces.[19]

Genitures, like satires and news-sheets, were short, punchy, easily copied and recopied. No wonder that they too led an active life: scholars exchanged them as eagerly as they did the letters to which they were often appended. All astrologers—even the humble authors of *Prognostica*—collected and interpreted the horoscopes of the great and powerful when they could and complained when they could not. Cardano himself remarked, in his *Pronostico,* that he could not predict the fate of the duke of Milan in all its details "since I do not have his nativity."[20] Cardano's geniture collection, in other words, marked the emergence into the wider arena of printing of a form of writing long pursued as a manuscript genre destined for local circulation and private discussion. That may help to explain its tone as well as its content.

The members of one group of astrologers, men both used to traditional forms of communication and passionately interested in increasing their stock of genitures, helped to give Cardano's book its final form. They also brought the revised text to the attention of a new, northern public. The cities of the Holy Roman Empire, in Cardano's time, were more prominent centers of research and publishing in the mathematical disciplines than most of their counterparts in Italy. Nuremberg, in particular, harbored flourishing traditions of astronomical instrument-making and scientific publication, as well as active scientific work.[21] The city, moreover, had become Protestant in the 1520s, and tight links were forged between it and the intellectual citadel of the Protestant movement, the Saxon town of Wittenberg. The intellectual powerhouse of Wittenberg's university, Philipp Melanchthon, found astrology as fascinating as Luther found it repellent.[22] He injected a substantial dose of the subject into the curriculum of the university, which he reformed. And the Electors of Saxony, like many German princes of the time, relied heavily on astrologers for political advice. The Nuremberg-Wittenberg axis buzzed with predictive messages in the form of horoscopes. Both cities attracted expert astrologers.

In 1536 and after, exactly the period when Cardano was composing and publishing the *Libelli,* Nicolaus Gugler studied medicine and astronomy in Wittenberg and Nuremberg.[23] The young German—he was born on 16 April 1521—heard lectures on standard medieval manuals of astronomy, the Sphere of Sacrobosco, and the textbook of Al-Farghani.[24] He also read and heard lessons of some sort, evidently from Johannes Schöner and perhaps Joachim Rheticus as well, on the art and science of astrology. Gugler learned that the discipline was ancient and honorable. Its knowledge, moreover, depended on close study of "the nativities of great men." These, Gugler noted, "can be rectified"—in astrology, normally a term for correction by one of a variety of standard systems meant to be used when the time of a nativity was uncertain—"only through universal and important configurations of the heavens, since they are dependent on such natural configurations, through which they are determined. These include universal events. Necessarily, then, particular events and the horoscopes of princes are rectified with this method, as Ptolemy tells us in the *Tetrabiblos.*"[25] It was significant, therefore, that a great conjunction had preceded the birth of the king of Poland—an event that Gugler's teacher analyzed at length, with reference to the belief of Zoroaster and Plato that the souls of individuals came down from the stars to enter their bodies at birth.[26]

Gugler, however, took down more than such generalities. He also copied out, presumably from his teacher's notebook, a series of horoscopes. These resembled Cardano's first collection in a number of ways. Like Cardano, Gugler recorded figures chiefly for the births of great leaders and intellectuals: Jesus, Moses, Charles V, Francis I, Philip of Hesse, and Friedrich of Saxony in the first category, Erasmus, Luther, Dürer, Melanchthon, Rheticus, and Schöner in the second. Like Cardano, too, Gugler and his teacher evidently discussed their genitures with more than one informant. The impression made by these notes is clear: horoscopes formed a central topic of conversation in Luther's own university.[27]

Gugler gave not one but two horoscopes for Martin Luther. The first of them, which Gugler described as based on an astrologer's computation, set his birth at three hours and 22 minutes after noon of 22 October 1484.[28] The second, Gugler remarked, gave "the certain hour which his own mother had revealed," and which Gugler found "not inconsistent with his deeds," nine hours past noon on 22 October 1484.[29] One point—common to both genitures—calls for comment. Though a wise mother knows the time when her child was born, both of the genitures Gugler recorded, the astrologer's and that based on the mother's testimony, date Luther's birth to a year not found in modern reference works. Many of Luther's contemporaries—and most modern historians—have agreed with a scrawled note in the margin of Gugler's collection. This states, "Paulus Eber said that he was born at the eleventh hour after noon on 10 November 1483."[30]

The story of this contradiction was worked out in large part by Aby Warburg. He showed, in pages of unmatched brilliance, that Luca Gaurico made an astrological pilgrimage through the Empire early in the 1530s. Evidently called to Berlin by Kurfürst Joachim I, Gaurico drew up a horoscope for his son.[31] Gaurico's prophecies had already impressed Melanchthon, who praised them to their author as so accurate "that you seen to have written not only a prediction, but also a history of these events, and long in advance."[32] In late April or early May 1532, Gaurico visited Wittenberg, delighting Melanchthon by his commitment to humanism (he regularly wrote Latin poetry) as well as by his expertise, and that of his two assistants, in astrology. Then he went off to Nuremberg, bearing enthusiastic letters of recommendation to Joachim Camerarius and others.[33] On his way through the Empire, Gaurico left numerous genitures behind him, as the manuscript collections in German libraries show.[34]

The genitures that Gaurico discussed with his new German friends included that of Martin Luther. Considerable uncertainty hung around this vital date. Luther himself, as Reinhart Staats has recently discovered, originally believed that he had been born in 1484.[35] As an astrological counselor to high clerics and a faithful Catholic, Gaurico wanted to do his best to damage the Protestant cause with the tools of his trade.[36] Melanchthon, who knew very well that "we are uncertain about Luther's birth," showed Gaurico several figures, and he "approved the figure for 1484"—for a time when a massive conjunction in Scorpio fell in the ninth house—that of religion.[37] By doing so, as Warburg showed, Gaurico evidently hoped to damage Luther's public image. The widely disseminated prophecies of Johannes Lichtenberger had given currency to the idea that an evil religious figure would appear around 1500. By associating Luther's birth with the great conjunction of 1484, Gaurico hoped to connect him with these images of evil. He also found reason to predict that Luther would die soon.[38]

Gaurico's tactics backfired. His behavior soon made him unpopular in the Lutheran circles that had at first welcomed him.[39] But Protestants like Melanchthon found the mythical birthday he approved for Luther so dramatic anyhow, changing the hour to move the ninth house away from Scorpio, that they held on to it despite its dire connotations. Versions of the 1484 nativity circulated widely, long before Gaurico himself managed to print it in 1552. Melanchthon, obviously, speculated about it, as did Schöner. Still another version of the 1484 horoscope appears in another manuscript collection of horoscopes, that of the Protestant astronomer Erasmus Reinhold, now in Leipzig.[40]

Luther now began to register his own dissent from what had quickly become the standard opinion about his birth year. In spring 1543, someone in his circle remarked, "Master Luther, many astrologers agree on your geniture, that the constellations of your birth showed that you would bring about a great change." Luther replied brusquely: "No one is certain about the time of my birth. For Phillip and I disagree by a year."[41] Evidently, he had come to accept his brother's view that he had been born in 1483, a year before the astrologers wanted to date his birth.

Some informant passed this new date on to Cardano. Not only did he draw up a figure corresponding to it, but he also included it prominently in his second, expanded horoscope collection—which became, for this and other reasons, a highly controversial document. Cardano stated that in doing so he meant to combat an error which had already received widespread applause. Luther's real birthday—which he set at 22 October 1483—was in fact even more ominous than the false one:

> Know that this—rather than the false one for 1484 which has achieved such wide circulation—is Luther's true geniture. A geniture should not be unworthy of so great a matter, or the event of such a geniture. I think that men who did not understand the fundamentals of this art corrupted it. For the other one does not match the power of this, and if you really want something to condemn, you can find reason for criticism here too.[42]

Once again, a discussion previously carried on in the obscurity of scholars' studies and transmitted in letters—a relatively quiet exchange of opinions among the learned—emerged into the light of publicity, outside the notebooks of the astrological aficionados. And as the texts reached print, they mutated—as Cardano, a reformist Italian Catholic, showed some sympathy for Luther by publishing his work with a Lutheran publisher, though he also remarked, as he probably felt he had to, that the very divisions among the Protestants showed that their cause was wrong. Luther himself, characteristically, was not impressed. When someone showed him a copy of Cardano's chart, he remarked, "I think this is worthless," and demanded, as Augustine had long before, how the astrologers could explain why Esau and Jacob had such radically different characters.[43] But the lively astrological discussion about his birthday continued nonetheless.

Even a young student like Gugler, in other words, knew how to erect a figure, had access to collections of interesting historical and current examples, and knew that controversies raged over the status and value of particular genitures. It seems possible that one or two others in his collection, besides Luther's, were not meant to be taken literally. Gugler's horoscope for Moses, for example, connected his birth with an undated great conjunction of Saturn, Jupiter, and Mars in the sign of Aquarius—more likely a reference to the parting of the waters than a serious effort to establish the date and data of his birth.[44] But most of them explored the characters and predicted the fates of prominent men in Gugler's own immediate world. In the intellectual marketplace of high Lutheran humanism, genitures enjoyed strong demand from everyone but Luther himself.

No one understood this situation better than another highly educated Lutheran whose profession required him to follow the patterns of supply and demand very closely: the Nuremberg publisher Petreius, whom we have already encountered. Though famous above all as the publisher of Copernicus, Petreius also took a serious interest in astrological texts, many of which figured in his list. Like Cardano, Petreius saw no sharp disjunction between astrology and astronomy. His preface to the book on nativities of Antonius de Monte Ulmi, which he brought out in 1540, offered one of the first public testimonies to Copernicus' importance. And his preface to an Arabo-Latin text which also appeared early in the 1540s confirmed his desire to obtain more astrological works and give them wider diffusion.[45]

Petreius not only looked for existing astrological treatises, but also tried to find astrological authors whom he could persuade to shape their works to fit his sense of the market. In 1549, for example, he wrote to Erasmus Reinhold, who taught astronomy in Wittenberg, inviting him to come and work in Petreius' house, where he would enjoy his own "stublin und gemach," or workroom. Petreius also outlined a new project for him to carry out there:

> So far as I know, I have never seen in print a short compendium, that is, which explains how to go about erecting nativities in the first place, and inscribing them into the celestial figure [the standard square diagram], and how the signs, planets and stars are to be divided up in the aforesaid figure, and into the twelve houses and the angles of the houses (and for that matter, what the angles are). You know all this better than I can indicate it.[46]

Petreius went so far as to indicate the format and type font he thought appropriate for such a book—a triumph of editorial optimism over experience, given that his author had not even begun to write. In one respect, to be sure, the book Petreius now wanted would not have resembled the various astrological publications I have surveyed up to now. He advised Reinhold to stick to general methods, rather than specific conclusions: "As to the predictions to be drawn from constellations of this kind, that should be omitted from this book. For plenty of those have been written and printed, and my feeling is that a compendium like this should be fairly salable."[47] But even this negative recommendation clearly reflected Petreius' expert command of the range of materials already available, as well as his publisher's instinct for connecting an author with an opportunity.

Petreius' advice to his author bears looking at from another point of view as well—Cardano's. The book he recommended as a model for the physical appearance of Reinhold's proposed work was "Cardanus de nativitatibus"—Cardano's genitures.[48] Petreius himself had reprinted this work, in much enlarged editions, in 1543 and 1547, making further publications of the same kind less attractive investments—even for himself. It was he—working in conjunction with scholars from the Nuremberg-Wittenberg axis—

who transformed Cardano's career, more radically than any of the other printers, learned and unlearned, with whom Cardano eventually worked.[49]

Cardano's contact with Petreius resulted from one of his cleverest efforts to publicize his work. In 1538 Cardano applied for and received an Imperial privilege for his *Practica arithmeticae.* Such documents normally forbade any publisher to reprint a given work for a period of ten years or more, thus ensuring that the original publisher enjoyed a monopoly. Cardano, however, asked for protection not only for the *Practica,* but also for a series of thirty-four titles, all of which he described as already completed; on this point he exaggerated, characteristically. He claimed that he wished to avoid having to apply separately for each work. But as Ian Maclean has shown, Cardano also wanted to advertise the fact that he had everything from collected letters to commentaries on Ptolemy and Euclid to books on astrology and dreams ready for the press.[50] And his plan worked. Petreius had a learned agent and adviser, the theologian Andreas Osiander, who saw the *De revolutionibus* of Copernicus through the press (and supplied it with a radically misleading anonymous foreword, in which he described Copernicus' theory as a mere hypothesis, though the author himself believed it to be the exact truth). Evidently Osiander noticed Cardano's list. As Cardano later recalled, "I had added a sort of catalog of my books, which I had either written or begun to write. And that book began to attain some diffusion in France and Germany."[51] Thereupon, he said, Osiander and Petreius went to work, bringing his writing on subjects that ranged from astrology to natural and moral philosophy to a wide European readership. Cardano thus achieved an end for which many Milanese authors longed in the first half of the sixteenth century: he found his books on the list of a prominent publisher in Northern Europe.[52]

As we have already seen, Petreius did more than reprint the first edition of Cardano's horoscopes, the crudely printed Milanese edition which Cardano himself described as "torn from me by misfortune rather than printed." "In order to give an example of his diligence, which he wanted to be quite clear to me," Cardano remarked, "he did his duty and asked if I wanted to add or correct anything." Cardano noted in his dedicatory letter to the new edition that he had added a variety of new materials, including fifty-eight more genitures, making a total of sixty-seven.[53] He appreciated his publisher's generosity and interest in his work, which he later described as typical of the better conditions enjoyed by German scholars.[54] And he insisted that "anyone who fails to understand the future using this concise, packed little book, will not do better after reading any number of others. For since the art is infinite, it can be taught only by judgment, not as a system."[55] Cardano presented his new, upgraded collection of genitures as a virtual wax museum, its galleries lined with effigies of heroes, monsters, and murderers, designed to provoke the wonder of all visitors:

> Here are expressed all the different forms of death, by poison, by lightning, by water, by public condemnation, by iron, by accident, by disease; and after long, short, or middling periods; also the various forms of birth that yield twins, monsters, posthumous children, bastards, and those in the course of whose birth the mother dies; and then of the forms of character, timid, bold, prudent, stupid, possessed, deceptive, simple, heretics, thieves, robbers, pederasts, sodomites, whores, adulterers: and also, with regard to the disciplines of the rhetoricians, the jurisconsults, and the philosophers, and those who will become the greatest physicians and diviners, and famous craftsmen, and also those who will become despisers of the virtues. I have also followed out the different incidents of life, explaining what sort of men kill their wives, suffer exile, prison, and continual ill health, convert from one religion to another or pass from the highest position to a low status, or, on the other hand, from a low fortune to kingship or power.[56]

Cardano promised those who walked the paper corridors of his collection the secrets of both natural and political power—including the genitures of not just one, but three popes who had reached their high estate from humble origins.

At this point in his astrological career, Cardano found himself confronted with a dilemma: how to move forward on two fronts at once, as both a local healer with a practice that he needed to enlarge and an international man of science with a potential readership to which he wanted to appeal. He had already worked up a style for explicating genitures, one which pleased and provoked. That no doubt explains why Osiander and Petreius went to such pains to improve and distribute his work. But Cardano still felt himself under attack on the local front, where his collection of horoscopes evidently had not convinced scoffers that he professed a real art. "Astrology," he complained, in a new dedicatory letter to Archinto, the patron who had supported the first edition of the book, "has as many enemies as there are ignorant men, as Ptolemy said." Some of them had smeared Cardano's name, "saying that I make public pronouncements only about past events." Accordingly, he added to the collection "the geniture of an illustrious boy." This would make clear Cardano's willingness to predict in public for a large audience, even to stake a claim that he had already succeeded in doing so: "his relatives will not allow me to lie. When I examined the geniture of his brother, which was crystal clear, I pronounced that he would have serious trouble in one eye, and have a mark made by iron on one cheek. In the fifth year after the geniture all these things happened, down to the smallest detail, so that the doctors were given far more trouble than they expected."[57] Cardano also invoked the prestige of Archinto himself, whom he called as a witness to another remarkable prophecy: "When a certain doctor asked for a yearly revolution, after he had experienced some happy ones, as I had predicted, I announced from the final one that he would die and stated the month"—just as Luca Bellanti had done for the skeptical Pico della Mirandola. "You recognize the man," Cardano told Archinto, "and they still have my written text. I also informed you about it in a private letter." Showing his usual tolerance for contradiction, Cardano wound up both by lamenting the unhappy condition of his times, which had led him to refuse to practice astrology no matter what pleas and fees he was offered, and by citing yet another bishop, who, without knowing it, "had the final trial of my art."[58] The upshot was clear: Cardano's collected genitures were merely the tip of a secret iceberg of astrological practice, the miraculous results of which, as the reader could now see, were vouched for not only by the astrologer, but by his clerical patron as well. Even as Cardano became an international author, in short, he emphasized the brilliant successes he had obtained as a local practitioner, perhaps in the hope of attracting still more of the fees and requests for help that he described himself as denying.

The local successes Cardano described so eloquently may have enhanced the appeal of his work to the unknown members of his larger reading public. But Cardano took care to offer them something else, something perhaps even more attractive: a rich body of information on the genitures of many contemporary rulers and intellectuals. Cardano also took care to reveal that he had obtained at least some of this information from Rheticus, another member of the circle of Petreius. Perhaps Rheticus actually contacted Cardano at Petreius' request.[59] More likely, a shared interest in astrological history brought Cardano and Rheticus together. In his *Supplement to the Almanac,* as we saw, Cardano argued that the movements of the sphere of the fixed stars determined the fates of cities and kingdoms.[60] Rheticus, for his part, loved such schemata. He believed in the 1540s that the Copernican system contained a solution to the riddles of world history as well as those of astronomy. Fifteen years later, he would propose an astrological system quite like Cardano's in a dedicatory letter to Ferdinand II.[61]

In any event, Cardano himself publicized his collaboration with the Protestant astronomer. In commenting on the horoscope of Savonarola that figured, with 66 others, in Petreius' 1543 edition of his *Libelli,* he wrote enthusiastically: "How could anyone describe more precisely what actually took place? One might be tempted to believe that this was made up, if my friend George Joachim had not sent me these last four horoscopes after I finished my little book. I saw to it that they were added."[62] The horoscopes in question stated the birth times, characters, and fates of Savonarola, Pico della Mirandola, Georg Peurbach, and Albrecht Dürer. Cardano's sixty-seven genitures thus became more than an individual enterprise. They swelled with the materials that were already circulating from notebook to notebook in the German world, bringing these into the public domain of print discussion. These additions firmly associated Cardano's researches with the most up-to-date and cosmopolitan astrological work of his time, done by men whose contacts in central Italy were clearly superior to Cardano's own. Publishing in Nuremberg not only brought Cardano's name and work to a much wider public, but made it possible for him to draw on a much wider range of informants and collaborators. The horoscope collection was and would remain a compromise: at once a set of affidavits about local successes outside Padua and Milan and a reference work depending on connections throughout Europe.

If the substance of Cardano's collection was sometimes borrowed, its style was largely his own. The horoscopes in collections like Gugler's included, for the most part, only astronomical and factual details: dates of birth and positions of planets. Occasionally, the owner or a later reader might note that the subject of a given horoscope had died. But the collectors, on the whole, made little effort to analyze the bodily or the mental constitutions of their subjects. Cardano, by contrast, treated the horoscope as a literary form, and one of remarkable flexibility. Like a nineteenth-century German composer writing lieder, he associated freely, changed moods and forms with startling speed. He found himself able to attack an incredibly diverse range of themes and incidents, while remaining within the boundaries of a single form.

Cardano's dedicatory letter to Archinto for the new edition promised strange deaths, bizarre lifestyles, and monstrous beings, and he provided all of these. Astrological courtesy prevented him from revealing the last name of Veronica—the shameless woman, born on 4 February 1480, whose husband murdered her for being the whore that Venus, in close conjunction with the dragon's tail in Capricorn, had made her.[63] Similarly, he could not name or even give the birth date of the effeminate cleric whose bad character and bad death he prophesied.[64] But he spared few other details, either about these characters or about the monstrous child, the woman who died by poison, or the child who wasted away, for all of whom he provided genitures.

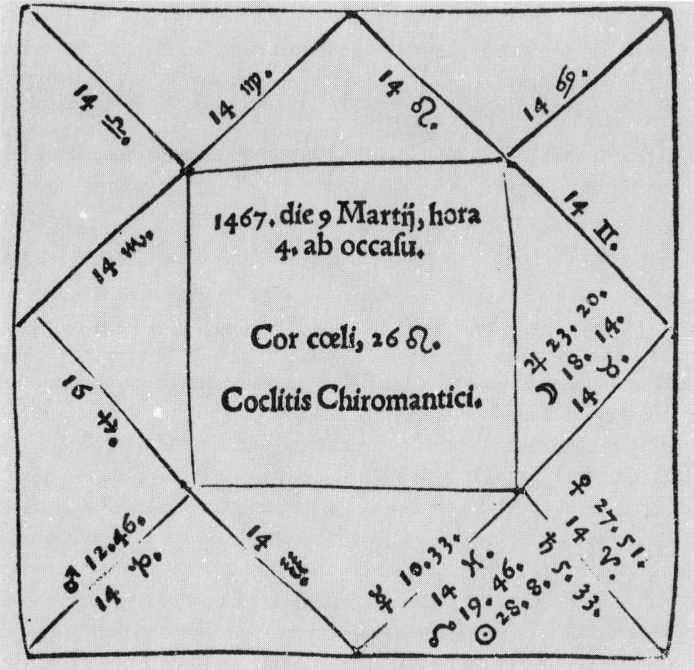

Figure 16 Cardano's geniture of Bartolomeo Cocles, born in 1467, from Cardano's *100 Genitures* (Nuremberg, 1547).

Cardano also began in this collection, for the first time, to reveal some of the wonderful characteristics of the patient he both knew best, and felt compelled by the morality of his craft to analyze with complete frankness: himself. Cardano had evidently drawn up his horoscope well before he published it: he complained that "certain men, by no means ignorant of this art, when they saw this geniture, denied that it could be mine. They argued that they found in it no trace either of the life I have led up until the present or of any dignity." Rebutting these unnamed—but clever—detractors, one of whom he elsewhere identified as his own friend Girolamo Cutica, Cardano insisted that his geniture, which he himself had erected "with minute care," corresponded precisely to the course of his life. He also revealed that the "savage conjunction" of the planets at the hour of his birth had done him terrible violence, producing "a weak digestion, a weak brain, ambushes, enemies, the loss of possessions, attacks, and innumerable sufferings that proved terribly dangerous, and unjustly harmed my reputation among the ordinary people."[65] The astrologer himself was a monster, or would have been, if he had not used his knowledge of his own weak body and perilous environment to save himself—a theme Cardano would pursue with endless patience and ingenuity in later years.

In 1538, Cardano promised his readers horoscopes of great men. The new edition contained many more of these, which he described as powerful confirmation of the general rules of the art—short summaries of which he scattered among the horoscopes themselves. Cardano's horoscope of Filippo Maria Visconti, for example, offered what he saw as an undeniable retrospective explanation of the subject's character as well as his entire life:

> No duke of Milan was more successful or more powerful, or more often victorious. He had three kings as his captives at one time. But since Mercury was forced into misfortune in Virgo by the sun and Saturn, and the cadent Venus, he suffered from stupidity, which was also determined by the moon in quartile with the sun and Saturn in opposition to Mars. Accordingly, he rejected the gifts of fortune and fell into the greatest possible difficulties, suffering no little harm. Finally, when the moon was overcome by both unfortunate stars, and by the sun, he was forced to have his wife beheaded publicly—a rare event, so much as to be a prodigy, especially since a ruler was involved. Let those who reject astrology come now and work out answers for these palpable miracles in human affairs—or let them think that I invented these genitures, which are taken from the public annals—or that I have deliberately set the planets into false positions, since his whole life fitted the decrees of his geniture so prettily.[66]

In this case, the stars in their courses fought against the unlucky duke. The malevolent planets lined up in malign aspects both to one another and to Mercury, the planet that bestowed cunning political intelligence. They deprived the duke of Mercury's aid even though it was in Virgo, not only its mansion but its *gaudium*—a position which enhanced its dignity.

Of Nero, whose birth Cardano set on 14 December C.E. 36, he wrote that the positions of Mercury, the sun, and Mars made him cruel, that of Venus made him lustful and perverse, and that of Mars and Saturn made his death a bad one—even though he also insisted that "it is simply not possible to seek the cause of gaining an empire or losing it in the geniture, as I have repeatedly said before."[67] A year or two later Cardano realized that Nero was actually born on 18 June C.E. 38, a date which yielded an entirely different set of planetary positions. He silently expunged his earlier analysis and substituted a totally new figure for the old one. Nonetheless, he still felt that his art enabled him to explain Nero's savagery and lust economically and effectively: "one snowflake is not more like another than this geniture resembles the actions, character, and fortunes of Nero."[68] What mattered in astrology was, in the end, less the rigorous astronomy that laid the foundations of the art than the dextrous application of astrological canons to interesting cases.

In the second edition, as in the first, not all the celebrities who found a place were princes. Cardano made his book into a small-scale lexicon of Europe's leading intellectuals. He explained the successes, in the realm of erudition and eloquence, not only of those whose genitures Rheticus gave him, but also of many of the most prominent Italian scholars of the period just before his own. Cardano's reader learned why the Carmelite monk and Christian epic poet Battista Mantuanus had wound up his difficult life as the favorite of many rulers and the author of works comparable to Virgil's in quality. He learned the causes for Savonarola's theological prowess, Andrea Alciato's rhetorical prowess, and Pico della Mirandola's universal prowess—though Cardano, like others, took care to point out that the stars had caused the early and predicted death, as well as the brilliance, of this great scholar who had "slanderously attacked astrology." Zesty tidbits of personal information like these fascinated even the most technically proficient of astrologers, and figured in their manuscript notebooks as well as Cardano's printed collections. Reinhold, for example, noted with fascination that the erudite botanist and bibliographer Conrad Gesner read "only with books held very closely before his eyes" and that Gregor Zechendorfer had undergone painful cutting for the kidney stone no fewer than five times even though "amazingly enough, he never ate cheese."[69]

Cardano, like most specialist astrologers before and after him, was no determinist. He followed Ptolemy in insisting that environment and other factors modified, and sometimes reversed, the judgments of the stars. In the case of Julius II, for example, the role of Mars explained in general terms the pope's perpetual efforts to make war. No planet appeared in the first house of his geniture, but the ascendant was in Scorpio. Scorpio, in turn, was the mansion in which Mars especially "rejoiced." Mars, accordingly, became lord of the ascendant even though it was itself in Gemini, across the sky. And the lord of the ascendant determined the subject's character and manners. But malign planetary influence, though necessary, did not strike Cardano as a sufficient explanation:

> Some of this perhaps resulted from the stars, but more from divine judgment, so that many were punished through him for their crimes. For his birth brought about the ruin of the Roman church. This gave rise to sects, first in Italy and then throughout the Christian world, and the partial loss of the supreme apostolic dignity of Saint Peter, whom alone Christ set over the others. The uncertainty about the succession offers no excuse for him. Was

> Christ's blood, was the divine law granted to mankind so that you, who should preserve the sheep, might rend them? That the members of Christ might lie in their blood, with more suffering than on the cross? For he hung there willingly for a few hours, and it was done by men who knew not what they did, and for the benefit of many. You, by contrast, fail to restore what has been damaged for so long.[70]

This sharp critical language marked a turn away from the enthusiastic papalist language of Cardano's 1538 horoscope for Paul III, in favor of the prophetic tone of the *Pronostico.* It must have done much to make Cardano's work—dedicated as it was to a Catholic patron, whom Cardano praised with great warmth in his horoscope—acceptable to Protestant readers.

Cardano's reworked horoscope collection was evidently the fruit of collaboration, and may very well have included more by way of information and suggestions from his German partners than he directly stated. Petreius' suggestions conceivably played an even larger role than the preserved documents reveal. Was the Milanese horoscope collector transmogrified into the recorder of a world of wonders and the sedulous biographer of scholars, all so that a publisher could feed the immense appetites of highly literate Lutherans for pamphleteering and pedantry? It seems certain both that Petreius or Osiander sent Cardano Luther's preferred date for his own birth, and that in accepting it, Cardano showed his continuing sympathy, if not for reformers like Luther, at least for efforts to reform the church. It also seems likely that Cardano or his editors removed the ardent praise of Paul III that figured in the 1538 edition of the pope's horoscope in order to make his work safe for Protestants. But most of the threads spun out at great length in Cardano's *Libelli duo* made their first appearance in the work he directed at his first, Italian public.

From prophecies of doom to horoscopes for humanists, his early publications show why he could work so well with intellectuals from a very different cultural and religious background. *Libelli duo* closely resembles, even in its sympathies, the Protestant Reinhold's horoscope collection, much of it compiled in 1545. Reinhold showed a similarly passionate interest in matters concerning the true religion. He noted the excommunication of George Podiebrand "because he was on our side prematurely," the career of Frederick of Saxony, "under whom the Kingdom of God, which Satan had so long oppressed, began to flourish," and the death of Pope Paul II, "that proud man; on 20 July 1471 he slept with a young man and was strangled in the act by demons."[71]

No wonder, then, that Cardano's newly gleaming little book, handsomely printed by Petreius, found readers across Europe—especially, but not only, in the north European milieu in which it had been solicited and reshaped. The book moved rapidly into circulation. Janus Cornarius, a medical man who worked, at times, as a corrector for the printing house of the Amerbachs in Basel, bought his copy in Marburg in October 1543.[72] He read his way through it with an attentive eye for detail, entering the death dates for Francis I and Henry VIII in 1547 as well as a cross reference to Cardano's own horoscope.[73] His attention was snagged by Cardano's worried query about whether Charles V might turn out to be another Philopoemen. So he explained the reference in the margin: "He was said to be the last of the Greeks. Captured by the Messenians, he was imprisoned in their treasury, drank poison, and died."[74] And he noted with fascination Cardano's account of the astrologer and palm-reader Bartolomeo Cocles, who, Cardano said, had put on armor, since he knew himself to be in danger—only to be felled by the blow of a club, because he had offended the ruler of Bologna, where he lived. "Mira res," wrote Cornarius: "an extraordinary thing."[75] Cornarius was not uncritical; he allowed himself one mild cut in passing at Cardano's notoriously messy Latin style, in which his skilled copy-editor's eye detected flaws.[76] But none of his notes suggest that he saw Cardano as anything but a solid source for astrological principles and data—even when he recorded, next to Cardano's prediction that Henry VIII would have a long life, the fact that he died in 1547 (Cardano himself was so embarrassed by the passage in question that he cut it, silently, from the 1547 edition of the genitures).[77] Other readers showed equal respect: the Lutheran intellectual Fridericus Staphylus, for example, had his copy of the 1543 edition bound up with such reputable companions as Johannes Schöner's treatise on astrology of 1539 and Rheticus' treatise on the Copernican system.[78]

Staphylus also used his copy of the text in what evidently became a typical way: as a notebook in which to record further nativities. True, he entered only one, a horoscope of the Nuremberg astrologer Schöner, which also appeared, with different house divisions, in Gugler's manuscript notebook prepared a decade before.[79] But other readers went about the job more systematically. The anonymous reader of a copy now in Vienna, for example, noted that Cardano had published, as the horoscope of Regiomontanus, what was really that of the astronomer's teacher Georg Peurbach.[80] He erected six figures, including one for Regiomontanus' true nativity, in the blank leaves at the end of the volume. And he emulated Cardano in method when he offered clear astrological explanations for Regiomontanus' brilliance: "Mercury, in his own house, makes a man brilliant, clever, alert in every art and science, especially in mathematics, philosophy, poetry,

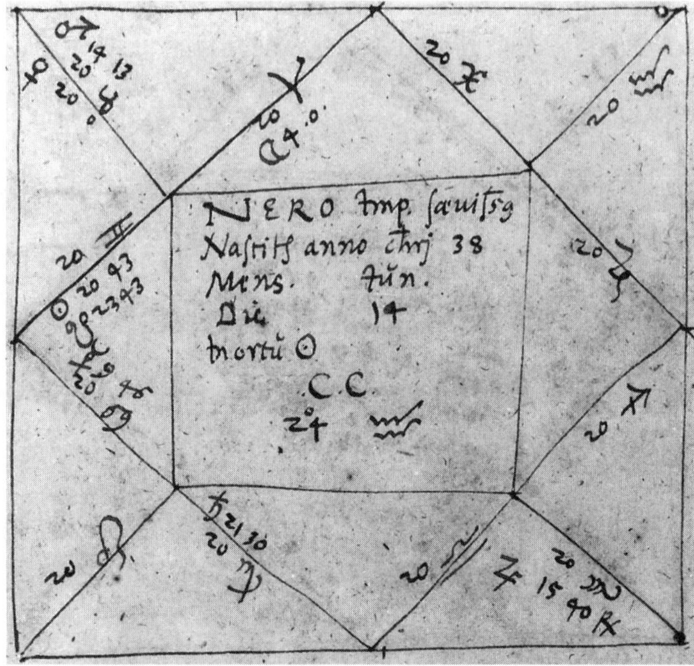

Figure 17 Cardano's geniture of Nero, from a manuscript collection bound with a copy of Luca Gaurico's *Tractatus astrologicus* (Venice, 1552). The compiler copied this geniture from the 1547 edition of Cardano's *100 Genitures,* in which this corrected version appeared.

and rhetoric, and he will be able to make with his hands everything that he sees."[81]

Melanchthon, an aficionado of astrology, went still further. He made his copy of the 1543 genitures into an elaborate notebook, offering alternate horoscopes for Paul III, Luther, and Angelo Poliziano and adding many new ones, from those of the dukes of Saxony and the royal house of Denmark to those of his own four children. He not only compiled these genitures, moreover, but examined the degree to which they predicted the subjects' lives. Comparing his alternate horoscope for Charles V with that given by Cardano, Melanchthon noted that the four planets in Pisces at Charles's birth, Jupiter, the sun, Venus, and Mercury, "temper by their power the malevolence of the others."[82] Of his daughter Anna, born in August 1522, with the moon, Mercury, and Venus all in Libra, he remarked that "because of these three in conjunction she produced lots of daughters."[83] This was a reasonable explanation, given that the moon was the feminine planet *par excellence,* Venice was feminine as well, and Mercury, which was of ambiguous nature, became feminine when in conjunction with a feminine planet. Melanchthon found Cardano's astrological history as intriguing as his reading of individual fates. He took careful notes on the passage in which Cardano used the doctrine of the great conjunctions to explain the rise of Christianity and Islam. These interests are not surprising: Melanchthon and the students of world history in his circle worked hard in the 1540s to apply astronomical data to the study of world history, in the hope both of fixing the precise dates of past events and of discovering their celestial causes.[84]

Not all of Cardano's readers found his work consistently compelling. Even those who began by taking his ideas and methods very seriously indeed sometimes found themselves frustrated by his practices. One of these—a standard one, as we have seen—consisted of using one or two aphoristic statements about the powers and effects of individual planets and configurations to identify the central features of a geniture, without explaining what criteria defined the aphorisms in question as the most relevant ones to the case in question. A medically informed reader, who apparently had met the Italian physician Antonio Brasavola and referred knowingly to Andreas Vesalius as well, made revealing notes in his copy of the second edition of Cardano's full collection, which appeared in 1547, with expanded introductory treatises. He began by summarizing Cardano's work in detail and even encouraging himself to commit parts of it to memory. As he read further, however, his dissatisfaction mounted. In *Supplement to the Almanac,* Cardano noted that Mars, when it appeared in a prominent position in a geniture, tended to cause a violent death. His geniture of the poet and humanist Poliziano showed Mars in the seventh house, in opposition to the ascendant. Cardano, accordingly, identified Mars as "lord of the ascendant," and used the planet's influence to explain why Poliziano lived away from his native land. But as the reader complained, in a marginal note directed at the author, he did not even mention the fact "which is surprising, in the light of your principles, that he did not die by violence."[85] Gradually, this reader came to see methodological incoherence as characteristic of Cardano's work. When Cardano criticized other astrologers for drawing up manuals in the form of long sets of unconnected individual precepts, the connections among which were unclear, the reader wrote bitterly: "here you offer a splendid critique of your own work."[86]

Evidently the Cardano of the 1543 *Libelli duo* counted as an authority, if not an infallible one, even in the eyes of expert readers like Melanchthon, and despite the errors and crudities some noticed in his work. An analogy may help to clarify his achievement. The first printed collection of Roman inscriptions, published by Iacopo Mazzocchi in 1521, was inaccurate and incomplete: it did not represent the highest level of antiquarian research then carried on. But it helped to create a community of scholars across Europe, many of whom learned their trade by comparing the printed text to the originals and annotating its many errors.[87] Similarly, the first printed collection of genitures did not necessarily represent the highest level at which astrology was practiced. But it clearly stimulated an enormous amount of interest, both for the information it conveyed and for the example it proffered.

One further note of Melanchthon's calls for a brief discussion. After erecting horoscopes for Philip of Hesse and his oldest son, Melanchthon remarked of the latter: "Gaurico explained this geniture to Duke George [of Saxony], and predicted that he would be like another Alcibiades."[88] This comment is suggestive in two ways. On the one hand, it confirms that Cardano was not the only Italian astrologer who tried to make his way, personally or virtually, in the north. Here as elsewhere he followed paths that Gaurico and others had traveled before him.[89] In fact, as we will see, Cardano's work represented not only a well-designed and empirically rich textbook of astrology, but an attack, as subtle as it was unmistakable, on this rival. Geniture collections became not only a profit center for publishers but a contested area for scholars—a quality which perhaps enhanced their appeal.

On the other hand, Melanchthon also suggests that horoscopes were more than dry, technical data sets produced by mathematically skilled intellectuals to satisfy their curiosity. They were politically sensitive and intellectually challenging documents, directed at powerful clients who were hard to satisfy, and often presented and discussed in a public forum where defeat could hardly be concealed. Cardano's first collection of genitures reveals little activity of this kind. But he would soon find himself in demand not only as a credible author and scholar but also as a reliable counselor for the rich and famous.[90]

chapter six

ASTROLOGERS IN COLLISION

MANY OF CARDANO's remarks indicate that the Renaissance astrologer worked in a highly public situation, an exposed position in which clients and competitors constantly threatened to undermine or ridicule him. The same clients who asked Cardano's advice deliberately gave him false data about the places and dates of their births, rather as some clients had, as a test, given medieval doctors the urine of dogs or horses to analyze as their own. Rivals lost no opportunity to criticize every aspect of Cardano's work. They attacked him, as we have seen, on the grounds that he confined himself to analyzing the horoscopes of individuals who had already grown up and made their careers—but did not dare to publish horoscopes the outcome of which he could not foretell.[1] Friends also turned into critics. As we have seen, Girolamo Cutica, whose technical prowess Cardano admired, argued with a nice sense of the paradoxical that the young man of monstrous character depicted by Cardano's geniture could not have turned into a brilliant success like Cardano.[2]

Astrologers had always confronted jealous competitors. The Assyrian scholars who worked up predictions for their rulers in the late eighth and seventh centuries B.C.E. sometimes attacked one another bitterly—though they also managed to collaborate regularly.[3] The astrologers who drew up horoscopes in sand tables in the public markets of medieval Baghdad and Damascus worked in a terrifyingly exposed position, ringed by crowds of articulate critics.[4] Even Ptolemy's dry textbook, the *Tetrabiblos,* came alive on the few occasions when he felt obliged to abuse the more primitive methods of his colleagues.[5] The lines of communication between the German astrologers whose situation Cardano envied also vibrated, and sometimes shook, under the impact of the malevolent messages sent along them.[6]

Cardano, however, like some of the controversialists we have already seen debating the relative merits of medicine and astrology, found new ways to establish his reputation and demolish those of his rivals. From the start, he took delight in his success as a print author—and especially in the fact that his astrological prowess had won him the attentions of Osiander, Rheticus, and Petreius. Late in life, as he ranged the rooms of his capacious memory, he still liked to dwell on this story, as his acquaintances knew. When Hugo Blotius issued his instructions for visiting Cardano, he told his young friend to assure the old man that "his works were read with great enthusiasm in Germany and Belgium."[7] In the end, Cardano had to pay for his early success in the Protestant world. As censorship took hold in Italy, his connections with prominent heretics became a cause for suspicion rather than congratulation.[8] At times, as will become clear, Cardano felt that his interest in astrology had done him more harm than good. But for most of his life, he glowed in the happy memory of his literary debut.

What Cardano never explicitly said about this debut, however, was that it represented much more than his entry to a calm, impersonal debate on general principles. He also made his work—sometimes deliberately, sometimes inadvertently—into his own effort to overturn the sand tables of his rivals. The first astrologer with whom Cardano came to blows was not the enemy he himself targeted, his fellow Italian Luca Gaurico, but his German ally Rheticus. The success of their 1543 publication—and the desire to learn the secrets of astrology which Cardano promised to disclose, but did not fully reveal, to his readers—led Rheticus to make a pilgrimage to Milan, where Cardano was now well established, actively treating patients and continuing to finish texts of various kinds for Petreius—a series that included not only Cardano's geniture collections but his most influential work in mathematics, the *Ars magna.* Cardano himself reported, in the new edition of his horoscope collection which he finished in 1546, that Rheticus had brought him essential new material:

> I always say that everything happens by a certain necessity. Just as I was considering adding some more horoscopes, by chance Georg Joachim Rheticus, a cultured man and an expert in mathematics, came from Germany to Italy. Immediately, this gentleman—who is honorable and meticulous in carrying out all of his duties—offered me some genitures of famous men which he had with him. [They included] those of Vesalius, Regiomontanus, Cornelius Agrippa, Poliziano, Jacob Mycillus, and Osiander. I added some of them to this work to make up a full hundred genitures; for I rejected all the questionable ones.[9]

Cardano did more than draw on Rheticus' collection. He printed the geniture of one of his own most prominent clients, the governor of Milan, Alfonso Davalos, remarking that "if what he gave me is his geniture, he will never be abandoned by good fortune."[10] He also included the geniture of his own pupil Ludovico Ferrari and that of Emperor Maximilian I, taking the latter—as he himself said—from a work by Schöner.[11] But Cardano's German friend clearly became his chief source, emptying the rich resources of the Nuremberg-Wittenberg collections into his hands. Cardano claimed more than once that he had far more genitures already established and interpreted than he had found room for in his publications. The eagerness with which he seized upon Rheticus' materials suggests that Cardano exaggerated his own industry and detective skill in retrospect.

The two men not only swapped their genitures, but also discussed them at length, and in their conversations lay the seeds of their quarrel. For the second revision of his *Libelli* Cardano added a number of treatises to his work, including one, a set of *Astronomical Aphorisms,* in which he tried to condense his experience as a reader of horoscopes into an elaborate set of rules for others to apply. General in formulation and apparently random in sequence, Cardano's observations amount to nothing more than a fuller list of the generalizations that he had originally tucked into and between the genitures in his collection. He did not evince the drive to quantify the effects of planetary influence and the range of possible planetary configurations that gave body and force to a similar work by John Dee.[12] Still, Cardano's rules for reading the sky fascinated a good many readers—like the anonymous reader who heavily underlined a copy of the text now in the British Library, on principles that remain uncertain:

> II. 132. To recognize a pestilence in a single region from the configuration of the stars alone is impossible.
>
> 133. *For general constitutions one must also observe comets and the other things that accompany them.*
>
> II. 170. Mercury in Leo makes eloquent men, in Aries men of pleasing speech.
>
> 171. *Mercury in Libra, or Aquarius, makes a remarkable intellect, such as it produces nowhere else; yet it has some effect in Capricorn too.*[13]

Evidently what now looks like a massive series of disconnected statements read to its original audience like *Word Perfect for Duffers*—a well-chosen set of indispensable hints for making the complex and unforgiving computer of the heavens produce the right results. Like Nostradamus' clients, who begged him to provide them with just a few "aphorisms" about their genitures, Cardano's readers found more in his cryptic pronouncements than meets the modern eye. Many expert astrologers tried to boil down their principal findings into short, irrefutable statements of principle. Reinhold, for example, also tried to hack simple interpretative rules from the thickets of angular relations that he observed in the genitures he compiled. "Those that have Mars in the fourth house, in a position of dejection, are unfortunate warriors," he remarked, founding this rule on the genitures of Frederick IV and Francis I, in both of which it held true.[14] Elsewhere, Reinhold—who took the unusual step of compiling a group of genitures of illustrious women as well as those of illustrious men—remarked still more curtly that "Venus in the twelfth house means a whore."[15]

Cardano also offered something of a justification for his pursuit of dozens of small rules rather than a few larger ones. He insisted that the craft of the astrologer did not lend itself to systematic treatment. It was simply too complex, the stellar message it dealt with too multivalent. The astrologer's art, Cardano liked to say, "is so sublime that it resembles the art of the jeweler: no full account of it can be given." Interpreting genitures, like cutting gems, required skills so diverse and actions so complex that words could not do them justice.[16] Cardano admitted that his aphorisms only hinted at the depths of this tacit knowledge. But they had more value than a useless effort to attain system and completeness.

Here and there in the *Aphorisms,* however, Cardano flavored his bare, oracular statements with individual genitures and anecdotes. When he did so, he adopted an assertive, dogmatic tone—more that of the prophet who had a direct link to a divine source than that of the astrologer struggling to take all the factors into account. Twice he reported, in detail, on the exchanges he had had with Rheticus over particular genitures. "When Rheticus," he wrote at one point,

> that expert on the motion of the stars, spent some time recently in Milan, he heard me say more than once that I had invented and taught an art, by virtue of which, once given a horoscope, I could predict many extraordinary things about the body, the character, and the major experiences of the subject, without knowing whose horoscope it was. He tried this out twice, and it worked. Finally on 21 March 1546 he came to me with the following horoscope, not informing me of the name or the subject, since even he did not at that time know the name. He asked me to say something about it, saying that a great event had happened in it. But he had set the third degree of Aquarius as the ascendant, since he had made it earlier, fixing the ascendant not on the basis of the given time but by his own computation. Looking at it, I said: "This man is Saturnine and melancholic." He replied: "Where do you get that?" I answered,

"because Saturn rules over the ascendant, and holds the degree opposed to it, and looks at it. And Saturn is in Leo, which adds to the sorrow." Then I added: "but he is capable of smooth and easy speech, and seems gentle and calm." He asked, "Where do you get that?" "Because," I answered, "Aquarius is a human sign, and Saturn produces men who are smooth of speech, and the head of the dragon—which is very important—is in the ascendant. It makes men who are gentle of speech and demeanor." As I examined it, he added, "You captured the man perfectly, it couldn't be done better, but it's not all that surprising. You always do this, and you yourself admit it's fairly easy. But please, go through the rest." To which I replied: "He will certainly die a bad death." "But how do you know that?" he asked, to which I replied, "He holds Saturn condemned, with the dragon's tail, in the seventh house. Therefore, my method says that he will die badly." "How?" he asked. "By hanging," I said. "How do you know that?" "Since Saturn and the dragon's tail, in the seventh house, show that he will be hanged." "But," I added, "after he's hanged, he will be burned." Looking at me in amazement, he asked, "How do you know that?"[17]

Not only did Cardano know the manner of the man's fate; he could also set its time (in his thirty-fifth year). For he knew that the ascendant was in Aquarius, even though Rheticus had not known the exact time of the birth. Aquarius is one of the "mansions" of Saturn. Accordingly, Cardano took Saturn as the lord of the ascendant: the planet that served as the "significator of manners," determining the individual's character.[18] Accordingly, the subject received Saturn's gift of speech, a gift enhanced by the presence of the dragon's head in the ascendant. Unfortunately, Saturn also brought the less welcome gift of a violent death when in a "solid" sign (Taurus, Leo, Scorpio, or Aquarius).[19] Cardano naturally turned out to have predicted the fate of the unknown subject—a counterfeiter named Francesco Marsili, born in Rome in 1505—almost perfectly (in fact, he had already been condemned to hanging and burning when they spoke, and would die at the age of forty-one). But Cardano found this out only when he went to ask the judge if he had condemned anyone to the fire. This confirmation of his "trial of the art," he remarked, could bear comparison with the achievements of the ancients.

Cardano proved equally deft—and Rheticus equally dim—when his German friend showed him a second figure. This Cardano interpreted at once as the geniture of a female magician and trickster in Milan, who would certainly be burned. After all, the malevolent planets Mars and Saturn were both in Leo, another solid sign, and in trine to—120 degrees away from—the ascendant, making her deceptive. The moon, in Scorpio, ensured that she "will be of very bad character, and a prostitute, and will suffer many misfortunes." The fact that Venus "saw" Mars and Saturn made her seem truthful; but she was in fact a liar. In this case, to be sure, Cardano could not attain to certainty about whether the subject would undergo a public execution. Otherwise, however, his marvelous method proved itself again.[20]

Rheticus, presumably, took no pleasure in seeing himself portrayed as Dr. Watson to Cardano's astrological Mr. Holmes. And he can hardly have enjoyed it when Cardano replaced his misidentified geniture for Peurbach with correct ones for Peurbach and Regiomontanus alike—only to denounce Regiomontanus as a plagiarist who had stolen his astronomical tables from the Ferrarese astrologer Giovanni Bianchini.[21] For years to come, Rheticus showed his displeasure with Cardano at every opportunity. He fumed at Cardano's commentary on Ptolemy's *Tetrabiblos* when it appeared in 1554, claiming that his former friend had deprived his fellow German Regiomontanus of the credit due him.[22] He encouraged another astrologer and diviner, Thadäus Hayck, to beat Cardano to the punch by publishing a large-scale manual of metoposcopy, the art of divining the mind's construction and the person's future from the face. Cardano, Rheticus said, "has been milking us with the vain hope of this art for years now."[23] As late as October 1561 he urged the Lutheran astrologer Paul Eber to have a student make a full collection of princely genitures and publish it—no doubt in the hope of finally supplanting Cardano in the book trade.[24] Not for the first or last time, comments that Cardano had probably made without much reflection turned a friend into an enemy.

If Cardano alienated his one-time publicist and benefactor, he infuriated his chief Italian rival Gaurico. From the start of his career, Cardano detested Gaurico—in the first instance because the older man had slighted his father, Fazio, in the preface to his edition of John Peckham's treatise on perspective, which appeared a few years after Fazio's. Gaurico denounced his unnamed predecessors for leaving the text in a corrupt state, boasting of the many textual errors he had corrected and the meticulous care with which he had divided the text into sections and assigned each diagram to its proper place. In fact, however, he seems to have produced his own edition simply by marking up a copy of Fazio's text, without giving any credit at all.[25] Cardano, accordingly, was predisposed to challenge Gaurico, and evidently circulated some of his criticisms at an early stage in his career.[26] As soon as Reinhold saw Cardano's enlarged geniture collection—probably sometime in 1545 or soon after—he realized that Cardano had set Luther's birth a whole year earlier than had Gaurico. More important still, the whole form of Cardano's astrology represented a challenge to Gaurico.

In the course of the fifteenth century, astrologers working at the court of Ferrara and elsewhere had created a new kind of astrology—one styled to appeal to erudite patrons like the Estensi, widely known for their belief in astrology, as well as the Medici and Sforza.[27] Though Pellegrino Prisciani and his colleagues still consulted the standard textbooks of Arabo-Latin astronomy and astrology which had circulated for centuries, they also began to study the huge literary astrologies of Marcus Manilius and Firmicus Maternus, to examine Byzantine treatises in Greek, and to copy the illustrations in the ancient treatises of Aratus and Hyginus. They stared with fascination at the strange divinities that ruled each 10-degree segment of the Zodiac, the so-called decan figures. These had originated in Egypt as groups of stars painted on the lids of coffins, but they had undergone a long series of metamorphoses in transmission from one language and culture to another, turning into demonic figures who haunted the Zodiac, qualifying and sometimes countermanding the influence of the Zodiacal signs and other constellations. Renaissance astrologers also revived the colorful, if entirely nonquantitative, doctrines of Manilius and Firmicus, dividing humanity into the "children" of the seven planets, and offering their clients general advice on that basis, as well as establishing and interpreting individual horoscopes. They found it possible to offer painters the materials from which they could construct powerful images of a cosmos in which the planets, represented as the gods of Greek myth, controlled the souls and actions of all mortals—a vision which Francesco Cossa and others splashed unforgettably across the walls of the Estensi's Palazzo Schifanoia in Ferrara.[28] Fashionable writers on astrology took equal pleasure in the pullulating exotic detail of Firmicus' treatise, which they recycled in more economical textbooks of their own. Gaurico remained loyal to this tradition throughout his many years of astrological practice and writing. He loved to decorate his astrological pamphlets with apposite quotations from the technically dubious but rhetorically brilliant astrological poem of Manilius. Even in a highly technical horoscope analysis, like the one that Gugler copied and studied, Gaurico was as likely to quote Firmicus as Ptolemy.[29] He offered humanistically educated patrons an astrology with a classical panache, rather than the crabbed scholastic Latin and arid lists of planetary positions on which some of his rivals concentrated.

In an age of readers trained to move through texts as a mine-disposal squad moves through a field, eyes peeled and toes delicately feeling for allusions, arguments did not have to be blunt or straightforward to have force. To undermine Gaurico, Cardano simply attacked Firmicus and the kind of astrology he had practiced, which he rejected as impious and impermissible for Christians. In the very first edition of his *Libelli,* as we saw, he made a point of rebutting Firmicus' effort to exempt kings from the power of the stars.[30] He abused Firmicus for failing to see that when Mercury and Jupiter both signified good fortune, a new Plato and Aristotle would be born.[31] And in the expanded 1547 edition of the genitures he made his attack on Gaurico direct and explicit. Reproducing and expounding one of the horoscopes Firmicus had included in his work, which he saw as a genuine horoscope for one of Firmicus' contemporaries, Cardano remarked that in the other horoscopes in the *Mathesis,* those of Plato, Paris, and other ancient heroes, "the impossible happens: Mercury is more than one Zodiacal sign away from the sun. It is clear, therefore, that he did not know the rules that govern the planets, that he did not understand the mathematics of their motions. That is clear anyhow, since he did not assign them their [precise] degrees."[32] In 1547, Cardano made the same argument even more pointedly: "The ancient writers on this art dealt with it in such a careless and absurd manner, that you can find examples in their books which are astronomically impossible. One must not only flee them, but also those who claim to rely on their books. They do not know the art, and most of them are sycophants."[33] For the encyclopedic astrology of the late fifteenth century, the tradition from which Gaurico emerged, with its inclusive welcome to texts of many kinds, its love of astrological imagery, and its willingness to downplay quantitative precision, in some cases, in order to deploy attractive, colorful symbols, Cardano claimed to substitute something more up to date and austere. He made his proposal, moreover, with all the polemical violence that had characterized the classical tradition in astrology, and in the newly expanded public world of print as well as in manuscript genitures which circulated before his book came out.

Gaurico took his time in replying, but his broadside, when he finally launched it, was powerful. His *Tractatus astrologicus* appeared in 1552. A substantial collection of horoscopes, it was organized more systematically than Cardano's, but covered much of the same ground. Like his younger rival, Gaurico offered figures for the founding of cities and the births of popes, princes, intellectuals, and artists. Like his younger rival, too, Gaurico commented on his materials with great flair, paying some attention to the technical details of planetary positions but more to the personalities and careers that they shaped. Despite Gaurico's respect for Firmicus, he even agreed with Cardano against his ancient authority that horoscopes could offer powerful information about the rulers of European states. On Cosimo I, the duke of Tuscany, for example, he wrote:

> If Cosimo de' Medici was born on 12 June A.D. 1519, at the second hour of the night, less a quarter of an hour, Luca Gaurico would prophesy that he would reach seventy-two, if he somehow managed to survive his fifty-second and sixty-third years. But others must decide what is portended by Mars, which lies by a platic computation on the western angle of the horoscope

> [the point opposite the ascendant], and Mercury, which is precisely there, Saturn as the ruler of the house of the horoscope and the moon in the Cacodaemon.[34]

This carefully qualified geniture, with its indication that it rested on the approximate, rather than the exact, position of Mars and its deference to the opinions of other experts, shows no particular polemical intent.

In other cases, Gaurico elegantly took advantage of his position as the later of the two to write, which enabled him to expose some of Cardano's errors without stooping to violent language. Gaurico's geniture of Henry VIII, for example, looks like a normal piece of what Warburg memorably called "astro-political journalism." His comment did at least partial justice to the sensational character of Henry's reign, if not to his own mastery of the details of current history: "The king of England was very learned and very rich, but a Lutheran; he had his wife beheaded, then his concubine, and himself died of a fever on 17 January 1547, at the age of fifty-five years, five months, and six days, because of the direction of the ascendant to Saturn."[35] Gaurico here used a standard doctrine—that Saturn, at certain angular distances, or "directions," from the ascendant, "is a terrible Direction . . . and threatens death, or danger thereof"—to explain the precise timing of Henry's death.[36] But he also reminded anyone who had read the first edition of Cardano's genitures that it had included a prophecy of long life for the English king—one that evidently rested on a misreading of the data which pointed so clearly to a fairly early death.

At the same time, Gaurico boldly ventured where Cardano had not dared to go. When Cardano boasted that his predictions had included brilliant successes, he appealed to unpublished documents in the hands of his clients and to the good faith and reputation for probity of his patron Archinto. Gaurico, by contrast, appealed to documents in the public domain, like the published prognostications in which, he reminded the reader, he had predicted in public and in advance the victory of Francis I at Marignano, his defeat at Pavia, and the imprisonment and release of Francesco Gonzaga.[37] Gaurico, moreover, was willing to offer public prophecies about the lives of prominent individuals—something Cardano had not risked since the very beginning of his career. Like Cardano, he praised other predictors—like the father of Marcello Cervini, an astrologer, who happily and rightly cried, "Today a pope is born to me" (neither he nor Gaurico, evidently, could read in the stars that Cervini's pontificate would last only three weeks).[38]

Commenting on the horoscope of the Florentine military man Pietro Strozzi, Gaurico took due heed of the dangers of a soldier's life, but still pronounced a bolder and more specific verdict than his rival had offered: "He will undergo danger, and harm from horses and the gun, and will suffer somewhat in his naughty bits. If he can profit by a good regimen to survive his unhealthy years, the forty-ninth and fifty-eighth, he will live eighty-two years. His death will result from a pestilent fever and a flow from his belly, outside his native land."[39] Despite the hedges which Gaurico planted on every side of this bet, he proved far less mealy-mouthed than his younger rival. Indeed, he insisted that he had once been tortured by the Bentivoglio of Bologna for predicting—correctly—their defeat by Julius II. "So," he reflected, "the truth hurt the poor prophet"—who could hardly have hoped for a stronger vindication of his qualities of both mind and character.[40]

When it came to the horoscopes of scholars, Gaurico commented on many of the same individuals as Cardano, and often in the same way, describing their physical appearance, their moral and physical health, and their careers. He often gave cheerful accounts of their deaths as well. Like Cardano, Gaurico enjoyed a salacious detail, and joined his rival in using the malign influence of Venus and Mars to explain why Francesco Filelfo "burned with wild lust for girls, and especially for boys."[41] Like Cardano, Gaurico dismissed Pico's critique of astrology, citing Luca Bellanti, "who refuted his arguments and childish little stories, but excused him as having been ignorant of astrology, though a philosopher of the very highest ability."[42] Like Cardano, he offered horoscopes for northern as well as Italian scholars—including Catholics of dubious orthodoxy, like Erasmus, and the Protestant arch-fiend Luther as well.

But here too Gaurico adopted a different style—one that rested, at least in part, on his position as a sophisticated intellectual who had spent long years in the Rome of the high Renaissance, rather than an aging provincial stuck in the country. Gaurico, after all, had computed the propitious time for laying the cornerstone of the new Farnese wing of the Vatican in April 1543—a story that he told very well:

> Luca Gaurico computed the hour and erected the celestial figure for the laying of the first stone of the foundation of the building near St Peter's. But Vincenzo Campanazzi of Bologna used an astrolabe to determine the suitability of the time, crying out with a loud voice, "Behold, the sixteenth hour from the accustomed setting of the clock is now complete." And at once Ennio of Veroli, cardinal of Albano, having put on a white stole and wearing a cardinal's tiara on his head, fitted into the foundation a great piece of marble, beautifully polished and adorned with the arms of Pope Paul III.[43]

Gaurico, in other words, was a consummate curial insider. When possible, he used this status to advantage, telling the reader not only public but private details of the lives of the scholars he had known—for example, that the Carmelite poet Battista Mantuanus had claimed, probably falsely, to have more books of Ovid than were found in the vulgate text. When he could he gave the precise amount, in ducats, of a given scholar's salary—then as now a matter of widespread interest. Gaurico's profiles of learned men, with their confidential-sounding information about each individual's appearance and religious life, had something of the character of a newsletter promising inside information for well-informed readers.

But Gaurico did not confine himself to subtle ways of denigrating the young whippersnapper from the north. He did not feel inclined to accept Cardano's apparent assessment of him, as incompetent to assess the technical value of an ancient authority. Instead, he went on the attack, again and again. Sometimes their disagreements were merely factual: if Cardano dated the birth of Julius II to 22 May 1445, Gaurico set it in 22 June—though the two men agreed that the Zodiacal sign of Scorpio had played a major role in framing his warlike character.[44] In other cases, however, their disagreements became clearer. Cardano, writing in 1543, used the horoscope of Andrea Alciato to explain his miraculous eloquence. Gaurico, writing almost ten years later, used the same horoscope to show that the malevolent influence of Saturn, credited by Cardano with making Alciato a great man, had killed him in 1546, in his early fifties.[45] In printing his horoscope for Luther, dated to the great conjunction year of 1484, Gaurico openly defied Cardano's effort to replace the reformer's mythical birthday with his natural one:

> Martin was at first a monk for many years. Then he threw off his monastic habit and married a tall abbess at Wittenberg, with whom he had two children. A remarkable and quite terrifying conjunction of five planets in Scorpio, in the ninth house, which the Arabs assigned to religion, made him a sacrilegious heretic, a bitter enemy of the Christian religion, and profane. From the direction of the ascendant to the conjunction of Mars he died as a man without religion. His guilty soul sailed down to the underworld, where Allecto, Tesiphone, and Megera tormented it through eternity with fiery whips.[46]

Here Gaurico mentioned, to give his account drama and color, the threatening planetary conjunction in Scorpio with which the 1484 date connected Luther's birth. But he also used an entirely different astrological fact—the angular distance from Mars to the ascendant—to explain the vulnerability to anger and madness which characterized Luther's death.[47] So much both for Cardano's insistence on setting Luther's birth date in 1483 and for his even-toned analysis of the resulting planetary configuration, which, he thought, had made Luther not the scorpion described by Gaurico but a theologian of great commitment to the cause of religion and unshakable firmness of purpose.[48]

Gaurico attacked Cardano from two sides at once—by emphasizing both the technical superiority of his methods and the human superiority of his experience and contacts. He highlighted his technical proficiency by using the so-called method of Alcabitius—not the simpler equal house method preferred by Cardano—to lay out the houses for Pico's figure. In fact, he made a point of rubbing Cardano's nose in the crudity of his horoscopes. Writing of the astrologer Paris Ceresarius, Gaurico remarked: "After passing the threshold of old age, he began to work on astrology, and computed the heavenly houses by equal numbers of degrees, and like a bumpkin. Schöner and Cardano imitated what he did."[49] Even when Gaurico took information from his rival, he stung him while stealing from him—as he did when complaining that the planetary positions he gave in his horoscope for Pico, which he had copied from Cardano, number for number—"were determined only in whole degrees," without the additional minutes. Gaurico's failure to recompute the planetary positions for Pico's figure seems curious in the light of his willingness to recompute the divisions of the houses: this suggests strongly that Gaurico cared more about discrediting his rival than about erecting the most accurate possible figure.[50]

The point of Gaurico's attack became sharpest of all, not surprisingly, when he turned to the geniture of his patron Paul III. Cardano, interpreting this under the influence of his patron, Paul's faithful servant Archinto, had discussed the pope's good fortune, wisdom, learning, and courage. Gaurico made clear, once more, that Cardano had simply missed the point, because his command of astrological data rested on too weak an evidentiary foundation and he followed classical authority too uncritically. In Paul's geniture, six planets appeared in the first four houses, and accordingly below the horizon, and invisible, at the hour of his birth. Though even Ptolemy had not realized it, Gaurico believed that he had the evidence to prove that the stars, when in this position, promised the long life that Paul in fact lived: "Luca Gaurico had it established by experience in around a thousand genitures, that those who had all the planets under the earth in their genitures lived longer than those who had them above the earth."[51] Not only Ptolemy needed correction, moreover. Cardano had consistently claimed to draw the opposite conclusion from the same evidence. So much for his claim to refound the art of astrology on a new, empirical foundation.[52] Gaurico here attacked one of Cardano's fundamental principles, mercilessly.

Cardano, evidently infuriated by an assault that he had gone out of his way to provoke, struck back immediately. In a little treatise of 1554 on interrogations—figures erected to determine the chance of success in a particular enterprise, like investing or marrying, at a precise time—he made bitter fun of Gaurico's account of how he had been tortured for the truth. Listing the unfortunate astrologers who had been punished over the centuries by state power, he mentioned that "Gaurico was racked by the Bentivoglio. He certainly had not foreseen this from the stars, though he threatened the family with ruin, basing his conjecture on the state of affairs more than the stars. For he was a remarkable con-man."[53] And when Cardano took over Gaurico's genitures of Henry II and Catherine de Médicis, he condescended to his elder just as Gaurico had done to him: "it is easy to infer that Gaurico did a very careful job of computing these births. But in the second figure he puts the moon six degrees farther east than the tables do"[54]—a nice way to avoid grappling with the problem that Gaurico computed his nativities more precisely than Cardano, for all the latter's claims to superior science. Still, counter-punches like these could not ward off Gaurico's attack, any more than the brief passage in Cardano's treatise of 1557 *On His Own Books,* in which he insisted that Gaurico had misconstrued his—and Ceresarius'—reasons for using equal houses.[55] In the course of the 1570s, Gaurico's complete works and Cardano's commentary on Ptolemy, with his rebuttal of Gaurico, were all brought out only three years apart by the same erudite Basel publisher, Heinrich Petri.

Reaching the public through print thus brought penalties as well as rewards. Cardano had been able to make a name and win a readership. But he had also struck blows without reckoning that his victim would probably return them, a lifelong habit of his. And he had failed to anticipate that his rival could find a printer and produce a product even more appealing than his own. Print made Cardano into a particular kind of author: informative, critical of his competitors, not unkind to learned Protestants. But it also enabled, even provoked, him to join in what amounted to undignified skirmishes with other writers whom his work enraged. For the first, though not the last, time in his career, Cardano saw his name linked for a long time to come with that of sharp opponents.

From the 1550s on, well-informed readers put Cardano and Gaurico side by side on their bookstands, struggling to deal with the tensions and contradictions that the comparison unleashed. Sir Thomas Smith, who eventually became a royal secretary and ambassador to France under Elizabeth, found himself in 1555 obsessively studying astrology, not sleeping for three months as he struggled to gain mastery of the art, which he had studied in his youth, but evidently not since. Smith knew Gaurico's work, from which he copied horoscopes; he even added his own astrological analyses—which concentrated on planetary positions and aspects—to the more biographical and historical captions provided by Gaurico.[56] But he chose to learn the art by reading over and over a copy of the 1547 edition of Cardano's work, which he annotated throughout in minute detail.[57] Smith's protégé Gabriel Harvey, friend and counselor to Philip Sidney and Edmund Spencer, worked through a copy of Gaurico's *Tractatus* in 1580. A dedicated and skillful reader of technical books of many kinds, Harvey regularly left notices of his reactions to his reading in the form of elaborate marginal annotations couched in a gloriously legible italic script. The notes that he left in his copy of Gaurico make it possible to watch him study and compare astrologers, horoscope by horoscope.[58]

Harvey read his Gaurico against a copy of Cardano's genitures, which unfortunately has yet to be identified (a relative of Smith's, he may have used Smith's copy, but if so he left no clearly identifiable notes in it). He clearly grasped that Gaurico had woven hostile, implicit references to Cardano into his text, and listed many of them in the margins of his book. At Gaurico's horoscope for Ceresarius, for example, Harvey noted that a later German astrologer, Johannes Garcaeus, had supported Cardano's method of dividing the houses.[59] He also remarked on Cardano's own efforts at self-defense: "An apology for Paris, and himself, is in c. 11 of Cardano *De motuum restitutione,* and there is another very short one in his work on his own books, which I have copied out at the end of his last treatise, here."[60] At the end of the book, Harvey copied out the relevant section from Cardano's self-defense, along with bibliographical information on his other astrological works, including his "marvelous horoscope of Christ."[61]

As Harvey read through the two books, he took careful note of both parallels and divergences. He was fascinated by Gaurico's publicly demonstrated prowess as a predictor. Reading the Italian's account of how a foolish rival had gone against him, prophesying the impending death of Charles V in the 1520s, Harvey wrote: "Gaurico's enemy: but a pseudo-prophet."[62] On the other hand, he also felt his Protestant sensibilities stirred, and irritated, when he read one or two of Gaurico's horoscopes and comments. That for Melanchthon, whom Gaurico knew, praised his poetry, his learning, and his skill as an astronomer, though it denounced his heresies. "On Melanchthon," reflected Harvey, "he speaks honorably enough, except about religion. Sadoleto spoke similarly about Erasmus, Melanchthon, Bucer, Sturm. He was more humane and frank than many other papists."[63] But when Harvey came to Gaurico on Luther, he strongly disapproved, finding Cardano (as repackaged by his German friends) much more attractive: "Compare Cardano, number 14 in his one hundred examples of horoscopes;

which is that of Luther. See also number 46, which is that of Henry VIII, the king of England. In them there are judgments far more worthy of note [than this one.]"[64]

Harvey's final reaction, after tracing his way along both complex, connected strands of this astrological double helix, was ambiguous. On the one hand, he found himself unable to resist the seduction of Gaurico's claims to both vast reserves of empirical evidence and practical experience in the corridors of papal power: "Certainly his vast experience should not be condemned, and the authority conjoined with all that knowledge—and that in the court of a prudent pope."[65] He also considered Gaurico's self-assurance—or arrogance—a persuasive sign of his superiority: "I think one should particularly note here that Gaurico dared to oppose his own astrological experience [Astrologicam Experientiam] to the ingenious observations of Ptolemy himself."[66] At the same time, however, Harvey was fascinated by the treasury of precise information and prudent comment offered him by Cardano's horoscopes, which he set alongside the curious *Lives of the Philosophers* by Diogenes Laertius, the more curious *Lives of the Sophists* by Philostratus and Eunapius, and the modern *Elogia* of Paolo Giovio as the sort of book that a "polytechnus," or aspiring courtier and versatile intellectual, should read with special care and attention.[67]

Harvey's ways of reading were always individual and often resolutely idiosyncratic. In this case, however, he had hit upon a comparative, politically sensitive approach directly suggested by the works in question. He was not alone. Richard Bruarne—an Oxford man, who became provost of Eton after being deposed for immorality from the chair of Hebrew at his alma mater—used his copy of the 1547 edition of Cardano much as Harvey used his Gaurico.[68] He filled its margins with content summaries and little hands pointing to vital pieces of information or argument. He erected figures on its blank pages. And he compared Cardano's book with Gaurico's, noting, for example, beside Cardano's geniture of Luther, that "Luca Gaurico writes that Martin Luther was born in 1484, on Wednesday 22 October."[69]

For the next half-century and more, geniture collections on the model Cardano first laid down continued to appear. The number of examples collected and studied rose to two and then three hundred. Discussion of the technical issues involved—from house division to the use of tables—continued, and precise computation gradually became easier, especially in the later sixteenth century, as how-to books that explained, point by point, how to compute planetary positions from Erasmus Reinhold's *Prutenic Tables* of 1552 and almanacs with precalculated tables of houses made the process of erecting a figure easier and easier.[70] Cardano, as the author of the genitures,

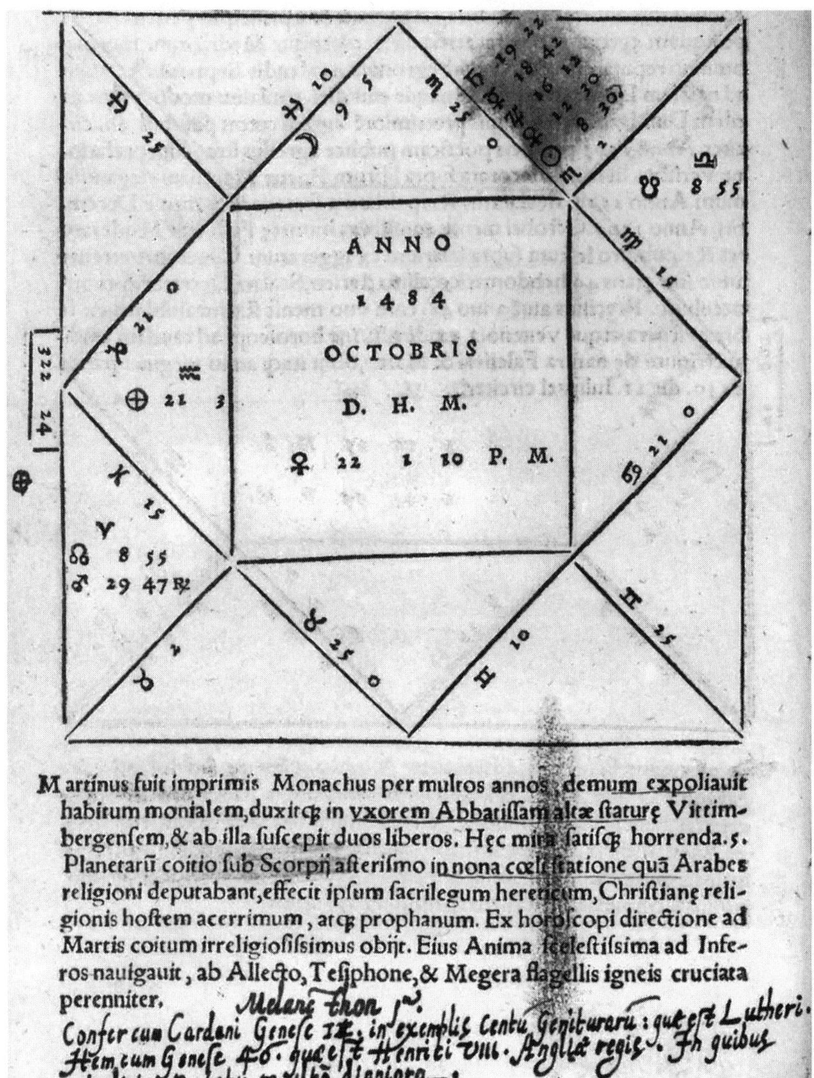

Martinus fuit imprimis Monachus per multos annos, demum expoliauit habitum monialem, duxitq; in vxorem Abbatissam altæ staturę Vittimbergensem, & ab illa suscepit duos liberos. Hęc mira satisq; horrenda. 5. Planetarū coitio sub Scorpij asterismo in nona cœli statione quā Arabes religioni deputabant, effecit ipsum sacrilegum hereticum, Christianę religionis hostem acerrimum, atq; prophanum. Ex horoscopi directione ad Martis coitum irreligiosissimus obijt. Eius Anima scelestissima ad Inferos nauigauit, ab Allecto, Tesiphone, & Megera flagellis igneis cruciata perenniter.

never ceased to be read. But he also never ceased to be compared with his own critics, like Gaurico. The same mechanisms of authorship which made Cardano a celebrity—when applied to the immemorial rivalries of the astrologers—reduced his work in the course of time to the humdrum status of part of the literature that every aspiring astrologer had to read. Had Cardano stopped with his publications of the 1540s, one suspects, he would not

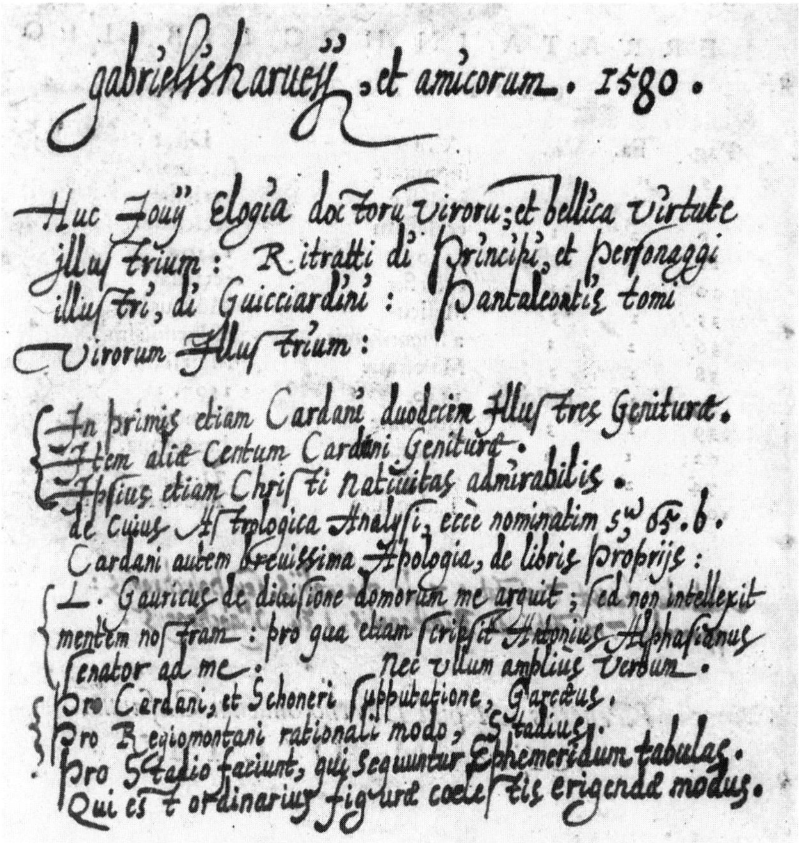
gabrielis harueij, et amicorum. 1580.

Huc Jouij Elogia doctoru virorum; et bellica virtute illustrium: Ritratti di Principi, et personaggi illustri, di Guicciardini: Pantaleontis tomi Virorum Illustrium:

In primis etiam Cardani duodecim Illustres Genituræ.
Item aliæ Centum Cardani Genituræ.
Ipsius etiam Christi natiuitas admirabilis.
de cuius Astrologica Analysi, ecce nominatim 5° 65.b.
Cardani autem breuissima Apologia, de libris proprijs:
L. Gauricus de diuisione domorum me arguit; sed non intellexit mentem nostram: pro qua etiam scripsit Antonius Alphasianus senator ad me: nec vllum amplius verbum.
Pro Cardani, et Schoneri supputatione, Garcæus.
Pro Regiomontani rationali modo, Stadius.
Pro Stadio faciunt, qui sequuntur Ephemeridum tabulas.
Qui est ordinarius figuræ coelestis erigendæ modus.

Figure 18 Two pages from Gabriel Harvey's copy of Luca Gaurico's *Tractatus astrologicus* (Venice, 1552). On the facing page is Gaurico's natal chart for Martin Luther (see the text); Harvey, in his notes at the bottom of the page, compares this to Cardano's chart for Luther, and praises Cardano's geniture for Henry VIII as well. Above is Harvey's substantial bibliographical note on Cardano, drawing attention to his "remarkable nativity of Christ" and other works. Harvey also quotes Cardano's brief defense of his method of dividing the houses from his *De libris propriis,* and compares his works to contemporary biographical compendia as a source for political and moral instruction.

have retained the dominant position among the astrologers of his time which the genitures briefly brought him.

Even in 1547, as the famous author of the standard collection, Cardano still felt beleaguered. In a *Peroration* to his aphorisms he returned to the traditional themes of the Ptolemaic astrologer. Once again he stressed that he had reformed astronomy and astrology, cleansing both disciplines of their useless and erroneous elements and putting the rest into a fully coherent, durable shape for the first time: "I have laid out, without errors, everything that could be done. And what is more, I have reduced it to an art that will last forever."[71] Once again he admitted that the stars could not shape everything that took place in the messy realm of matter beneath them. Once again he insisted, in the immemorial way, that the stars and planets stamped those born under them in unmistakable ways: "It is clear beyond a doubt that all who are born, when they are in a soft and malleable condition, and newly born, receive the influence of the stars like wax, when it is taken off the fire, or lead, when it is first poured and forced into a mold. All these genitures, which I did not invent, but which—except for my own—were taken from others, may serve as evidence."[72] And once again, Cardano could not resist the temptation to corroborate his most general principles by producing, at random, a particular correlation between the stars and the bodies of his clients: "One may also produce another proof. Those who have the luminaries in their constellations cannot avoid having eyes that are nearly white, and unlike those of others in their shape, and generally very large."[73]

None of these arguments was really conclusive. None of them could really sustain Cardano's claim to have devised and practiced a distinctive art—much less to have "defended from insult an art which has been made infamous by the errors of those who practice it."[74] Cardano himself acknowledged as much. Writing a preface to a collection of some of his shorter medical works, he wrote bitterly that others had impelled him to study astrology, not because they hoped he could accomplish something but because they considered the whole art worthless. His original reputation in the field had rested on little or no knowledge of the art. Even his triumphant recovery of "that astrology which teaches us how to predict the future, and which I showed was as accurate as any other art, including medicine," had won him no greater credit: "In the old days, when I was a medical man and ignorant of astrology, I was taken for an astrologer, and not for a medical man. Now, as their ill-will grows a little weaker, I am entirely a medical man, not an astrologer."[75] Writing about astrology, by itself, could not win Cardano the preeminence that he hoped for. Inevitably, he returned to the set terms of the astrological tradition. But when he did so, he did not confine himself to writing about the art. In the course of the 1550s, Cardano's practice of astrology changed, and his ways of writing changed with it.

chapter seven

THE ASTROLOGER AS POLITICAL COUNSELOR

On the Sunday after St. Scolastica's Day (10 February) 1520, Georg Helmstetter received ten gulden from the bishop of Bamberg, for whom he had written "a nativity or judgment." The fee was substantial: the astrologer Johannes Schöner, who worked for the bishop as a bookbinder, was given less than four gulden for binding a work by Erasmus.[1] But the size of Faustus' reward should not occasion surprise. A tireless self-advertiser, he had haunted the inns of Germany's wealthy free imperial cities for years, bragging about his power to carry out many forms of prediction. More important still, the job he carried out for the bishop was genuinely taxing. Compiling a full analysis of a single client's horoscope required not only a fair amount of computation, but also an elaborate qualitative interpretation of the quantitative data. The astrologer had to decide which of the client's planets and their configurations would have the most powerful effects on his physical constitution and temperament, his prospects for marriage, children, travel, health, and length of life, and his other associations and experiences, and then to work out how the positive and negative influences balanced out. The astrologer also had to take into account the country in which the client was born, the genitures and qualities of his parents, and many other factors. Such genitures sometimes included not only a detailed commentary on the client's own natal stars, but similar analyses of the geniture's "revolutions"—the day and time in each year that corresponded to those of the client's birth—for many years to come. Horoscopes for fathers of families sometimes included those of their wives and children as well. These time-consuming and difficult services naturally demanded a high recompense.

All astrology, like all politics, is local. Cardano made his name in northern Europe, as we have seen, as a writer on the subject. But he built up his professional experience as an astrologer, and enhanced the glamor of the geniture collection he was building, by working with prominent Milanese. For example, before 1543 the musician Francesco de Canona, whose skill on the lyre *(testudo)* had won him the respect of Popes Leo, Clement, and Paul, "showed me his horoscope, and I picked out the year in which he would attain rank and rewards."[2] Probably after 1543, Alfonso Davalos, the marchese del Vasto, who served as the Spanish governor of Milan, "gave me" his geniture, which, if genuine, Cardano found extremely promising.[3] Cardano also drew up genitures for other well-known local figures, like the humanist and specialist in pure Ciceronian Latin, Marco Antonio Maioragio.[4] Evidently Cardano did not personally know all of the contemporaries whose natal charts he published and annotated. Of the medical man Antonio Brasavola, for example, he noted that "I have never seen the man; but he ought to have a large frame."[5]

But it seems likely that most of the short genitures he published were the result of personal transactions. Maioragio, for example, thought enough of Cardano to include him, as a major character, in one of his Latin dialogues. And Davalos took a strong interest in powerful occult forms of knowledge and prediction: he supported Giulio Camillo, the architect of a famous "memory theater," a massive information-retrieval device in the shape of an amphitheater, designed to offer rapid access to all the words and phrases used by Cicero, sorted by a system that matched the structure of the universe as a whole.[6] Late in life, Cardano recalled that he had enjoyed the friendship of Andrea Alciato—an opponent of astrology, but also Milan's star intellectual, a brilliant jurist much sought after by universities in other cities.[7] Observers of the highest Milanese circles recognized Cardano as one of the stars that regularly moved there. His name appeared in a Milanese political satire of the 1550s, which described him as "a great astrologer" and quoted his description of the effects of the superior planets on those of choleric disposition.[8] No wonder then that his early work in astrology included consultations for prominent friends.

Cardano's publishing and personal contacts of the 1540s must have reinforced his sense that many great men set considerable store by predictive abilities like his—especially in the Holy Roman Empire. Highly proficient German astronomers like Rheticus took a serious interest in astrology. More important still, high Protestant political figures were also fascinated by the subject, and filled with hope that it could afford guidance through the dangerous political and military situation they faced, as Charles V, having dealt with the French and the Turks, turned his attention to ridding his domains of heresy. Erasmus Reinhold, astronomer and dean of arts at Wittenberg, carried on a lively correspondence with his patron, Albrecht of Brandenburg, in the 1540s—the years in which Reinhold was also drawing up the first Copernican tables of planetary motion, the *Prutenicae Tabulae,* which he finally issued in 1551. Just after the winter solstice in 1545, for example, Reinhold replied with some formality to a princely request for particular genitures with explications:

> Since Your Highness gave me to understand in conversation that Your Highness wished to have a more substantial explanation of some nativities, I have sent this letter to express my will to serve you. I will apply myself to this task, if Your Highness will let me know which genitures he would like to have explained. For I am too busy with my lectures to explain many of them, as the computation takes a long time. But since Your Highness has such a good opinion of these arts, and defends the cause of letters so virtuously, I will freely explain some genitures to Your Highness as a way of declaring my gratitude.[9]

Fifteen months later, Reinhold wrote again to explain why he had not yet produced the genitures Albrecht wanted. He pleaded both pressure of work and the perils of wartime.[10] Reinhold seems genuinely to have preferred the abstract delights of computing astronomical tables to the money which—as he explained in 1549—he could easily have earned by providing "judgments of nativities for kings, princes, and other famous men."[11] Nonetheless, he erected nativities for pay when he could not avoid it—as his unpublished notebook of genitures obviously confirms.[12] Cardano, whose work found such acclaim in Germany, must always have known that his astrological studies might lead to challenging and profitable tasks outside Italy, as they had for Gaurico.

In the event, the great northward journey of 1552, which transformed Cardano's life in so many ways, also gave him the chance to experience the political uses of his art—and to draw up horoscopes larger in scale and richer in detail than those he published at first. As Cardano moved through French and English society, he found himself lionized—so he later recalled—by prominent medical men and intellectuals. He also found himself confronted by prominent lawyers and statesmen, like the great cleric who first invited him to northern Europe, John Hamilton. He was traveling the twisting, complicated corridors of an existing political and social system—one in which entrepreneurs of power over nature like John Dee had already established a position as advisers to men of power over the state. Despite many legends to the contrary, Dee and his patrons were not obsessed with occult ways of knowledge. Dee belonged at least as much to the Renaissance tradition of practical engineering and navigation as to that of scrying and natural magic, and offered Queen Elizabeth and William Cecil practical advice and technical knowledge of many kinds.[13] Nonetheless, he and some of Queen Elizabeth's most tough-minded, pragmatic counselors believed that astrology could yield indispensable predictions, both political and personal. Not only Dee, but Thomas Smith, royal counselor, ambassador to France, and author of a lucid Aristotelian study of the English constitution, collected the genitures of important people and analyzed them.[14]

A common interest in medical astrology evidently brought Dee and Cardano together. Dee entered the note which records their meeting in the margins of his copy of Ficino's *De vita;* it suggests how a serious interest in astral influences, natural magic, and curious substances could unite experts and patrons in inquiry. "I saw a stone," Ficino remarked, "at Florence, brought from India, where it had been dug from the head of a dragon. It was round, in the form of a coin, and naturally and neatly decorated with a great many points, which were rather like stars. When vinegar was poured on it it moved a little way in a straight line, then to the side, and soon began to move in a circle, until the vapor of the vinegar dispersed."[15] He interpreted the stone as one of many gems capable of drawing down the power of particular planets, in which those who owned and wore them could hope to share. This particularly luxurious form of astrological therapy, a highly appropriate one for the consumerist elite of Medicean Florence and generations of courtiers after them, combined very old traditions of talismanic magic, which had flourished through much of the Middle Ages, with a neo-Platonic cosmology and an attractive offer of customized service for the client of high birth and culture.[16]

Cardano eagerly collected celestially powered stones like these, contenting himself with tales about them when he could not inspect them himself.[17] In a marginal note in his copy of Ficino's book, Dee recalled how he and Cardano studied a similar specimen in the presence of some distinguished bystanders: "I saw a stone like this one, and of the same quality, in 1552 or 1553. Present were Cardano of Milan, John Francis [Cheke] and Monsieur Braudaulphin, the ambassador of the French king, in the ambassador's house at Southwark."[18] In the same period, Cardano drew up extended horoscopes for both Cheke and the French ambassador, Claude Baduel, as well as for King Edward himself. Astrology, in other words, brought Cardano into contact not only with a wide circle of readers but also with an extended—and presumably generous—circle of clients.

Cardano's longer genitures did not differ radically in principle from the short ones he had first collected. Like his original genitures, they took the classic form of square diagrams showing the twelve houses and the positions of the planets. Like the original genitures, they were cast in a relatively simple way. Cardano no longer used the simplest of all methods, that of equal houses, but the more complex one attributed to Alcabitius in his day, which involved the use of trigonometry as well as arithmetic.[19] But in more than one case, Cardano made a new point in his analyses. His inspiration for producing the geniture at all lay not only in the "singularity" of the individuals concerned, but also in the links of friendship that bound him to them.[20] The creation of genitures thus gave Cardano the opportunity to develop, as well as to portray, his relations with the political eminences of his time.

One obvious case in point is the horoscope Cardano drew up for Archbishop John Hamilton. Called from Milan to heal this rich and powerful sufferer from a pulmonary disease, Cardano relied for the most part on his medical skills (he had embarrassingly claimed, in print, to have a cure for such diseases, and did his best to live up to what he now knew had been his own false hopes).[21] But he also drew up a full geniture for Hamilton, which would serve—or so he claimed—as an "image" of Hamilton's "constancy, prudence, humanity, and patience," his "almost incurable disease," and Cardano's "skill in this art—and the truthfulness of the art."[22] Hamilton was evidently enough of a grandee, however, that Cardano did not venture to discuss his astrological results directly with the archbishop. Cardano may not have trusted his social skills, which often failed him, as he ruefully admitted. Or he may have carried out a rational calculation, of a kind common in all areas of early modern society and especially sensible for someone working in a foreign country: that he would make more progress by approaching the great man through an intermediary, as one prayed more effectively by invoking the aid of a saint, than by trying to go directly to the top. At all events, he recorded the animated conversation in which he had alerted Hamilton's physician, Gulielmus Casanatus, to his astrological findings. Given the symptoms Hamilton suffered, Saturn must be in the sixth house, which governed sickness, and the moon would approach it when the disease began (presumably to manifest itself again). In a few days, when Cardano's prediction was verified, Casanatus "related all this to your highness, not without wonder."[23] In this case Cardano did not claim more for his geniture than scientific veracity, though he did reveal that it had helped him to impress the doctor who had called him in for consultation.

Cardano made no bones about the connection between horoscopy and networking. One of the most elaborate genitures that he created in the course of his time in the north was for his medical colleague Casanatus. Cardano found a number of flattering things to say about the man whose invitation had led to the great adventure of his life. Casanatus too was an adventurer, who had moved from his native Burgundy to Scotland, "where very few foreigners live." He was erudite, liberal, warm, and "all courtier, as if he had been born at court."[24] Above all, he had a geniture that corresponded in many, though not in all, respects to Cardano's: "The question of friends is very remarkable. As I said, this geniture is given here as an example, but, to use Ptolemy's terminology, it corresponds with mine, the place of the moon in his with the place of the moon in mine, and the place of the sun with the place of the sun. And where he has the sun, I also have Venus and Mercury, and the lord of the ascendant is the same, namely Venus."[25] In the end, Casanatus' geniture proved both that he had made the ideal intermediary between Cardano and the archbishop and that Cardano had been better suited than he to diagnose the archbishop's illness.[26] Astrology, in Cardano's hands, not only created ties of affection but gave them a precise cosmic justification.

Cardano's use of genitures to weave a network of connections rested on ancient precedent. Ptolemy confidently explained that the stars could predict both friendships and enmities for any given pair whose nativities were known.[27] Renaissance astrologers applied these methods, for example, when determining the chances that a husband and wife would find happiness together.[28] But they also used them to investigate their own prospects of establishing solid relations with the prominent. Regiomontanus, according to one account, found reason for hope in the geniture of Ladislas of Hungary: "The ascendant of my nativity is no more than 12 degrees away from the ascendant of his; given his birth, he will offer me the offices of friendship. Similarly, the moon in his nativity is in the position of Jupiter in my nativity; and Mars in his nativity is in the position of the sun in mine."[29] Cardano, in short, acted as an up-to-date but conventional astrologer when he used genitures to predict and form relationships.

When Cardano worked for fellow intellectuals like Cheke and Baduel, however, his astrological inquiries became, effectively, exercises in collaboration. Some of his conversations with his clients remained on a businesslike level, at least as he portrayed them. In his discussion of Cheke's case, for example, Cardano recorded a set of precise details, as dry as they were vital, that only a client could have given him: "The following remarkable things happened to him. In the year 1540, on the seventh day of September he suffered from an acute fever. On 5 May 1552 he suffered from consumption. On 10 June 1544 he was made tutor to the king [Edward]. On 11 January

1549 he almost lost his original [place of] honor. On 11 May 1547 he married."[30] A little later, Cardano made the nature of the interview he had conducted with his informant even clearer: "I said that in the year 1549, on 11 January, he almost lost his office."[31] Evidently, the astrologer asked the client a long series of questions about the remarkable circumstances of his life, whether medical, personal, or political. Then he worked out the planetary conditions which had caused them, taking the client's horoscope as well as the immediate situation into account (in Cheke's case, the sun's movement into opposition with Mars, among other factors, was clearly connected with his barely averted fall).[32] One hears the faint echo of lost hours of businesslike consultation, perhaps based on questionnaires, in which the astrologer supplied the worried client, after the event, with reasons to explain his successes and failures.

The geniture Cardano drew up for another intellectual, King Edward himself, was even longer and considerably more digressive than that for Cheke. It offered another, and much more discursive, version of consulting-room conversation. Edward, Cardano recalled,

> was still in his fifteenth year when we met. He asked—for he spoke Latin as elegantly and readily as I—"What are the contents of your books *De varietate rerum?*" For I had dedicated them to him. I replied: "First of all, in the first chapter I reveal the cause of comets, which has so long been sought for." "What is it?" he asked. "The light of the planets," I answered, "coming together." "But," the king asked, "the stars are moved in different directions. How can it be that the comets are not broken up or moved by their motion?" I replied: "They are moved, but much more rapidly than the planets, because of the difference of aspect—just as happens with a crystal and the sun, when a rainbow shines on the wall. For a small change produces an immense difference in place." Then the king asked: "But how can that happen without some matter being subject to [the light]? For the wall serves as a subject to the rainbow." I answered, "It's like what happens in the Milky Way and in the reflection of lights. When many candles are lit at the same time, they produce a certain bright white light in the middle."[33]

"Therefore," Cardano commented, "you can tell the lion by his claw, as the saying goes"—a humanistic adage underlining his respect for the prince's scientific prowess. The conversation sounds superficially unrelated to the astrologer's task, but any informed reader would have seen the connection at once. Cardano's conversation with the erudite and clever young king, presumably carried on as he prepared the analysis of Edward's geniture, moved naturally from astrology to the closely related subject of comets. True, Aristotle had argued that these must exist in the atmosphere, not in the heavens, which were free of change. But even Ptolemy, the most Aristotelian of astrologers, had seen comets as useful for predicting changes in the weather and discussed them in the *Tetrabiblos* (2.13).

Many intellectuals who denied the uses of classical astrology, like Luther, accepted that comets were portentous.[34] When Cardano took the radical step of treating comets as heavenly phenomena, caused by the intersecting light rays of the superior planets, he provided what some readers found an impressive and plausible reason for astrologers to continue discussing them.[35] Not only the way that Edward asked his questions, in other words, but their very nature confirmed the boy's precocious understanding of natural philosophy and astrology—and presumably helped the astrologer in his task of character analysis.

Some of Cardano's other clients had not only brilliance and learning, but also political insight and experience, and he took care to suggest that their conversations had revealed these qualities as well. He remarked, for example, that he published his geniture of the jurist and bibliophile Aimar de Ranconet against the expressed wishes of his subject. As often with Cardano, his telling of the story carries a larger lesson:

> This magistrate has gravity, combined with a marvelous humanity; erudition combined with experience. He is as dutiful, and as affectionate toward scholars, as anyone. And though his estate is modest, nevertheless his collection of select books suggests that he wishes to imitate the secretary Epaphroditus. [Nero's secretary, sometimes identified by earlier scholars, though no longer, with the man to whom the Jewish historian Josephus dedicated two of his works]. He fervently asked me not to include his horoscope here. His pleas revealed his judgment and humanity, but he did not obtain what should not be obtained: that is, that I should omit mention in this highly appropriate place of the man for the sake of whose friendship alone I could well have visited France. I confess that I have never encountered anyone like him in my own country—anyone, that is, who so combined humanity with his official position, and assessed me as he did. Though I appeared before him in rags, I could not make him despise me; though I spoke simply, I could not make him look down on me. Then I said to myself: "Here is a rare bird, one that looks inward, and is not taken in by the false appearance of what is right."[36]

Cardano, in other words, approached Ranconet in disguise—or at least dressed and behaving in an eccentric way. The French lawyer proved that he could judge human nature by seeing through the bizzareries of Cardano's conduct to the sage within. So did Cheke, who—Cardano recalled—refused to despise the astrologer even though he wore as humble a guise as he could, "so that I could recognize, and not be recognized."[37]

Cardano, in other words, made his consultations with these political intellectuals into pragmatic intelligence tests, which they in turn passed without difficulty. He carried out his transactions with his clients on a political and moral, as well as a quantitative and technical, level. Not surprisingly, his analyses of their characters often concentrated on the qualities that would serve them in public life—or fail to do so. His commentaries on their genitures turned into brief but graphic character sketches, by no means without insight. In Cheke, for example, the fixed stars that occupied significant points in his geniture had produced a highly intelligent trimmer without a central core of conviction:

> For the head of Medusa, which is of the nature of Saturn and Jupiter, means the priesthood and a high position in the administration of the law. Along with Procyon, which is of the nature of Mercury, this star makes a man who loves learning and is gifted at carrying out enterprises. He will be especially gifted at knowing how to accommodate himself to time and place. And he will attain the highest level of brilliance and glory accessible to humanity, and the reputation for almost divine wisdom, unless the common constitutions of the stars prevent him.[38]

Of Baduel, Cardano said even more, his tone frank, sharp, and admiring:

> This birth is remarkable for fortune and intellect and character and bodily form. He is a tall man, rather larger than he should be, fat and thickly built. With this form, he is clever, not unskilled in mathematics, polite, splendid, affable. Sly in affairs, he is prudent and energetic, and has helped his king greatly with his wisdom . . . He will not be more successful or better placed in anything than in journeys, embassies, and expeditions, in which he will suffer the risks and slanders caused by envy. Nonetheless he will reach the highest offices. This birth has some extraordinary contradictions: though plagued by illness, he will reach old age; he kept a good temperament, though he lost his wife; he was fat and clever; a beneficent man, he became the object of slander; and so on.[39]

Cardano's exercise in oxymoron, etched in contrasts as sharp as those of a Petrarchan poem, showed that he could sum up a complex individual at a glance—exactly as the great men summed him up. Astrological, like political, experience qualified the one who had it to play a role in the great world of affairs.

Cardano himself did so, and in a dramatic way. He drew up, perhaps at Cheke's suggestion, a horoscope for young King Edward of England. He provided a copy of it—presumably in a legible, and even luxurious, manuscript form—for the king's household to keep.[40] And in it he evidently found celestial configurations to account for the boy's obvious brilliance: his ability at languages, his mastery of dialectic, natural philosophy, and music, and his fine, princely bearing.[41] Cardano saw evidence that Edward would be a dextrous negotiator and a handsome man. He would marry well, even though his chances for a long and healthy life were diminished by the fact that the malign planet Saturn appeared in the first house of his geniture, which determined the subject's life chances. As we have seen, the identity of the planet that ruled the ascendant played a powerful role in Cardano's interpretations of genitures. In this case, though, the malign planet did not dominate the rest.[42] Edward, Cardano predicted, would at first run down his estate but then enlarge it. He would undertake modest journeys to the south, north, and east. And he would show himself wise and modest beyond his years.

In offering character analyses at this level of depth, detail, and sometimes sharply critical tone, Cardano followed the norms of his craft, providing a service for which members of the European elite regularly paid large sums. Since the later Middle Ages, at least, French and English royals had paid astrologers to produce genitures for them. Like Cardano's, these regularly went into great detail—personal and political, medical and psychological. Like Cardano's, they regularly described the client's character and physique in sharp, even biting terms.[43] In the course of the sixteenth century, moreover, astrologers regularly provided detailed geniture analyses for clients and their children, ranging from members of the Imperial and royal families through aristocrats to wealthy entrepreneurs and bourgeois.[44]

Any number of the most eminent patrician intellectuals of the early sixteenth century took advantage of astrological consultations of this kind. Francesco Guicciardini, for example, evidently felt a serious and sustained interest in the geniture created for him by Ramberto Malatesta. Like Cardano, Malatesta showed all the abilities of a deft Hollywood scenario writer as he laid out the many adventures predicted by the stars for his brilliant, saturnine, well-connected client. One can only speculate whether Malatesta derived these conclusions from the principles he invoked, which closely resemble those we have already seen being put into operation, or from his own close personal observation:

> [On journeys] But it is true that to go from the sun and Saturn in its retrograde arc, this shows that you must make many voyages. In them you will encounter many problems and grave risks, and so confront and become involved in many violent incidents, and so suffer a serious weakness and infirmity. But at the same time I warn you that when the time comes, you must be cautious and prudent to avoid some evil befalling you.

[On intellect] But when I consider again that Mercury is lord of the geniture, I say that you are a man of parts, brilliant, able to master all the sciences, and seriously devoted to the study of the secrets of astronomy. And when it comes into conjunction with Venus, according to the opinion of Firmicus Maternus, you must therefore be rich and involved with wealth in many forms, and plunged into the pleasures of women.

[Dangers on account of wealth] And so because of your obtaining these things, you will be exposed to various dangers and inconceivable difficulties.

[Honor] [I say] that Mars, being in its elevation, reveals government and control of arms and soldiers. And so it shows a man who can judge the lives and deaths of others, and the lives and deaths of many are placed in his hands. And thus it picks out a man adorned with the insignia of many offices, and also a man decorated with many honors . . .

[Ecclesiastical offices] But he will deal with letters and religious offices, and will become dear to great men on account of his good honors. And enemies will be raised up against him often, in sudden actions, but he will put them down with his strength and virtue.

[Adultery] And he will also corrupt the wife of another man or another's spouse.[45]

Willibald Pirckheimer, similarly, received not only a detailed geniture and analysis but regular astrological consultations from his friend Lorenz Beheim—as well as a geniture for his friend Dürer, which rightly predicted or explained his fame, his love of travel, and his desire for many women. Beheim even gave Pirckheimer instructions on how to read genitures on his own.[46]

Such services always took time and usually cost money. But the loss of Cardano's letters makes it impossible to reconstruct the economics and other technical details of his practice. Fortunately, a good many letters to and from one of his most successful rivals have survived. These suggest both the range of questions that a private horoscopist could deal with and the forms his compensation could take. Michel de Nostradamus made his name—as Cardano tried to—by publishing prognostications which combined astrological and prophetic methods and languages.[47] Once established as a celebrity, however, he shifted the pattern of his business, emphasizing the provision of charts, often short-term, for individuals of means. One of his favorite clients, the Augsburg merchant Hans Rosenberger, first approached him in November 1559 through an intermediary, Lorenz Tubbe. Tubbe wrote to Nostradamus, enclosing Rosenberger's geniture and asking his advice. He made clear that his client had refined tastes in astrological matters, since he had already benefited from the advice of

Cyprian Leowitz, a recognized expert, who had lived for some time in his household.[48]

Nonetheless, Rosenberger cast himself at Nostradamus' feet:

> In the Tyrol, a county of upper Germany, lives a certain nobleman who loves mathematics and all who study and teach it. That is why he has had some excellent mathematicians in his household for more than three years. He came across your astrological predictions, and because of their certainty he venerates you and wants me to discuss his nativity, which he sent me, with you. He hopes you will have the time to explain the following points, in your own manner, on the basis of astrology. First, on the basis of the principles of directions, what about the chances for his mining enterprises in 1559 and the years to come, as you see that his life is prolonged? For he has been spending a great deal on mines for some time. Secondly, what do you hope he will receive by way of honors and offices in each year? Thirdly, what of his health, fortune, and problems? Once he has these points explained by you—unless you wish to use your art to warn him about something else—he writes and commands me to pay you an honorable fee.[49]

Though Nostradamus eventually sent the analysis requested, it was in French and illegibly written, to Tubbe's dismay. He could make nothing of it and begged for a Latin translation for Rosenberger.[50]

Negotiations continued, and by 1561 Rosenberger was writing personally to Nostradamus to offer him, as an honorarium, a silver goblet gilt in the German fashion; to ask for genitures for his sons Karl and Hans; and to complain that he too could not read the French astrologer's handwriting.[51] The relationship continued for some time to come, and profitably—at least for Nostradamus. He not only offered celestial guidance for his client's mining operations, but also profited from the Augsburg connection he had made to write genitures for other grandees—including the two Habsburg princes Rudolf and Ernst, the sons of the Holy Roman Emperor Maximilian II.[52] By the end of his life, as Jean Dupèbe has written, Nostradamus "was in constant receipt of requests: his boutique, which employed several secretaries, had the appearance of a prosperous little factory."[53] Cardano's form of custom astrology, in short, was normal practice among the successful astrologers of his time; and so was the way he used his art, one eye on the main political chance, to rise to a position in which he could hope to reach the ear-trumpets of the very powerful. In offering advice at court and to high courtiers, he was not transgressing boundaries, pushing into territory where astrologers should not tread, but going where others had gone before and would go after him.[54]

Cardano rapidly found that the glimmering Greenland of high talk at high tables had its fissures and crevasses, into which the ambitious astrologer could easily fall. Technical failures of computation or prediction could normally be forgotten, glossed over, or explained away. Cardano, as we have seen, tacitly revised his geniture of Nero when he realized he had set it on the wrong day. Technical inconsistencies could normally be shown to be only apparent, not real—especially since Cardano's art of horoscopic interpretation rested on elastic guiding assumptions. "Some enemy of astrology," he wrote, reflecting on Casanatus' geniture, "will rise up here and demand, 'Where are the signs of his journeys? Where are the signs of his long stay outside his native country? For here it is the luminary, not Mars or the Lot of Fortune, which is cadent from the angle [in the fifth house].'" Cardano, however, had a ready answer: "Listen, my good man: two modest signs make one big one, and three a very big one."[55] The position of the moon in the fifth house, where Mars "looked at" it, the position of Saturn, and the fact that Casanatus himself came from a people much given to travel determined that he would make long journeys—even though the moon, Mercury, and Mars did not appear in the ninth house of his horoscope, which normally determined the subject's travels.[56] In hindsight, Cardano's conduct looks unattractive. As in his reframed geniture for Nero, he fudged his data when they proved refractory. From his own point of view, however, he was simply operating in full awareness that horoscope interpretation required an inexpressibly complex, partly intuitive balancing of factors, a process in which errors and revisions were inevitable.[57] His model was hermeneutical, not geometrical. In any event, problems like these simply stimulated Cardano to develop elaborate and credible arguments about his way of reading.

But glaring errors of fact could neither be tacitly corrected nor explicitly explained away, especially when made in documents prepared for very prominent clients. The *Liber xii geniturarum,* as Cardano had to admit when it appeared, recorded one of the most glaring of his own. Despite his doubts about the "debility" of Edward's life, Cardano had predicted marriage, a more or less normal lifespan, and some years of rule for him. But by the time his book appeared in 1554, the young king had died, without issue. Aghast, Cardano still insisted that he had hedged his predictions about with enough reservations to ensure that he had not committed a professional foul: "From this," he wrote, "it is clear that we should not pronounce about the length of life for weak genitures, unless we have first consulted all the directions, processes and entries of the prorogatives [the places that extend life]. And if I had not made a reservation on this point in the prediction that I gave them, they could rightly complain about me."[58]

This technical plea did not satisfy Cardano, however—and he probably saw that it would not satisfy his readers either. Accordingly, he added what he called the "more important cause" of his failure to predict Edward's death. Here he told the story of what he had done for his client. Cardano had spent, he claimed, around a hundred hours just on Edward's geniture and its prorogative places. His normal method of taking the directions of sun and moon, he said, would inevitably have led him to discover the lurking disaster: "The matter would have been clear at once: the danger of death—for I am not such a great man that I would dare to say certain death, even though that could have been pronounced quite safely, given the large number of testimonies that agreed on the point—as well as treason, riot, the translation of the kingdom into other hands, and the rest."[59] Cardano could not have kept these horrors to himself, moreover: "the goodness of my nature would have forced me to make the prediction."[60] And such a prediction could only have brought disaster upon its maker:

> I would have been forced to state my opinion. Imagine my fears; imagine the rumors. Some would have said my prediction was vain and stupid. Others would have said another ruler had bribed me with money to overturn someone, or alienate the king from him. Still others would have said that I made this up in the hope of gain. What help would I have found, what hope, among peoples unknown to me? They do not even spare their own fellow countrymen—not even their king, who was still a boy, who could not have defended himself, much less me.[61]

The credulous young king, in the power of men already determined to betray him, could easily have been turned against Cardano: "Therefore it was certain that I would never return home—and that even if matters turned out for the best, with how little reward it would have been for my great danger and perturbation of mind."[62] Cardano, in short, would have been lost, caught in the terrible toils of professional duty and bound to speak the truth, but unable to do so without ruining his own life. The truth, moreover, would probably not have helped the poor young king, caught as he too was in the haunted corridors of a corrupt Elsinore, surrounded by powerful older men who wanted him dead.

Cardano, however, managed to have his meat and his manners too. He insisted that he simply had not done the extra half-hour of computation that would have shown him the king's future. He brashly pointed out that he could easily have claimed accurate foreknowledge, smoothly disguising his technical failure as an adroit application of courtly prudence: "I could, in the manner of certain astrologers, have pretended that I knew what was coming, and had kept silence out of fear; that would have been easy in an event as conspicuous as this. But I was far from even thinking of this, much less from foreseeing it."[63] Instead, he had simply left the country. Cardano's sympathy for poor Edward had grown to the point that he felt nauseated to see the young king controlled and exploited by others. A tyranny was clearly taking shape, as members of the English elite battened on the goods of the Catholic church which had been distributed among them. Cardano, accordingly, said that he had followed the dictates not of the stars but of his native prudence, and departed with his work incomplete.[64]

Edward's case revealed, in other words, not the limitations of the astrologer's art but the dangers of the high position he hoped to occupy. Cardano was hardly the only ambitious, low-born astrologer to offer a royal or noble patron inaccurate advice. Gaurico, for example, told the Habsburg archduke Ferdinand that he would defeat the Turks, lead the sultan in triumph with his arms bound behind him, and become more important than the emperor himself—all this at a time when the Habsburgs were lucky to keep the Turks from taking Vienna, and many years before Charles V laid down his heavy crown.[65] But Gaurico made this prediction only in an unpublished custom geniture—one neither he nor its recipient had any interest in making public. Cardano, by contrast, had to explain his error—and did so by reference to the power of Providence, which had preserved him from spending the little extra time that would have revealed the truth, and of native prudence, which had led him to cease work. Otherwise he would have faced a political dilemma that no level of technical expertise could solve. Paradoxically, Edward's case showed that the court astrologer could not, in some circumstances, carry out his principal duty of telling his client the complete truth.[66]

When Cardano emphasized the political problems that hedged around the astrologer's drawing board, he self-consciously drew attention to a long-established feature of the astrological tradition. Like many other medical men of the time—and like his astrological rival Gaurico—Cardano was a good humanist as well as a good astrologer, one dedicated to close philological study of ancient texts and the traditions to which they belonged.[67] Accordingly, he did historical research to drive home his thesis about astrology and politics—a point to which I shall return later on. He noted that the astrologers of the Roman imperial court had faced exactly similar problems. When Tiberius, in his exile on Capri, took advice from his astrologer Thrasyllus, a slave (or the emperor himself) stood ready to hurl the seer into the ocean if he lied. After the astrologer predicted that recall to Rome would come soon, Tiberius asked what he foresaw for himself. The future, Thrasyllus replied, looked very dark—and by this melancholy answer saved his life. Only Thrasyllus' ability to predict his own death, in other words, enabled him to avoid it: the astrologer entered the quicksands of court life with a heavy professional burden, under which he could easily sink. Many had. Domitian's astrologer Ascletarion, for example, paid for his prediction of the emperor's death with his own (which he had foreseen). In insisting on telling Domitian the truth nonetheless, Ascletarion displayed his technical ability and his professional ethics at one and the same time.[68]

Extinction threatened Roman astrologers more than once—especially in the later years of the Empire, when their way of explaining politics and history came into conflict with those of the Christian church and the emperors, since both claimed dominion over the universe. As we have seen, Firmicus Maternus, astrologer and Christian bishop, proposed a solution which became popular. Emperors, he explained, being gods, escaped the control of the planets.[69] Many Renaissance astrologers agreed, but Cardano, from the outset of his career, rejected both the ancient authority and his message. Firmicus, he accurately insisted, was a grammarian, not an astrologer: he collected bits of astrological doctrine but showed no understanding of the technical core of the art.[70] The high-flying astrologer might face a politically delicate situation, but he could not escape it simply by ducking responsibility for high politics.

The more gifted the astrologer, in short, the more hazardous his career. Cardano drove this point home more than once. But his experience of high risk was not unusual in the trade. Gaurico made the same point more directly, as we have seen, when he described the outcome of the accurate prediction he had made "in a certain printed forecast." The astrologer warned that Giovanni Bentivoglio would destroy himself and his house if he did not humble himself before Julius II. Bentivoglio condemned him to "four tortures of the arms"—the same terrible torture under which Tommaso Campanella would bear up, many years later, until his tormentors declared him insane—and twenty-five days in prison. When Julius II soon defeated the Bentivoglio and leveled their palace to the ground, he bore out Gaurico's prediction, but that did nothing to mitigate the astrologer's long-remembered pain. "Thus the truth hurt the poor prophet," Gaurico wrote years later.[71]

Cardano, as we have also seen, referred to this saying contemptuously in his own little book on interrogations.[72] No wonder, then, that even Cardano's most prominent astrological catastrophe did not diminish his faith in the predictive power of the stars—any more than the less prominent one that took place in 1559, when Aimar de Ranconet, whose virtue and learning he had praised so warmly, died in prison, accused of having made his own daughter pregnant. Cardano simply recalled that—even though he had failed to predict the disaster in this case too—he had at least warned Ranconet to take extra precautions, since Mars and Saturn threatened him with a great misfortune. No doubt, he remarked, the conjunction of the moon with Mars in opposition to Jupiter had dealt Ranconet the final blow.[73]

If anything, the experience of providing detailed, elaborate genitures for living clients and dead celebrities made Cardano's enthusiasm for his art blaze up even higher. He found himself making astrological experiments of a sort—as when, in curing a melancholy woodcutter whose infant son had just died in a fall, he drew up the child's geniture to determine the cause of the sad event, and discovered that the malevolent planets threatened that he would die "by accident and ruin."[74] He also found himself returning to the study of genitures—like those of Erasmus and Paul III—that he had first established many years before with undimmed enthusiasm and close attention to a wider range of details.

Even more sustained—indeed, it became a lifelong preoccupation—was Cardano's effort to investigate his own geniture in 1553. He had erected a figure for his own birth long before, as we have seen, and discussed it with friends and rivals in Milan, and versions of this appeared in his 1543 and 1547 collections of genitures. But in the *Liber xii geniturarum* Cardano analyzed both the astronomical and the astrological details of his own case with a microscopic attention to detail that he had never shown before. Evidently he found the process rewarding—so much so that he repeated it, twenty years later, as he developed his topical, analytical autobiography, *On His Own Life*, from a further analysis of his geniture.

Cardano's geniture will call for more detailed study later on. For now, what matters above all is his justification for including it in what he had advertised as a collection of "illustrious" genitures. Cardano admitted that it might seem inconsistent to include his own geniture with those of really great men like Erasmus and Cheke. But it genuinely deserved attention. It revealed an incredible variety of talents and incidents—more variety, in fact, than any of the others. It had a further, unique advantage: it was wholly known to its analyst. Indeed, Cardano described it as "so precisely examined that you would find it hard to find a comparable example."[75] Above all, Cardano's data proved the basic verity of the principles of Cardano's art of prediction. "It has been confirmed," he wrote, "by the previous edition. In the ten years that have passed since then, many of the things publicly predicted in it have taken place; and nothing that was not foreseen. Therefore everything that has happened in my life fits this figure so precisely that I seem to have laid down a history rather than a prediction, and a decree of the stars."[76] For all the misadventures that beset his career as a predictor, for all the risks and pitfalls he had encountered, Cardano's work on individual genitures left him more convinced than ever that he was the master of a high and powerful science. No wonder that he also felt capable of writing the first detailed, up-to-date commentary on the one true classic in the field—Ptolemy's *Tetrabiblos,* his deep respect for which had grown as his experience of astrology increased.

chapter eight

CLASSICAL ASTROLOGY RESTORED

Cardano began his career as an astrologer already concerned about what his discipline had been like, and what it had achieved, in the ancient world. One of the first Milanese celebrities whose geniture he published, as Germana Ernst has observed, was the humanist and jurist Andrea Alciato.[1] In the early years of the sixteenth century, Italian scholars were only beginning to acknowledge the challenge to their preeminence in eloquence and erudition presented by northern humanists like Erasmus and Guillaume Budé.[2] By the 1540s, the literary balance of power had clearly shifted. Cardano praised his fellow countryman as one of the rare Italians who could challenge, and even outdo, the northerners:

> I am not unaware that my city has some citizens who are so highly adorned with every virtue that the addition of their horoscopes would yield considerable profit here. But I have added the geniture of Alciato alone, since I could do so without incurring any suspicion of flattery. For in his lifetime he published a good many things worth reading, when others could scarcely manage that, and amid that throng of barbarian commentators he retained a pure Latin and added to it another language, Greek. He is the only one who rivals both Budé and even Erasmus for eloquence, and in my judgment successfully. Moreover, he attains a far higher—really an absolutely higher—level of gravity, as one can see by comparing letters to letters and speeches to speeches. Therefore I did no wrong in adding this geniture to my work.[3]

Evidently Alciato's geniture eminently deserved its place near that of Erasmus.

But if Cardano unreservedly admired Alciato's humanistic style of jurisprudence, with its historical and philological approach to the Roman *Corpus iuris,* he had more mixed feelings about another, and even more popular, side of the lawyer's literary activities. In 1531, Alciato devised and published the very first example of what became one of the most fashionable genres of writing in the Renaissance: the emblem book. This was a collection of short compositions, each of which had three elements: an image, often taken from Greek or Roman mythology; a title or caption; and a short poem in Latin commenting, sometimes obliquely, on the message offered by the words and picture above it.[4] Alciato's emblems, with their visually and verbally pointed morals, were the object of learned commentaries and the target of widespread imitation. Academies and schools required their members to create and devise emblems, which rapidly became the fashionable learned counterpart to the mottos and *imprese* so popular in Italian and northern courts.

Two of Alciato's emblems focused on astrology. One of them, which posed the chained Prometheus as its central image, warned readers not to look too high, since some forms of knowledge were and should be inaccessible to men: "The hearts of those wise men who aspire to know the fortunes of the heavens and the gods are gnawed by cares of many kinds."[5] The other showed Icarus falling into the ocean after the wax of the wings made for him by Daedalus had melted. Entitled "Against the astrologers," the emblem explicitly warned that any effort to ascend by thought into the heavens must end in a disastrous fall.[6] The elements of Alciato's satire were conventional, of course, but his authority endowed them with considerable weight. Cardano, accordingly, felt obliged to justify discussing Alciato at all. Following the precedent set by Alciato himself, who had become famous for his efforts to explain Roman laws by setting them back into their historical contexts, Cardano resorted to history. The record, he argued, both explained why astrology had a bad reputation and proved that this was no longer deserved:

> [Alciato] could properly have been omitted here, since he wrote that this art is fallacious and deserves public punishment, relying on certain laws which, at the time [when they were passed], were severe and just. For the world can barely contain the incompetence of these rascals, who either from greed or hope endanger empires by issuing false predictions, without knowledge, study, or judgment. But custom has invalidated these laws, for in the course of time it became clear that this discipline, when properly practiced, has been a great gain for the human race.[7]

Cardano did not pursue the point further in his comments on Alciato's geniture. But he added at the end of his little collection of genitures and texts a short and flowery text "In Praise of Astrology." His inspiration for doing so may not have been wholly Milanese. Printers like Petreius often added to the technical works they brought out in astronomy and astrology

112 ASTROLOGIA.

Quæ ſupra nos, nihil ad nos.

Caucaſia æternum pendens in rupe Prometheus
Diripitur ſacri præpetis ungue iecur.
Et nollet feciſſe hominem: figulóſque peroſus
Accenſam rapto damnat ab igne facem.
Roduntur uarijs prudentum pectora curis,
Qui cœli affectant ſcire, deûmque uices.

Figure 19 The astrologer as Prometheus, from Andrea Alciato, *Emblematum libellus* (Lyons, 1550).

short rhetorical texts by literary intellectuals. These placed the more rebarbative and inaccessible technical areas into a moral, literary, or historical frame. They also filled up extra space at the ends of gatherings of pages, which might otherwise have remained empty—a costly luxury which printers tried to avoid. Petreius may well have asked his author to add this final flourish. In any event, Cardano used the opportunity creatively. He traced the history of astronomy and astrology back to the origins of human civilization, crediting Moses himself with using the new moons, the equinoxes, and seven, the number of the planets, to set the feasts of the Jewish year in their proper places.[8] The Greeks, Egyptians, and Phoenicians, who observed the heavens "more curiously, but not more reverently," developed the discipline of astronomy.

Cardano listed the usual suspect heroes from the ancient Near East, like the Egyptian Hermes Trismegistus and the Chaldean Berosus.[9] References of this kind were conventional. Even in antiquity, Greek and Roman scholars saw astronomy as a discipline of staggering antiquity and spread myths about the priests who had created it in their ancient temples. Lecturers on astronomy in Renaissance universities regularly recited the same pedigree before plunging their students into the details of epicycles and mean motions. Gaurico, ever Cardano's heart's abhorrence, devoted more than one passage of heated rhetoric to the mysteries of astronomy in the ancient East.[10]

Cardano, however, also followed Alciato into the humanist's own territory, that of Greek myth. He boldly reinterpreted the stories that Alciato had read, and others to which he jumped by easy association, as evidence of the high prestige that astronomy and astrology had long enjoyed. Orpheus, he argued, had expressed the harmonies of the universe with seven distinct chords, choosing the number to reflect the harmonies of the universe itself. More strikingly still, Cardano treated the disastrous overreachers of Greek myth not as men who had tried to know too much but as astronomers whose ambitions had outrun their technical grasp. All of them had been honored, duly, by their fellow countrymen, who gave them mythical status: "Phaeton, because he investigated the path of the sun, Endymion, because he investigated that of the moon; Atlas, because he investigated that of the stars and the Zodiac; Daedalus, about whom they made up the tale that he flew; and Icarus, who, because he had not fully mastered his inherited discipline, is said to have been hurled headlong into the sea of ignorance."[11]

Myth after myth, properly analyzed, revealed the nonmythical effort that the Greeks had put into exploring the heavens. Tiresias the prophet gained the reputation for changing sexes, Cardano argued, because he declared that some of the stars were feminine and others masculine. The tale of the Argonauts and the Golden Fleece recorded, in altered form, the rivalry of the Greek kings who had tried to be the first to work out when the sun actually entered Aries and the spring equinox took place.[12] Even the central classics of the Greek literary tradition included a substantial dose of astronomy and astrology.

Following the precedent of ancient readers of Homer like the allegorist Heraclitus, Cardano interpreted the encounters of the gods in Homer and Virgil as descriptions of the planets in conjunction and opposition, and their relations with human heroes as analyses of the celestial influences that had shaped their bodies and characters:

> What do you think Homer and Virgil had in mind, when they continually made the gods quarrel or fight, the Homeric ones for the Greeks or Trojans, the Virgilian for Turnus or Aeneas? Clearly that some of the stars favored the one party, and others the other. That is the explanation of those numerous meetings and counsels of the gods. For it is quite absurd to believe that the gods acted this way, like men. But it is even more absurd to believe that those poets did not mean to hide a deeper sense under the literal one, when they wrote these things, but that these great poets engaged in the pointless enterprise of devising a story like a Chimera, one of no use at any point. Therefore when they said that Venus favored Aeneas because he was very handsome, or that Juno, that is, fortune, and the moon favored Turnus, or that Apollo, or the sun, favored Hector because he was strong and just, they had in mind, concealed under the veil of fable, the genius or star that ruled each one at birth.[13]

Astrology, in short, formed part of the basic fabric of Greek and Roman civilization. The true humanist—the one who really understood ancient literature and religion—would come not to mock but to praise it.

In applying the literary methods of humanism to the study of ancient science, Cardano was hardly alone. Throughout the later fifteenth century, a host of Italian humanists had devoted themselves to finding, translating, and explicating the classics of Greek science. Sharp controversies had broken out about the interpretation of such central texts on the natural world as the *Almagest* of Ptolemy, a systematic and immensely difficult treatise on astronomy, and the *Natural History* of the elder Pliny, a great rag-and-bone shop of ancient medicine, natural history, and much else. Debate raged about who had the right to explicate and emend such texts: the humanists, with their honed tools of textual commentary and their knowledge of the bad habits of scribes, or the natural philosophers, with their command of the subject matter. This was no joking or trivial matter in many cases: the interpretation of a standard text about theriac or *materia medica,* for example, could be a literal matter of life and death for patients. Calendar reform, which underpinned the correctness of the entire liturgical year, depended—or was at least thought to depend—on the interpretation of ancient sources.[14] By Cardano's time, however, more and more individuals commanded both sets of skills. Andreas Vesalius, for example, studied anatomy both by mastering the Greek text of Galen and by exploring the skeletons and body cavities of corpses. Medical men like the erudite Cambridge scholar John Caius proved as zealous as any teacher of grammar or rhetoric at such basic scholarly tasks as collecting the fragments of lost works and hunting the manuscripts of unavailable ones.[15]

Cardano's rereading of Greek myth made a very decorative gesture toward a humanistic study of ancient astrology. But it was nothing more than that. As a dedicated reader of astrological literature, Cardano knew very well that Pico della Mirandola had demolished the very myths about the ancient Near Eastern origins of astrology that he retailed in his praise of the discipline—a fact that may explain why he concentrated so heavily on the Greeks and treated astrology not as a discipline fully revealed in early times to primeval sages, but as one that human effort had developed over the centuries.[16] If Cardano really wanted to use the techniques of humanistic scholarship, as well as those of observation, to build or restore astrology's reputation, he had to wield considerably sharper tools.

These proved suprisingly easy to find. Cardano, as we have seen, was a medical man as well as an astrologer. Galen, the chief ancient medical authority, had devoted himself to scholarship as well as to empirical inquiry. He commented at length on the older medical texts attributed to Hippocrates, using all the tools of philology to remove spurious works from the medical canon and purge corrupt ones of their textual errors.[17] He also made clear, over and over again, that he saw Hippocrates as the ideal physician, and the study of the Hippocratic works as a basic duty of the scientific medical man. These points were hardly lost on Renaissance scholars and publishers. In 1525, just as Cardano was completing his medical training, Fabio Calvo published the first Latin translation of the complete works of Hippocrates; in 1526, Aldo Manuzio brought out an edition of the Greek texts. Suddenly, modern scholars could read the texts which Galen had studied so intensively. Cardano—like many others—found the experience exhilarating in the extreme. Hippocrates played a key role both in his sense of his own enterprise as a scientist and in his plans to renovate the practice of medicine.[18]

Nothing impressed Cardano more in Hippocrates' work than the *Epidemics*—a collection of dry, unemotional, and detailed case histories, which he studied throughout his life. He read the text in part as a model kind of inquiry into nature, based on the study of particulars and therefore highly credible. But he also saw it as a model for the study of prediction—a model which did not offer abstract rules, but "narrate[d] only the essence of the thing and [did] not teach what should be done"—just as astrology, carried on in his style, became an indescribably complex art, too ramified to be described fully in words.[19] From fairly early in Cardano's career as an astrologer, he evidently began to wish that his art—which had its Galen, or at least its authority from the imperial age, in Ptolemy—had also had a Hippocrates who had laid out in well-chosen case histories the technical basis of the art.[20]

Certainly Cardano came to see the matter this way in hindsight. In 1556, recalling his earlier career in one of his many works about his own life and writings, he described his "astronomical judgments" in terms which made it seem as if his geniture collecting had always reflected his plan to remake astrology on a medical model: "The tenth book is on the examples of two hundred genitures. The book begins, 'Hoc totum quod nos ambit' ['All that surrounds us . . .']. It is around two hundred leaves long. This book is to the commentaries of Ptolemy as the books of the *Epidemics* are to those of the *Aphorisms* in medicine."[21] Cardano's actual published geniture collections, however, tell a different and less dramatic story. Neither the primitive text of 1538 nor the more substantial one of 1543 made clear that Cardano had the model of Hippocrates in mind. Nor did Cardano mention Hippocrates when discussing his early astrological work in the first full version of his autobiography, which was composed in 1543, even though he had long since made himself so intimately familiar with the Hippocratic text that he used it as a unit of measure when describing how long his own works were.[22]

In 1546, however, Cardano put the finishing touches to the full version of his hundred genitures, adding to them, as we have seen, a long collection of *Astronomical Aphorisms* in which he tried to condense the principles of astrology, unsystematically but accessibly. Any summary would do injustice to the multifarious contents of this staccato, hard-to-follow textbook. Much of it covered such conventional topics as the effects of particular pairs of planets in conjunction or opposition, the meaning of eclipses and comets, and the connections between particular planets and signs of the Zodiac and particular places on earth that were the concern of astrological geography. Some of the more unconventional remarks reflected Cardano's reading not of classical but of very modern astronomical literature—as when he noted, startlingly, that "Copernicus seems not to have been altogether wrong when he thought that only the moon revolves around the world of the elements, as its center. For it really works very differently than the other planets."[23] Evidently Cardano's connection with Petreius, who published Copernicus' book and probably supplied Cardano with his copy of it, had as much impact as his medical career on his astrological thought.[24] But the Hippocratic inspiration of the textbook as a whole seems clear, not only from Cardano's use of the Hippocratic form of the aphorism but also from the particular one with which he began: "Life is short, art is long"—a tag from Hippocrates which no literate reader could fail to identify.[25] Equally clear is the larger theme—also closely connected with medicine—of the need to reform astrology by a systematic program of study, which would include a reexamination of the ancient sources as well as the collection of new materials.

Cardano never made his program—if he had one at this point—entirely explicit. But a number of points emerge very clearly from the mass of his disparate remarks. Like a good humanist, Cardano believed that the best way to refound his art was by direct and reverent study of its classic author: "The difference between Ptolemy's precepts and those of all the others who have followed him is bigger than the difference between emeralds and mud."[26] Cardano surveyed the writers of the intervening period with complete contempt. All of them had committed such gross errors as to make intellectual failure inevitable. Mere "grammarians" like Firmicus Maternus in antiquity and Giovanni Gioviano Pontano in modern times had simply not known what they were doing in this technical, quantitative art. More technically adept astrologers who used the Alphonsine Tables were still misled by the erroneous placement of the fixed stars in their desk reference. Seeing, as they thought, that fortunate individuals had the luminaries in conjunction with unfortunate fixed stars in their horoscopes, and vice versa, they had lost faith in the art. Others despaired of sorting out the true from the false in the great mass of astrological texts and prescriptions. Still others decided that neither the meanings nor the positions of the fixed stars were yet determined, and therefore gave up on astrology altogether.[27]

Cardano, accordingly, claimed that he had begun—much in the manner of the medical humanists of his day—by clarifying the valid astrological principles already to be found in Ptolemy's great and difficult book, the *Tetrabiblos:* "Ptolemy set down the roots of the art. I have explained his obscure sayings, supplemented those that were lacking, and settled those that were ambiguous."[28] But simple textual commentary would not do the job. In medicine, after all, neither Hippocrates nor Galen sufficed, on his own. The same held for astrology: "How stupid it is to try to stick to Ptolemy alone, since he passed down to us only the smallest part of this enormous art. If Galen had done the same, remaining content with Hippocrates, we would have no medicine at all."[29] In short, Cardano had to admit that "the art is still imperfect." Mature astrologers had reasonably enough despaired of living long enough to see how the lives of the infants whose horoscopes they could compute would turn out.[30] The sensible astrologer had to admit that all his predictions were provisional.

Still, Cardano did see one way in which he might make progress. Ptolemy, he noted, must have drawn on sources now lost: "It is likely that he had the miraculous writings of the Chaldeans and Babylonians from many centuries, and of the Egyptians as well"—a comment stimulated by Ptolemy's own references to older manuscripts and Egyptian methods.[31] In the "peroration" to the *Aphorisms,* Cardano referred to yet another set of ancient astrologers—the Roman imperial ones, Thrasyllus and Ascletarion, whose work for the dangerous emperors Tiberius and Domitian had earned them undying fame.[32] Many other writers on astrology and related subjects, even after Cardano's time, condemned these Roman astrologers as magicians who had only managed to predict future contingent events precisely because they made illicit use of demonic aid.[33] Cardano, by contrast, assumed that they were astrologers like himself—perhaps more adept, but still humans working with human capacities on humanly acquired data.

Could one possibly hope to restore—by collection of all available data—some version of the lost materials on which Ptolemy had built? Could one hope to recreate—by close study of texts and contexts—some form of the high Imperial astrology which Ptolemy had practiced? The evidence, though inconclusive, suggests that Cardano had begun to think in these terms by the mid-1540s at the latest. As we have seen, the experience of working at a court reinforced the analogy, in Cardano's own mind, between his own situation and that of his ancient predecessors. It seems at least possible, then, that Cardano came to view the traditional activity of horoscope collecting in a particular new light. Cardano's collections, with their data about ancient genitures, like that of Nero, as well as modern ones, gradually came to reflect his desire to call back into being the lost Hippocratic astrology to which Ptolemy's work formed a Galenic conclusion, and to fuse the two into a new and more perfect whole.

On his way to treat Hamilton in 1552, Cardano stopped for some days in Lyons. Thanks to a chance encounter with a schoolmaster on the last day of his stay there, he received a copy of Ptolemy's *Tetrabiblos* as a gift. The decision to travel up the Rhone on a boat, rather than on horseback, gave him the time to study the work in detail.[34] In the course of his northern tour he managed to draw up a very substantial commentary on the *Tetrabiblos*, which he published with his detailed analyses of twelve horoscopes and other subsidiary works, as a new basis for astrological studies.

Cardano went to work with almost no secondary literature to help him: "It is strange," he remarked, "that there are so few commentaries on this very famous and useful book."[35] He knew the medieval commentary ascribed to Haly ibn Rodoan, which had long been available to Western astrologers in Latin translation, and the Greek scholia more recently translated into Latin by Giorgio Valla. Otherwise, however, he found it necessary to cut his own way through the tangled technicalities of Ptolemy's text, as well as to reconstruct the larger context into which a reader should set it. Cardano's account has the sound of boasting about it: the lone hero, dapper and determined, must walk the mean streets without a partner to help him.

In fact, a number of Western astrologers had gone before Cardano. Conrad Heingarten, for example, wrote an enormous commentary on the text, emphasizing both the technical difficulty and the urgency of the enterprise, and praising Ptolemy himself in terms that Cardano would have accepted:

> His books contain the roots and rules of all of judicial astrology, set out in natural and rigorous form. This was so obscure, thanks to his extreme brevity and the great gravity of his language, that scarcely anyone could understand it. I have undertaken to interpret it, opening up his closed sentences in order to help students and make the reading of Ptolemy more accessible. For he clearly outdoes all other writers on astronomy, as the moon in its golden splendor outshines all the lesser stars.[36]

Like Cardano, Heingarten knew and drew on Haly's commentary. He thought it too corrupt, however, to serve on its own as a basis for understanding the text (Cardano, by contrast, excused Haly's errors by inferring that he had had to work with a bad translation of Ptolemy).[37] Heingarten—and the professors who worked systematically through the text in university courses on astrology—could have offered Cardano a good deal of material to draw on.[38] Commentators less ambitious than Cardano, after all, regularly injected large amounts of foreign matter, often word for word, into the lecture courses that became their published glosses on great texts. Commentary often amounted less to a creative act than to a massive program of intellectual recycling.

From the outset, however, Cardano attacked his text in a novel manner. The analogy with medicine constantly on his mind, he followed Galen's example in asking philological questions before philosophical ones. He insisted, for example, on authenticating the *Tetrabiblos* in some detail, using the same tests for style and consistency with which Galen had authenticated (or deauthenticated) the works ascribed to Hippocrates: "It is clear that this is the man who also wrote the *Almagest,* both because he himself says so in the preface of this work, and because no one else could have accomplished so subtle a treatment of the art, and also from the similarity of the style, for he shows himself as the philosopher at all times."[39] Cardano also made clear his debt to Galen's method—which enabled him, more prescient in this respect than some German philologists of the nineteenth century, to accept Ptolemy's authorship of the *Tetrabiblos*—when he denied the authenticity of the other astrological work normally ascribed to Ptolemy, the Arabo-Latin *Centiloquium.*

Haly, struck by the prominence of interrogations—astrological inquiries about particular endeavors and journeys—in the *Centiloquium,* had wondered why Ptolemy omitted them in the *Tetrabiblos.* Cardano dismissed the question as based on a false assumption. In fact, the inconsistency revealed that the other work was a later forgery. Galen, who had unmasked similar forgeries among the Hippocratic texts, not only provided the decisive arguments Cardano used to unmask the work, but neatly explained its origin. The all-consuming desire for books of the ancient rulers who created the great libraries at Alexandria and Pergamum stimulated the production of forgeries:

> It is easy to see, both from the presence of these [interrogations and elections] and from the quite different opinions on the same points offered by Ptolemy in this book and by the author of the *Centiloquium,* that Ptolemy did not write the *Centiloquium.* But the preface to the *Centiloquium* is an important counter-argument, since it mentions Syrus and this book [as Ptolemy's genuine prefaces did]. But Galen explains this, saying: "In the old days, kings who were trying to establish great libraries bought the books of famous men at very high prices. By doing so they caused men to ascribe their own works to the ancients."[40]

The reader of Cardano's commentary, in short, moved from the start in a new intellectual atmosphere, one never quite identical with that of the astrological tradition as it had developed in the West since the twelfth century.

The medical analogy from which Cardano began had many functions. He continually bore in mind that Ptolemy and Galen belonged to the same cultural moment—the great flowering of Greek-language philosophy, rhetoric, and natural philosophy that took place in the late first and second centuries C.E. True, earlier scholars had noticed the chronological coincidence.[41] But Cardano made it one of the pillars on which his interpretation rested. He tried to explain why ancient culture had reached such a high point in the age of the Antonines, arguing that only the theory—itself unclassical—of the great conjunctions of Jupiter and Saturn could account for such widespread developments in many fields of study.[42] And he identified substantial similarities between what he called "the prognostic part of philosophy, which teaches us to know in advance," and the segment of classical medical doctrine dedicated to prognostics.[43]

Typically, Cardano's evaluation of the two arts fluctuated, even in the course of the commentary. Sometimes he emphasized the higher metaphysical and epistemological standing of astrology, sometimes the great practical efficacy and higher public esteem of medicine.[44] But Cardano did not hesitate to draw connections on any number of specific issues, both in Ptolemy's method and in his conclusions. Ptolemy, he argued at one point, based his theses, like any "skillful teacher," on the most obvious kinds of evidence: "For the risings and settings of the stars produce such obvious changes in the weather, that all writers on natural phenomena use them to set down their weather observations. The most prominent medical writers, including both Hippocrates and Galen, used these rather then the position of the sun to distinguish the seasons of the year from one another."[45] The general analogy between scientific medicine and scientific astrology became clear to any careful reader of Cardano's commentary.

So did his passionate desire to reconstruct the lost evidence on which Ptolemy's astrology actually rested. Cardano speculated endlessly on the nature of the materials that Ptolemy had reworked to produce his lucid, systematic treatise, which entirely lacked the sort of precise, dated observations that filled large sections of the *Almagest.* His own textual evidence about these lost sources took two forms, neither highly precise. Ptolemy himself referred, repeatedly, to "Egyptian" and "Chaldean" methods for solving certain problems, describing in enticing detail the "ancient manuscript" from which he had derived information about them.[46] Even before he started his commentary, Cardano had decided, as we have seen, that Ptolemy must have had such materials at his disposal, and in quantity. As he worked through the text, accordingly, he inferred, wherever he struck what seemed to him an especially solid inference from empirical data, that Ptolemy had compiled the material in question from his ancient Near Eastern sources.

In 1.18, for example, Ptolemy described the four triplicities, or groups of three out of the twelve signs of the Zodiac, each of them forming an equilateral triangle in the heavens, each of them linked to one of the four elements, and each of them governed by a particular planet:

Aries, Leo, Sagittarius	northern	Jupiter
Taurus, Virgo, Capricorn	southern	Venus
Gemini, Libra, Aquarius	western	Saturn
Cancer, Scorpio, Pisces	eastern	Mars[47]

True, Cardano felt that in "our regions," the planets might have different effects. But he was sure that Ptolemy's doctrine deserved credibility, since it derived from the lost Near Eastern sources he had drawn on elsewhere as well:

> Moreover, the east makes men given over to pleasure, like Venus. The north makes them furious and strong and frightful, as Mars does. The west makes them moderate, polite, pleasant, as Jupiter does. And the south makes them sorrowful, melancholy, fearful, cruel, and nervous, as Saturn does. But Haly says that the principles laid down by Ptolemy match experience. It is therefore plausible that Ptolemy's teaching attains a high level of certainty, and that it is particularly consonant to the observations of the Egyptians and Chaldeans.[48]

Similarly, Ptolemy's solid doctrines on the power of the fixed stars clearly rested "on the observations of the Chaldeans and Egyptians."[49]

Cardano knew, however, that this argument posed certain problems of its own. Pico had shown that the astronomical observations Ptolemy recorded were none of them earlier than the eighth century C.E., and most of them much later. The notion that ancient astronomy had taken its definitive form on the pyramids of Egypt and Mesopotamia, though still very popular, clearly lacked any historical foundation. Cardano, however, found another potential source: Ptolemy could have had access to the work of Chaldean and Egyptian astrologers working in or near his own day.[50]

Here too, the lives of the Roman astrologers on which Cardano had been ruminating for some time gave food for thought. Connecting the stories that he had read about them in the Roman historians with Ptolemy's brief indications of his sources, Cardano offered a dazzlingly original hypothesis about the transmission of Near Eastern astrology to the Alexandrian astronomer. Early in his career, he had tried to reconstruct the achievements of the Roman astrologers—to identify, for example, "the secret of the ancients" with which Ascletarion had produced his "remarkable prediction" of the death of Domitian.[51] Now he concluded that the very predictors whose adventures with their emperors filled him with fascination and alarm must also have become Ptolemy's informants:

> When he adds that the Egyptians enhanced the art, he means both them and certain provinces near them, like the Chaldeans, of whom Suetonius reports that they predicted to Nero his rule and his murder of his mother. When she heard this, she said: "Let him kill me, so long as he rules." One of these was Thrasyllus, who predicted to the exiled Tiberius that he would rule over Rome, and who gained too much authority, because Tiberius lived in a criminal way. Another was Sulla, the astrologer of Caligula, who also predicted both his reign and his assassination, both of them unexpected. He too enjoyed great authority. Ascletarion was less successful with Domitian, but even more illustrious, thanks to the double and very remarkable events that he predicted [the emperor's death and his own]. The man who predicted Gordian's reign, using instruments and the time, came from the same race. Thus it is clear that the Chaldeans and Egyptians were unbelievably celebrated in this art. When Ptolemy had collected their writings, he assembled them in this book, but so briefly, that the better part of the art is lacking. It would have been better if, like the great Hippocrates, after he had created his art, he had also composed a book giving individual examples, corresponding to the *Epidemics*. For it would have shed much light on understanding the things written in this book, and have provided much reason for belief against those who continually rail that this art is vain.[52]

Cardano took every opportunity to track down new scraps of information about these astrologers, whose lost works had provided the empirical basis for Ptolemy's theory. He repeatedly mused that Ptolemy had "probably" had these treasures, "but he apparently neglected them." More daringly, he speculated eagerly about the treasures—like imperial horoscopes—which these works might have contained: "It would have been so useful to have examples of the horoscopes of Domitian and Nero, with precise indications of the times. This would have helped not only to enhance the glory of the art of astronomy, but also to cultivate and extend the discipline itself."[53] And he tracked the fragments of pre-Ptolemaic astrology into every nook and cranny of the astrological literature. Even while Cardano was on his initial voyage down the Rhone, working largely without books, he recalled that Firmicus Maternus had cited certain early works "of the Chaldeans and Egyptians, which came into his hands," and promised to make a systematic collection of these—not an easy task, since Firmicus' own incompetence as an astrologer had made him corrupt the materials he used almost beyond repair.[54] After Hieronymus Wolf brought out a summary of the *Tetrabiblos* ascribed to Porphyry and another Greek commentary on Ptolemy, Cardano declared himself unimpressed by the technical skills of these ancient commentators but grateful, once again, for new historical information: "Porphyry—who is useful for nothing but mentioning names—refers to Thrasybulus and Petosiris, who had a great reputation before Ptolemy, and whom he calls 'the ancients'; and also to the Egyptians Antigonus and Psnanus."[55]

All commentators on Ptolemy—including the Greek ones—noticed his references to earlier sources. Heingarten, for example, eloquently evoked the astrological and astronomical skills of the Egyptians:

> Those Egyptians were the wise magicians of antiquity. For by study and practice they became great men in the sciences and in all the forms of wisdom with which men help themselves. And we know this from the chronicles of the ancient sages and through what remains of their works, from many thousands of years ago down to the present day . . . And the Chaldeans are the ones from Babylon who followed the Egyptians in the study of astronomy.[56]

But most such descriptions, like this one, remained pleasingly vague. Cardano, by contrast, discussed what he could find out about the Egyptians in detail. And the more he learned, the less he liked. The older Egyptian astronomers, he declared, provided tenets "so absurd and full of nonsense that Porphyry ruined the whole art."[57]

At least some of Cardano's historical work, in other words, had a distinctly negative result: it revealed that Egyptian astrologers had sometimes employed methods as absurd and inconsequential as those of the Arabo-Latin astrology, which Cardano had long despised. The quality of Ptolemy's work—and that of his immediate predecessors—emerged more sharply than ever from this investigation of the background. When Joseph Scaliger argued, in his commentary on Manilius, that the Roman astrological poet preserved the remains of a primitive Near Eastern astronomy and astrology, he very likely owed a debt to Cardano, whom he criticized, as well as to Pico, whom he praised, for his ability to attack some founding myths of Renaissance thought.[58]

As Cardano worked on his commentary, then, he found himself faced with a double, and sometimes contradictory, task. Part of his work consisted in textual explication, strictly defined: a systematic effort to work out the meaning, bases, and applications of the many doctrines briefly summarized in Ptolemy's clipped, schematic little book. Cardano devoted enormous effort and intelligence to this task, as well as to the related one of carefully singling out for condemnation the many astrological practices and doctrines popular in his time that did not fall within Ptolemaic guidelines. At the same time, however, Cardano regularly discussed materials and methods that his author had omitted—including both the empirical materials that Ptolemy had used, but not reproduced, and certain astrological theories that he simply had not known or believed in, even though they were consonant with his views. Cardano's book swelled to enormous size, and the two subsequent editions each stretched even further to incorporate new materials and ideas.

As a commentator, Cardano sometimes revealed a clear sense of Ptolemy's historical place and period. The *Tetrabiblos* began, for example, with substantial arguments in favor of the morality and utility of Ptolemy's art. Cardano knew from the literature of Ptolemy's time that he had directed these passages against philosophical critics of astrology, whom he could identify. By doing so he showed that these passages carried out a clear function in the economy of Ptolemy's book, making good his claim—and Ptolemy's—to be teaching astrology in a rigorous manner:

> In Aulus Gellius, Favorinus, a famous philosopher who lived not long before Ptolemy, defamed the art of astrology as the ambitious will. He cited two grounds in particular: that future events cannot be known and that if they could be known, knowledge of them would not be useful to mortals. In the last two chapters of his prologue, Ptolemy offers a full and careful reply to these criticisms. By doing so, moreover, he reveals the end of his art. For as Galen puts it in his book on the constitution of the art of medicine, each art is established by resolution from knowledge of its end. Ptolemy could not possibly establish his art in this book without first explaining its purpose.[59]

Like Ptolemy, Cardano argued, carefully and with many reservations, that astrology was useful even though it did not offer absolutely certain knowledge about the future.

Favorinus had insisted—in line with a major current of thought in the Stoic school he adhered to—that knowledge of future disasters, being unchangeable, would plunge its possessor into a useless despair. The wise man would live for the moment—in a highly moral way, of course—rather than worrying about what was to come.[60] Cardano, explicating Ptolemy, made clear that the ancient astrologer had never claimed to offer absolutely valid predictions about what would happen, but only probable inferences about future conditions. A prudent man could take these into account in order to avoid their messier practical and emotional consequences:

> Ptolemy replies, briefly, that the future can be changed. But Favorinus will say, that if events can be changed, they are not the future. But Ptolemy will answer, that future events are not in themselves the future, but in a relative sense. Thus if I know in advance that great heat and thirst will kill my sheep, who are feeding on a high mountain, then if I dig a cave and well for them they will not die.

> Therefore astrology does not deal with future events, but offers only a comparison of events with their causes. But it is because of these that they will take place.[61]

As so often, Cardano's astrology lends itself to parody when seen in retrospect. Like good economists, the ancient author and his modern annotator explain in chorus why their discipline matters to humanity even though it cannot, and supposedly does not try to, predict specific outcomes with absolute certainty. Much of Cardano's practical advice—like the suggestion that one travel in as large a group as possible, since if most of the passengers on any given ship are not foredestined to die in a wreck, the danger is lessened—has all the precision and intelligence of a modern discount broker's newsletter.

In fact, however, such satire has less substance to it than meets the eye. Recent work on ancient philosophy has emphasized its therapeutic side. Stoics, Skeptics, and Epicureans clearly set out to alter the emotions, and thus to improve the lives, of those who read them, to show those capable of taking in their message that the wise man must accommodate himself to the order of the universe, learning to take delight in its power and beauty and not to resent its occasional failure to reward him with health or wealth. In doing so, as Martha Nussbaum, among others, has argued, they emphasized "the dignity of reason," the need to train their pupils to reach the right conclusions by the independent exercise of a disciplined mode of thought.[62] Nussbaum is not kind to the astrologers: "What sets philosophy apart from popular religion, dream-interpretation, and astrology," she argues, "is its commitment to rational argument."[63] Ptolemy and Cardano would have found this distinction hard to swallow. They saw themselves as offering their readers a sharp-edged set of tools with which to free themselves from slavery to external circumstances—not by learning to see around them but by schooling themselves to predict them. They felt certain that knowledge of the future would enhance, not diminish, the mastery of the self: excess passion could be contained more easily, after all, by those who saw the occasions for it coming, in advance. Astrology, like philosophy, offered a discipline of life—and one adapted to the needs of the man who recognized himself as human and knew that his happiness was inextricably bound up with the fates of his body, his household, and his nation.

Cardano laid great emphasis on the precision and delicacy of the astrologer's craft, at least as Ptolemy defined and explicated it. Emulating Galen, he warned his readers that they must begin by assuming that Ptolemy's text reached an extraordinary level of profundity and subtlety: "For we must think of Ptolemy just as Galen wrote of Hippocrates' books on difficulty in breathing—that is, that he wrote nothing common or widely known, but that everything in him is unique and recondite."[64] From Ptolemy's references to the incompetence of his competitors in antiquity, Cardano constructed a general denunciation of the charlatans who, by his account, had afflicted good astrologers at all times and places: geomancers, numerologists, those who translated the names of their clients' parents into numerical form and assigned planets and signs to these numbers; worst of all, those who, from desire for gain, had devised the art of taking the celestial prospects at a given moment through interrogations and elections.

Without making any effort to show that these devices of the modern almanac had ancient roots, Cardano ridiculed them as exactly the sort of bad astrology Ptolemy had had in mind:

> Consider, gentle reader, how much ridicule has been caused by those who, by selling their client an astrological interrogation on some single point, brought him to a disastrous end, while many, in the same situation, enjoy great success without taking the advice of an astrologer. Let me choose one of many examples, with a clear and remarkable result, and that of a man known to me. Ludovico Sforza was the ruler of the province of Milan. He supported a greedy astrologer who was completely ignorant of astrology (for he was one of those whom Ptolemy rightly criticizes), enriching him with a great fortune of a hundred and more big golden talents. In return for this compensation, this gentleman assigned him the time at which he should begin every enterprise, and in such a ridiculous way that the prince, in other respects a man of great wisdom, had to mount horses in the midst of storms, and lead the whole courtly host of his supporters through rainstorms, through the muck and mud, as if he were in hot pursuit or headlong flight of enemies.[65]

No wonder that poor Ludovico wound up his career in jail, deprived of his domain, beaten and humiliated.

In treating Ptolemy as a wise man besieged by idiots and mercenaries, Cardano certainly projected his own situation backward into the past. But by doing so he did not merely distort the ancient text and its context. Geoffrey Lloyd, Vivian Nutton, Tamsyn Barton, and other historians of ancient medicine and astrology have emphasized in recent years that all ancient students of nature—especially those who offered clients advice for a fee—worked in a brutally competitive social world. No licensing authorities existed in an ancient city to distinguish the Hippocratic doctor or Hipparchan astrologer who knew his craft in depth from the healers who flanked them in the marketplace, offering other forms of prognostication and cure. Only the most persuasive speech—and the strongest technical arguments—could fortify one practitioner's position impregnably. Indeed, Barton argues that the labyrinthine technical complexity of ancient astrology—its emphasis on the multiple intersection of stellar and planetary influences, impossible to analyze fully in any written text—served above all to reinforce the astrologer's authority, since no amateur could hope to reach the jewel at the center of the maze without expert guidance.[66] Cardano would never have admitted that he—or Ptolemy—owed his prominence to persuasive abilities, rather than operational knowledge of nature. But he would certainly have recognized modern historians' vision of the highly competitive world in which the ancient astrologer worked, since he adumbrated it so clearly in his own writing.

Cardano also drew from Ptolemy some of his many portraits of the ideal astrologer. When Ptolemy remarked that the problems of his discipline lay not in it, but in those who professed it, Cardano heartily agreed. In modern as in ancient times, astrologers provided their critics with innumerable examples of professional malpractice:

> Giovanni Marliani, a man of excellent judgment, used to say quite rightly that if you wish to make predictions, then just say the exact contrary of what the astrologers either promise or threaten. They have erred so badly as to make their entire art not only worthless, but infamous. For they do not spend even a hundredth part of the effort or the industry or the diligence or the time that they should spend. For not only do we go wrong from negligence at the point when we seek to inquire into the future; we must work hard when learning the art itself.[67]

Adequate preparation involved not only technique, but attitude. The astrologer must realize that his predictions were always fallible. Ptolemy had confessed as much—like the author of book 7 of the Hippocratic *Epidemics,* who had admitted that a suture of the head had fooled him. Just so, the astrologer in training must learn that his art, even when restored to the high level of Ptolemy's, would never enable him to predict the future as certainly as animals and ecstatic seers could do by their direct, if fortuitous, inspiration.[68]

But the astrologer must fulfill positive demands as well. Ptolemy—himself the most searching critic, as well as the most systematic expositor, of classical astrology—made clear that the positions of the stars at a client's birth could not possibly account for every twist and turn of his future life and career:

> But in an inquiry concerning nativities and individual temperaments in general, one can see that there are circumstances of no small importance and of

> no trifling character, which join to cause the special qualities of those who are born. For differences of seed exert a very great influence on the special traits of the genus . . . and the places of birth bring about no small variation in what is produced. For if the seed is generically the same, human for example, and the condition of the ambient the same, those who are born differ much, both in body and soul, with the difference of countries. In addition to this, all the aforesaid conditions being equal, rearing and customs contribute to influence the particular way in which a life is lived. Unless each one of these things is examined together with the causes that are derived from the ambient . . . they can cause much difficulty for those who believe that in such cases everything can be understood, even things not wholly within its jurisdiction, from the motion of the heavenly bodies alone.[69]

Cardano, who had long since begun to insist on the difficulty of making accurate predictions, was predisposed to see this passage as central to the *Tetrabiblos.*[70] Ptolemy, he argued, had intended both to stress the need for the subtlest horoscopes possible and to show that "a certain hidden power" often enhanced or mitigated the power of the stars:

> For I have seen those who suffered more misfortunes, and more often, than the stars seemed to promise, and vice versa. For more dangers seemed to threaten both my daughter and my younger son than actually took place, and my daughter, though it seemed she would be quite weak, has scarcely ever caught a serious illness. And I have experienced far greater things, with regard to honors, and actions, and my life, than the stars seemed to promise.[71]

Throughout his commentary, accordingly, Cardano found repeated occasion to point out the limitations of his chosen art.

As we have seen, weather prediction had formed part of Cardano's astrology from the beginning of his career. He never completely lost his optimism about astrological meteorology. In book 2 of the *Tetrabiblos,* for example, Ptolemy remarked that "the sun creates the general qualities and conditions of the seasons, by means of which even those who are totally ignorant of astrology can foretell the future."[72] Cardano took this as his cue to give instructions for the amateur who wished to make useful observations: "I advise anyone who wishes to predict the weather at a given time of the year to observe the risings and settings of the stars for three or four years, day by day, and in addition to observe carefully the winds and the state of the skies in his area. And he should note down how they agree with one another, and their conditions, and make a table usable throughout the year."[73] The result, a text rather like Ptolemy's own *Phaseis,* which listed the risings of the stars and their effects, would be very useful—if only for the maker's own location. Cardano also devoted considerable effort to clarifying Ptolemy's meteorological doctrines—for example, by supplying an elegant circular chart with the names and directions of no fewer than thirty-two winds, for help with which he warmly thanked John Hamilton's doctor, Casanatus—clear evidence that Cardano discussed the Ptolemy commentary, as well as Hamilton's and Casanatus' own horoscopes, with him.[74]

At the same time, however, Cardano insisted that meteorology had its absolute limits. Ptolemy described himself as moving, when he came to the subject of weather, to "a more subtle [or detailed] kind of investigation."[75] Cardano took the phrase as firm evidence that his apparently self-confident classic author had undergone a dark night of the soul, and rightly so, when he found himself confronted by this excruciatingly difficult set of problems. The winds, after all, posed agonizing problems to both the philosophers who wanted to explain them and the astrologers who hoped to predict them. Even Aristotle had dared only to say that they were hot and dry exhalations, a thesis Cardano thought quite problematic.

> But what follows from this is very, very difficult. For when it rains at Gallarate the central road at Cardano has a clear sky, even though these two towns are barely a mile apart. What art or conjecture can be subtle enough to work out this difference and explain the other, in so small a distance, which is as a point compared either to the visible extent of the sky or the surface of the earth? This question tortured me for a long time, and, I think, tortured Ptolemy as well, which was why he had to add those words "to a more subtle kind of investigation." Undoubtedly this is the strongest objection which can be made to an astrologer. But medicine is not to be despised because it cannot cure cancers. No art, in fact, no matter how wonderful it is, can embrace and achieve everything of importance. Much is missing from medicine, from geometry, a great deal from music; nor have the grammarians and rhetoricians and dialecticians perfected their arts.[76]

Astrology, like other arts, was the imperfect product of human effort and history. It would continue to change and improve in the future.

Like Ptolemy, Cardano repeatedly scrutinized the weakest points in astrology's structure, citing evidence against as well as for its powers. He himself had failed to predict basic events in his own life, the celestial causes of which "I did not see, though I easily could have seen them."[77] No wonder, then, that astrology, for all the soundness of its basis in astronomy and all its richness in technique, did not enjoy the esteem of its sister art of prognostication. The human intellect was simply too weak to read every detail written in the stars: "And that is why the pronouncements of medical men about the future have nothing silly about them, and are founded, so to speak, on really solid arguments, while those of the natural philosophers, and even more those of the astrologers and theologians, are footling, and such that not one of them agrees with another."[78] Astrology as Cardano conceived it extended its tentacles into every area of human life, but some of them were not yet strong enough to move the objects they encountered.

Influential segments of Cardano's commentary amounted to little more than an effort to work out in detail the implications of what Ptolemy only hinted at in his brief, schematic text. At one point Ptolemy asserted, without offering much argument, that the choice of certain angular relationships between the planets as their significant astrological aspects had a justification in music. For the ratios of the significant angles to one another corresponded to the chief musical ratios. For example,

> quartile (90 degrees) is in sesquialterate ratio (3/2) to sextile (60 degrees), corresponding to the musical diapente;
>
> trine (120 degrees) is in sesquitertian ratio (4/3) to quartile (90 degrees), corresponding to the musical diatessaron.[79]

Cardano explicated this argument at length, offering lucid diagrams as well as systematic commentary. Such explanations, he admitted, had little to do with the practice of astrology, but seemed to him necessary "because of the calumniators" of the art, solid though it clearly was. Tangential though Cardano thought this passage was to the kind of astrology he wanted to practice, it fascinated one of his most insightful readers, Johannes Kepler, who glimpsed in it a solid justification for the reformed astrology, empirical in its foundation and general in its bearing, with which he hoped to replace the ancient art of individual horoscopy.

As one might expect, much of Cardano's more general commentary has the look of a normal Renaissance encyclopedia, of the sort that he himself wrote. Astrology, for all its weaknesses, could account for the birth of monsters, as Ptolemy explained at some length.[80] Cardano took this as the occasion to print the horoscope of a pair of conjoined twins born while he was at work, whom he described with a pathologist's dry precision:

> It was born in England, while I was there, on a manor known as Middleton Stoney, eight miles from the famous University of Oxford, and it was posthumous. The father was called John Kemer (that is how it is written in English). There were two girls, joined at the navel, which had coalesced into one as if the side of one were inserted into the other, belly to belly, back to back, with one navel, one vulva, one anus, which was between the left thighs and the buttocks. Therefore the left thighs kept their position, as when boys play while sitting, but one right thigh and a foot, combined with the other, had fused. That foot, accordingly, had nine toes. On the first two days they did not want to suck milk

> from the mother because the birth had been so tiring, and were fed on cows' milk. On the third day they suckled with their mother. Sometimes the one napped while the other remained alert, because from the navel upwards, each had its own separate members. The one lived until 18, the other until 19 August.[81]

Cardano could explain the appearance of the monstrous twins without difficulty: Gemini, a sign with two bodies, had been the ascendant and ruler of the horoscope, and the positions of the remaining planets—especially the malevolent planets Mars and Saturn—had deformed the children. But the details of their bodies may well have interested him and his readers just as much—especially at a time when erudite men collected and copied the leaflets that fluttered through European marketplaces giving details of monstrous births, both human and animal.[82] Similarly conventional interests were at play when Cardano, following Haly, used Ptolemy to explain the birth in extremely cold and hot regions of "anthropophagi, whose faces are horrid, and so different from normal human ones that they scarcely seem human"—another class of horrific-looking beings that greatly fascinated writers and readers, turning India and Brazil into the sixteenth-century counterpart of Roswell.[83]

For all his insistent loyalty to Ptolemy and all the traditionalism of his attitude, Cardano did not confine himself in the commentary to questions that his ancient master might have raised—or to the sorts of answer that Ptolemy would have proposed. Ptolemy, for example, though he saw comets as significant, devoted only a brief discussion to them. He remarked that some "naturally produce the effects peculiar to Mars and to Mercury—wars, hot weather, disturbed conditions, and the accompaniments of these."[84] But he said little about how to observe or measure them, merely listing some of the traditional types, like "beams" and "trumpets." Cardano, however, argued that Ptolemy "dispatched the history of the comet briefly not because comets are of little or even modest importance, but to avoid leading the reader to despair by the enormousness of the subject."[85] Ambitiously, Cardano set out to provide the missing material. He described comets and related phenomena at length, quoting the extensive observations recorded by Regiomontanus, Pontano, Nifo, and others to give a sense of the different periods and appearances of true comets. And he made clear why he devoted so much attention to a phenomenon traditional astrologers had not analyzed at length. Comets shared the qualities of Mars and Mercury, Cardano claimed, because those two planets produced them (or rather, as he made clear in his work *On the Variety of Things*, their rays, which intersected in the crystalline matter of the heavens, did so, combining to produce the swift-moving, bright comets observed on earth.)[86] In passages like these, the closed, coherent cosmology that had supported astrological beliefs and practices since ancient times, and to which Ptolemy himself had given such powerful expression, seems to be breaking up. In the course of the 1570s, more accurate observations of the new star of 1572 and the comet of 1577 would place that system under powerful external pressure. Cardano's commentary reveals, in glimpses, the internal stresses that his cosmos was already experiencing.

In the final analysis, however, Cardano returned to astrological traditions, many of them nonclassical, and framed Ptolemy's text in them. Ptolemy saw astrology as a tool for understanding the fates not only of individuals, but of whole nations. But he took space, not time, as his organizing principle for predictions on the grand scale, trying to connect eclipses and conjunctions that took place in particular signs or involved particular planets with the lands that were under their direct governance. Cardano, however, read Ptolemy's text through a screen of astrological tradition—in particular, the Sasanian tradition, well established in medieval astrology, that the conjunctions of Jupiter and Saturn had determined the course of world history as a whole, their effects changing as they passed from one trigon, or group of three Zodiacal signs, to another.[87] Developing ideas that had fascinated him since the 1530s, when he wrote his first predictions and drafted his *Secrets of Eternity*, "and drawing on the Islamic tradition that he elsewhere rejected," Cardano inserted into his commentary a prediction in the same quintessentially un-Ptolemaic style.

Characteristically, he began by denouncing existing texts on the subject as worthless, because based on inadequate observations. Then he offered his own, purportedly individual variation on the same theme:

> There are certain general signs to be had from the great conjunctions, and they are that the conjunctions in the watery signs, which belong to the trigon of Mars, mean many wars and the invention of mechanical devices, because of Mars, and malign contagious diseases because of Scorpio and Cancer, and the combination of Mars with Venus or with the moon, and serious heresies. The religion of Muhammad and some others began under that trigon. But in the first trigon, that of Aries, are produced worldly empires and monarchies, because of the rule of the sun and Jupiter, which mean peace in the world. But this cannot happen unless one becomes the ruler of all. Wise and remarkable men also appear, and great dearths, because of the rule of the planets that are hot and not very moist. Therefore, after the year 1583, down to the year 1782, before the middle of the year, a monarchy will take shape, and one will rule all. But in the second trigon, that of Taurus, earthquakes will take place, and

> floods, and many comets, because of Capricorn, in which Saturn and Mars dominate, and the weakness of planets which should be in authority, Venus and the moon. And the things which have taken shape under the watery trigon will fall apart. But when the conjunction reaches the trigon of the human signs, that is, Gemini, then the monarchies made by the trigon of Aries will fall apart, and in their place a new monarchy will arise, and because of the rule of Saturn and Mercury there will be many wise man, and the arts will flourish, and there will be many deceivers. And men will be very wicked, and great vices will form as they take their pleasures, and many comets will be seen in the sky because of Mercury.[88]

The commentary on Ptolemy's great textbook, in other words, resounded with the same traditional strains that had marked Cardano's first astrological overture, his long-forgotten *Pronostico.*

Cardano never ceased to tinker with this material. He explored the astrological conditions—also to be found in the great conjunctions—that had brought printing and many other spectacular arts and discoveries into being in his own time.[89] And he fleshed out his astrological history with more and more precise detail, arguing that the empires of the Medes and Charlemagne and the rise of Tarquinius Priscus were all correlated with great conjunctions.[90] In making these arguments, Cardano, as he knew, broke with his ancient authority—who, he said, had omitted the long-term effects of the great conjunctions "because they take place more slowly, and are less visible, and belong more to prophets than to astrologers."[91] Cardano's work was nowhere more conventionally unclassical than in passages like these. They resembled in style and substance alike the compendia of more conventional astrologers like Cyprian Leowitz, who issued what became the standard work on the great conjunctions in history.[92]

But if Cardano used ordinary materials to make his historical framework for Ptolemy, his workmanship was resolutely unconventional. For centuries, astrological historians had offered explanations, as he did, not only for the rise and fall of kingdoms but for those of prophets and religions. Though many believed that Guido Bonati had died for the sin of explaining Christ's birth and mission astrologically, such correlations continued to find a place in astrological literature through the Renaissance.[93] Cardano, however, took the most audacious step of all. He placed a horoscope for Jesus in the very heart of his work, in the commentary on book 2. And in it he explicated, step by step, the geniture of the Christian savior.

Cardano's geniture of Jesus sums up many of his aspirations, achievements, and weaknesses as both astrologer and historian of the astrological tradition. As he established it, he took for granted that he knew when Christ

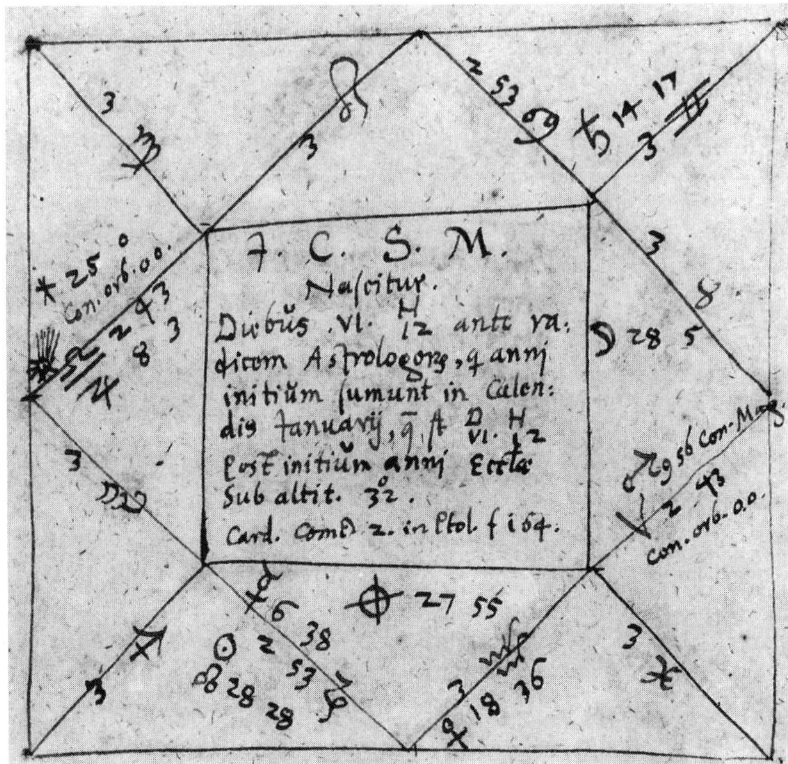

Figure 20 Cardano's geniture of Jesus, from a manuscript collection bound with a copy of Luca Gaurico's *Tractatus astrologicus* (Venice, 1552). The compiler took this from the first edition of Cardano's commentary on Ptolemy's *Almagest.*

was born: at midnight on 25 December. God had timed the event to coincide with several significant celestial conditions and phenomena: no fewer, in fact, than ten of them. At least three especially visible markers revealed the approach of a great prophet, one who would exercise a profound and long-lasting influence. The constellation of Libra in the eighth sphere coincided with the Zodiacal sign of Libra in the ninth. A powerful comet announced both great disturbance in the world and the great fame of the prophet who would cause it. And the presence of Jupiter in the ascendant revealed that the prophet would be eloquent, winning in his ways, and precocious. The heavens declared the glory of the son of God, in ways that no contemporary could have failed to notice. Other heavenly signs were more subtle. Cardano pointed out that the bright star Spica Virginis was near the ascendant, making the subject more eloquent. He also noted that the autumnal equinox was in the mid-heaven, and that a great conjunction of Saturn and Jupiter had taken place only six years before Christ was born. Fixed stars, planets, and comets predicted the glory and suffering of the Savior.[94]

This list included both traditionally accepted signs of Christ's coming and Cardano's new ones. The star of the Magi had, of course, provided an astrological foundation for Christian belief for centuries—though Cardano innovated, as usual, in his treatment of details. Ficino, for example, had explained the star as a comet, magically produced in the atmosphere. Cardano took it as a celestial portent—even though, by doing so, he admitted the possibility of new appearances among the celestial spheres.[95] Cardano did not call attention to this point, though no learned reader could have missed it. His silence is puzzling.

Still more puzzling, however, was the silence that Cardano maintained with regard to a number of other problems. Abu Ma'sar had already set Christ's birth in the Zodiacal sign of Libra, for example. He had argued that the first decan of Libra—the star daemon that dominated the first ten degrees of the sign, and that took the form of a pure, modest, elegantly dressed virgin, feeding a child—represented Jesus' mother, the Virgin Mary.[96] Pico della Mirandola rejected this theory, along with other efforts to analyze the geniture of Jesus. He reckoned that Libra had begun to rise on the evening of 25 December at around 10:00 p.m. By midnight, the tenth degree of Libra would have reached the horizon, and the first decan, with its theologically dangerous resemblance to the Virgin, would have ceded authority to the second.[97]

Tiberio Rosselli, a young Padua-trained philosopher, defended the astrologers against Pico's criticism a generation later. To retain the first decan of Virgo in the ascendant, he noted that the authoritative teachings of the church specified not the exact time of the Savior's birth, but only that of the angels' appearance to announce it, at midnight. Jesus could, in other words, have been born at some earlier point in the evening. The astrologers, Rosselli claimed, had needed to know only the night on which Jesus was born. Then they used their knowledge of his career and qualities to set the astrologically appropriate time for his birth. So much for the impious questions that had evidently been hurled at Rosselli by skeptical young men—men of the sort who would reappear in the Chatauqua tents of the nineteenth century, demanding to know where Cain had found his wife: "With that," Rosselli remarked, "we reply to the objection that was raised at Florence: who timed the birth of Christ with an astrolabe, to determine the sort of death he would suffer?"[98] For all Rosselli's confident rhetoric, however, he still found himself forced by the discrepancies and gaps in the Gospel accounts to lay out and discuss three possible, differently timed genitures for Jesus, in order to show that Saturn and Mars occupied positions in each of them that predicted the Savior's career and death. The geniture of Jesus, in other words, was contested ground, especially in the years around 1500, when prophets abounded. Anyone interested in the problem knew that nothing about it was as simple as it seemed.

Cardano claimed that he had worked out his geniture of Jesus in the 1530s, at a time when these earlier discussions and the Arabo-Latin literature that gave rise to them were still fresh in the minds of astrologically sophisticated readers. But he ignored them, and the technical problems that they raised, when he simply assumed that he knew when Christ was born. He also failed to point out that his interpretation of the geniture laid special weight on astrological factors which Ptolemy had not invoked, and some of which had entered astrology after his time, like the theory of the great conjunctions. Cardano assumed that the ascendant was in Virgo, but instead of discussing the stellar daemon that had mattered so much to Pico and Rosselli, he mentioned only one fixed star, Spica Virginis. He did not even record the fact that his own interpretation of Saturn's influence, which he thought had aged Jesus prematurely, did not match the influence attributed to the planet by his predecessors, who had seen it as predicting the Savior's death. In its eclecticism, its combination of professions of respect for Ptolemy and use of non-Ptolemaic theories, and its arbitrariness, Cardano's geniture is typical of his work.

Cardano's decision not to mention the earlier literature helped to make his geniture of Christ notorious: it earned him charges of impiety from Joseph Scaliger and others who read his commentary, but did not set it into the context of the medieval and Renaissance discussions from which it emerged. Cardano's avoidance of the problems his predecessors had raised enabled his critics to treat him, unfairly, as a wild innovator.[99] Like most of his predecessors, he insisted that he did not mean to suggest that Christ's divinity, or his miracles, or his sanctity, or indeed his new dispensation had their ultimate origins in the stars. But he did mean to say something almost as powerful: "Christ had an admirable nativity, and nature attributed to him everything that could be worked out by the combined action of the heavens, and our law is by nature one of piety, justice, faith, simplicity, charity, established in the best possible way, and it will have no end, unless it does so after the restoration of the ecliptics, which will bring a new state of the universe into being."[100] He went on to argue that a strictly Ptolemaic reading of

Christ's horoscope revealed exactly the events recounted in the synoptic Gospels, down to the precise wording, and in the early history of the church. Ptolemy, he admitted, "perhaps did not ever find out about this birth." But Ptolemaic astrology matched Christ's birth so closely that only two conclusions could be drawn. Either Ptolemy had used Christ's horoscope as the basis of his art, a conclusion Cardano dismissed as "stupid and ridiculous"; or—as Cardano did not quite say—Ptolemy had indeed framed an art that enabled its practitioner to watch the very functioning of the universe over time—and to predict it with the precision of one foretelling the operations of a perfectly precise machine, its gears and pistons moving without friction as their designer had ordained.[101] On the one hand, Cardano's Ptolemaic astrology insisted on its own limits. On the other, it claimed to hold the keys to the kingdom of universal knowledge. The assessment—as so often in Cardano—seems inconsistent, even unstable, when viewed in minute detail. One way to understand why may be, after this close-up view of Cardano the astrologer, to pull the camera back and watch him comparing astrology to its rival predictive arts, so many of which he also practiced.

chapter nine

RIVAL DISCIPLINES EXPLORED

SOON AFTER CARDANO started to write his first large work on astrology—so he recalled almost twenty years later—he had a vivid dream, which encouraged his ardent pursuit of his career as a writer:

> One night, having taken off my body, I thought that I was in the heaven of the Moon with the soul of my father. But since I did not see him, he said, "Behold, here I am; I have been given to you as your companion." Then I began to ask him a great many questions. Answering these, he told me, among other things, where I was, and that after seven thousand years I would rise into the heaven of Mercury. Then, after as many years again, into that of Venus, and then into that of the Sun, until I reached paradise, which is the summit of the universe. I heard this with great pleasure. I could have considered it an empty dream, if I had not afterward written so much that apparently matched the meanings of the planets—so much that I seem to have embraced everything relevant to the interpretation of the dream. For paradise can mean my books on the *Arcana aeternitatis;* the vast number of stars which are in the eighth sphere, my books *De rerum varietate* and *De subtilitate;* the sphere of the sun, my books on the art of medicine, for that art took its origin from Apollo. Arithmetic and Geometry belong to Mercury, and humor to Venus, and moral philosophy to Jupiter; and the interpretation of dreams to Saturn and the Moon, like everything else which pertains to divination. The books on gambling belong to Mars.[1]

The arts of astrology and astronomy provided the general frame of Cardano's account. In imagining himself climbing, slowly, from one sphere to another, Cardano obviously had in mind a standard image of the heavens like the famous one from the beginning of Hartmann Schedel's *Nuremberg Chronicle*—one in which the earth, with all its change and imperfection, formed the turbulent center of a set of perfect, unchanging crystalline spheres. Their concentric rings served as a ladder for the ascent of the soul.[2] But Cardano also recalled enough of the technical details even while asleep to remember the Alphonsine Tables and their period of 7 × 7,000, or 49,000 years—even if he transferred it from the existence of the cosmos as a whole to the life of his single soul. When awake, moreover, and trying to interpret the experience, he used astrology in still another way to tease out the deep symbolism of the dream. The character and qualities of each of the planets, Cardano inferred, supplied the key which enabled him to work out what they meant for his own future career.

Literary reminiscences shaped other elements in Cardano's account. He was hardly the first to imagine making a long, slow ascent through the sphere of the fixed stars. The Florentine humanist and poet Matteo Palmieri, on pilgrimage to Val di Nievole in 1451, dreamed that the spirit of Cipriano Rucellai appeared to him:

> He said that the planets were carried around by eternal law in their unceasing course and that the fixed stars stood in their boundaries. All that space was carried around in its course and full of angels and good beings. When he had said this, Matteo asked him where he himself was located. To this he replied, "A little past the moon." Then Matteo said to him, "Why then, you're in Mercury." But he answered, "I am measured out in the mean circumference but the star never touches me." Then Matteo asked if they could come to us. He replied, laughing: "We can. I come as I wish to."[3]

Both Cardano and Palmieri, in their turn, no doubt had echoes of Dante reverberating in their heads as they imagined the souls ascending through the heavenly spheres, acquiring virtue as they went.[4] These intellectuals' recollections of their nighttime experiences—like those of Descartes, two generations later—swarmed with "the allegoric devices, the *emblemata,* the rhetorical conventions . . . which organize not only this particular dream but baroque sensibility as a whole"; they were "rhetorically dramatic . . . choreographic and sententious, as ours are not."[5] Historians have tried again and again to read between the lines of such materials, to separate—for example—manifest from latent content. But such efforts result only in the importing of anachronisms and the distorting of the sources. At this distance in time, it is impossible to separate a written account from some purported original dream, and pointless to substitute a modern analytical language for Cardano's.[6] The historian can only try to reconstruct the ways in which the astrologer himself connected the interior life of dreams to the cosmic dance of the stars.

It seems paradoxical, at first sight, that a dedicated and proficient astrologer like Cardano—one who spent so many of his nights awake, scrutinizing the mechanically precise choreography of the heavens, and so many of his days at work, scanning the cold tables of numbers in astronomical ephemerides—also paid such close attention to the soft-edged murmurings and obscurities of his dream life. Cardano, after all, saw the stars not just as the signs but as the causes of future events. In predicting and verifying their motions, he watched the steel gears of fate and history carry out their precise, inalterable motions.

The language of dreams, by contrast, for all the images and terms that connected it to that of the waking world, was inevitably obscure. It consisted only of signs of what was to come, not of causes. Yet Cardano trusted dreams as firmly as planetary motions. He tried almost as hard to make the interpretation of dreams into a coherent art as he did to improve astrology—that is, in the terms used by his contemporary Caspar Peucer, he expended as much effort on the interpretation of dreams, which served only as signs, as on the interpretation of the stars and their movements, which really caused events.[7] And he used a wide range of other disciplines as well in his desire to gain control over the world and make predictions about its future course, analyzing materials whose colors, values, and intensities varied as widely as those of the pigments on a painter's palette. As Cardano applied these other disciplines, he made clear that astrology afforded him what he saw as powerful, but also as limited, knowledge of the universe.

Cardano himself never suggested that he saw it as unnatural to practice both quantitative, formal astrology and less precise, more interpretive, kinds of divination. This was only natural. For professional astrologers had never made, in practice, the kinds of absolutist claims that most critics, and a few defenders, of their art had ascribed to them in theory. Since late antiquity, at least, most of the clients who consulted astrologers—like those who consulted doctors and, for that matter, priests—had been eclectics. They chose their medicines for melancholy from a varied repertoire, including sacred as well as secular healers and cures. The Mediterranean medical *koiné*, an "inherited conglomerate" of magic and medicine, lasted as long and changed as gradually as astrology itself. And its component disciplines always rested on radically divergent premises.[8]

In Cardano's time, as for centuries before, an Italian who felt too lethargic to carry on a normal life could consult a doctor, an astrologer, or an exorcist—or make a pilgrimage to a shrine known to heal the sick. In southern Italy one could also hire specialists in this disease: musicians, who played the so-called tarantella to induce the patient to dance himself back to health.[9] Bitter complaints circulated about the charlatanry of individual doctors, astrologers, and exorcists. Sometimes a critic went so far as to argue, in a polemic or a satire, that all practitioners of astrology or one of its rival arts were quacks. On the whole, however, most patients seem to have believed, to some extent, in the competence of most healers and advisers. They chose to consult a particular one on grounds that are often anything but clear—especially since practitioners of sacred and scientific, learned and popular arts of healing regularly borrowed procedures from one another, and only gradually began to try to define specific areas as exclusively their own.[10]

Astrologers, for their part, normally did not find this form of competition wrong or unfair. On the contrary, Cardano's predictive practices were as eclectic as his customers' demands. He recognized that astrology could not yield information on everything that a client might need to know. In particular, Cardano worried constantly about the popular "catarchic" form of astrology—the form which took as its task not detailed inquiry into a client's geniture, but the erection of a figure for a given place and time and only, meant to produce an answer to one specific question: whether to take a voyage, make an investment, or find a spouse. Cardano warned that patients often mistook such inquiries for talismans, figures able not only to inform them about the disposition of the heavens, but to change it. Though Marsilio Ficino and other influential theorists of astrology and natural magic had urged their clients to use talismans to avert malevolent planetary influences and attract favorable ones, Cardano generally viewed such practices with disapproval.[11] For all his insistence that any given client's fate was determined as much by nation, upbringing, and later experiences as by the planets, he retained the ancient idea that the planets shaped each newborn as a hot seal shaped wax. Other factors might well modify this original process, but no form of magic could reverse it. Cardano also insisted that astrological interrogations could yield misleading results about such vital questions as the legitimacy or illegitimacy of a child. In such cases, he warned, the astrologer's art could cause misery, and even bloodshed—but it did not rest on, and could not provide, secure knowledge. Even at his most aggressively self-confident, in other words, Cardano recognized that astrology had limited powers.[12]

Cardano not only treated astrology critically, but also lavished time and attention on other arts of prediction. As a prominent physician and professor of medical theory, Cardano developed, as we have seen, a European reputation for successful diagnosis and treatment of diseases that other practitioners could not cure.[13] At his most self-confident—or boastful—he insisted that he could read a given patient's future, and infer the nature of his condition, with absolute security, from his appearance and symptoms—even when these would have fooled his competitors. Cardano's miraculous successes in therapeutics, he admitted in his autobiography, should "occasion no astonishment, since I also had a perfect command of the part of medicine concerned with diagnostics."[14]

Ever a willing gambler, Cardano made bets that he could pinpoint the cause of death for any patient who died:

> Accordingly, a great many who openly hoped that they could accuse me of error dissected bodies: for example, those of Senator Orsi, Doctor Peregrino, and Giorgio Ghislieri. In this case, does it seem remarkable that I predicted that the disease would be in the liver, even though his urine was excellent? And that his stomach would be intact, even though it caused him constant pain? After that they performed many other dissections in secret, but never found that I was wrong, and never dared to take my wager.[15]

Anatomy lessons in the sixteenth century were public events, held in theaters which provided a dramatic setting, often attended by grandees who had no professional interest in medicine, and regularly made more entertaining by the students, who grouped themselves into gangs and loudly urged their professors to debate with one another.[16] Cardano recalled with pleasure that every public anatomy of a nobleman which he had attended while at Bologna, from 1562 to 1570, had turned into a ritual of humiliation for his numerous critics. Time and again, the surgeon's knife laid bare undeniable facts that confirmed Cardano's unexpected but infallible conjectures.[17] Medicine, like astrology, both worked wonders and revealed them to be the results of natural laws previously unknown.

Some sixteenth-century intellectuals held, at least in theory, that astrology could provide the rigorous intellectual framework within which the doctor worked on his subjective, messy tasks. The movements of the planets and luminaries—so textbook after textbook stated, continuing a tradition that stretched far back, through the Middle Ages, into the ancient world—should determine the proper time for the doctor to let blood, carry out surgery, or prepare a prescription.[18] Cardano—himself both astrologer and medical man—might well have accepted this point of view, subordinating the more earthbound and qualitative art of medical prediction to the more noble and quantitative art of astrology, as Pomponazzi had. But he did nothing of the sort.

Cardano drew up horoscopes for some of his patients—himself, for example, and Archbishop Hamilton—and for other medical men. He also argued, in a long passage of his commentary on Ptolemy, that one could sometimes use the movements of the planets to explain the onset and course of a disease, day by day. He even suggested that one could interrogate the heavens about the sex of a pregnant woman's unborn baby.[19] In the course of the same text—a short treatment of the sort of catarchic, short-term astrology widely practiced by contemporary medical men in England—he asserted, as forcefully as in any other passage of his work, the superiority of astral to other forms of knowing the future: "For the predictions of astrologers, when made using the rules laid down in this book, are far more solid than the knowledge of the doctors of our time about disease: for the account of astrology given here is extremely careful, while medicine is handled with great negligence."[20] But elsewhere in the same large book that included this work—the commentary on Ptolemy which Cardano himself identified as his crowning achievement in astrology—he admitted that medicine, though epistemologically less profound than astrology, was practically superior to it, and that medical men enjoyed a far better reputation with the public than astrologers.

Cardano, in other words, saw astrology and medicine as fundamentally independent arts of prediction. Neither relied on the other for its basic principles. Neither required the other to attain its most remarkable results. Neither consistently attained a higher rate of success than the other. Cardano's own brilliant achievements in both spheres showed not that they belonged to a single, coherent intellectual enterprise but that he had a miraculous ability—the ability first attested to by his youthful dreams—to do valid, original research in many different disciplines, and to write up his results in important books.

Accordingly, Cardano's palette glowed with many colors, not just the black and gold of astrology and the red of medicine. In the course of the 1540s and 1550s he came to see himself—like his father—as able not only to understand the natural processes that governed the world, but to use the astonishing powers of natural magic to change their effects. He devoted two great and bizarre books, *On Subtlety* and *On Variety*, to this subject. In them his natural philosophy spreads out before the reader like a vast night sky, marred here and there by turbid black holes but also illuminated by brilliant pinpoints of insight. When writing as a natural philosopher, Cardano envisioned the terrestrial world as a constantly changing rather than a largely stable entity: a vast organism, one in which not only animals and plants but minerals as well grew with time. The physical and spatial configurations of all beings explained their apparently miraculous effects on one another, just as the configurations and connections of bodily organs explained their interactions. Sympathy and antipathy, proximity and distance provided the terms to identify and explain these effects.

For example, Cardano confronted the problem of why a candle made of human fat would flame up and spatter when near a deposit of treasure, and then suddenly go out. "Sympathy" made this apparently bizarre event predictable and explicable. Fat contained blood; blood in turn contained mind and *spiritus.* And *spiritus* was the super-glue of the Renaissance magician's cosmos, a subtle matter that pervaded the universe, providing a channel for communication between the celestial and the terrestrial worlds. Mind and *spiritus* were full of the desire for gold once felt by the human they had formerly belonged to. No wonder, Cardano argued, that they spurted up in the presence of the desired object. No wonder either that modern interpreters have insisted that when Cardano set out to investigate the natural world, he usually ended up commenting on a given body of information, most often one—like this—drawn from books or hearsay, not obtained by first-hand investigation.[21]

Cardano's books were certainly omnium-gatherums. They ranged from the sublime realm of magical talismans to the quintessentially low one of treatments for toothache (even here, however, the marvelous occurred: Cardano found that while rocking a painful tooth with his right hand did not help matters, doing so with his left hand, with the fingers in a particular position, miraculously eased even severe pain.)[22] Even Cardano's expressions of skepticism resembled those of the Azande medicine men studied by E. E. Evans-Pritchard; he often challenged the proficiency of individual rivals, but not the validity of the art they practiced.[23] When Cardano criticized those who believed that the figures on talismans gave them power, he did not urge a reconsideration of talismanic magic and action at a distance. Nor did he subject to any criticism his own firm conviction that "living" materials, like gold and gems, could draw power from the stars.

Yet Cardano could discuss the marvelous properties ascribed to many natural objects with considerable critical distance. The elder Pliny had devoted a long passage of his *Natural History* to the wonders of saliva. It could bring epileptics out of their fits, ward off witchcraft, cure snakebites, and alleviate pain. If you regret having inflicted pain, Pliny advises, merely spit on the hand that delivered it and you will alleviate the pain you caused. This assertion, *mirum* though it seems, is *experimento facile;* try it on a draft animal and see. Henry Cornelius Agrippa, whose *De occulta philosophia* offered would-be magi a rich stock of more elaborate recipes and talismans, included this humble technique as well.[24] Cardano ridiculed both Pliny's argument and the method that underlay it. He also offered a psychological counter-explanation for the fact Pliny cited. Often, he suggested, one feels ambivalent about inflicting pain and hits less hard than one thinks one is hitting. That explained why pain disappeared after the short time it took to spit into one's hand. In any event, Cardano pointed out, pain is a labile phenomenon, which, like fire, requires continuous "generation" to keep it in existence.[25] Most important, though, was Cardano's analysis of how Pliny went wrong. He had used a form of inference both normal and deceptive: he assumed that something that often happened was necessarily an instance of a universal scientific law. Like so many other students of the natural world, Pliny had failed to sift his experiences with enough care and precision to find out the truth.

As Cardano's discussion of saliva suggests, his brand of natural magic was alluringly varied in both content and method. Petreius, in his blurb for the first edition of *On Subtlety*, claimed that Cardano's book offered its readers "the causes, powers, and properties of more than fifteen hundred varied, uncommon, difficult, hidden and beautiful things, all of them observed by the author, in various places, by personal trials. Anyone who reads these things and the works of a great many of his predecessors will agree with me that they are not only delightful to know, but also more useful, both for private and for public purposes, than a great many earlier writings, which are less important even if they form part of philosophy."[26] Cardano himself emphasized how much his contemporaries loved the rare and surprising:

> Things heard are more enjoyable than things read: and among the things one reads, those written in foreign languages are more fun, and the rarer books give more delight. All of these effects have one cause: rarity. For rare things are to be found in rare books, which are known to relatively few; and the things which are found in difficult books are more rare, because fewer people know them; and the things which are heard are the rarest of all, as they are told to us alone. Therefore nothing can be more delightful than conversations about great and secret things. Things known to everyone seem devoid of value, even if they are quite valuable. That is why priests wanted to describe their ceremonies in an obscure way: they would have seemed of no value at all if they had not been covered up in dark shadows.[27]

On Subtlety, accordingly, resembled at times a verbal equivalent to Aldrovandi's museum, with its strange minerals, dried flowers, and brilliantly detailed, colorful pictures of rare birds and snakes. Cardano composed an artificial world of wonders for readers eager to read about mountains so high that the ashes of sacrifices burned on them remained there for a whole year; wells in the Carpathians, the water from which could transmute iron to bronze; and magnets, the touch of which could give a needle the power to enter one's flesh without causing pain.[28] Often *On Subtlety* seems designed as much to mystify as to explain. Cardano himself, after all, warned readers of the 1554 edition that "many will read, but few, if any, will understand everything written here, since there is much hidden beneath the rind of the text which is of greater value than what is explained in it."[29] Here and elsewhere Cardano offered a book on occult forces written in an occult style.

Yet Cardano—like Vannoccio Biringuccio, Giambattista della Porta, and Georgius Agricola, whose works on similar themes exploded into the book market in the 1540s and after—also offered, paradoxically, to explain the wonders that he retailed.[30] Cardano made a specific promise to readers of the revised edition of 1554, which he described as "the finished work *On Subtlety,* of which you had only the shadow in the previous editions." In it they would find clear explanations, derived by the author from his own experience, of the "varied strengths and properties, and uncommon, and hidden and difficult causes" of "twenty-two hundred very beautiful things," Cardano wrote, enlarging the promise made in the blurb to his first edition four years before.[31] The work, in short, would unmask itself, removing by explanation the very mysterious qualities that made its content attractive.

And indeed, from the start Cardano included in his work, along with the hidden qualities of elements and fountains, devices and explanations redolent of another, mechanistic kind of natural magic: the magic of the Renaissance engineer, like Filippo Brunelleschi, whose ability to lift a young man dressed as Jesus through the roof of a church on Ascension Day or to stage pageants consisting of carts that moved by themselves was as astonishing to his Florentine public as any act of conjuring.[32] Thus not only did Cardano describe how, "at Milan, just as I was writing this, a certain man washed his face and hands in molten lead"; but he also tried to explain the techniques that made this possible.[33] He recounted feats of technology as eagerly as those of prestidigitation, dwelling with pleasurable interest on the Brescian craftsman who made a clock small enough to fit on a ring and still powerful enough in its mechanism to strike the hour; a ship whose oars were set in motion when a woman struck a gong; and a tiny lead scorpion with which the craftsman killed his wife's lover while escaping detection.[34]

In cases like these Cardano's natural magic shared the reflective, partly self-critical, quality of his astrology. Sometimes he treated the effects of occult powers as psychological and therapeutic, not physical. Sometimes he insisted that raw data unexamined and unverified could not yield scientific laws. And often he explicated not the hidden virtues of stones but the openly available ones of mechanical devices. In doing so, Cardano resembled contemporary magicians like John Dee, who astonished his public, at different times, both by creating a mechanical scarab that seemed to fly and by conversing, through a scryer, with angels. The Jewish natural philosopher Abraham Yagel, recently studied by David Ruderman, showed a comparable range of interests and used a comparable range of techniques.[35] Sometimes, indeed, Cardano adumbrates such prophets of the New Science as Francis Bacon, who called for the meticulous sifting of data, but also took a deep scientific interest in the way his warts fell off in sympathy with the rotting lard he had nailed above his window. A magician with some sanity in his method may have more to do than historians have thought with a methodologist whose sanity was tempered by a good deal of magic.

Like Cardano's astrology, his art of dream interpretation occupied his attention over a span of many years. As early as 1543, writing his first elaborate autobiography, he emphasized the role that dreams had played in his intellectual life. His work of the 1530s on mathematics, for example, rested partly on the art and his own diligence in it, partly on chance, "so that I made a great many discoveries through my dreams. These also encouraged me to continue looking for solutions, which in the event never escaped me."[36] Another dream of the same period encouraged Cardano to go on writing, so powerfully "that its image still torments me."[37] Yet another both led Cardano to write about the life of Christ and frightened him so much that he did not dare publish the text.[38] Another inspired him to learn Greek.[39]

Cardano had eminent authority for believing that knowledge obtained in dreams could supplement expertise acquired while awake. Galen had said as much. And a vast range of manuals of dream interpretation assured Cardano that a careful, systematic study of dreams could yield principles for interpreting them, normally as clues to the immediate future rather than, as they would be for Freud, keys to the dreamer's past mental states. Galen's contemporary Artemidorus had collated dreams and established rational categories into which to put them—much as Ptolemy, in Cardano's view, had collated genitures.[40]

Accordingly, Cardano set out early in his career to make the interpretation of dreams into a coherent predictive art. In the *Somnia Synesia,* which did not appear until 1562, he recounted a long series of his own dreams in meticulous, often fascinating detail. He also devised an elaborate and plausible explanation for the predictive power of dreams. Admitting that dreams took many forms and had many different levels of clarity and obscurity, Cardano emphasized that both the cause and the object of a vision must be clearly established for a dream to achieve real clarity. Only when the stars inspired a vision of a person or object already known to the dreamer would the interpretation of a dream arrive at certainty.[41] Cardano celebrated the powers of this art with phosphorescent enthusiasm—and stern warnings against its abuse by the incompetent:

> All forms of revelation celebrate the interpretation of dreams as divinely granted, useful, and an admirable form of divination . . . No one ever felt ashamed to confess himself an interpreter of dreams, though other forms of divination were despised and many mocked them. But Moses forbade its common use—as he did that of many other dangerous pursuits—to prevent the adulteration of truth with falsehood and useful things with useless ones, and predicting directly from dreams as if no art were needed to interpret them, and the spread of sinfulness among the people because of their trust in false prophets. Just as only medical men are entrusted with healing, and priests with dealing with the divine, and jurisconsults with giving judgment, so only the wise may interpret dreams.[42]

Like astrology, in short, Cardano's art of dream interpretation required from its practitioners expert knowledge, profound wisdom, and a sense of personal honor.

Unlike astrology, however, dream interpretation did not always rest on a coherent set of technical principles. True, Pomponazzi argued, in his brilliant polemic on incantations, that the movements of the heavenly bodies could explain all portents and omens, from statues that wept and bled to the apparitions seen, while dreaming or while awake, by so many ancient heroes "that I could cite an infinite number of examples on dreams from Plutarch and a great many other writers, all of which I omit."[43] More conventional thinkers, however, disagreed. Caspar Peucer argued that some men were born with brains naturally predisposed to shape the dreams which they had for purely physiological reasons so that they also predicted the future accurately. Drunkards, on the other hand, had disturbed thoughts even when awake, and the wildness of their dreams reflected only their condition. And divine beings—from God on down to angels and devils—inspired still other dreams: "Diabolic in nature are all those dreams with which the devil showered pagans once upon a time, when they spent the night at the shrines of idols, wrapped in the skins of sacrificial victims, in order to obtain these illusions"—as well as those of modern Anabaptists and magicians.[44]

Like Peucer, Cardano did not believe that dreams were caused in every case by the predictable motions of the stars and planets. Instead, he too tended to explain such rapid and unpredictable flashes of insight into the future as inspired by supernatural beings. Like Cardano's astrology, his belief in other channels of communication with divine beings was inherited, at least in part. His father, Fazio, for whom Girolamo had a deep respect, had believed that he possessed the power to contact God and his angels directly. True, the fine state of preservation in which Fazio's corpse had been found when his tombstone was replaced twenty years after his death proved not that he had been a saint but that he had benefited from pure air, plenty of exercise, and a moderate diet.[45] But Girolamo treated with great respect his father's firm belief—one typical of pious Catholics in the years around 1500—that one who prayed on bended knee, at 8:00 A.M. on 1 April, to the Blessed Virgin, asking her to intercede with her son and adding the Lord's Prayer and a Hail Mary, would gain whatever favor one asked for. Girolamo tried this prayer himself, and on Corpus Christi of the same year found himself cured of a disease. Later the same prayer helped him to cure his gout.[46]

Above all, Cardano remembered with fascination his father's stories of visions and conversations with daemons. Fazio claimed to have had conversations with these superior beings over some thirty years. On one occasion, a written record of which Girolamo found, seven of them—all Averroists—visited Fazio, holding a theological disputation on the eternity of the world. They told him that they inhabited the air and could live up to three hundred years. Cardano admitted that the story had an air of falsehood, since the daemons' arguments "do not agree closely enough with our religion, and my father, with all his daemons, was no more successful, or richer, or better-known than I am, who has never seen a daemon."[47] On the other hand, "my father could have replied that he predicted many things, which could never have been known so far in advance without the aid of daemons: for example, that the emperor would at last end up in control in Italy, which did not happen until thirty years later."[48] Perhaps the daemons manifested themselves only because Fazio was a particularly pure and holy man; perhaps because he conjured them with a special formula he had learned from a dying Spaniard.[49] In either event, Cardano left the reader of *On Subtlety* with the clear suggestion that his father had conversed directly with spirits—though he himself seemed to deny the possibility of such communication.[50]

In *On Variety,* Cardano went much further. He described, at great length, the world and habits of the daemons who inhabited the upper realms. He also described—again at great length—his own remarkable powers of perception: for example, his ability to see images of whatever he wished, "not with my mind, but with my eyes." He made clear that he regarded his dreams, and related ways of perceiving the future through symbolic interpretation, as special gifts that he owed to the daemons:

> The third [of my special qualities] is that I see an image of everything that will happen to me in my sleep. I might indeed venture to say, indeed I can truly say, that I recall being warned in advance, and in exceptional cases long in advance, about every good or evil or indifferent thing that has happened to me. The fourth is that traces of things that will happen to me—though very faint ones—appear on my fingernails. Black and livid marks, and in the middle finger, are the signs of bad events, white ones of good events. Those in my thumb indicate honors, those in my index finger wealth, those in my ring finger studies and matters of great importance, those in my smallest finger minor discoveries. Closely concentrated marks indicate matters that are firmly established; if they are like stars, they indicate things less certain and more public and full of verbiage.[51]

Immediately afterward, Cardano insisted that his reader should consider these signs purely "natural."

But Cardano protested too much. Later in the work, in the detailed discussion of daemons to which Cardano devoted book 16, he described at horrific length the ways in which they interacted with humans:

> They come, sometimes, when called, or produce the image of one coming. Sometimes they are gentle and wise, and predict certain future things, surrounding them with a thousand ambiguities and mingling them with lies. Others choke humans, or, if they cannot do that, drive them to despair. They make some think they are entering their bodies. They kill the sons of others, not on their own, but by a certain art, in exactly the same way that men use net and trident to kill fish on the bottom of the sea.[52]

Cardano advised against becoming acquainted with daemons, since, like tyrants, powerful men, and wild animals, they made dangerous company. He assured his readers that "I certainly know that no daemon or genius accompanies me." But then he gave the game away: "If one accompanies me and I am unaware of it, since I have been warned so often by dreams, then, since God has given him to me, I will revere God alone, and thank him alone for whatever good things happen to me."[53]

Like Fazio, Girolamo suspected that the daemons had picked him out. Like Fazio, he could tell dozens of stories about the strange revelations of the future that he had obtained not by artistic readings of the stars or dreams but by direct mental or bodily revelation. The interpretation was obvious, even if Cardano resisted it. Many of his dreams came to him not through the regular action of the stars but through the direct intervention of a higher being or beings—as Cardano himself finally admitted, without making any more show of resistance, in his work of 1557 on his own books. Cardano's dreams spoke in the language of revelation as well as that of Aristotelian natural philosophy. Like Cardano's natural magic, in other words, his ways of reading dreams were multiple in nature, and sometimes rested on radically different assumptions about the nature of the experience.[54]

Cardano used other arts as well. He developed a theory of physiognomics and one for palmistry (though he also denounced both arts, on occasion, as false).[55] At the end of his life, he wove into his autobiography vast, asymmetrical webs of explanation, describing the astrological configuration of his birth, the dreams that propelled him to take vital actions, and the clues to the future that he had discovered in a vast range of everyday phenomena: in the smell of hot wax, where there were no candles; in the buzzing of a great wasp; even in what he frustratingly called "the obstinate behavior of my clock," without explaining it further.[56] "We are permitted," Cardano argued in his autobiography, "to draw conclusions from the smallest things, if they last unusually long. I have shown elsewhere that as a net consists of individual, uniform holes, so everything in human life consists of tiny things, which are repeated over and over again, and grouped, like clouds, into a variety of figures."[57] Cardano had lived—so he believed as his life drew to a close—not only in a world of wonders, but in one of signifiers. And he was never certain whether his ability to read some of these derived from regular natural processes which he had learned to decode or from the direct intervention of the divine being that accompanied him. Cardano—like other magicians of his period—scrutinized his own body and experience for the sorts of unusual marks, odors, and sounds that were, in other cases, interpreted as the signs of sainthood.[58] He even credited himself with the possession of a "splendor," a divine or nearly divine form of illumination, which gave him his unique understanding of the world—exactly the quality that experienced assessors of the supernatural like Giovanni Francesco Pico della Mirandola looked for in genuine female saints, since it enabled them to be sure that their own illuminations and purgations came from God, not the devil.[59] But Cardano himself suggested this sacralizing interpretation of his experience only hesitantly, and as one hypothesis, though he may well have considered it correct.

Cardano inferred the past and future from the regular motions of the planets. But he also placed special weight on events that appeared to violate the normal laws of nature. Not only twentieth-century intellectuals, but some Renaissance ones saw the application of these two approaches as a contradiction in terms. The fifteenth-century humanist and architect Leon Battista Alberti claimed that his considerable gifts as an analyst of characters, a diviner of others' intentions, and a predictor of future events rested on both a personal gift and a formal mastery of astrological technique.[60]

Philipp Melanchthon's son-in-law, Caspar Peucer, scrutinized this problem in his *Commentary on the Principal Forms of Divination,* which appeared in 1553. He described the widely held view, which Martin Luther also shared, that divine providence normally expressed itself through the birth of misshapen animals and similar portents. The abnormal shape of a two-headed calf, for example, offered a key which could unlock much of the immediate future. Peucer admitted that eclipses, by contrast, were regular celestial events, which took place regularly and foreseeably. He found it entirely plausible that a reader might object strenuously to his ascribing to them "portentous" content.[61]

Some students of the future took objections like these to heart. A later astrologer and interpreter of hands and faces, the Marburg professor Rudolf Goclenius, argued that a single, empirical approach unified all his efforts to predict the future. He insisted that those "who nowadays show off some sort of monsters in crystal balls" must have relied on diabolic aid.[62] And he rejected all such "superstitious" forms of divination in favor of precise, case-by-case observation of such particulars as the cruciform mark he had seen on the foreheads of seven men, "including two great men." All of them had died by violence, five of them by beheading. From such regularities in the data rigorous predictions could follow, and only from them.[63]

In practice, however, the culture of prediction, in Europe as elsewhere, usually proved flexible enough to employ conflicting, and even contradictory, methods.[64] Peucer (and Melanchthon) read the world much as Cardano did, even if doing so required a high tolerance for inconsistency. Peucer insisted that the stars played the role of divine signs, especially when they underwent eclipses. Eclipses in the past, after all, had regularly preceded or accompanied great and tragic events. God himself, moreover, had declared as much: "Erunt vobis in signa." Logically, Peucer could not explain why astrology should work; theologically and empirically, however, no doubt arose, as empirical and scriptural evidence both confirmed.[65] The nominally Catholic jurist Jean Bodin interpreted the fates of countries in a similarly eclectic way. True, he rejected astrological history, attacking Cardano and Gauricus alike. But he developed elaborate numerological rules to determine the fates of lands and dynasties, trying to set absolute limits for the duration of any given state. At the same time, he drew on the Hippocratic tradition, using the climates of the lands from which peoples originally came to explain their characters.[66]

Bodin also had a tutelary spirit, which guided him with a variety of signs, many of them quite dramatic—at least to judge by his third-person description of them:

> Every morning at three or four o'clock the spirit knocked at his door, and sometimes he rose, opening the door, and saw no one, and every morning the spirit kept it up. And if he did not rise, the spirit knocked again, and went on waking him until he rose. Then he began to be afraid, thinking, as he said, that this was some evil spirit. And he therefore went on praying to God, without missing a single day, asking God to send him his good angel, and he often sang the Psalms, almost all of which he knew by heart. Well, he has assured me that the spirit has accompanied him ever since, giving him palpable signs: touching him, for example, on the right ear, if he did something that was not good, and on the left ear, if he did well.[67]

Bodin's daemon came to him in direct response to his prayers and rituals, while Cardano's arrived without being summoned. But the similarity of their dealings with the two men seems as striking as the differences in the way they entered their lives.[68]

Cardano's fellow astrologers resembled him most closely of all. Ptolemy had already claimed that astrologers could predict which individuals would have prophetic gifts. Haly included a sample horoscope of a prophet in his commentary on the *Tetrabiblos;* Pomponazzi, in his turn, cited Haly as an authority and listed other cases in which astrology and prophecy had gone together.[69] Gaurico boasted of his divine gift for foretelling the future as well as of his quantitative skills as astrologer and astronomer. He devoted considerable space, in his collection of horoscopes, to explaining the astrological causes of the success of nonastrological prophets. When Giovanni de' Medici, just having escaped French captivity after the battle of Ravenna, came to Mantua, Gaurico took him to see "a certain monk with a wooden leg, named brother Serafino, an old man." He promised that Serafino would draw from the lines in Giovanni's hands "precise predictions of the future events" of the cardinal's life. After three days of silent palmistry, carried out every day before lunch in a little garden, Serafino told Giovanni that the Medici would soon return to Florence and that Giovanni himself would soon become pope. These apparently ludicrous predictions proved entirely accurate, showing that Serafino was, as Gaurico had claimed, a "Chyromanticus egregius."[70]

Later astrologers like Simon Forman and John Dee assumed without further ado that astrology formed only one of the many colors on the palettes of predictive methods that they deftly wielded.[71] They inserted numerous accounts of visions and encounters with spirits into their astrological diaries, and looked as eagerly as Cardano for every predictive art that could complement astrology. Dee, for example, eagerly underlined Synesius' statement, in his work on dreams, that "everything is signified by everything, since all things in the one great animal of the world are related, and these are like letters of every shape, signed in the universe as in a book, some Phoenician, some Egyptian, some Assyrian. The wise man reads them." "This," Dee remarked in the margin, "is my Cabala of being."[72]

As Dee's example suggests, the eclecticism of the Renaissance astrologers was no innovation. Revealing parallels occur in Roman astrological literature and in the neo-Platonic circles of late antiquity. Censorinus, writing his strange little book *De die natali* in C.E. 238, cited not only the horoscope of Rome drawn up for Varro by Lucius Tarrutius of Firmum but also the twelve vultures seen at Rome's founding when he tried to determine the length of the city's future.[73] Proclus, the quintessence of the divinely inspired sage, used astrology and theurgy together to defend the holy city of Athens.[74] The brilliant astrologer Sosipatra wielded both the astrological principles she learned from two mysterious Chaldeans and the mystical power of her own divine prophetic gift when she carried out the wonderful deeds described by Eunapius in his lives of the sophists—a text which became widely available in 1568, when Hadrianus Junius' edition and translation appeared.[75] And the prominent orator Aelius Aristides closely followed the advice of Asclepius as he drove himself desperately through exercise and medication to regain his lost health and powers. Willem Canter, the Flemish scholar who translated Aelius' *Sacred Tales* in the 1560s, described without any irony how "Asclepius, whom he reverently worshipped, cured him at last, against hope and even against the order of nature, with a vast number of drugs, baths, fasts, vomitings, bleedings, races, speeches, travels, and other similar things, which he ordered him in dreams to carry out."[76] Canter's reaction to Aelius' work—which has sometimes impressed more recent scholars as pathological—occasions no surprise. He spoke the same language of symbols and causes, having learned at the knee of his Parisian teacher Jean Dorat to appreciate the powers of ancient prophets and magicians.[77]

The eclectic wonder-workers of late antiquity loomed large in Renaissance visions of what prediction should be and do. The English humanist Gabriel Harvey, who read both Cardano and Gaurico, compared the modern palm-reader Serafino, whom he read about in Gaurico, to the ancient eclectic diviner Sosipatra (the comparison redounded to her, not his, advantage): "But how much truer and more certain was Sosipatra's divination, which rested, as it seems, on the astrology and physiognomy of the Chaldeans, and was furthered by certain cabalistic principles and trials."[78] Gabriel Naudé, who wrote the first biography of Cardano, thought it obvious that his superstitious, gifted protagonist stood in the tradition of later

Platonism.[79] Cardano himself no doubt inspired this interpretation with the long passage in which he connected his work on daemons to the Platonic tradition, which he traced back to Hermes Trismegistus himself—as well as with many other segments of his work, like his admiring description of the miraculous prophetic powers of the astrologer Paris Ceresarius.[80]

Tradition, in other words, required the astrologer to possess not only technical rules, but also secret forms of knowledge accessible only to the initiated.[81] Without knowing the rules, the astrologer could not claim to practice a mathematical science. Without knowing secrets that no rules could convey, thanks to a special, divine gift, the astrologer could deploy only a lifeless aggregate of techniques. Renaissance theorists of many arts, from painting to courtiership, raised the question of the relation between rules and spontaneity, discipline and inspiration, system and *sprezzatura*. Evidently astrologers found they had to raise it too. But in claiming a divine gift, astrologers often departed from the technical basis of their art, following clues that lacked any mathematical or astronomical basis. The divinely gifted astrologer became a divinely gifted specialist in prediction of all sorts. Cardano has been seen as eccentric because he insisted on his own divine help, tried to fuse or combine all sorts of predictive disciplines with his own, and at the same time admitted that forms of prediction that relied on inspiration rather than art could reach their results "exquisitius"—"more precisely"—than astrology.[82] In fact, in such cases the lover of scientific "subtlety" agreed, for once, whole heartedly with his predecessors and contemporaries.

But Cardano went further—or showed a larger tolerance for contradiction—than most. More than once, he portrayed himself and his colleagues as inhabiting an austerely Cartesian cosmos filled with matter and men in motion, propelled only by impersonal forces or personal emotions. No occult forces or sympathies of any kind, visible or invisible, pervaded this cosmos—which Cardano himself described as inaccessible to any of his traditional predictive discipline. In his treatise *De ludo aleae*, Cardano considered the possible outcomes of throws of dice. He insisted that a simple mathematical formula could predict the probability of a successful one. Determine the number of favorable outcomes that a throw of two dice may have; divide them by the whole number of possible outcomes; and you have the probability that any given throw will win. Cardano explicitly denied that any outside force could modify this strict quantitative rule. He treated dice as rigid pieces of matter dancing to the music of mathematics, their steps unaffected by sympathy, antipathy, prayer, or incantation. Cardano's mathematical rules were often wrong, sometimes because he uncritically followed the beliefs and practices of the gamblers of his time. But the style in which he formulated and explained them remains significant.[83]

Cardano's reflections on ethics and politics also describe a cold, hard world, one of men whose actions, and their outcomes, he found as predictable as the motions of billiard balls struck by cues. In his *Arcana aeternitatis,* his *Proxeneta,* and elsewhere Cardano reflected at length on how one attains success in human affairs. He admitted that the stars and the power of numbers set absolute limits to the life spans of states and individuals. But in the realm of day-to-day and year-to-year history, he insisted, men chose their actions and determined their fates. They acted for material motives; they succeeded if and when their means were adequate to their ends; their actions and institutions were valuable only insofar as they promoted success. Thus he recommended polygamy for kings, not for moral or magical reasons but because he thought it the only rational way to produce enough offspring to secure a line of succession. Without polygamy, natural decrease would put an end to every royal family in time. But without the Turkish custom of exterminating excess princes, civil wars would blaze up. Cardano praised the paradoxically humane "barbarity" of the Turks, at least on this one point.[84] In radical contrast to Montaigne, to whom he has often been compared, Cardano interpreted the cannibalism reported by European visitors to the New World not as a complex, provocative feature of a culture different from his own but as the result of a total lack of edible animals. Men ate men only because hunger had made them so ferocious as to lose any affection, even for their own offspring, whom the Indians gobbled up as eagerly as, according to Montaigne, they ate adult male prisoners.[85]

When Cardano analyzed gambling and politics, the tones of Machiavelli and Guicciardini suffused his style. He used their brutal images, like Machiavelli's famous comparison of fortune to a woman who must be beaten into submission—which Cardano quoted, putting it into the mouth of a French ambassador explaining the actions of Henri II (admittedly, these ended in disaster).[86] He accepted their chilling tacit assumptions about the nature and development of human history, which lost the definite order and divine purpose that it had when he analyzed the past and future as an astrologer. The cosmos of Cardano the politician seems far less cozy, far less orderly, than that of Cardano the astrologer and magician.

Sometimes, Cardano's accounts of the human world expressed an even bleaker modernity, a despairingly clear sense that many events happened not because of divine order or stellar influence or human will, but simply from blind chance. As he was leaving Milan for Bologna, Cardano almost lost his store of unpublished manuscripts. He found them, he tells us, only because he had broken his garter. When climbing into his carriage to leave, he realized that he had to urinate. After urinating he could not do up his hose, and found no new garters for sale in the three haberdasheries in the neighborhood. He turned back to obtain one of the new pairs of garters he had left in a chest in his house. And once the chest was opened he saw, his hair standing on end with horror, the manuscripts that he thought he had taken with him. Some weeks later, the house in question was broken into and the contents of the chest taken. "If it had not been for my garter," Cardano wrote, "I should not have been able to give my lectures, I should have lost my position, I would have become a beggar, all those monuments would have perished, and I should have died soon of grief. And all this depended on an instant! Alas for the condition—or rather the wretchedness—of mankind."[87]

Chance and fortune, human will and accident, seem to hold dominion over all. In this light, the whole project of rational prediction is reduced to a mere dream—a quixotic fantasy rather than a firm handle on the future. Yet elsewhere in the same text, Cardano insisted that "fortune has no power over an art: for a barber does not need the help of fortune to give a haircut, or a musician to sing or play; and therefore it has no power in medicine either"—even when his own medical predictions reached their most miraculous pitch of brilliance.[88]

Paradoxically, even a form of divination Cardano rejected could somehow yield a valid message. On his way to treat John Hamilton, Cardano went, invited by a schoolmaster, to watch a boy who claimed to be able to read the future by scrying, in a bowl of water. The demonstration failed, but the schoolmaster had a copy of Ptolemy's *Tetrabiblos*, which he gave Cardano. This chance encounter led to the composition of his commentary: "I believed," Cardano wrote, "that this was a divinely offered opportunity, which I could not evade."[89] The borders between rational control and irrational inspiration never became entirely fixed.

In the early seventeenth century, as Johannes Kepler tried to refound astrology on what he regarded as a basis "in agreement with nature," he set out to draw a clear line between the realms for which astrology could offer useful prognoses, like the weather, and those for which it could not, like the politics of the Holy Roman Empire. He frankly confessed to an unidentified nobleman that "astrology can cause grave harm to kingdoms, if a cunning astrologer wants to abuse human credulity," and that his own imperial master, Rudolf II, was "credulous." Accordingly, he deliberately distorted the astrological predictions of political affairs that he produced for his patrons in order to bring about what he saw as good—irenic—political ends. For

Kepler, political and astrological knowledge belonged to radically different domains and served radically different purposes. Only an astute political analysis should dictate the actions of a wise ruler. Astrology, for its part, had its virtues but "should entirely depart from the senate, as well as from the minds of those who now wish to persuade the emperor to adopt the best course, and it should be kept entirely out of the emperor's sight."[90]

Cardano, by contrast, never saw his own experiences of the autonomy of politics and the power of change as reasons for rejecting astrology, either in the political or in the personal sphere. Though he sometimes explained particular events in terms that denied belief in occult influences, he consistently resorted to astrology, as a practice, a well-used set of tools, worn and polished by the use of decades. Even though some of his late comments suggest that he had less faith in astrology than in medicine, he still used it, as we will see, to organize his last substantial work, his autobiography. Cardano's ability to wield other, radically different tools at the same time should occasion little surprise. Many scholars nowadays use computers to write and fax machines to submit the conference papers in which they unmask all of modern science as a social product, a game like any other. Though they hold that the laws of fluid dynamics are only one way, no more valid than many others, of describing the motion of air over wings, they take airplane trips to participate in the self-congratulatory discussions that ensue. Compared to the sterile credulity of modern arts of analysis, Cardano's arts of prediction look bright, warm, and solid enough to explain their appeal to the wide range of intelligent readers they attracted and informed.

Students of the Renaissance often approach the natural philosophy of the period through the brilliant chapter of Michel Foucault's *Les mots et les choses* that describes "the prose of the world."[91] Here Foucault portrayed Renaissance thought as an enormous game of snakes and ladders, a huge set of interlocking Möbius strips along which the intellectual could move from one text or object only to another which was connected to the first by physical or verbal similarities. For Foucault, Cardano exemplified the dreaming Renaissance sage, obsessively commenting on new shades of influence and antipathy but never able to see any of the disciplines he practiced—much less their underlying assumptions—from a critical distance. Modernity could arrive only when the surrealistically coherent structure in which Cardano and others lived finally collapsed, so that a new, classical one could take its place. The astrologer's world could not harbor elements of an anti-astrological sensibility.

In fact, however, Cardano—like most of his contemporaries and many of us—inhabited a mental world which had many mansions. These ranged from enchanted memory castles to austere observatories. Some of these dwellings he inherited; some he built from scratch; most of them he rebuilt and redecorated. He moved with ease, if not with comfort, from one set of assumptions to another, as the requirements of a subject or the facts at hand seemed to dictate. No overarching system unified all his beliefs and arguments. And no single language, no prose of the world or anything else, spoke through him. A hard and irreducible individual, a knowing and thinking subject, Cardano modified, manipulated, or invented contradictory languages as he needed them. He was not always sure why he used them as he did, or on what assumptions they rested, or even whether the predictions he spoke came to him from his own intellect, the stars, or daemonic inspiration. But he knew and said that he stood at the center of a cosmos that his own mind could mirror only in a fractured, incoherent way.[92] He deserves to be heard.

chapter ten

CARDANO ON CARDANO

About the year 1534, in the gray of dawn, at a time when I had not yet come to any decisions about my life and everything was going from bad to worse, I saw myself, in my sleep, running along the base of a mountain which rose to my right. With me ran an enormous crowd of people of every estate, sex, and age: women, men, old men, boys, infants, the poor and the rich, all dressed in different ways. So I asked where we were all running. One of them answered, 'To death.' This terrified me. Since the mountain was on my left, I turned in order to have it on my right, and began to grasp the vines which were on the mid-slope of the mountain, up to where I was, and climb. They were covered with the sort of dry leaves, with no grapes, that one normally sees in the fall. The climb was hard at first, since the base of the mountain, or rather the hill, was very steep. Afterward, however, once I had managed this part, I climbed easily, using the vines. Once I reached the summit and felt as if the power of my will was going to let me pass even beyond it, sheer, naked rocks appeared. I came close to plunging headlong into the depths of a foul, deep, and shadowy abyss. Though forty years have passed, the memory of this dream still fills me with depression and fear."[1]

The scene then changed, with a speed and lack of narrative logic that demand the description "dreamlike." Cardano found himself entering a rural hut, hand in hand with a young boy in an ash-colored suit. Then he woke.

This vividly detailed story is only one of dozens that Cardano told in his autobiography—the rich text which he wrote just before he died in 1576. Like Cardano's dream of his father's spiritual ascent through the celestial spheres, his dream of struggle in this world resounds with echoes of Dante. Any Italian reader would have been reminded at once of Dante's evocation of the terror that filled him whenever he relived his vision of the "selva oscura."[2] Like many of Cardano's other anecdotes, this one gleams with the polish that came from years of retelling and revision. Cardano had described the same dream for the first time almost twenty years before, in his second treatise on his own books. Already in the first early version, Cardano had set the dream at dawn and described the ascent of the mountain, the varied crowd with which he ran, and the terrifyingly dusty answer he received when he asked about their common destination: "To death."[3] But Cardano had also described the mountain in detail before explaining how he had climbed it, using the vines for handholds, and put the conversation with his informant curiously late in the story.[4]

These inconsistencies Cardano ironed out in the second draft, which appeared in the 1562 version of *De libris propriis.* There he separated his run with the crowd from his later solitary climb, making many minor stylistic changes as well.[5] Yet even at the end of Cardano's life, he continued to refine his recollections—or his narrative. Both the details he gave about the direction from which he saw the mountain and the description of the sharp, sheer rocks he saw on its summit appeared for the first time in the autobiography.

Cardano interpreted the dream as flexibly as he described it. In 1557, at the height of his productivity and fame, he saw it as a premonition that he would win the immortal glory he had always wanted, while most mortals hurried only to their deaths. The divine being that looked after him, he argued, must have sent it.[6] Yet he did not know the meaning of every detail: "I do not yet understand what the hut and the boy reveal."[7] By 1562, the boy's identity had become clear: "he is Ercole Visconti, my pupil, who entered my household immediately after my son's marriage: for the age, the time, and his appearance match perfectly, and the rest of the things that happened in the dream." The rural hut also had a clear sense: tranquillity of mind. Cardano found it reasonable that this vision from the 1530s took almost three decades to understand. Like any good prophecy, it became clear only after the events which it announced took place.[8] This interpretation sounds definitive.

In fact, though, the passage of time shed less light, not more. The old Cardano still saw the dream as a whole as describing the shape and character of his future life. But he now could not decide if the little boy he encountered represented the good spirit who accompanied him through life, a favorable omen, or his grandson, a less favorable one. And he connected the terrifying vision of the abyss with the execution of his elder son for murder.[9]

Cardano's narrative of his own life—as the analysis of this one segment suggests—was his most sustained literary and intellectual achievement. It amounted to a summation of his lifelong effort to understand and explicate his own experiences, and a systematic demonstration of the unique powers of analysis and prediction that he had dedicated his life to developing. The text embodied Cardano's definitive effort to trace the complex, riven web of relationships that connected his body and soul to the cosmos and the forces that ruled it. Though not published until the mid-seventeenth century, it has consistently fascinated and often appalled later readers.[10] Goethe admired the work's unbuttoned, informal style: "It is not the doctor in a long robe, who instructs us from the height of the pulpit: it is the human being." Georg Misch, the historian of autobiography, treated it as the Renaissance's definitive effort to portray an individual personality in an analytical way. Cardano's life was to that of Benvenuto Cellini, he wrote, echoing a famous passage from Jacob Burckhardt, as philosophy to poetry.[11]

Cardano constructed this complex work—as we have already seen—from existing blocks of material, many of which he had quarried and shaped long before. He also imitated a wide range of literary models. *On His Own Life,* in short, can hardly serve as a reliable guide to the events of Cardano's early life or middle years: often the sources make it possible to reconstruct these more precisely in a modern library than Cardano could, working from memory and by inexact self-quotation, in his Roman chambers. But the work's defects, seen from the point of view of a biographer hungry for facts, can be turned into advantages if one reads the text not as a query for materials but as an interpretation in its own right. True, historians' recent fascination with the many modes of life-writing has not so much clarified as complicated the contours and history of this enterprise. Rudolf Dekker, James Amelang, Kaspar von Greyerz, and others have begun to collect and assess the many kinds of "ego-document," high and low, fancy and plain, written for publication or for one family or a desk drawer, produced in early modern Europe. They have achieved a dizzying increase in the number of documentary genera and species any serious student of the field must take into account when assessing a particular specimen.[12]

Even the narrower history of autobiographical writings composed in formal Latin by formally educated men has become more sinuous and complex in recent years. Thomas Mayer and Daniel Woolf have rightly emphasized that all Renaissance biographies and autobiographies written by the learned were the products of a rich literary and rhetorical tradition. Even a Benvenuto Cellini, who represented himself as a craftsman without training in letters, manipulated literary models in his *Life.*[13] The humanist who stood up not to bury but to praise a dead colleague, hurling all the usual evidences of virtue and all his own well-worn metaphors into the one fragile basket of an individual's life, did the same—and, as his readers were expected to know, deployed more conventional themes than Cellini had used. In the end, all Renaissance humanists forced the facts of their subject's life to fit the often inconvenient outlines of existing literary lasts.[14]

The task of the student of such texts is, accordingly, not to reduce them to historical rubble by showing that they misrepresent the facts, but to identify the models that writers used in particular cases, to analyze what these enabled them to achieve, and to tease out, where possible, the tensions between remembered or recorded experience and available literary forms. These questions, though easy to pose, are often hard to answer. Any erudite man writing a life could draw on the high, instructive biographies of heroes and commanders by Plutarch and Suetonius, the irresistibly gossipy lives of philosophers by Diogenes Laertius and Eunapius, and many other prototypes. Few if any of them distinguished carefully between different schools and genres of classical biography, as more recent philologists have tried to do, or saw biography and autobiography as fixed genres with clear rules. And none of them went to work with the characteristically modern notion in mind that their subject was a unique individual to whose every peculiarity they had to do justice.[15] These conditions require great delicacy on the part of any interpreter.

Cardano's autobiography, like its subject, was unusually labile and complex. He had already drawn up a whole series of approximations—three or four earlier autobiographies, three explications of his own horoscope—when he began to write his final version of his life. He also knew and cited a wide range of ancient prototypes, as we will see. Once again, however, the art of astrology played a central role. Its methods provided the frame that organized Cardano's account as a whole; its traditions helped to determine the topics he discussed and the details he included; and its intellectual capaciousness, its easy tolerance for contradiction, enabled Cardano to make his book a partial mirror of his fractured self.

In some respects, *On His Own Life* resembled other humanist autobiographies—as, indeed, did Cardano's earlier treatises on his own books. He made clear that he had solid classical precedent for his efforts to chart the course of his own life. In his previous works, as in parts of *On His Own Life,* autobiography grew out of bibliography. From 1544—when the first, very short form of *On His Own Books* appeared—Cardano traced his life literary project by literary project, explicating in detail how he had decided to write each work, what form it had taken, and how it had finally reached print or failed to do so. Though the bibliographical segments of *On His Own Life* were relatively short, they condensed what had grown into richly circumstantial accounts of how he had produced such popular and influential treatises as *On Subtlety:*

> Something happened at the same time—something quite remarkable and unusual, which I mentioned in my books *On Subtlety.* Because of that dream I wrote twenty-one books on that subject, which have often been printed. The work is 280 folios long. The text begins, *Propositum nostri negocii est de Subtilitate tractare* [The intention of this work is to deal with Subtlety] . . . I wrote it, in the first instance, on 1 page; then on 4, next on 7, from which I increased it to 50. Finally, when it was first published, it reached 80; but it is now a full 160. When it was first printed at Nuremberg (for it has also appeared in Paris, Lyons, and Basel) that dream finally ceased.[16]

Cardano provided similar details for each of his books, including both the dreams that brought them into being and the details of the literary work that went into them.

In setting out to preserve his intellectual biography, Cardano followed well-known precedents, which he cited. Galen, the ancient medical man with whom Cardano wrestled throughout his life, had written a detailed text *On His Own Books.* He did so both to establish the canon of his genuine works and to inform his readers about the numerous forgeries that were in circulation under his name. Erasmus, for whom Cardano had deep respect, also produced a detailed bio-bibliographical text. This laid out the lines on which he wanted his literary executors to organize his *Complete Works.*[17]

From the beginning, however, Cardano aspired to more than listing his books and describing their contents. He connected them, as we have seen, with portents that indicated their divine, or at least providential, origins. He also discussed matters not directly connected with his literary life at all—like the history of his many illnesses. Readers of the 1562 version of *On His Own Books* learned that Cardano had suffered from impotence for ten years.[18] *On His Own Life* revealed far more. Cardano recounted the discharges that he suffered, from head and stomach alike; the loss of his teeth; his gout, his hemorrhoids, and his ruptures. He described in even more detail his "great flux of urine, which seized me in the year 1536 (who would have believed it?). Though I have suffered from this for almost forty years, passing from sixty to one hundred ounces of urine in a single day, I live well. I am not wasting away, as my rings show [since they did not slip off his fingers], and do not suffer from thirst."[19] He also left unmentioned no detail of the regimens with which he tried to preserve his health: "I like to spend ten hours in bed . . . For dinner I like to have a dish of vegetables, most of all mangel-wurzel, sometimes also rice or endive salad."

A serious student of diet, Cardano gravely analyzed his tastes in fruit, meat, and seafood (he preferred the tender flesh of river crabs to the tougher flesh of their ocean-crawling relatives), and laid down systems for cooking and exercise:

> The heart of the matter can be reduced to seven categories: air, sleep, exercise, food, drink, medication, and moderation. There are fifteen species: from air, sleep, exercise, bread, meats, milk, eggs, fish, oil, salt, water, figs, rue, grapes, or strong onion. There are fifteen kinds of preparative: fire, ash, the bath, water, the stew-pan, the frying-pan, the spit, the gridiron, the pestle, the edge of the blade, the back of the blade, the grater, parsley, rosemary, and laurel. Exercises include turning the mill-wheel, walking, riding, playing ball, carriage driving, the form of fencing in which makers of arms are expert, riding, the saddle, sailing, the finishing of paper, massage, or bathing.[20]

Cardano, his satisfaction undiminished by the occasional incoherencies of his list, bragged that he "had reduced the whole matter, as in theology, to a few main points, by deep thought and brilliant reasoning: without this splendor some points which are absolutely clear may seem a little puzzling to you."[21] The sacred light of Cardano's divine mind had devoted itself to the same arts of living that had always most concerned medical men and astrologers.

When Cardano recounted these details about the functions and care of his body, as Nancy Siraisi has shown, he wrote in part as a doctor, following classical precedents. The medical writing of the later Middle Ages included increasingly detailed *Consilia,* or reports on individual cases and their treatment. In the Renaissance, models for medical narrative multiplied. The author or authors of the *Epidemics* ascribed to Hippocrates and made available, with his other works, in 1525–26, case histories recounted in precise, emotionless detail. Galen told medical stories more vividly, and with more emphasis on the doctor's active role, in *On Prognosis.* Cardano's long narratives of his own diseases and their cures mirrored the detailed, highly personal accounts of others' diseases and cures that he included in a wide range of medical and philosophical works. The chapter of *On His Own Life* that dealt with Cardano's early impotence, for example, was no more startlingly frank than the section of *On Drawing Profit from Adversity* in which Cardano had discussed the same episode, in print, more than ten years before. Cardano's public already knew that he had "left them all dry" for ten years—even when he spent three nights in a row in bed with the same girl, trying with characteristic grit to overcome his problem. Cardano also knew and drew on the vast advice literature of his time. This provided systematic rules for every imaginable sphere of hygiene, including not only diet, on which a vast literature had grown up in both Latin and Italian, but also such delicate areas as personal hygiene and sexual intercourse. In some ways, his autobiography amounted to one vast case in point, a cautionary tale for readers of such books: the story of how following their rules had helped, and failing to follow them had hindered, one man's progress through life.[22]

Astrology, however, did more than any other single discipline to fix the shape and style of Cardano's most elaborate self-portrait. He began his life—as he had begun several of his previous efforts to understand his character—by investigating his own geniture. The text that he produced, moreover, was not a linear narrative but a topical account, one organized into short chapters. Some of these told stories, but more of them summed up the significant points about Cardano's "birth" (2), "stature and bodily appearance" (5), "health" (6), "forms of exercise" (7), and "dietary habits" (8)—exactly as the shorter topical paragraphs of his commentaries on his own horoscope had done in 1543, 1547, and 1554. His life became a unique combination of astrological character analysis and Suetonian autobiography: a fruitful combination of two radically different prototypes.[23] Astrology inspired Cardano's passion for giving the exact number of days which many activities had required and producing sums of these, sometimes slightly inaccurate; they corresponded to the planetary "directions" and "progresses" that identified the precise points of opportunity and vulnerability in the life of an astrologer's client.[24] More important, Cardano's art of prediction made possible one of his most remarkable, and most creative, achievements as a writer. By concentrating less on the long-term movement of his career than on the forces which recurred throughout his life, he produced an autobiography which did not make the author's life fit the teleological narrative logic of an adventure or a conversion, but set out to isolate the permanent traits of his character.[25] The old art of the geniture could be stretched to produce results, in the realm of introspective writing, that challenged comparison with those of Michel de Montaigne's new art of the essay.

Astrology shaped content as well as form, since it played a crucial role in Cardano's willingness to reveal the secrets of his bedrooms and bathrooms. Ficino described, in his influential *Three Books on Life,* the many problems that beset the learned, threatened as they continually were by the loss of vitality and the encroaching, destructive force of Saturn and melancholy. According to Ficino's model of human life, the wise man would pay close attention to the thousands of lines of influence that connected every organ and part of his body and soul to particular stars and planets. He would use every possible means to influence these for the better, from enjoying the beauties of a flowery meadow in spring to sucking the milk of a young woman or the blood of a young man—both of whom Ficino carefully described as willing participants in these operations. Only rare scents, powerful talismans, and lovely sights could keep the savant's liver and lights safe from the influence of the malevolent planets that constantly aimed their harmful rays at vital organs. The wise man's body, in short, was highly permeable, its internal organs accessible to scrutiny and responsive to powerful smells and sights.[26] Such images of the body seemed very compelling to a wide range of sixteenth-century writers, as Montaigne's *Essays* and Shakespeare's plays clearly show. Joseph Scaliger cried out in irritation, as he read Montaigne, "How silly, to write that he liked white wine." But the hundreds of readers who devoured edition after edition of the *Essays* evidently wanted to read the meditations of someone who cared as much as they did about whether wine was served in a pewter or a crystal goblet, and what it felt like to pass a large and painful stone.[27]

Like Ficino, Cardano found in astrology both a theory that accounted for the problems and powers of his body and a language for describing them in public. As early as the 1540s, in the first detailed version of his horoscope that Cardano published, he told his readers in an urgent series of paratactic clauses how Saturn had almost killed him a decade before:

> And it was 1538, and I was afraid I would die, and no illness appeared with which I came down, but only a flow of urine, which generally exceeded thirty ounces in a single night, and I had to get up four times to urinate, and it was without heat. And I, understanding the cause, was helped by hot applications, and the great quantity ceased at once. Hence I do not have to get up at night at all. Still, the quantity of urine remained larger than I used to produce.[28]

Cardano apparently felt a certain embarrassment in describing his bodily functions so precisely. He admitted that he would have preferred to explain "another geniture, since it is very hard to speak correctly about oneself." But the arguments in favor of giving details about his own life and fate had overcome these objections: "Since this is the only geniture that I truly know, and I have worked on it for more than thirty years, I therefore preferred, as I generally do, to satisfy scholars at my own risk."[29] The astrologer's punctilious desire to provide solid information and doctrine led Cardano, for the first time, to reveal in public those details of his own organism which would become an increasingly prominent feature of his medical and philosophical writing as well. No wonder that a seasoned reader of Cardano like Sir Thomas Smith described, in detail, in his own astrological autobiography the fever, scabies, pustules, and toothaches that had made his later childhood and youth a torment.[30] The astrologer could not ignore such private problems any more than Freud could have ignored his own mental and emotional development, dreams, and desires—however painful he found it to recall and record their history. In a biography framed as a retrospective version of one of the detailed luxury horoscopes Cardano had written for himself and his favored clients, one which described and interpreted at the outset the position of the stars at his own birth and then traced their effects in brief, topical chapters on the usual subjects, from family and wealth to journeys and illnesses, the subject's body could not be ignored.[31]

Neither could his mind and soul. Astrology played a central role in Cardano's searching analysis of his own character. He included in the versions of *On His Own Books* divergent but detailed accounts not only of his proud successes, but also of his abject failures. Describing his early life in Sacco, for example, he wrote:

> I also wrote another book *De pituita,* and another on venereal matters. Because a cat spoiled both of these, before they were completed, by pissing on them, I threw them away. I also wrote another book on chiromancy, which I transferred later into my books *On Variety.* In other words, during the entire period of six years that I practiced medicine in that town, I worked very hard, but with little profit for me and much less for others. I was caught up in incoherent thoughts and useless projects.[32]

In *On His Own Life,* these brief mentions of problems and failures swelled into pitiless dissections of Cardano's besetting weaknesses. From his own account, he emerged as a figure of fun, a wacky professor who made himself ridiculous even by his irregular way of walking. Staggering along the street, gesturing wildly, Cardano hardly showed the dignity for which he strove so hard as a philosopher and writer.

In fact, he made clear that he dressed badly, spoke poorly, offended everyone with whom he dealt, and failed to discipline either himself or those under his care:

> Sometimes I go out in rags, sometimes in fine robes; sometimes I am taciturn, sometimes talkative; sometimes I am happy, sometimes sad . . . In youth I took little care of my hair, and did so rarely, since I was intent on more important things. I move in an irregular way, sometimes quickly, sometimes slowly; at home I go around with my legs bare to the ankles. I lack piety and have an uncontrolled tongue, and my temper is so quick that I am sick with the shame it causes me . . . Among my faults I recognize that one is especially glaring and serious: I prefer to say exactly what will offend my listeners, and I persist in this deliberately and fully conscious of what I am doing. Yet I know how many ene-

> mies doing so has made me. This shows the strength of one's nature, especially when combined with long-established habits. Yet I avoid this when dealing with my patrons, and the powerful: it would be enough to avoid fawning on them, or at least flattering them . . . I am as solitary as I can be, even though I understand that Aristotle condemned this sort of life, saying, "A solitary man is either a beast or a god." But I have explained this. With a similar kind of foolishness, and with as great a loss to myself, I keep servants who are utterly useless to me, or even a source of shame. I have also accepted as gifts all sorts of little animals, kids, lambs, hares, rabbits, storks, which made the whole house filthy . . . I have made many, even a great many, errors because I wanted to bring in whatever I knew, whether it was much or little, whether I did so appropriately or not—so much so that I injured those I had meant to praise, as in the case of Aimar de Ranconet, president of the Parlement of Paris and a great scholar, a Frenchman.[33]

Cardano thus admitted that he lacked the central virtue of the ambitious courtier and professional: prudence.[34]

The most famous stories in Cardano's autobiography—the anecdotes about the spirits who had played major roles in his life, the strange phenomena that he witnessed, and the magical properties of his body and soul—were calculated to detract even further from his credibility. True, saints' lives swarmed with similar instances of the paranormal and the supernatural. But the consistent, rigorous holiness of saints' actions and emotions, not the power of their ecstasies and visions, won them sainthood. If anything, spiritual directors and church authorities looked with suspicion on visionaries. Those who were flailed by demons, consoled by the Virgin, and nourished only by the Host often found themselves not elevated as the sources of a special grace but condemned as pretenders to it.[35]

Aspirants to sanctity who believed, or whose followers believed, that they had signs of heavenly favor written on their bodies were as likely to meet with derision as with adoration. Dominicans denied that St. Francis had really received the stigmata. More radically still, Petrarch suggested that the power of Francis' own devotions had produced them, and Pomponazzi pointed out that astrology could also explain their presence in purely natural terms—even though he professed his acceptance of the church's supernatural explanation for them. Bodily marks and prophetic utterances were in any event a largely female province. The many wonders printed on and created inside the bodies of saintly women in the later Middle Ages demonstrated not only their holiness, but also the special softness and impressionability of their female flesh. Spiritual companionship could be hazardous to the reputation in many ways.[36] No wonder that Bodin—ever more prudent than Cardano—disguised the story of his own dealings with a daemon by telling it in the third person, as a narrative about a pious friend.[37] When Cardano told of his dealings with the spirit world, he did so—as he must have known—at the cost of his own reputation for veracity and common sense.

Autobiographers never tell all: they merely give more or less successful and consistent impressions of having done so. Cardano's confessions were not so full and frank as they appeared. He did not describe in identifiable detail the sexual inclinations that led him to pedophilia and brought him legal penalties—only the indignation that he felt when his own son-in-law accused him of this heinous crime, and the deft way that he had exposed the implausibility of the charge.[38] In this and other cases, Cardano's flood of lesser revelations—like the room full of bric-a-brac which surrounded the *Purloined Letter,* left out on a stand in full view, in Poe's story—distracted attention from traits which might well have done him more discredit than those he admitted.[39]

Similar efforts at camouflage appear when one inspects Cardano's attempts to revise the more technical segments of his work. Cardano did not try to hide all of his errors. In the last version of his geniture, he admitted that he had at first put the moon in the twelfth house, not the eleventh, and failed to see that it was the aphete (the planet that determines the length of life). Hence the astrologers had gone wrong, "and I with them, and I went chasing after nonsense." "And this error," Cardano bitterly remarked, "was the cause of great evils for me: it is better to be ignorant of the arts than to understand them incorrectly." He also admitted that he had suffered from a fever for forty days not in his fifty-sixth year, as he had predicted, but in his fifty-fourth. So far, so frank.

But Cardano chiefly emphasized his triumphs: his survival in his thirty-eighth year of an eclipse, which others had misinterpreted as malign, and of the flux that seized him in his thirties; his provision of prophecies that corresponded perfectly with events; his creation of the first profound and accurate astrology since Ptolemy's. To bolster the impression that he was infallible he suppressed important elements of his earlier geniture. In the 1550s, for example, Cardano noted that his sixty-eighth year would be very dangerous. Worse still, the ever-changeable Mercury would reach the malign quartile aspect with the ascendant at the end of his seventy-fourth year. This might well cause him to contract "a disease which takes many different forms, and which can easily prove mortal when it attacks someone weakened by age." Evidently Cardano stayed free of disease—and felt free to celebrate by dropping any mention of his failed prediction. He boasted that he had created a truly scientific astrology by being brave enough "to publish examples." But even in his most elaborate case study, his commentary on his own geniture, he failed to admit how many miscalculations he himself had had to conceal or to forget along the way.[40]

Cardano's assumptions and prejudices also shaped his account, often in vital ways. Unlike some other astrologers, Cardano does not seem to have systematically collected women's genitures. And as Germana Ernst has observed, though he dramatically described how he met and fell in love with his wife, he showed little interest in the roles that women had played in the formation of his character or the development of his career. Though he included his parent's genitures in his commentary on his own, he discussed only his father's chart at length. Of his mother he wrote, revealingly: "And because she was a woman, I shall not say much, except that she was clever, wise, noble, honest, and loved her sons."[41] Similarly, Cardano's testimony about his *familia,* for all its rich detail, reveals little about the place of his wife, his daughter, or female servants in what was, for many years, a large and busy household.[42]

Still, many readers found it bizarre that Cardano voluntarily revealed so many weaknesses of character.[43] Naudé, for example, reproached Cardano in his preface to the first edition of the text with having destroyed his own social and intellectual position. Certainly, some writers of ego-documents, working in a reflective old age, abandon all social and political ambition. But Cardano did not. In 1570, only a few years before his death, he composed the *Proxeneta,* a manual for successful life at court. Here Cardano advised the courtier to maintain silence above all. Any revelation about one's means or emotions could only help one's competitors.[44] Yet Cardano the autobiographer graphically revealed his mistakes and character flaws to readers and rivals alike. In the age of Baltasar Gracián's cold morality, the philosophy of the personality hard and featureless as a billiard ball, Cardano's frankness—or at least his volubility—represented a basic violation of the rules of prudence.[45] Cardano keenly felt the strength of this objection to his habits of self-description—and his general lack of reticence. In *On His Own Life* he admitted that he had failed to maintain prudent behavior with Aimar de Ranconet "because I did not rely on those certain rules which I later discovered, and which men of social ability generally know."[46]

In fact, however, such excuses were not typical. Usually Cardano stated that he had deliberately broken the normal rules of literary self-presentation—the rules that the prudent writer would follow in all cases. He had done so, once again, out of his sense of professional duty. The astrologers of the later Middle Ages and Renaissance saw it as absolutely vital to explore the flaws in their customers' characters—even the worst of them—so far as basic self-preservation allowed.[47] In some contexts, of course, unpleasant character traits could serve practical purposes. When a Vienna doctor drew up horoscopes for the children of Maximilian II, he felt impelled to reveal that Maximilian's eldest daughter would show a masculine severity, inclining to be both irritable and vengeful. However, he also commented that these qualities showed that she was well equipped for public responsibility.[48] In other cases no such compensations appeared for the defects written in the stars. When Tommaso Campanella produced a horoscope for Sir Philibert Vernat while both lay in the royal prison in Naples, he had to explain that his young customer tended toward sexual passivity and could even have become a pervert, had he not been a northerner. The client barely escaped both sterility and priapism.[49] Astrology offered a means of understanding one's own character—and not allowing it to become one's destiny. But only frank speech about the unspeakable could serve a client so deeply afflicted by the maleficent planets as Vernat—or as Cardano himself.[50]

Cardano, as we have seen, admitted in the 1540s that he felt uneasy when revealing the secrets of his body. In the *De vita propria* Cardano remarked that he had harmed himself by learning, through astrology, that he was likely to die between the ages of forty and forty-five—especially when his own worry was repeated by others, becoming a widely-diffused rumor.[51] The early versions of his horoscope, however, said of his mind and character only that the stars had given him "deep thought, study, diligence, and a great tolerance for work"—as well as "a deceptive memory, though also a capacious one."[52] But in the longer analysis of Cardano's geniture which appeared in his edition of Ptolemy, he described his own character unsparingly, quality by quality, juxtaposing epithet to epithet to create a magnificently saturnine pointillist portrait of a man tortured by his own faults: "pious, faithful, a lover of wisdom, a contemplative, a deviser of many things, a brilliant mind . . . modest, curious about medicine, interested in miracles, an architect, tricky, deceptive, bitter, a specialist in mysteries, serious, hard-working, laborious, diligent, ingenious, living for the day, frivolous, a despiser of religion, full of resentment for past injuries, envious, sad."[53] Cardano made clear exactly how, as he saw it, his professional duty as an astrologer had forced him to violate the normal canons forbidding discreditable public confessions:

> The occasion was provided here for giving those who take pleasure in this art something of considerable value. For no horoscope was ever so precise or certain, or so carefully examined. And I could not know anyone's mind, behavior, and hidden deeds as fully as my own thoughts, lusts, and desires, and the basic impulses of my own mind. But, as the saying goes, nothing is perfect in every

> way. If I open the sealed cells of my mind not only to one person—which many would see as a grave error; not only to friends—which almost no one does in an honest way; but to everyone, telling what I thought and what I deeply wished to remain secret; if I start to praise myself, or to criticize myself, what will I seem, if not a clear case of insanity and stupidity? If I am silent, what use will I be to students of the discipline? Let love of truth and public utility win out. It should seem not so much shameful that I have praised or criticized myself, as appropriate that I have exposed myself, in my desire to attain truth and wisdom, to the calumnies of the spiteful and the abuse of the insane mob.[54]

When Cardano laid bare his follies and foibles in *On His Own Life,* in short, he followed the rigor of his own commitment to astrology, as he had worked this out many years before. In withstanding the pain of serving as the subject in his own public anatomy lesson, he played the hero of science, in his own eyes at least; and the deeper the humiliation he risked, the greater the bravery of his attempt.

Behind this first line of defense, Cardano erected a more conventional inner wall. In his commentary on Ptolemy he explained that when he published his detailed analysis of his own bad character, he portrayed himself not as he was, but as he would have been—if he had not taken measures to avoid the sins and errors to which the stars made him specially liable:

> True, my conduct is such—for nothing else belongs to me alone—that it seems impossible to praise it without boasting or to criticize it without madness. But here I am speaking not of what I have actually acquired through philosophy and education, but of my natural conduct, which is such that Socrates, who had similar attributes, was not ashamed to be called foolish, incompetent, and self-indulgent. For our natural disposition is one thing, but that of our studies and self-discipline, which form each person's actual conduct, is quite another.[55]

The skilled astrologer examined every detail of his physical constitution in order to devise the proper regimen to keep himself healthy. In exactly the same way, he sounded the depths of his moral constitution in order to devise ways of keeping himself honorable.

Cardano's moralizing vision of astrology was conventional. Erasmus Reinhold introduced his collection of genitures with a stern reminder about the role of astrology in forming a client's moral sense: "When we see which vices the stars or our temperaments make us prone to engage in, we must govern our conduct with greater care, so that our evil desires do not win out."[56] When Sir Thomas Smith examined the geniture of his own illegitimate son, he arrived at deeply depressing results: "This configuration makes him unfit to master formal studies, slow of intellect, credulous, changeable, fickle, very prone to error, sly, unfaithful, rash, hasty, forgetful, and deceitful." Though discouraged, Smith refused to despair: "He is the sort who will someday deserve to pay a great penalty for his own crimes—if this is not corrected by a great deal of good training."[57] Smith meant what he said. He assigned his younger relative, the humanist Gabriel Harvey, to read Livy's account of the Punic Wars with his son, so that scholarly discipline could implant the backbone that his inborn character lacked.[58] The boy was thus properly equipped to play his role in breaking resistance to English rule in Ireland—at least until his own servants murdered him.

Cardano, similarly, tried to make productive use of the connections between the stars that haunted him and his own character. Sometimes he resisted the stars; often, however, he used his astrological characterology as a form of moral therapy. The second chapter of *On His Own Life* described what may be the most striking example of his success at treating himself. Cardano confessed there, not for the first time, that he had been impotent as a young man, for ten years. The position of the stars at his birth, he argued, accounted for this wretched condition. They had almost made him the sort of monster that his readers found so chillingly attractive to read about—and they certainly maimed him. Even the beneficent planets which had occupied significant positions in Cardano's geniture had only been able to mitigate the malevolent influence of Mars, which was in quartile (a malign aspect) to the moon: "Because Jupiter was in the ascendant and Venus was the ruler of the horoscope, I was harmed only in my genitals, so that from my twenty-first to my thirty-first year I could not sleep with women and often mourned my sad lot, envying all others for theirs."[59]

Cardano's explanation of his problem stood out for its impersonal character.[60] In sixteenth-century Europe, impotence and fear of impotence were pandemic—a terrible threat in a society in which no family found it easy to reproduce itself, infant mortality was high, and connections through marriage alliance were vital to collective survival. Everyone knew, moreover, that witches caused this dreaded condition. The German woods, so the Dominicans Heinrich Kramer and Johannes Sprenger argued in the *Malleus maleficarum,* swarmed with evil women who knew how to create, with diabolic help, the devastating illusion that they could steal men's penises and hide them in birds' nests. Though strict theology denied them the power actually to remove bodily organs, the rhetoric of visual images suggested that their sleight-of-hand could have horrifyingly real effects (consider, for example, the sausage-like objects that witches grill in the works of the gifted misogynist Hans Baldung).[61]

This widely disseminated fantasy contributed greatly to the late sixteenth-century witch craze, and had its adherents in Cardano's own adopted city of Bologna: but it did not infect Cardano.[62] Though more skeptical than many about the diabolic pact, in principle Cardano believed in witchcraft.[63] He refused to write a testimonial for a woman accused of it (to be sure, Cardano characteristically interpreted the invitation to do so as a trap set by his enemies).[64] But though he speculated about the role that witchcraft might have played in his troubles, he refused to blame a particular woman for his own impotence—even one of the young ones with whom he made energetic, if ineffectual, efforts to relieve his condition.[65] Over time, his passive reliance on the stars produced better results than the hectic activities in which he engaged while in bed with his partners. Astrology worked: and it worked again when it enabled him to survive and go on working after the terrible death of his son. Cardano found then that placing a certain stone in his mouth made him forget his pain: for as we have seen, he believed—though he did not call attention to the point—that the stars imbued gems and other stones with their power to affect human temperaments and emotions. Cardano never ceased to rely on the stars, and they never entirely failed him. Even in his last years of house arrest in Rome, he emerged as a powerful figure, actively participating in the meetings of the Roman doctors' guild and enlarging, as well as modifying, his early books in the vain hope of gaining approval for new editions.[66] Only "the monstrous condescension of posterity" has made it impossible to see how effective Cardano's impersonal, theoretically warranted therapies really were.[67]

Astrology, in short, provided not only the large-scale predictions, but also the fine-grained character analyses and precisely adjusted psychological therapies, that early modern intellectuals needed. According to Peucer, even the most penetrating and effective psychologists of all—the devil and his minions—used astrology to understand, and thus to undermine, the characters of the humans whom they wished to lead into temptation:

> They have precise knowledge of the natures, powers, and effects of the celestial bodies, and know that they were created to the end that each part should move and change the elementary nature in its own way, and produce various effects on it by combining primary qualities with one another in various different ways. They understand and observe that these qualities and another secret power of the stars have a miraculous ability to affect the temperaments of men. And they note with absolute accuracy what effects each star either stands for or produces and brings about in any given place or ordering.[68]

If devils needed astrology to understand and alter the human character, then human students needed it all the more.

No wonder that some of the most penetrating character analyses of the time—like John Aubrey's wonderfully brash *Brief Lives*—began as horoscope collections (no wonder either that modern editors, showing a typical disdain for astrology, have thoroughly obscured these origins in their dealings with Aubrey's manuscripts).[69] The late seventeenth-century Rye merchant Samuel Jeake, whose astrological diary has recently received an exemplary edition from Michael Hunter and Annabel Gregory, found in astrology, even more than in his Puritan beliefs, the inspiration for his meticulous examination of the timing and meaning of all the disasters and near disasters he suffered in an eventful life. Gabriel Harvey showed real insight when he systematically compared the horoscope collections of Gaurico and Cardano to Paolo Giovio's *Elogia* of great men, with their rich characterological "montages" of virtues and vices.[70] The good astrologer—like the good biographer—promised to teach his disciples to read, and even to rewrite, the book of human character itself.

The drive to make his own experiences morally instructive led Cardano to what superficially seem extremes of self-contradiction. As an astrologer—and as an autobiographer—he struggled with time, trying to uncover the hidden logic of his past and to show how accurate predictions could yield valuable therapies for his own and others' futures: "in my own view," he wrote, "I was particularly able at examining my own experiences, thanks both to the great length of my life and to the great number of my misfortunes."[71] More than once, however, Cardano tried to replace this perspective with a radically different one: one in which time past and future mattered little or not at all, in which the moral philosopher tried to oust the astrologer.

In one chapter he insisted, not very convincingly, that he had never strongly desired honors:

> The desire for honor drains away our wealth, since it makes us avoid strenuous effort and the other opportunities for gain, as we dress ambitiously, give banquets, and support numerous servants. It also urges us to die, in more ways than I can mention: in duels, wars, quarrels, disgraceful lawsuits, attendance on princes, inappropriate high living, intercourse with wives or courtesans. We risk the high seas, we claim that it is honorable to fight for our country. The Brutuses were characterized by their willingness to die in combat, Scaevola burned his right hand, Fabricius refused [Pyrrhus'] money. The last example was perhaps the action of a wise man, the others of fools or maniacs. There is no reason to brag about your fatherland. What is a fatherland but a conspiracy of petty tyrants to oppress the weak, the timid, and those who are basically innocent?[72]

In another chapter Cardano rejected fame just as strongly, insisting that he wished "only to have it known that I have lived, not what sort of man I was"—an ambition that Sir Thomas Browne dismissed as "frigid."[73] In yet another he insisted that the true lesson of life was that the wise man would live joyously even though mortal life offered no security, enjoying such little but undeniable goods as rest, cleanliness, telling stories, and playing with pets.[74]

As he drafted these hortatory passages, Cardano clearly followed the model of the ancient writer he cited at the very beginning of his work, Marcus Aurelius, "that very wise and excellent man, as it is believed, whose example I follow as I set out to write about my own life."[75] Marcus' work—like that of Eunapius—belonged to the substantial number of philosophical texts from the Imperial age that reached the book market only in the middle of the sixteenth century. It had in fact been translated into Latin only a few years before Cardano wrote, by the experienced editor and press corrector Gulielmus Xylander.[76] Not an autobiography but a mixture of self-scrutiny, advice book, and diary, perhaps never meant to be read by others, Marcus' work denied at every point the importance of time and history: "How quickly," he wrote, "do all things pass into nothingness: bodies in the world, and in time even the memory of them."[77] He dismissed his own battles with the enemies of his Empire as the squabbles of so many dogs over a bone, the human body as a putrescent bag of viscera, the human mind as the prey of dreams and fantasies. The wise man would cease trying to learn either what others thought and felt or what might happen to him in the future, in order to enjoy the present alone, as philosophy taught him to. And he would see even the present in proportion, as the fleeting moment that it was.[78] His book offered not the details of a single life but the general principles which could bring contentment.

As Xylander perceptively explained in his preface to the text,

> Like most scholars, I consider that Antoninus not only wanted to set out in the form of commentaries the matters with which he had concerned himself and the rules, examples, and arguments by which he trained himself to play the roles of man, citizen, emperor, and philosopher in a worthy manner, but also to show the true and direct way to attain tranquillity of mind and the happiness which man can gain in this life.[79]

At times, as Cardano sat in his Roman solitude, the detachment of the Stoic emperor clearly tempted him, and he tried to teach himself and others the same lessons. Like the Stoic humanist Justus Lipsius, Cardano tried to remake his self as he meditated on it, to turn his act of life-writing into a moral exercise that could result in the transformation of his sinful, emotion-wracked soul.[80]

Most of the time, however, Cardano resisted what he saw, in moments of despair, as the truth of Marcus' message.[81] In the same prologue in which he cited Marcus' example, he also wrote that he himself meant not to teach but simply to describe: "my life is presented without adornment, and not to instruct anyone: it consists of the straight story alone, and describes a life, not great disturbances."[82] He never ceased trying to work out the meanings of each tiny experience, including apparently trivial events. In fact, he seems to have taken special pleasure in describing evanescent experiences, which other writers, who lacked his astrologer's sense of the vital importance of tiny clues, might have missed:

> The second remarkable quality appeared when I was four, and lasted about three years. On my father's orders, I rested in my bed until around the third hour of the day, and when I woke up before that time, I spent whatever time was left before the set hour watching a delightful spectacle. I was never disappointed in my expectation that it would take place. I saw various images, like airy bodies, which seemed to consist of little rings like chain mail, though up to then I had never seen chain mail. These images rose from the lower right-hand corner of my bed, in a semicircle, slowly, and sank down again to the left, so that they entirely disappeared. There were pictures of castles, houses, animals, horses with riders, plants, trees, musical instruments, theaters, men in different kinds of clothing and dress, flute-players, especially ones with their pipes, actually playing, though no voice or sound was heard. There were also soldiers, peoples, fields, and the shapes of bodies, ones which are hateful to me even now; groves, forests, and other things which I can no longer recall, and sometimes there was a veritable chaos of things moving together very rapidly, not in such a way that they became jammed up together, but so that they reached a very high speed. These images were transparent, but not so much so that they seemed not to be there, and yet they were not so dense that one could not see through them. But the tiny rings were opaque and the spaces they enclosed were wholly transparent.[83]

None of Cardano's visions of spirits called forth from the vasty deep had the vividness of this charming childhood memory.

Cardano even tried to trace, in some detail, the course of his past emotional life, to find a language capable of conveying the flavor of different times as he remembered them:

> My happiness in any given period is to be measured by comparison to the whole—as, for example, when I lived in the town of Sacco. Among giants, one must be the smallest; among pygmies, one must be the biggest. Nonetheless, the giant is not small, nor is the pygmy big. Thus, even though I was happy

> while I was in the town of Sacco, it does not follow that I was happy at some time. I gambled, I worked at music, I took walks, I feasted, and though I did little work on my studies, I had little trouble and few fears. I was respected, I was looked up to, I had the chance to meet Venetian nobles, it was the flower of my time. Nothing in my life has been more pleasant than this period, which lasted five and a half years, from September 1526 to February 1532. I chatted with the mayor; the communal palace was my kingdom and my pulpit. Yet it is clear from the fact that my happy dreams carry me back to that time not only that it has not only passed away, but that even its memory has been stretched into a single thread, preserved by the feeling of pleasure.[84]

In passages like these, the astrologer stood up to the philosopher, and came away the winner. The interpretation of time took precedence over the realization that time had no larger meaning and purpose. The study of experience, in all its close-grained and resistant detail, proved more absorbing and attractive than detachment from experience. Astrology offered a language for describing the indescribable, the momentary, the felt, in late recollection. "Let all your last thinks be thanks," Cardano could have said—if he had read W. H. Auden—as he told and retold the years and minutes of his life, recollecting adventures and dreams in the partial tranquillity of his last year. Time had not lost its meaning for him, in his own life or in history as a whole—even if his gloom sometimes led him, in his own latter days, to fear that the discoveries of the New World and of printing, which he had once celebrated, might indicate the imminent arrival of the end of time itself.[85]

Cardano's autobiography, in other words, amounted neither to a proud declaration that his arts of prediction were wholly valid nor to a modest, dour retraction of his belief in them. Sometimes he wrote as if his pursuit of astrology had cost him time and reputation—as when he complained that his enemies at Bologna "brought me bundles of horoscopes, so that I might give judgment on them as if I were a soothsayer and a prophet, and not as a professor of medicine."[86] More often, however, he continued to ask the astrologer's questions and to use the astrologer's methods. It even seems likely that he set out to write his own life because he had astrological reason to think that his time was almost up. Cardano had predicted he might fall ill and die in 1574, if he actually lived so long, in his commentary of 1554 on his own horoscope.[87] *On His Own Life* framed Cardano's experiences, tragic and triumphant alike, in the terms that he had always used to understand the jagged course of his life and feelings: as the movements of a being veering as the planets pushed in one direction, his own partly intact will resisted them, and the superior being that Providence had assigned to him intervened on his behalf.

If the basic tools of astrology remained stable over the centuries and millennia, their applications—as we have repeatedly seen—depended on the changing needs and situations of their users and their clients and readers. Cardano—like other Renaissance writers from Petrarch onward—felt the need to scrutinize his interior life, mental and physical; to identify the many ways in which his life conflicted with the ideals he professed; and to dramatize these conflicts, not as travails overcome, in an Augustinian narrative of conversion completed, but as torments still felt. His autobiography became as much a dialogue, in the end, as Petrarch's formal dialogue with Augustine, the *Secretum:* the painful history of a debate, in the course of which each half of his divided heart addressed the other, but no final conclusion was ever reached. The mosaic-like format of the commentary on a horoscope proved the ideal mirror for Cardano's fractured soul.

Cardano's astrology, like that of his competitors, offered its practitioner the mastery of time lived and time to come. It equipped him with the tools he felt he needed to report on and evaluate his mental and physical world. In its assumptions and methods, it belonged to the classical tradition. But in the way he applied it, it fitted seamlessly into that culture of endless curiosity and self-scrutiny which historians have long identified with the Renaissance. In fact, Cardano provided basic ingredients for the modern vision of his own period. In an age conversant with Latin, his curious and uncanny autobiography attracted many readers until late in the nineteenth century. Jacob Burckhardt still took it as a given, in his essay of 1860, *The Civilization of the Renaissance in Italy,* that he did not need to describe or analyze *De vita propria,* since all his readers would be familiar with it. It may seem paradoxical that Burckhardt saw the work of an astrologer as connected to the passionate introspection and zealous cult of fame that marked the Italians of the Renaissance as the first moderns. Though Burckhardt was fascinated by some of the forms that astrological practice and theory took in medieval and early modern Italy, he did not see the art as an integral part of Renaissance culture. For the most part, in fact, he treated it as an obstacle to the free development of individuality. But he recognized, as later historians sometimes have not, that a practitioner of this ancient discipline could describe the condition of modernity.

chapter eleven

THE ASTROLOGER AS EMPIRICIST

CARDANO'S ASTROLOGY was, in a way characteristic of its time, an empirical art. It rested on the belief that a sufficiently large collection of carefully established genitures would provide a solid foundation for astrology as a whole. Everyone interested in astrology, from eager proponents to angry opponents, knew that an individual nativity could be faked or corrupted, that any given astrological principle might be falsified by the discovery of contradictory instances. But almost everyone also believed that a finite number of cases would suffice to settle all the outstanding questions, rigorously and fully. John Aubrey, for example, blamed the defects of the art not on its principles but on its practitioners. And he described his own *Brief Lives* as the sort of foundational database that could repair all major defects:

> Ital. Prov: *É Astrologia, ma non é Astrologo.* we haue not that Science yet perfect. 'Tis one of the Desiderata. The way to make it perfect is to gett a supellex of true Genitures. in order wherunto I have with much care collected these ensueing, wch the Astrologers may rely on; for I have sett downe none on randome, or doubtfull information, but from their owne mouthes, qd NB.[1]

Like Aubrey's general sentiments, his particular astrological practices reflected his continued faith in the solidity of Cardano's astrological work. He quoted Cardano and Schöner side by side, as equally valid sources of interpretive principles: "for sayeth Cardan, Jupiter in sexta domo morbos denegat aut leves praestat. Schoner also sayeth, si Venus Mercurius et Sol Lunam aspicientes inveniuntur, Natus erit longaevae vitae, et sanus."[2] Like Cardano, Aubrey carefully recorded many of the sources from which he had drawn genitures.[3]

Like Cardano too, Aubrey admitted that his knowledge was not always soundly based. He preserved a letter from Anthony Wood, for example, which made clear how hard even a well-born and erudite informant could find it to provide an astrologer with all the necessary data: "My Nativity I cannot yet retrive: but by talking with an ancient servant of my father, I find I was borne on the 17 of Decemb. but ye year when I am not certain? 'twas possibly about 1647. Jo: Selden was borne the 16 of Decemb. and Sr Symonds Dews the 17 but of these matters I shall tell you more when my trouble is over."[4] Aubrey tried consistently to assure himself, and his potential readers, that he had reason to trust his data and their sources.

Like Cardano, Aubrey took a special interest in strange cases, the lives and deaths of executed criminals, for example.[5] And like Cardano, Aubrey knew that astrologers saw themselves as expert on individual psychology—above all, that of erudite and saturnine scholars like those who generally practiced the art. On that pertinacious self-scrutinizer "Democritus Junior" (Sir Thomas Browne), for example, Aubrey reflected, ironically: " 'tis whispered, that non obstante all his Astrologie, and his booke of melancholie, that he ended his dayes in that chamber by Hanging himselfe."[6]

Even those less enthusiastic about astrology than Aubrey accepted the terms on which Cardano had based his discussion. Pierre Gassendi, for example, savagely attacked incompetent astrologers in his *Syntagma.* But he based his criticism on exactly the same sorts of evidence on which Aubrey had rested his defense. Gassendi examined Nostradamus' genitures of notables, comparing them to the lives they actually led. For Antoine Suffren, he gleefully pointed out, Nostradamus had predicted a long beard, discolored teeth, and a bowed back; but the gentleman in question actually kept his jaw clean-shaven, his teeth white, and his back erect to the end of his life.[7] By compiling such particulars, Gassendi hoped to expose the systematic flaws in astrological practice. There were occasional dissenters. John Dee, as we have seen, tried to make a rigorous mathematical analysis of all the relations that could obtain among the planets and stars in a given geniture—an enterprise which, taken to its logical conclusion, would have shown the impossibility of ever collecting enough empirical data to support the kinds of general statement Cardano and his colleagues regularly made. But in this respect Dee remained an isolated figure. Cardano's Hippocratic, case-by-case approach remained the model for an empirical, critical astrology until deep in the century after his death.

But Cardano's astrology was empirical in a second, more alien sense as well. It represented an effort to study, as directly as possible, his own body and soul and those of many others. Unlike Cardano's dogged efforts to compile data, his notion of how to study them, and the ways in which he tried to put it into practice, are strikingly unfamiliar now—and do not much resemble the interpretive ways of the New Philosophers of the seventeenth century. Cardano drew his hermeneutical tools, as we have seen, from the astrological tradition. And they focused his attention on a specific range of connections between the minutest and most ephemeral phenomena of consciousness, the drifting thoughts and uncontrolled feelings that he recorded so intently, and the highest, most changeless, and most beautiful entities in his universe: the planets and the stars.

The astrologer's way of tracing the connections between the heavenly and the human body was peculiar. Philosophers who imagined themselves as looking down to earth from the dizzying vantage point of the heavens normally did so in order to distance themselves from trivial concerns, to master the deeper realities of the cosmic order. Marcus Aurelius—whom, as we have seen, Cardano tried to use as his guide into the moral life—laid special weight on this form of mental discipline. His constant efforts to show that things of the world and the body had no substantial worth, as Carlo Ginzburg has recently argued, represented an effort to make alienation from all everyday concerns the mark of wisdom. And the royal road to alienation lay through a consistent effort to contemplate the vast expanse of space and time in the universe—and thus to remove oneself from the momentary concerns, which were revealed, when they appeared before this immense backdrop, as worthless. Marcus Aurelius' sometimes puzzling questions and riddles formed organic parts of a rationally conceived program of mental and spiritual exercises.[8]

For Cardano and other astrologers, by contrast, the cosmic perspective that lent distance had a radically different value. It concentrated their attention on the local and the ephemeral. Examining the stars that shone at a client's birth, watching the movements of the planets during an illness, made the contours of the client's permanent character, even the minor ones, and the details of his short-term case history, even its ephemeral fluctuations, stand out with a new clarity. Distance enhanced the astrologers' promiscuous attention to the kinds of detail philosophers disdained. Their cosmic viewpoint focused and intensified their intimate contact with the emotional and the corporeal side of each individual life, as if a viewpoint on the celestial pole or at the mid-heaven actually magnified the minute details of individual life on earth. In the world of the astrologers, opposition might not be true friendship, but distance could be true intimacy.[9]

Cardano's cosmos and his body intersected at every moment and at every turn. The corruptible and changeable was thus invested with something of the deep and permanent interest of the celestial sublime which governed it. The ancient, authoritarian tradition of astrology, with all its stiff templates for classifying and judging human character and action, could still provide a flexible and precise way to describe and judge the intimately human. In this special, sixteenth-century sense, astrology could become a disciplined, empirical inquiry into the depths of the self. It both prescribed profound exercises in characterology and introspection and stimulated inventive exercises in expressing and recording their results. Some of those who lost faith in the explanatory mechanisms that Cardano and other astrologers still employed, or claimed to have lost it, like Giambattista della Porta, retained their confidence in the readings of human bodies and spirits that the astrologers had obtained. Della Porta, writing after a papal bull of 1586 had forbidden the practice of astrology, explicitly denied the influence of the stars. But he cast his *Celestial Physiognomics* in astrological terms nonetheless. The seven different natures of the planets still provided the basic categories with which he classified the human temperaments.[10]

As consistently as their contemporaries who scrutinized politics and history, the Machiavellians who looked for "the effective truth of things" and the Stoics who wrote their selves into a disciplined state, the astrologers and their clients used rational means to explore their worlds and their selves, and to master them. Like the disciplines now called psychology, political theory, and moral philosophy, which are still considered both rational and indispensable, astrology provided sixteenth-century scholars and rulers with what most of them saw as fundamental tools for analyzing and controlling their societies, their bodies, and their souls.

NOTES
BIBLIOGRAPHY
INDEX

NOTES

The notes that follow provide, when Cardano himself is quoted, page references both to his original publications and to his ten-volume *Opera omnia,* ed. C. Spon (Lyons, 1663; hereafter *O*). This work, reprinted in Stuttgart–Bad Canstatt in 1966 and in New York in 1967, is widely available in major libraries throughout the West. Passages from Cardano, accordingly, have usually not been quoted in the original, except when *O* omitted them, as it did most of his Latin prefaces; or mangled them; or transmitted only the last version of a passage that Cardano reformulated substantively from one edition to the next. In other cases, readers will find in *O* a reasonably acceptable version of Cardano's words. Passages from his contemporaries have generally been quoted when they derive from manuscripts, manuscript notes in printed texts or fifteenth- and sixteenth-century books, but not when they were readily available in modern editions.

1. *The Master of Time*

1. F. d'Amboise, *Discours ou traité des devises* (Paris, 1620), 32: "L'vsage et les affaires apprennent assez combien le tems commode et l'opportunité sont à rechercher, ie vis H. Cardan ja fort vieil à Rome, la chambre duquel estoit paree de rouleaux, TEMPVS MEA POSSESSIO, sans peinture."
2. M. de Montaigne, *Journal de voyage,* ed. F. Rigolot (Paris, 1992), 26 January 1581, 99–101.
3. L. B. Alberti, *Opere volgari,* ed. C. Grayson (Bari, 1960–1973), I, 177. Cf. R. Glasser, *Time in French Life and Thought,* tr. C. G. Pearson (Manchester, 1972); J. Le Goff, *Time, Work, and Culture in the Middle Ages,* tr. A. Goldhammer (Chicago, 1980); G. Dohrn-van Rossum, *History of the Hour: Clocks and Modern Temporal Orders,* tr. T. Dunlap (Chicago, 1996).
4. G. Cardano, *De subtilitate* 18 (Basel, 1553), 523 = *O* III.651: Cf. also Cardano, *De propria vita liber,* ed. G. Naude, 23, 2d ed. (Amsterdam, 1654), 64 = *O* I.15. Cardano describes as his fourth "observatio specialis" "ut temporis summam haberem rationem."

5. F. Chabod, *Storia di Milano nell'epoca di Carlo V* (Turin, 1971); G. Lubkin, *A Renaissance Court: Milan under Galeazzo Maria Sforza* (Berkeley, 1994). Milanese cultural life certainly did not die out. For its continued vitality in a number of spheres see C. M. Pyle, *Milan and Lombardy in the Renaissance: Essays in Cultural History* (Rome, 1997).
6. Cardano, *De propria vita liber* 9 (1654), 28–31 = *O* I.7–8.
7. N. G. Siraisi, *The Clock and the Mirror: Girolamo Cardano and Renaissance Medicine* (Princeton, 1997), 5, 29, 33, 207.
8. See the versions of this story in Cardano, *De propria vita liber* 30 (1654), 79–80 = *O* I.19; and in *Liber xii geniturarum, O* V.521; cf. the episode described in *De ludo aleae liber* 20 (*O* I.271).
9. Cardano, *De propria vita liber* 48 (1654), 192–199 = *O* I.45–47.
10. Cardano, *De subtilitate libri xxi* (Paris, 1551), xvii, fol. 278 ro = *O* III.626.
11. Cardano, *De libris propriis* (Lyons, 1557), 96 = *O* I.77–78.
12. See the fine analysis by I. Maclean, "The Interpretation of Natural Signs: Cardano's *De subtilitate* versus Scaliger's *Exercitationes,*" in *Occult and Scientific Mentalities in the Renaissance,* ed. B. Vickers (Cambridge, 1984), 231–252.
13. Siraisi, 225–227.
14. C. Gregori, "Rappresentazione e difesa: Osservazioni sul *De vita propria* di Gerolamo Cardano," *Quaderni storici* 73 (1990), 225–234.
15. On the Babylonian "forerunner to the genethlialogical branch of astrology that emerged in the hellenistic Greek world," see A. Sachs, "Babylonian Horoscopes," *Journal of Cuneiform Studies* 6 (1952), 49–75; F. Rochberg-Halton, "Babylonian Horoscopes and Their Sources," *Orientalia* 58 (1989), 102–123 (quotation from 110); D. Pingree, *From Astral Omens to Astrology: From Babylon to Bīkāner* (Rome, 1997), chaps. 1–2. On seventeenth-century Rome and London see respectively G. Ernst, *Religione, ragione e natura* (Milan, 1991), chaps. 10–11, and P. Curry, *Prophecy and Power* (Princeton, 1989).
16. See in general S. J. Tester, *A History of Western Astrology* (Woodbridge and Wolfeboro, 1987), and, for the Greek and Roman worlds, T. Barton, *Ancient Astrology* (London, 1994). On contemporary astrologers' beliefs and practices see T. W. Adorno, *The Stars Down to Earth and Other Essays on the Irrational in Culture,* ed. S. Crook (London and New York, 1994), and H. Wiesendanger, *Zwischen Wissenschaft und Aberglaube* (Frankfurt, 1989).
17. Though Babylonian astrologers devised procedures and assumptions which remained central to Hellenistic astrology, their main concerns were quite different: see F. Rochberg-Halton, "New Evidence for the History of Astrology," *Journal of Near Eastern Studies* 43 (1984), 115–140; "Elements of the Babylonian Contribution to Hellenistic Astrology," *Journal of the American Oriental Society* 108 (1988), 51–62; Pingree.
18. For two useful case studies in the transformations that astrology underwent in early modern England see M. E. Bowden, "The Scientific Revolution in Astrol-

ogy" (Diss., Yale, 1974), which deals with theory and practice, and Curry, which deals with the political and social context.

19. A. Pagden, ed., *The Languages of Political Theory in Early Modern Europe* (Cambridge, 1987); J. Goody, *The Culture of Flowers* (Cambridge, 1993); A. Hollander, *Sex and Suits* (New York, 1994).
20. G. G. Pontano, *De rebus coelestibus libri XIV* (Basel, 1530); cf. C. Trinkaus, "The Astrological Cosmos and Rhetorical Culture of Giovanni Gioviano Pontano," *Renaissance Quarterly,* 38 (1985), 446–472.
21. See E. H. Gombrich, *Symbolic Images* (Oxford, 1972; repr. 1978), 66–69.
22. For a good introduction to this cosmological tradition as it was known and illustrated in early modern Europe, see S. K. Heninger, *Touches of Sweet Harmony* (San Marino, 1974). The account given in the text above naturally ignores many nuances and some questions of great importance—for example, that of precisely when it came to be believed that certain stars were malevolent. For a very helpful discussion of the ancient, late antique, and patristic sources on these questions see A. Scott, *Origen and the Life of the Stars* (Oxford, 1991; repr. 1994).
23. J. C. Eade, *The Forgotten Sky* (Oxford, 1984), describes astrological terminology and techniques. For a richly detailed study of the nature and development of the different methods for laying out horoscopes, see J. North, *Horoscopes and History* (London, 1986). For a full study of one Renaissance horoscope and its interpretation, see R. Reisinger, *Historische Horoskopie* (Wiesbaden, 1987).
24. J. North, "Astrology and the Fortunes of Churches," *Centaurus,* 24 (1980), 181–211. See further D. Pingree, *The Thousands of Abu Ma'Shar* (London, 1968); E. S. Kennedy and D. Pingree, *The Astrological History of Masha'Allah* (Cambridge, Mass., 1971).
25. L. Smoller, *History, Prophecy, and the Stars* (Princeton, 1994). Smoller provides an excellent general introduction to medieval and early modern astrology.
26. M. MacDonald, *Mystical Bedlam* (Cambridge, 1981). For some similar forms of astrological practice in Italy, though not concentrated on medical problems, see P. Zambelli, "Da Giulio II a Paolo III. Come l'astrologo provocatore Luca Gaurico divenne vescovo," *La città dei segreti,* ed. F. Troncarelli (Milan, 1985), 299–323.
27. F. Cumont, *L'Egypte des astrologues* (Brussels, 1937), as described by O. Neugebauer, *The Exact Sciences in Antiquity,* 2d ed. (Providence, 1957; repr. New York, 1969), 56.
28. A. Warburg, *Heidnisch-Antike Weissagung in Wort und Bild zu Luthers Zeiten,* SB Akad. Heidelberg, 1919 (Heidelberg 1920), repr. in Warburg, *Gesammelte Schriften: Studienausgabe,* ed. H. Bredekamp et al. (Berlin, 1998), I, 1.2; E. Garin, "Magic and Astrology," *Science and Civic Life in the Italian Renaissance,* tr. P. Munz (Gloucester, Mass., 1978); Garin, *Lo zodiaco della vita* (Rome and Bari, 1982).

29. E. Casanova, "L'astrologia e la consegna del bastone al capitano generale della repubblica fiorentina," *Archivio storico italiano* 5th ser. 7 (1891), 134–144. See more generally A. J. Parel, *The Machiavellian Cosmos* (New Haven and London, 1992).
30. Angelo Decembrio, *De politia litteraria*, MS Vat. lat. 1794, fol. 6 verso. For later evidence about the role of astrology in the Ferrara of the Estensi, see G. Biondi, "Minima astrologica. Gli astrologi e la guida della vita quotidiana," *Schifanoia* 2 (1986), 41–48.
31. See, e.g., the famous astrological woodcut that Dürer provided for the 1496 syphilis broadsheet of Theodoricus Ulsenius, on whom see B. Lawn, *The Salernitan Questions* (Oxford, 1963), 113–128, and P. Dilg, "Der Kosmas-und-Damian-Hymnus des Theodoricus Ulsenius (um 1460–nach 1508)," *Orbis pictus*, ed. W. Dressendörfer and W.-D. Müller-Jahncke (Frankfurt, 1985), 67–72. On the image itself—and the way in which prophetic images from astrological pamphlets pervaded Dürer's thought—see J. M. Massing, "Dürer's Dreams," *Journal of the Warburg and Courtauld Institutes* 49 (1986), 238–244.
32. See J. L. Heilbron, introduction, in *John Dee on Astronomy = Propaedeumata aphoristica (1558 and 1568)*, ed. and tr. W. Shumaker (Berkeley, 1978).
33. F. Guicciardini, *Ricordi*, C 57; *Maxims and Reflections of a Renaissance Statesman*, tr. M. Domandi (New York, Evanston, and London, 1965), 56. For the original text see F. Guicciardini, *Opere*, ed. V. de Caprariis (Milan and Naples, 1953), 110.
34. See *I Guicciardini e le scienze occulte*, ed. R. Castagnola (Florence, 1990). For Salutati's views see his *De fato et fortuna*, ed. C. Bianca (Rome, 1985), 115. A similar argument appears in Montaigne, *Essais* I.11: "Des pronostications."
35. Ptolemy *Tetrabiblos* 1.3.
36. N. Siraisi, *Medieval and Early Renaissance Medicine* (Chicago and London, 1990).
37. A. Murray, *Reason and Society in the Middle Ages* (Oxford, 1978; repr. with corrections, 1985), 208.
38. For the Black Death, see the materials collected by H. Pruckner, *Studien zu den astrologischen Schriften des Heinrich von Langenstein* (Leipzig and Berlin, 1933), and G. W. Coopland, *Nicole Oresme and the Astrologers* (Liverpool, 1952); for syphilis, see the texts assembled in *Die ältesten Schriftsteller über die Lustseuche in Deutschland, von 1493 bis 1510*, ed. C. H. Fuchs (Göttingen, 1843), and the analysis of P. Zambelli, *L'ambigua natura della magia* (Milan, 1991), chap. 4.
39. D. P. Walker, *Spiritual and Demonic Magic from Ficino to Campanella* (London, 1958); W.-D. Müller-Jahncke, *Astrologisch-magische Theorie und Praxis in der Heilkunde der frühen Neuzeit, Sudhoffs Archiv*, Supplement (Stuttgart, 1985); see also M. Ficino, *Three Books on Life*, ed. and tr. C. V. Kaske and J. R. Clark (Binghamton, 1989). (Alchemy, of course, played the most central role in Paracelsus' system.)
40. P. Pomponazzi, *De naturalium effectuum causis sive de Incantationibus* (Basel, 1567; repr. Hildesheim and New York, 1970). See the classic analysis by E. Cas-

sirer, *The Individual and the Cosmos in Renaissance Philosophy*, tr. M. Domandi (New York, 1963), chap. 3; M. Pine, *Pietro Pomponazzi: Radical Philosopher of the Italian Renaissance* (Padua, 1986).

41. H. E. Midelfort, *Mad Princes of Renaissance Germany* (Charlottesville and London, 1994).

42. See A. Warburg, *Images from the Region of the Pueblo Indians of North America*, tr. M. Steinberg (Ithaca, 1995); J. Krois, *Cassirer, Symbolic Form, and History* (New Haven, 1987).

43. M. Foucault, *Les mots et les choses* (Paris, 1966). Cf. I. Maclean, "Foucault's Renaissance Episteme Reconsidered: An Aristotelian Counterblast," *Journal of the History of Ideas* 59 (1998), 149–166.

44. K. V. Thomas, *Religion and the Decline of Magic* (New York, 1971).

45. See O. Murray, review of R. MacMullen, *Enemies of the Roman Order, Journal of Roman Studies* 59 (1969), 261–265 at 262–263.

46. See e.g. O. Neugebauer, "The Study of Wretched Subjects," *Isis* 42 (1951) = *Astronomy and History* (New York, Berlin, Heidelberg, and Tokyo, 1983), 3; *The Exact Sciences in Antiquity;* Neugebauer and H. B. Van Hoesen, *Greek Horoscopes* (Philadelphia, 1959); D. Pingree, *Thousands of Abu Ma'Shar* (London, 1968); Pingree and Kennedy, *Astrological History of Masha'-Allah;* Pingree and B. Goldstein, *Levi ben Gerson's Prognostication for the Conjunction of 1345* (Philadelphia, 1990); *The Astrological Papyri from Oxyrhynchus*, ed. A. Jones (Philadelphia, forthcoming). See most recently L. Taub, "The Rehabilitation of Wretched Subjects," *Early Science and Medicine* 2 (1997), 74–87. For the works of F. Rochberg-Halton see e.g. notes 15 and 17 above.

47. North, "Astrology and the Fortunes of Churches"; *Horoscopes and History; Chaucer's Universe* (Oxford, 1988; repr. with corrections, 1990).

48. V. I. Flint, *The Rise of Magic in Early Medieval Europe* (Princeton, 1991).

49. See e.g. P. Zambelli, "Da Giulio II a Paolo III"; "Astrologi consiglieri del principe a Wittenberg," *Annali dell'Istituto Storico Italo-Germanico in Trento* 18 (1992), 497–543.

50. See *Elias Ashmole (1617–1692): His Autobiographical and Historical Notes. His Correspondence, and Other Contemporary Sources Relating to his Life and Work*, ed. C. H. Josten, 5 vols. (Oxford, 1966); A. Geneva, *Astrology and the Seventeenth Century Mind: William Lilly and the Language of the Stars* (Manchester and New York, 1995).

51. See esp. T. Campanella, *Articuli prophetales*, ed. G. Ernst (Florence, 1977); Ernst, *Religione, ragione e natura.*

52. Nostradamus, *Lettres inédites*, ed. J. Dupèbe (Geneva, 1983); P. Brind'Amour, *Nostradamus astrophile* (Ottawa and Paris, 1993); Nostradamus, *Les premières centuries ou propheties*, ed. P. Brind'Amour (Geneva, 1996).

53. For the development of Foucault's thought see e.g. D. Macey, *The Lives of Michel Foucault* (London, 1993; repr. 1994). Cf. I. Maclean, "Foucault's Renaissance

Episteme Reconsidered: An Aristotelian Counterblast," *Journal of the History of Ideas* 59 (1998), 149–166.

54. Österreichische Nationalbibliothek MS 6070, fol. 25 recto-verso: "Alii se faciles praebent, omniumque facillimum se exhibet Vlysses Aldrovandus qui [ms: cui] horti simplicium qui Bononiae ad Palatium Legati seu gubernatoris est incumbit. Domi etiam hic musaeum habet maxime mirabile, omni herbarum fruticum, caeterarumque rerum naturalium, quae sub oculos cadunt, genere, refertissimum." On Blotius see H. Louthan, *The Quest for Compromise: Peacemakers in Counter-Reformation Vienna* (Cambridge, 1997), 53–84.
55. Cf. G. Olmi, *L'inventario del mondo* (Bologna, 1992), and P. Findlen, *Possessing Nature* (Berkeley and Los Angeles, 1994). Note that Cardano visited Aldrovandi's museum (ibid., 140).
56. Österreichische Nationalbibliothek MS 6070, fol. 25 recto: "Cardanum salutaturis cautio esse debet, ne ipsum in os laudent, ut paucis rem absolvant, rogentque num quos alios libros propediem aedendos expectare possint."
57. The best short accounts of Cardano's life remain that in O. Ore, *Cardano, the Gambling Scholar* (Princeton, 1953), and *Dictionary of Scientific Biography,* s.n. Cardano, Girolamo, by M. Gliozzi. See also A. Ingegno, *Saggio sulla filosofia di Cardano* (Florence, 1980); the important studies collected in E. Kessler, ed., *Girolamo Cardano: Philosoph, Naturforscher, Arzt* (Wiesbaden, 1994); and Siraisi, *The Clock and the Mirror.*
58. G. Ernst, "'Veritatis amor dulcissimus': Aspetti dell'astrologia in Cardano," in Kessler, 158–184, and in Ernst, *Religione, ragione e natura,* 191–219.
59. Cardano, *De interrogationibus libellus,* in Ptolemy, *Quadripartitum,* ed. Cardano (Lyons, 1555), 206–208 = *O* V.560. An English translation of this passage by Jo. Bowker is preserved in Bodleian Library MS Ashmole 176, 214 ro–vo.
60. Firmicus Maternus *Mathesis* 2.30, previously quoted by Barton, *Ancient Astrology,* 2.
61. Cardano knew Artemidorus' work from the 1539 Latin translation, which made it available to him close to the beginning of his career as a writer, and on which he drew extensively in his own treatise on dream interpretation. See L. Grenzmann, *Traumbuch Artemidori* (Baden-Baden, 1980).
62. Artemidorus 1.11–12, 4.20. On Artemidorus' work see S. F. Price, "The Future of Dreams: From Freud to Artemidorus," *Past & Present* 113 (1986), 3–37; M. Foucault, *The History of Sexuality,* III: *The Care of the Self,* tr. R. Hurley (New York, 1986), pt. 1; J. Winkler, *The Constraints of Desire* (New York and London, 1990), chap. 1.
63. See Ernst.
64. See A. Blair, *The Theater of Nature: Jean Bodin and Renaissance Science* (Princeton, 1997).
65. Cf. Taub and H. King, "Beyond the Medical Market-Place: New Directions in Ancient Medicine," *Early Science and Medicine* 2 (1997), 88–97.

2. *The Astrologer's Practice*

1. For this and what follows see above all A. Bouché-Leclercq, *L'astrologie grecque* (Paris, 1899): J. C. Eade, *The Forgotten Sky: A Guide to Astrology in English Literature* (Oxford, 1984): J. North, *Horoscopes and History* (London, 1986); North, *Chaucer's Universe* (Oxford, 1988; repr. 1990). A classic case study is W. Hartner, "The Mercury Horoscope of Marcantonio Michiel," *Vistas in Astronomy*, 1, 1955.
2. L. B. Alberti, *Della famiglia*, Opere volgari, ed. C. Grayson (Bari, 1960–1973), 291–292.
3. See R. Reisinger, *Historische Horoskopie* (Wiesbaden, 1997), for a very full discussion of how a geniture was drawn up and interpreted by the astrologer Joachim Carion.

3. *The Prognosticator*

1. Cardano, *Pronostico*, ed. G. Ernst, in *Girolamo Cardano: Le opere, le fonti, la vita*, ed. M. Baldi and G. Canziani (Milan, 1999), 461. Cf. Psalms 31:10.
2. See L. Smoller, "The Alphonsine Tables and the End of the World: Astrology and Apocalyptic Calculation in the Later Middle Ages," *The Devil, Heresy, and Witchcraft in the Middle Ages: Essays in Honor of Jeffrey B. Russell*, ed. A. Ferreiro (Leiden, Boston, and Cologne, 1998), pp. 211–239.
3. Cardano, *Pronostico*, ed. Ernst, pp. 461–462.
4. Ibid., pp. 462–463, 463–464. For the year 1800 cf. Ernst and Smoller.
5. Ibid., p. 470.
6. Ibid., p. 469.
7. Ibid., p. 471.
8. For Luther's views on portents see esp. R. Barnes, *Prophecy and Gnosis* (Stanford, 1988).
9. Cardano, *Pronostico*, ed. Ernst, 469.
10. See G. Ernst, "'Veritatis amor dulcissimus': Aspetti dell'astrologia in Cardano," *Religione, ragione e natura* (Milan, 1991), 196–197: Ernst was the first to call attention to the *Pronostico*.
11. On the ambiguities of the language of political prophecy see H. Dobin, *Merlin's Disciples* (Stanford, 1990), esp. chaps. 2–3.
12. See B. R. Goldstein and D. Pingree, *Levi ben Gerson's Prognostication for the Conjunction of 1345* (Philadelphia, 1990).
13. R. Rusconi, *L'attesa della fine. Crisi della società, profezia ed Apocalisse in Italia al tempo del grande scisma d'Occidente (1378–1417)* (Rome, 1979), esp. 85–101, 164–169.
14. J.-P. Boudet, "Simon de Phares et les rapports entre astrologie et prophétie à la fin du Moyen Age," *Les textes prophétiques et la prophétie en occident (XII–XVIe siècle)*, ed. A. Vauchez (Rome, 1990), 327–358 (quotation at 342).

15. R. Westman, "Copernicus and the Prognosticators: The Bologna Period, 1496–1500," *Universitas: Newsletter of the International Centre for the History of Universities and Science, University of Bologna,* December 1993, 1–5.
16. See in general A. Warburg, *Heidnisch-Antike Weissagung in Wort und Bild zu Luthers Zeiten,* SB Akad. Heidelberg, 1919 (Heidelberg, 1920), repr. in Warburg, *Gesammelte Schriften: Studienausgabe,* ed. H. Bredekamp et al. (Berlin, 1998), I, 1.2; G. Hellmann, *Beiträge zur Geschichte der Meteorologie* (Berlin, 1904–1922); F. Saxl, "The Revival of Late Antique Astrology," *Lectures* (London, 1957), I, 73–84; D. Cantimori, "Note su alcuni aspetti della propaganda religiosa nell'Europa del Cinquecento," *Aspects de la propagande religieuse* (Geneva, 1957) = *Umanesimo e religione nel Rinascimento,* 2d ed. (Turin, 1975), 164–181; C. Webster, *From Paracelsus to Newton* (Cambridge, 1982; repr. 1984), chap. 2; M. Reeves, ed., *Prophetic Rome in the High Renaissance Period* (Oxford, 1992). L. Thorndike's *History of Magic and Experimental Science* (New York, 1941), 5–6, describes and summarizes a vast number of prognostications written and circulated in the Renaissance. C. Vasoli analyzes the efforts of Annius of Viterbo to fuse prophecy with astrology in *I miti e gli astri* (Naples, 1977), chap. 1. The collection of studies edited by P. Zambelli, *"Astrologi hallucinati": Stars and the End of the World in Luther's Time* (Berlin and New York, 1986), casts a new light on the most notorious single episode of (false) prognostication, the flood of 1524, as well as its larger context. The as yet unpublished Habilitationsschrift of Barbara Bauer offers a more extensive and profound treatment of the transmission and reception of astrological doctrines in this period than any published work.
17. See J. Kepler, *Gesammelte Werke,* ed. M. Caspar et al. (Munich, 1937–), XI, pt. 2, 7–264, and the useful Afterword, ibid., 442–465; on Kepler's astrology see also G. Simon, *Kepler astronome astrologue* (Paris, 1979), and J. Field, "A Lutheran Astrologer: Johannes Kepler," *Archive for History of Exact Science* 31 (1984), 225–268.
18. Ioannes de Rogeriis, *Ad Christianissimum Gallorum Regem Prognosticon anni 1537* (Rome, 1537), British Library C 27 h 23 (17), Aii ro: "Labente anno gratiae 1537 Turcarum Rex cum exercitu suo non irruet contra christicolas in Italiam, nec erit cruentum aliquod bellum, nisi fortasse armorum plurimi apparatus et mavortii tumultus. Nihilosecius plebei et proceres suorum Regum ac Principum tyrannides experientur acerbas et a militibus plurimum exagitati."
19. Ibid., Aii vo: "Cosmus Medices, si venit in lucem horoscopante tertia capri decuria, non longo tempore Florentiae sceptra tenebit"; [Aiii ro]: "Et ante finem anni 1538. eius imperium diruetur, & anima ipsius nefanda ibit ad infernos non reditura lacus. Et (uti speramus et sydera portendunt) impia Machometi secta penitus diruetur ante exitum anni 1543"; ibid.
20. Ibid., Aii ro: "Erunt dein calores maximi per totam ferme aestatem. Autumno magni flabunt venti."

21. C. Vasoli, "Giorgio Benigno Salviati (Drajisic)," *Prophetic Rome*, ed. Reeves, 121–156 at 123.
22. K. Schottenloher and J. Binkowski, *Flugblatt und Zeitung* (Munich, 1985), I, 196.
23. P. Brind'Amour, *Nostradamus Astrophile* (Ottawa and Paris, 1993), pt. 1. The rich material collected in this work—the best-informed and most technically competent study of an astrological practitioner of the Renaissance—deserves far more attention than it has yet received. For further evidence of the care with which *prognostica* were studied by serious intellectuals, see K. Peutinger, *Briefwechsel*, ed. E. König (Munich, 1923), 33–34, 386–392.
24. D. J. Price, *The Equatorie of the Planetis* (Cambridge, 1955), 104–107.
25. Cf J. M. Millas Vallicroza, *Estudios sobre Azarquiel* (Madrid, 1950).
26. O. Cane Gaurico, *Pronostico del anno M.D.XL.* (N.p., 1540), British Library C 27 h 23 (24), [A i vo], [A iii vo—A iv ro].
27. Cardano, *Pronostico*, ed. Ernst, 473. On the *Apocalypsis Nova* see A. Morisi-Guerra, "The *Apocalypsis Nova:* A Plan for Reform," *Prophetic Rome*, ed. Reeves, 27–50.
28. Cardano, *Pronostico*, ed. Ernst, 463. Ibn Ezra saw astrology as explaining essentially all sublunary events, and some of his astrological works which were translated into Latin give the impression that he was a complete determinist: see e.g. *In re iudiciali opera*, tr. Pietro d'Abano (Venice, 1507), xliv vo–xlv ro, lxxxiv vo–lxxxv ro. But he also seemed to state, in certain contexts, that the soul—or at least the souls of Jews who followed the Torah—could not be constrained by the power of the stars. See Y. Langermann, "Some Astrological Themes in the Thought of Abraham Ibn Ezra," *Rabbi Abraham Ibn Ezra: Studies in the Writings of a Twelfth-Century Jewish Polymath*, ed. I. Twersky and J. M. Harris (Cambridge, Mass., and London, 1993), 28–85, esp. 42–61; D. B. Ruderman, *Jewish Thought and Scientific Discovery in Early Modern Europe* (New Haven and London, 1995), 28–29.
29. Cardano, *Pronostico*, ed. Ernst, 465.
30. See e.g. D. M. Fontana, *Ad Illustrissimum Dominum D. Iohannem Benti. de Aragonia etc. . . . Prognosticon in annum 1501* (Bologna, 1501), British Library C 27 h 19 (1); J. Benatius, *Prognosticon anni MCCCCCII* (Bologna, 1502), British Library C 27 h 23 (2); J. Grünpeck, *Pronosticon anni MDXXXII usque ad annos MDXXXX* (Regensburg, 1532; repr. Milan, 1532), British Library C 27 h 23 (15).
31. L. Smoller, *History, Prophecy, and the Stars* (Princeton, 1994).
32. A. P. Gasser, *Prognosticum astrologicum ad annum Christi MDXLIIII* (Nuremberg, 1543), A2 vo, B3 vo–C vo.
33. Ibid., B2 vo–B3 vo, B2 ro–vo. Resemblances between the work of prognosticators in very different social and religious environments were often due in part to their reading of one another's work (the creation of such pamphlets often involved more reprocessing than original composition). Gasser, for example, bought and read the prognostications of the Ferrarese astrologer Antonio Arquato; see Cantimori, 170–171 and n.

34. For Cardano's early career see O. Ore, *Cardano: The Gambling Scholar* (Princeton, 1953), chap. 1, and N. Siraisi, *The Clock and the Mirror: Girolamo Cardano and Renaissance Medicine* (Princeton, 1997).
35. Cardano, *De propria vita liber,* ed. G. Naudé, 25, 2d ed. (Amsterdam, 1654), 67–68 = *O,* I.16. Cf. Ernst, 197 n. 16.
36. I. Maclean, "Cardano and His Publishers, 1534–1663," *Girolamo Cardano: Philosoph, Naturforscher, Arzt,* ed. E. Kessler (Wiesbaden, 1994), 313.
37. Maclean, 335–336, shows that Cardano adapted Luke 4:24.
38. See e.g. D. Kurze, "Prophecy and History: Lichtenberger's Forecasts of Events to Come," *Journal of the Warburg and Courtauld Institutes* 21 (1958), 63–85; P. A. Russell, "Astrology as Popular Propaganda: Expectations of the End in the German Pamphlets of Joseph Grünpeck (d. 1533?)," *Forme e destinazione del messaggio religioso,* ed. A. Rotondò (Florence, 1991), 165–195; Reeves, ed., *Prophetic Rome;* and *"Astrologi hallucinati,"* ed. Zambelli. On the relation between political crises and prophecy, see J. M. Bremmer, "Prophets, Seers, and Politics in Greece, Israel, and Early Modern Europe," *Numen* 40 (1993), 150–183 at 167–172.
39. See in general F. A. Yates, *Giordano Bruno and the Hermetic Tradition* (London, 1964), and D. Cantimori, *Eretici italiani del Cinquecento* (Florence, 1939). On the prophets mentioned in the text see L. Lazzarelli, "Epistola Enoch," ed. M. Brini, in *Testi umanistici sul l'Ermetismo,* ed. E. Garin et al. (Rome, 1955); D. Weinstein, *Savonarola and Florence* (Princeton, 1970); D. Ruderman, "Giovanni Mercurio da Correggio's Appearance as Seen through the Eyes of an Italian Jew," *Renaissance Quarterly* 28 (1975), 309–322. P. O. Kristeller's *Studies in Renaissance Thought and Letters* (Rome, 1956) remain fundamental.
40. G. Zarri, *Le sante vive: cultura e religiosità femminile nella prima età moderna* (Turin, 1990).
41. For Cardano's belief that he lived in a time of multiple prodigies, see *De propria vita liber* 41 (1654), 146–147 = *O* I.34–35.
42. See A. A. Long, "Astrology: Arguments For and Against," *Science and Speculation,* ed. J. Barnes et al. (Cambridge and Paris, 1982), 165–193.
43. See N. Oresme, "Tractatus contra astrologos," in *Studien zu den astrologischen Schriften des Heinrich von Langenstein,* ed. H. Pruckner (Leipzig, 1933); G. Pico della Mirandola, *Disputationes contra astrologiam divinatricem,* ed. E. Garin (Florence, 1946–1952); A. Grafton, *Commerce with the Classics* (Ann Arbor, 1997), chap. 3.
44. L. Bellanti, *Defensio astrologiae* (Venice, 1502).
45. C. H. Fuchs, ed., *Die ältesten Schriftsteller über die Lustseuche in Deutschland, von 1493 bis 1510* (Göttingen, 1843), 16–17.
46. Ibid., 130. On this controversy see the excellent treatment of P. Zambelli, "Astrologi consiglieri del principe a Wittenberg," *Annali dell'Istituto storico italo-germanico in Trento,* 18 (1992), at 501–505, and J. Arrizabalaga, J. Hender-

son, and R. French, *The Great Pox* (New Haven and London, 1997), chap. 5. Cf. Ernst, 201–202.

47. Fuchs, 148–149, 150–152, 154.
48. Ibid., 162, 167, 208, 283.
49. A. Nifo, *De nostrarum calamitatum causis liber* (Venice, 1505), 27 ro; *Ad Apotelesmata Ptolemaei eruditiones* (Naples, 1513), sig. [A] vo.
50. Nifo, *De nostrarum calamitatum causis liber,* 16 ro, 32 ro.
51. A. Pighius, *Adversus prognosticatorum vulgus, qui annuas praedictiones edunt, et se astrologos mentiuntur, astrologiae defensio* (Paris, 1518), 2 ro–vo: "genus quoddam hominum indoctissimum, qui ridicula quaedam annorum prognostica annis singulis emittunt in vulgus, et mendacia sua omnia, sua sortilegia, suas superstitiones in astrologiam referunt."
52. Ibid., 12 vo: "Praeterea in signandis diebus et temporibus congruis pro phlebotomia, pro sumendis pharmacis, et in universum, pro singulis medicinae operibus perficiendis (in quibus certum aliquem lunae ac totius caeli statum eligere aut evitare est vel necessarium vel operae precium) non turpiter solum, sed et periculosissime errasse: cogentes chirurgos et medicos, astrologiae imperitos, intempestiva phlebotomia aut pharmaco interficere miseros infirmos, aut infirmiores reddere"; 13 ro: "Quod etiam suo exemplo plurimos Antwerpiae praesertim (ubi iam nemo medicam artem audet profiteri nisi divinet cum reliquis) ad tam insignem iniuriam sibi inferendam concitaverit."
53. Cf. Ernst, 191–219.
54. J. Stoeffler and J. Pflaum, *Almanach nova plurimis annis venturis inservientia* (Venice, 1506),)(2 recto: "Hoc anno nec solis nec lune eclipsim conspicabimur. Sed presenti anno errantium siderum habitudines miratu dignissime accident. In mense enim Februario 20 coniunctiones cum minime, mediocres, tum magne accident, quarum 16 signum aqueum possidebunt. Que universo fere orbi climatibus regnis provinciis statibus dignitatibus brutis beluis marinis cunctisque terre nascentibus indubitatam mutationem variationem ac alterationem significabunt, talem profecto qualem a pluribus seculis ab historiographis aut natu maioribus vix percepimus. Levate igitur viri Chistianissimi capita vestra." Cf. P. Zambelli, "Da Giulio II a Paolo III. Come l'astrologo provocatore Luca Gaurico divenne vescovo," *La città dei segreti,* ed. F. Troncarelli (Milan, 1985), 299–322; *"Astrologi hallucinati",* ed. Zambelli.
55. A. Nifo, *De falsa diluvii prognosticatione* (Florence, 1520), [A] vo.
56. O. Niccoli, *Prophecy and People in Renaissance Italy,* tr. L. G. Cochrane (Princeton, 1990).
57. Ibid., 167.
58. See A. Warburg and R. Barnes, *Prophecy and Gnosis* (Stanford, 1988). Barnes calls attention to Leonhard Reinmann's prediction of a popular rising in a *practica* published in 1523 (143).
59. Niccoli's attractively neat chronology is accepted by W. Christian, Jr., *Apparitions in Late Medieval and Renaissance Spain* (Princeton, 1981), 184, and by

Bremmer, 168. J.-M. Sallmann, however, suggested that sixteenth-century Italy witnessed a "glissement" rather than a break in the world of prophecy. See his review of Niccoli in *Annales: Economies, Sociétés, Civilisations* 47 (1992), 144–146 at 146. For a very different approach see A. Seifert, *Der Rückzug der biblischen Prophetie von der neueren Geschichte: Studien zur Geschichte der Reichstheologie des frühneuzeitlichen deutschen Protestantismus* (Cologne and Vienna, 1990).

60. L. Roper, "Stealing Manhood: Capitalism and Magic in Early Modern Germany," *Oedipus and the Devil* (London and New York, 1994), 125–144.
61. See *"Astrologi hallucinati,"* ed. Zambelli, and, more recently, Zambelli, "Eine Gustav-Hellmann-Renaissance? Untersuchungen und Kompilationen zur Debatte über die Konjunktion von 1524 und das Ende der Welt auf deutschem Sprachgebiet," *Annali dell'Istituto Storico Italo-Germanico in Trento* 18 (1992), 413–455, discussing and criticizing recent literature, esp. H. Talkenberg, *Sintflut: Prophetie und Zeitgeschehen in Texten und Holzschnitten astrologischer Flugschriften, 1488–1528* (Tübingen, 1990).
62. See T. Campanella, *Articuli prophetales,* ed. G. Ernst (Florence, 1977); Ernst, *Religione, ragione e natura;* J. M. Headley, *Tommaso Campanella and the Transformation of the World* (Princeton, 1997); and, for the fullest study of the relation between Campanella's astrology and social revolution, G. Bock, *Thomas Campanella* (Tübingen, 1974). Admittedly, Campanella used magical means to mobilize impoverished followers whom he saw as exploited by the Roman clergy and others in power. But he himself came to maturity in a highly sophisticated urban intellectual world, on which see the classic work of R. Villari, *The Revolt of Naples,* tr. J. Newell with J. A. Marino (first ed. 1967; Cambridge, 1993).
63. M. D. Reeves, *The Influence of Prophecy in the Later Middle Ages* (Oxford, 1969); cf. the classic study by L. Festinger et al., *When Prophecy Fails* (Minneapolis, 1956).
64. Cardano, *Aphorismi astronomici,* VII.34, *Libelli quinque* (1547), 282 ro = *O* V.76.
65. See Zambelli, "Da Giulio II a Paolo III." Cardano evidently tried one more *Pronostico* (or one more edition of the first one): Ernst, 197 n. 16.

4. The Astrologer

1. Venatorius (Thomas Gechauf, 1490–1551) was a prominent Nuremberg mathematician and preacher who wrote numerous exegetical and theological works.
2. On Gasser see K. H. Burmeister, *Achilles Pirmin Gasser 1505–1577* (Wiesbaden, 1970–1975). I cite A. P. Gasser, *Prognosticum astrologicum ad annum Christi MDXLIIII* (Nuremberg, 1543), A vo: "Communis amicus noster Ioachimus Rheticus haud aliter me ad aedendum prognosticum istud impulit atque elephantum anima serpentes e latibulis suis extrahere fertur."

3. Gasser, *Prognosticum astrologicum,* A vo: "Cum enim hactenus ego Mathematicis disciplinis privatim soli mihi oblectamento fuissem, illisque citra invidiam satis otiose semper domi vacassem, voluit ille omnino ac pro sua in me authoritate persuasit, ut relicta umbra et speculatione (quam θεωρίαν vocamus) in arenam et forum usque descenderem tandem, ac publice etiam quid astronomia, cum in actum exit (unde practicae adpellationem annuis iudiciis obvenisse autumo) circa earum proventus, antequam fiant, discernendos possit, studiosis testatum facerem."
4. See in general N. Swerdlow and O. Neugebauer, *Mathematical Astronomy in Copernicus's De Revolutionibus* (New York, 1984), esp. chap. 1; G. J. Rheticus, *Narratio prima,* ed. H. Hugonnard-Roche et al. (Wroclaw, 1982).
5. F. Cardano, ed., J. Peckham, *Perspectiva communis* (Milan, 1482/3?), ep. ded. to A. Griffo (title page vo = [a vo]): "In tanta librorum cuiuscunque generis copia divino quodam imprimendi artificio comparata appetentes huius clarissime urbis insubrium impressores novi quidquam in medium afferre quod esset studiosis non mediocriter profuturum: persuasique mea opera id effici posse: me illud efflagitantes convenerunt. Cupienti ergo mihi horum expectationi non deesse: remque pretio dignam edere cogitanti: occurrit in primis prospective opus: cum ceteris Aristotelicis libris plene [ed.: plane] intelligendis: tum eiusdem methaurorum tertio maxime necessarium. nam que oculi mirabiliter vident: occulta multorum ratio unico eius suffragio prospici: facileque dignosci potest. Itaque ne tanto posteri beneficio essent immunes: summo corrigendum labore suscepi: opus viro etiam doctissimo nedum mihi grave futurum: tum quod ardua eius est materia: consumatissimoque mathematico indiget: tum quod in librorum id genus raritate exempla nisi admodum depravata non offendi. Accidebat ad castigatam figurarum signationem: que codice etiam bene emendato vix deprendi potest: ex casus positione quam maxima difficultas: ex quo forte factum est: ut in hunc usque diem: perinde ac res ignota latuerit: non quod viros me longe doctiores defuisse putem: Quorum doctrina exactissime emendari potuisset: non enim mihi tantum arrogo: sed quod laboris pertesi rem ipsam: licet maxime utilem: intactam reliquerunt: quam ego pro communi doctorum utilitate: summo meo incommodo corrigendam: imprimendamque esse duxi. Verum opinatus huic meo incepto patronum: qui et litteris: et autoritate plurimum valeret: vindicari oportere: te Ambrosi griffe virum et optimum: et doctissimum: animi vigore: et gravitate Camillo: scientia atque facundia appiis: Scipioni dexteritate: animique alacritate: Tito quintio monitis salutaribus persimilem maxime delegi. Accipe igitur has laborum meorum primitias: qui tuo muniti presidio calumniatores non formidabunt: Multosque tibi viros devincient: Quando tuis auspitiis opus se egregium consecutos esse animadverterint. Vale: meque mutuo ama."
6. Cardano, *Libelli duo* (1538).
7. Ibid., *De supplemento almanach* 1, Aij ro = O V.576.
8. Ibid.

9. Ibid., chap. 2, Aij vo = *O* V.576.
10. Ibid., chap. 14, B ro = *O* V.586. On the uses of Hyginus and Aratus see F. Saxl, "The Survival of Late Antique Astrology," *Lectures* (London, 1957), I, 73–84; J. Seznec, *The Survival of the Pagan Gods,* tr. B. F. Sessions (New York, 1953); S. C. McCluskey, *Astronomies and Cultures in Early Medieval Europe* (Cambridge, 1998), pt. 3.
11. Cardano, *De supplemento almanach,* chaps. 13–14, B ro = *O* V.586.
12. Ibid., chap. 6, Aiiij vo–Aiiiij ro = *O* V.578.
13. Cardano, *De temporum et motuum erraticarum restititutione,* 2, *Libelli duo* (1538), Aiiij vo–Aiiiij ro = *O* V.1–2.
14. Cardano, *De temporum et motuum erraticarum restitutione,* 3, *Libelli duo* (1538), [Ciij ro–Ciiij ro] = *O* V.3–4; cf. A. Grafton, *Joseph Scaliger* (Oxford, 1983–1993), II, 122–126.
15. Cardano, *De temporum et motuum erraticarum restitutione,* 8, *Libelli duo* (1538), [Diij ro–Diiij vo] = *O* V.8–10.
16. Cardano, *De supplemento almanach* 17, *Libelli duo* (1538) = *O* V.587–588; L. B. Alberti, *Ludi matematici, Opere volgari,* ed. C. Grayson (Bari, 1960–73), III, 150–151.
17. J. Stoeffler, *Ephemerides,* ed. P. Pitatus (Tübingen 1548), Prooemium, 2 ro: "Sed neque tamen ipsius Stoeflerini Ephemerides in planetarum congressibus atque stellarum fixarum motibus ab omni erroris crimine purgantur. Quod cernentibus sensibiliter innotuit in coniunctione magna Saturni et Martis anno domini 1536. Quae vigesimoquinto Maii in eiusdem diariis annotatur, cum tamen diebus circiter tribus coelo palam praecessisse, ac vulgaribus per dies plures etiam praevenisse visa sit."
18. See T. Brahe, *Opera omnia,* ed. J. L. E. Dreyer (Copenhagen, 1913; repr. Amsterdam, 1972), II, 57, 155. See also Dreyer's notes, ibid., 444, 448–449.
19. See in general D. P. Walker, *Spiritual and Demonic Magic from Ficino to Campanella* (London, 1958); F. Yates, *Giordano Bruno and the Hermetic Tradition* (London, 1964); M. Ficino, *Three Books on Life,* ed. J. R. Clark and C. V. Kaske (Binghamton, 1989); W.-D. Müller-Jahncke, *Astrologisch-magische Theorie und Praxis in der Heilkunde der frühen Neuzeit* (Stuttgart, 1985).
20. M. Ficino, *Opera omnia* (Basel, 1576; repr., ed. P. O. Kristeller, Turin, 1959), I, 763.
21. Nicolaus Ellenbog to Petrus Seuter, 12 October 1534, in F. Baron, "Who Was the Historical Faustus? Interpreting an Overlooked Source," *Daphnis* 18 (1989), 297–302 at 301: "Figuram signavit caeli cum duodecim domibus, sed gradus signorum (qui omni modo hinc necessarii sunt) praetermisit. Sed nec planetas cum suis signis et gradibus apposuit."
22. P. Brind'Amour, *Nostradamus astrophile* (Ottawa and Paris, 1993).
23. Cardano, *De supplemento almanach* 22, *Libelli duo* (1538) = *O* V.590. The passage concludes with mock-biblical profundity: "Ob hoc christiani erigite capita: qui potest capere, capiat."
24. Ibid., chap. 26 = *O* V.591–592.

25. Ibid., chap. 10 = *O* V.584.
26. Ibid.
27. Ibid., chap. 22 = *O* V.590.
28. For Cardano's effort to account for the fall of Rome in this work see A. Demandt, *Der Fall Roms* (Munich, 1984), 100–101. Cardano's arguments on the longevity of states combine numerological and astrological considerations: *Arcana aeternitatis,* 11–13, *O* X.17–28.
29. Cardano, *De supplemento almanach* 10, *Libelli duo* (1538) = *O* V.585.
30. Ibid., chap. 23 = *O* V.590.
31. T. Barton, *Power and Knowledge* (Ann Arbor, 1994).
32. Cardano used the same form of his name in his *De malo medendi usu* (Milan, 1539), but then dropped it. Even at the end of his life he remarked with evident pride on the possible relationship of his family and the Castiglione, and on the similarity—but not the identity—of their arms; see *De propria vita liber,* ed. G. Naudé, 1, 2d ed. (Amsterdam, 1654), 00 = *O* I.1, and 33 (1654), 107 = *O* I.25, and cf. M. Milani, *Gerolamo Cardano* (Milan, 1990), 57.
33. See *Dizionario biografico degli italiani,* s.v. Archinto, Filippo, by G. Alberigo. Cardano described his friendship with Archinto in *De propria vita liber* 15, (1654), 49–50 = *O* I.12. See also F. Secret, "Filippo Archinto, Cardano et Guillaume Postel," *Studi francesi* 29 (1965), 173–176.
34. In his dedicatory letters to the *De restitutione* of 1538, Cardano said that his work took up questions which had arisen in the course of a conversation on calendar reform that came up in the pope's presence (*Libelli duo,* 1538, C 1 verso): "Cum in Sanctissimi Pontificis Pauli Tertii conspectu sermo obiter de errore motus astrorum, qui ex prepostera temporum supputatione provenerat, incidisset, venit mihi in mentem ut quam brevissime et erroris quantitatem et corrigendi modum perstringerem, idque quam citius per occupationes liceret." Cardano explained in his *Libellus de libris propriis, cui titulus est Ephemerus,* published with his *De sapientia* (Nuremberg, 1543), 57 = *O* I.57, that he wrote these works "intelligens pontificem astronomia delectari." In *De propria vita liber* 4 (1654), 14 = *O* I.4, he described his brief contact with the pope.
35. Cardano, *Libelli quinque* (1547), ep. ded. For Cardano's horoscope of Archinto, see geniture 32.
36. Cardano, *De supplemento almanach* 25, *Libelli duo* (1538), [Biiij vo] = *O,* V.591 [in part]: "Quam plurimas genituras habere oportet, atque temporum considerationes: ac sic in eventibus planetarum inter se concursus ac ad fixas observare in directionibus revolutionibusque. Cumque ex eadem configuratione idem effectus provenerit, saepius statuendum est de congressu illo, aut natura fixarum secundum proprietates illius eventus, ut etiam in reliquis praedicere possimus."
37. See O. Neugebauer and H. B. Van Hoesen, *Greek Horoscopes* (Philadelphia, 1959). Cardano's rival Gaurico was able, working with or through his brother

Pomponio, to use the manuscript of Valens in the Vatican Library, Vat. gr. 191, from which he drew horoscopes for his *Tractatus astrologicus* (Venice, 1552). For the history of this manuscript and its presence in the library, see *Vettii Valentis Anthologiarum libri novem,* ed. D. Pingree (Leipzig, 1986), ix–x.

38. E. S. Kennedy and D. Pingree, *The Astrological History of Masha'allah* (Cambridge, Mass., 1971), esp. 129–190.
39. See J. North, *Horoscopes and History* (London, 1986).
40. H. M. Carey, *Courting Disaster: Astrology at the English Court and University in the Later Middle Ages* (New York, 1992). Worked examples of horoscopic figures with commentary also occurred in Luca Gaurico's *Praedictiones super omnibus futuris luminarium deliquiis in finitore Venetiano, anno humani verbi MDXXXIII examinatae, Figurae coelestes Venetiarum, Bononiae, et Florentiae . . .* (Rome, 1539). The charts in question were computed for the moments when a number of eclipses took place and three cities were founded.
41. When the astrologer projects the paths of the sun and moon outward onto the sphere of the Zodiac, the path of the moon intersects the ecliptic, or the sun's path, at an angle. The head of the dragon is the ascending node, the point at which the moon's path passes upward through the sun's. The tail of the dragon, or descending node, is naturally opposite to the ascending. Many astrologers indicated the position of this as well, though Cardano did not, presumably because he thought it too obvious to mention.
42. Cardano, *De temporum et motuum erraticarum restitutione* 11, *Libelli duo* (1538) = *O* V.12.
43. See North, *Horoscopes and History.*
44. Cardano, *Libelli duo* (1538), Eij ro = *O* V.458 [in part]: "Nec temere aut levi ex causa harum geniturarum aliquam subiungimus, cum unaquaeque aliquid admiratione dignum habuerit. Horum autem principum tam clara virtus eximiaque faelicitas mundo refulsit: ut plurium saeculorum testimonium etiam per historias sit habitura: quamquam extrema [extremus?] non absque summo infortunio finem habuerit: filiorum exilio: regni privatione: proditione: carcereque in quo etiam miserabiliter extinctus est: illud autem omnibus comune fuit, ut eorum acta virtutesque diligenter noverim." For the place of wonder in early modern natural philosophy, see L. Daston and K. Park, *Wonder and the Order of Nature, 1150–1750* (New York, 1998).
45. Cardano, *Libelli duo* (1538), Eij ro = *O* V.458.
46. Ibid.
47. Ibid.
48. Ibid., [Eiij ro]-[Eiiij vo] = *O* V.460 (geniture 3).
49. Ibid., f ro–vo = *O* V.460.
50. Ibid., Eii ro–vo = *O* V.458.
51. Firmicus Maternus *Mathesis* 2.30.4–5; see M. T. Fögen, *Die Enteignung der Wahrsager* (Frankfurt, 1993), 278–282.
52. Cardano, *Libelli duo* (1538), Eij vo = *O* V.458.

53. Ibid., fiij vo = *O* V.462 (geniture 7).
54. Ibid., fiiij ro–[fiiij vo] = *O* V.463 (geniture 8).
55. Cf. e.g. Ioannes de Rogeriis, *Ad Christianissimum Gallorum regem prognosticon anni 1537* (Rome, 1537), British Library C 27 h 23 (17); Cardano, *Libelli duo* (1538), [fv vo] = *O* V.464: "Admirantur quidam felicem genituram infelici exitu terminatam, et prudentiam detestantur, quae tam impium [1663: infaustum] finem habuerit."
56. Cardano, *Libelli duo* (1538), [fv vo]: "Hic cum in hoste etiam virtus laudetur sive dissimulatione sive propria natura omnibus predecessoribus suis melior est, fide hostibus illesa, minore barbarie ac crudelitate."
57. Ibid., [fv ro]: "Oportet autem meminisse coniunctionis que in anno 1524. in Piscibus et in anno 1544. in Scorpione celebratur: non enim parum legi illi favent he constitutiones, quum Arieti Cancer quartum est signum et Leoni Scorpius et Sagittario Pisces. Attolite igitur viri capita vestra et incumbenti periculo et virtute et religione resistite. Qui enim coelos moderatur supra coelos est. Et virtus periculi et terroris sola expers mortem ac interitum nescit."
58. Ibid., fij vo–fiij ro: "nutantem ecclesiam multis heresibus ac male ob luxum audientem magna ex parte restituit: hereses compescuit nec irritavit. Karolo Quinto contra Turcas pugnanti auxilio fuit. Regem Gallorum maximas et diutinas discordias cum Karolo agitantem conciliavit industria labore mansuetudine ac aequitate. Nec minus in privata vita."
59. See Alberigo.
60. Cardano, *Libelli duo* (1538), [fvi vo]: "Has igitur exposui exempli causa genituras: post hec promulgatis ex Medicina libris edam clarissimorum aliorum genituras: Iulii Caesaris Octavianique Imperatorum: ac eorum mortem: Ciceronis Neronis pluriumque aliorum insignium virorum: aut virtute: aut fortuna: aut eventu clarorum: quorum series in septimo et decimo libris astronomicorum iuditiorum descripta est."

5. *Becoming an Author*

1. Cardano, *Libelli duo* (1538), Eij ro: "horum autem principum geniture a me quantum fieri potuit sunt explorate: nisi consulto qui dederint peierarint: nam ex pluribus locis easdem semper nacti sumus."
2. On Regiomontanus see N. Swerdlow, "The Recovery of the Exact Sciences of Antiquity: Mathematics, Astronomy, Geography," in *Rome Reborn,* ed. A. Grafton (Vatican City, Washington, D.C., New Haven, and London, 1993), 125–167; for his correspondence with Bianchini see A. Gerl, *Trigonometrisch-Astronomisches Rechnen kurz vor Copernicus: Der Briefwechsel Regiomontanus-Bianchini* (Stuttgart, 1989).
3. Cf. in general W. Eamon, *Science and the Secrets of Nature* (Princeton, 1994).
4. Cardano, *De propria vita liber,* ed. G. Naudé, 34, 2d ed. (Amsterdam, 1654), 110 = *O* I.26.

5. Cardano, *Pronostico generale,* ed. G. Ernst, in *Girolamo Cardano: Le opere, le fonti, la vita,* ed. M. Baldi and G. Canzini (Milan, 1999), 464; cf. n. 19.
6. See J. Dupèbe's introduction to Nostradamus, *Lettres inédites* (Geneva, 1983), 18 and n. 43, and P. Brind'Amour, *Nostradamus Astrophile* (Ottawa, 1993), 318–319, 372–373.
7. Cardano, *Libelli duo* (1543), genitures 5 and 21. On Corbetta and Capella see S. Albonico, *Il ruginoso stile* (Milan, 1990). For Corbetta's gift see Cardano, *Libelli duo* (1538), Eij ro: "Gualterii Corbete singulari familiaritate utebamur: ipse sponte genetliacam figuram etiam obtulit."
8. Cardano, *De iudiciis geniturarum* 3, in Cardano, *Libelli* quinque (1547) 51 vo–52 ro = O V.436.
9. See L. Thorndike, *History of Magic and Experimental Science,* 8 vols. (New York, 1923–1958), V, 244–247, though he understandably failed to see that Niccolò and Costanzo were one and the same astrologer.
10. Cardano, *Aphorismi astronomici* (1547) 249 vo = *O* V.56.
11. Cardano, *Liber xii geniturarum,* in Ptolemy, *Quadripartitum,* ed. Cardano (Lyons, 1555), 116 = *O* V.532.
12. Cardano, geniture 55, *Libelli duo* (1543), aa iii ro–vo = *O* V.486.
13. See B. Castiglione, *Gallorum Insubrum antiquae sedes* (Milan, 1541), 113.
14. Cardano, geniture 21, *Libelli duo* (1543), Q ii ro–vo = *O* V.473.
15. Cardano, *Aphorismi astronomici, Libelli quinque* (1547), 232 vo = *O* V.46.
16. Ibid., 234 vo = *O* V.52, V.56.
17. G. Zanier, *Ricerche sulla diffusione e fortuna del 'De incantationibus' di Pomponazzi* (Florence, 1975).
18. J. Hutton, *The Greek Anthology in France and in the Latin Writers of the Netherlands to the Year 1800* (Ithaca, 1946; repr. with corrections, New York, 1967); A. F. Marotti, *Manuscript, Print, and the English Renaissance Lyric* (Ithaca and London, 1995).
19. H. R. Woudhuysen, *Sir Philip Sidney and the Circulation of Manuscripts, 1558–1640* (Oxford, 1996); H. Love, *Scribal Publication in Seventeenth-Century England* (Oxford, 1993).
20. Cardano, *Pronostico,* ed. Ernst, 473–474; cf. Ioannes de Rogeriis' similar explanation of why he could not predict the fates of the children of Francis I in his *Ad Christianissimum Gallorum regem Prognosticon anni 1537* (Rome, 1537), British Library C 27 h 23 (17), [Aiii vo]: "De liberis suae maiestatis nihil vaticinari possumus, cum geniturae ipsorum nondum circunferantur, neque ad nostras manus pervenerint"—a clear reference to the regular system of manuscript circulation which had long since taken shape.
21. See in general E. Panofsky, *Albert Dürer* (Princeton, 1943); G. Strauss, *Nuremberg in the Sixteenth Century* (New York, 1966); J. Chipps Smith, *Nuremberg: A Renaissance City* (Austin, 1983); *New Perspectives on the Art of Renaissance Nuremberg,* ed. J. Chipps Smith (Austin, 1985).
22. See in general S. Kusukawa, *The Transformation of Natural Philosophy: The*

Case of Philipp Melanchthon (Cambridge, 1995); P. Zambelli, "Astrologi consiglieri del principe a Wittenberg," *Annali dell'Istituto Storico Italo-Germanico in Trento* 18 (1992), 497–543; eadem, "Der Himmel über Wittenberg: Luther, Melanchthon und andere Beobachter von Kometen," ibid. 20 (1994), 39–62.

23. The development of Gugler's interest in the field is documented by Bibliothèque Nationale (hereafter cited as BN), Paris, MS lat. 7395. The relevance of this codex to Cardano's collections was first noted by P. McNair. See his remarkable article "Poliziano's Horoscope," *Cultural Aspects of the Italian Renaissance: Essays in Honour of Paul Oskar Kristeller,* ed. C. H. Clough (Manchester and New York, 1976), 262–275. For the circumstances in which the text was compiled see BN, Paris, MS lat. 7395, 1 ro: "Sphaera Iohannis de Sacrobusto in compendium digesta anno Domini MDXXXVI per me Nicolaum Gugler. Astronomiae et Medicinae studiosum. 1536"; rear cover: "Est scriptus iste liber Witaebergae per Nicolaum Gugler anno salutis nostrae 1536. Tunc temporis Astronomiae et Medicinae studiosum."
24. For Gugler's birth date, see BN, Paris, MS lat. 7395, 331 ro; for the lectures he heard, ibid., 1 ro–36 ro, 60 vo–85 ro.
25. Ibid., 87 ro: "Quapropter magnorum hominum nativitates non nisi per eas rectificantur quando et a talibus configurationibus naturalibus dependent quia per illas statuuntur. He quia universalia includunt particularia necessario et per hunc modum principum geniturae rectificantur, prout et Ptolo. in quadri: nos admonet."
26. Ibid., 87 ro–vo.
27. Ibid., 326 ro.
28. Ibid.: "Mar. Lutheri nativitas explorata per philonem annus et dies conveniunt. Hors est incerta. Anno 1484 die 22 Octobris. Hora 3 mo. 22 post meridiem."
29. Ibid: "Γένεσις Mar: Lutheri iuxta horam certam quam eius mater indicaverat. Est non inconveniens cum eius gestis. Anno 1484 die 22 Octobris hora 9 post meridiem."
30. Ibid.: "Paulus Eber dixit quod natus sit 1483. die 10 Novembris hor. 11 post m."
31. On Gaurico and the Kurfürsten of Brandenburg see G. Schuster and F. Wagner, *Die Jugend und Erziehung der Kurfürsten von Brandenburg und Könige von Preussen,* I, Monumenta Germaniae Paedagogica, 34 (Berlin 1906), 325, 496.
32. Melanchthon to Gaurico, ep. ded. in Ioachim Camerarius, *Norica* (Wittenberg, 1532), written apparently in early March 1532; *Corpus Reformatorum,* ed. C. G. Bretschneider et al. (Halle, 1834—), II, 570–571 at 570. Melanchthon to Ioachim Camerarius, 12 March 1532, *Corpus Reformatorum,* II, 571–572.
33. See Melanchthon to Ioachim Camerarius, 2 May 1532, *Corpus Reformatorum,* ed. Bretschneider et al., II, 586; Melanchthon to Ioachim Camerarius, ca. 18 May 1532, ibid., 587–588 at 588; Melanchthon to Hieronymus Baumgartner, ca. 18/19 May 1532, ibid., 588–589.
34. Munich, Staatsbibliothek, clm 27003, and Leipzig, Stadtbibliothek 935, now in the Universitätsbibliothek (hereafter cited as UB), Leipzig; see A. Warburg,

Heidnisch-Antike Weissagung in Wort und Bild zu Luthers Zeiten, SB Akad. Heidelberg 1919 (Heidelberg, 1920), repr. in Warburg, *Gesammelte Schriften: Studienausgabe,* ed. H. Bredekamp et al. (Berlin, 1998), I, 1.2, 498–499.

35. R. Staats, "Luthers Geburtsjahr 1484 und das Geburtsjahr der evangelischen Kirche 1519," *Bibliothek und Wissenschaft* 18 (1984), 61–84.
36. Gaurico may well have drawn up the highly critical horoscope of Luther that the reformer saw and mocked as early as 1524: Warburg, 499, quoting Luther to Georg Spalatin, 23 March 1524.
37. Melanchthon to Andreas Osiander, 30 January 1539, *Corpus Reformatorum,* ed. Bretschneider et al., IV, 1052–1053 at 1053. The astrologers divided on the hour of Luther's birth as well as the year; see Warburg, 498–503, 647–648.
38. J. C. Eade, *The Forgotten Sky: A Guide to Astrology in English Literature* (Oxford, 1984), 220–221.
39. For the evidence, which is incomplete, see Melanchthon to Ioachim Camerarius, 2 June 1532, *Corpus Reformatorum,* ed. Bretschneider et al., II, 595–596 at 595; Melanchthon to Ioachim Camerarius, 29 June 1532, ibid., 600–601, partly reprinted in Warburg, 498–499.
40. Warburg, 500–502, and plate II; for more details see E. Kroker, "Nativitäten und Konstellationen aus der Reformationszeit," *Schriften des Vereins für die Geschichte Leipzigs* 6 (1900), 3–33.
41. See Warburg, 500, 542, quoting *Tischreden* 5573, April 1543.
42. Cardano, *Libelli duo* (1543), [Niiij vo] = *O* V.465.
43. Warburg, 543.
44. BN, Paris, MS lat. 7395, 323 ro.
45. On Petreius see in general M. Teramoto, *Die Psalmmotettendrucke des Johannes Petreius in Nürnberg (gedruckt 1538–1542)* (Tutzing, 1983); for his scientific publishing in general, and a translation with commentary of his preface to Antonio de Monte Ulmi, see N. Swerdlow, "Annals of Scientific Publishing: Johannes Petreius's Letter to Rheticus," *Isis* 83 (1992), 270–274.
46. Berlin-Dahlem, Geheimes Preussisches Staatsarchiv, HBA A4 223: "Item meins wissens / so hab ich bisher in truck nit gesehen ein kurtz Compendium, scilicet quomodo primo erigendae sint nativitates et inscribendae in schema caeleste, et quomodo signa, planetae et stellae in tale schema, et in 12 domos, et in angulos domorum (et quid anguli sint) dividenda, welches ir besser wisset, den ichs anzeigen kan." Such invitations could make a great difference to an author, especially of a highly technical work. After Petreius died, Reinhold had to publish his *Prutenic Tables* in Tübingen. As he complained in a letter of 26 July 1551 to Hartmann Beyer (Staats- und Universitätsbibliothek Carl von Ossietzky, Hamburg, Supellex epistolica 45, folio, fol. 393 verso–394 recto [copy]): "Fateor ingenue in hac prima editione mihi multa fuisse certis de causis praecipitanda et omittenda, praesertim cum Typographus tanto a me intervallo abesset."
47. Berlin-Dahleim, Geheimes Preussisches Staatsarchiv, HBA A4 223: "Was aber

die praedictiones sindt ex talibus constellationibus, das dorft man nicht herein setzen / den von solchen viel geschrieben und getruckt ist, und deucht mich ein solch Compendium solt nicht unkeuflich sein."

48. Ibid.

49. For strikingly similar transactions between an astrologer and a publisher see Nostradamus, *Lettres inédites,* ed. J. Dupèbe (Geneva, 1984), 29–33, 36.

50. I. Maclean, "Cardano and His Publishers, 1534–1663," *Girolamo Cardano: Philosoph, Naturforscher, Arzt,* ed. E. Kessler (Wiesbaden, 1994), 337–338 (text of the 1538 privilege); 314–316.

51. Ibid., 316 n. 26, quoting Cardano, *De libris propriis* (1557) = *O* I.67. For a parallel see the two lists, one of "Libri ab Antonio Mizaldo Monluciano hactenus editi et elaborati" and one of "Libri quos idem Mizaldus partim domi paratos habet, partim hodie perficit ac elaborat," appended to A. Mizauld, *Ephemerides aeris perpetuae, seu popularis et rusica tempestatum astrologia, ubique terrarum et vera et certa* (Antwerp, 1555), 151 ro–153 vo.

52. See M. Gudius et al., *Marquardi Gudii et doctorum virorum ad eum epistolae* (Utrecht, 1697), 126, where Marco Antonio Maioragio, writing in 1547, asks an intermediary to tell the Basel publisher Oporinus: "mihi nihil esse antiquius, quam ut per eum notus in Germania fiam"; see in general the letters that appear ibid., 126–128.

53. Cardano, *Libelli duo* (1543), ep. ded., Aiij vo: "Cum Ioannes Petreius Calcographus Norimbergensis, suae quam mihi perspectam esse cupit diligentiae exemplum praestiturus, libellum Astronomicum, alias fortunae iniuria a me extortum potius quam impressum, praelo denuo excudi curaret, rogavit quod sui officii erat, si quid vellem vel adiicere vel emendare. Quod ego hominis votum, ut dignum cui assentirer, non neglexi, aliasque praeter reliqua quinquaginta octo genituras superaddidi."

54. Cardano, *Libelli quinque* (1547), ep. ded.

55. Cardano, *Libelli duo* (1543), ep. ded., Aiij vo: "Atque illud citra iactantiam dictum sit, qui huius libelli compendiosa brevitate futura non intellexerit, neque ea quam numerosa librorum multitudine intelliget.Nam cum infinita sit ars, iudicio non disciplina doceri potest."

56. Ibid., ep. ded., Aiij vo–[Aiiij ro]: "nempe in his primo omnis mortis varietas expressa est, veneni, fulguris, aquae, publicae animadversionis, ferri, casuum, morborum: tum et circa illa tempora diuturna, brevia, media: tum variae nascendi formae geminorum, monstruosorum, posthumorum, spuriorum, eorumque quibus in puerperio mater extincta est: tum etiam morum, timidi, temerarii, prudentis, stulti, daemoniaci, fallacis, simplicis, haereticorum, furum, siccariorum, pediconum, cinaedorum, meretricum, adulterorum: atque etiam circa disciplinas, rhetorum, iureconsultorum, philosophorum, quique archiatri et divinatores, artificesque clari, tum etiam contemptores virtutum sint. Eandem circa casuum vitae differentiam secuti, docuimus quales fuerint, qui uxores occiderint, qui exilio, carcere, perpetuaque valetudine vexati, qui ex

lege in legem transierint, aut ex supremis honoribus in humilem statum, contra qui ex humili fortuna in regnum aut potentiam perveniunt: inter quos trium Pontificum hac ratione geniturae explicantur."

57. Ibid., ep. ded., [Aiiij] ro: "Addidimus et illustris pueri genituram, ut quod nobis obiici solet dilueremus, nos publice de praeteritis tantum pronunciare . . . Non mentiri me sinent parentes eius, cum alterius fratris genituram inspexissem, quod dilucide conspicuum erat, pronunciasse futurum, ut oculo graviter laboraret, et in gena ex ferro vestigium haberet. Anno quinto geniturae subsecuta omnia ad unguem, ut medici omnes diutius quam sperarent fatigarentur." Luca Gaurico was subjected to the same criticism by Pietro Aretino, who called him "il Gaurico profeta dopo il fatto"; Aretino to Fname Vergerio, 20 January 1534, quoted by P. Zambelli, "Da Giulio II a Paolo III. Come l'astrologo provocatore Luca Gaurico divenne vescovo," *La città dei segreti,* ed. F. Troncarelli (Milan, 1985), 299–323 at 318 n. 48. For a nice parallel to Cardano's citation of a successful prediction, see T. Rosselli, *Apologeticus adversus cucullatos,* in P. Zambelli, *Una reincarnazione di Pico ai tempi di Pomponazzi* (Milan, 1994), 120.
58. Cardano, *Libelli duo* (1543), ep. ded., [Aiiij ro–vo]: "Cuidam medico annuam revolutionem reposcenti, cum aliquot felices quas praedixeram expertus esset, extrema moriturum, mensemque mortis pronunciavi, quod et consecutum est. Agnoscis hominem, et nostra adhuc apud illos scriptura manet. Significavi et id tibi privatis literis. Porro ingrata temporum conditio efficit, ut nullis precibus aut praemiis, tum ob negocia, ad artem exercendam impelli possim. Est ibi Romae Theudensis episcopus, qui incognitus extremum et ultimum experimentum meae artis habuit."
59. Both Petreius' eagerness to publish astrological materials and his collaboration with Rheticus are documented by his letter to Rheticus of 1 August 1540, in Antonius de Montulmo, *De iudiciis nativitatum liber praeclarissimus* (Nuremberg, 1540), sig. A ij verso; see also McNair and Swerdlow. Their relations soured, however, after Osiander equipped the work of Copernicus with his deceptive preface, making it less likely that Rheticus collaborated with Cardano on this work.
60. Cardano, *De supplemento almanach* 10, *Libelli duo* (1538), sig. [A vii recto–A viij recto) = *Libelli duo* (1543), sig. D ij verso (*Opera omnia,* V, 584–585) = O V.584–585.
61. G. J. Rheticus, *Narratio prima,* ed. H. Hugonnard-Roche et al. (Wroclaw, 1982), 47–50; K. H. Burmeister, *Georg Joachim Rhetikus, 1514–1574: Eine Bio-Bibliographie* (Wiesbaden, 1967–68), 3: 133–134.
62. Cardano, horoscope 64, in *Libelli duo* (1543), sig. cc ij verso = *O* V.490.
63. Ibid., horoscope 24, R ro–vo at R ro = *O* V.474 ("Pepercimus pudori familiae, ne eius nomen adiiceremus . . .").
64. Ibid., horoscope 35, [Tiiij vo] = *O* V.479 ("Effoeminati").
65. Ibid., horoscope 19, Piij vo—[Piiij vo] at [Piiij ro]= *O* V.468–469.

66. Ibid., horoscope 42, sig. [Xiiij ro–vo] = *O* V.481.
67. Ibid., horoscope 40, X vo–Xii ro at Xii ro: "Causam vero imperii ex genitura, vel amissionis, quod saepius praefati sumus, minime quaerere licet."
68. Cardano, horoscope 40, *Libelli quinque* (Nuremberg, 1547), 143 vo = *O* V.480–481: "Haec est vera Neronis genitura, nec nix nivi similior, quam haec genitura gestis moribus ac fortunae Neronis." In fact, of course, snowflakes are not identical. See also genitures 22 (*O* V.474), 30 (*O* V.477), and 50 (*O* V.485).
69. UB Leipzig, MS Stadtbibliothek 935, 183 vo: "Non nisi admotis ad oculos libris legit"; 186 ro: "hic nimio dolore calculi quinquies de vita in dubium venit. Toties enim scissuram passus est, & quod mireris, caseum nunquam comedit."
70. Cardano, horoscope 48, *Libelli duo* (1543), Z ro–Zii ro at Z ro–vo = *O* V.484. Cf. also geniture 27 (*O* V.476).
71. UB Leipzig, MS Stadtbibliothek 935, 40 ro: "Quia antea fuit nostrarum partium"; 53 ro: "Sub hoc incepit florere Regnum Christi, antea diu a Sathana oppressum"; 164 ro: "Homo superbus Anno 1471 20 Iulii concubuit cum Iuvene & in actu a Demonib. strangulatur."
72. Houghton Library, *IC5.C1782.543l, signed on the title page "Janus Cornarius Med. Physicus" and, in the bottom margin, "Marpurgi, mense Octob. 1543."
73. Ibid., [Miiij vo], Yiij vo.
74. Ibid., Miij vo: "Hic dictus est Graecorum ultimus et ab Messeniis captus in thesaurum carcerem coniectus, hausto veneno interiit."
75. Ibid., Pij vo. Note the emphasis on wonder; cf. L. Daston and K. Park, *Wonders and the Order of Nature, 1150–1750* (New York, 1998).
76. In the *Encomium* of astrology which the 1543 edition of his work included, Cardano remarked that the art was excellent "quippe cum sola, et ante alias omnes, astrorum primo cursus, dignitates, tempora, atque hinc deos ipsos etiam esse docuerit"—"because it alone, and before any other art, was the first to teach about the movements, dignities, and times of the stars—and thus that the gods themselves existed." By the two words "ante alias," before others," Cornarius wrote "ergo non sola"—therefore it wasn't the only one" (dd iij vo).
77. Cardano, horoscope 46, *Libelli duo* (1543), [Yiiij ro]; cf. *O* V.483 for the shortened text.
78. Houghton Library *GC5.C7906.540a. Later in life, Staphylus converted to Catholicism.
79. Ibid., verso of last blank in Cardano, *Libelli duo* (1543); cf. BN Paris MS lat 7395, 326 vo.
80. Österreichische Nationalbibliothek 72 X 5, note on horoscope 66, Aiij ro: "Non est verum: sed Peuerbachi preceptoris eius."
81. Ibid., rear blanks: "Mercurius in domo sua facit hominem ingeniosum, astutum, cautum in omni arte et scientia industrium, presertim in mathematica, philosophia, poesi, et arte oratoria, eritque aptus facere cum manibus omnia quae videt."

82. Österreichische Nationalbibliothek 72 J 123, M ij vo: "Hi planetae coniuncti mitigant sua potentia caeterorum malitiam."
83. Ibid., unnumbered blank at end: "propter hos tres coniunctos multas gignit filias."
84. Ibid., N ro: "Legem Christianam fovet igneus Trigonus, Mahumeti Aqueus"; "Christum praecessit coniunctio"; "Mahumetem non max [sc. Coniunctio] sed magna in initio praecessit." On astronomical and chronological studies in Melanchthon's circle see A. Grafton, *Joseph* Scaliger (Oxford, 1983–1993), II, 126–131. A similar collection of horoscopes, compiled and interpreted for the most part by a scholar with strong connections to both Görlitz and Wittenberg, is bound with a copy of Luca Gaurico, *Tractatus astrologicus* (Venice, 1552), in the Herzog August Bibliothek, Wolfenbüttel, 35.2 Astron. Its title reads: "Farrago thematum genethlialogicorum collecta per A. R. G. L. Witebergae," and it includes themata for the world, the Virgin Mary, and Christ as well as for many historical figures. The compiler drew the geniture of Christ from "Card. Comen. in Ptol. f. 164" (*Tractatus astrologicus,* 126 verso); he also used Cardano's 1547 *Libelli quinque,* from fol. 143 verso of which he drew the geniture of Nero that he copied on fol. 127 recto (a marginal note in a different hand reads: "Hanc veram esse affirmat Cardanus"), and from fol. 305 verso of which he drew the horoscope of Giovanni Iacopo Medici that he gave on fol. 134 recto.
85. Cardano, *Libelli quinque* (1547), Munich, Staatsbibliothek 40 Astr. U 35a. "haec ad unguem tenenda erunt" (24 vo); on geniture 94, that of Poliziano: "Mirum eciam quod iuxta principia tua violente morbo non obierit" (178 verso).
86. "Hic egregie taxas te ipsum" (ibid., 242 recto, on Cardano's critique of those who wrote "inconnexa . . . simul" on astrology).
87. See A. Grafton, "The Ancient City Restored: Archaeology, Ecclesiastical History, and Egyptology," in *Rome Reborn,* ed. A. Grafton (Vatican City, Washington, D.C., New Haven, and London, 1993), 87–123 at 97.
88. Österreichische Nationalbibliothek 72 J 123, [Xiiij vo]: "Gauricus hanc genesim Duci Georgio explicavit, & praedixit velut Alcibiadem aliquem futurum." The same geniture and text appear in Reinhold's collection, UB Leipzig, MS Stadtbibliothek 935, 29 ro.
89. For an earlier case, see the elegant study by J. Armstrong, "An Italian Astrologer at the Court of Henry VIII," *Italian Renaissance Studies,* ed. E. F. Jacob (London, 1960), 433–454.
90. It seems at least possible that Petreius continued to shape Cardano's career as a writer even after his own death in March 1550. By 1554, Cardano had begun to bring his works out in Basel, where the firm of Heinrich Petri became his main publisher. Cardano probably owed his Basel connection at least in part to the famous Italian exile community there. See e.g. his undated letter to Celio Secundo Curione, Hamburg, Staats- und Universitätsbibliothek Carl von Ossietzky, Supellex epistolica, 59, folio, fols. 67 verso-68 recto (copy), with its

budget of authorial news: "Nunc nihil novi est. Totus sum in emendandis libris de varietate rerum, in quibus spero meliore me fortuna usurum quam olim existimaveram. Sed moles negotiorum et operis me opprimit." (68 recto). But Petreius had a family connection to the Petri: during his period as a student at Basel, he learned his trade working as a corrector for Adam Petri. It thus seems at least possible that Cardano came to the house of Petri as something of a legacy. For Cardano's publications with Petri see F. Hieronymus, *1488 Petri/Schwabe 1988. Eine traditionsreiche Basler Offizin im Spiegel ihrer frühen Drucke* (Basel, 1997), II, 1015–1059.

6. *Astrologers in Collision*

1. Cardano, *Libelli duo* (1543), ep. ded., sig. [A iiij recto]: "Addidimus et illustris pueri genituram, ut quod nobis obiici solet dilueremus, nos publice de praeteritis tantum pronunciare."
2. Ibid., horoscope 19, sig. [P iiij recto]: "Itaque cum quidam non huius artis expertes eam [Cardano's geniture] vidissent, meam esse posse negarunt, argumento sumpto, quod nec vitae qua hucusque fungor nec ullius dignitatis vestigium invenirent." Cf. Ptolemy, *Quadripartitum*, ed. Cardano (Lyons, 1555), 47 = *O* V.108; 171–176 = *O* V.151; Cardano, *De iudiciis geniturarum* 21; Cardano, *Libelli quinque* (1547) (= *O* V.450); *De interrogationibus*, in Ptolemy, *Quadripartitum*, ed. Cardano (1555), 206 (= *O* V.560).
3. See the lively account in U. Koch-Westenholz, *Mesopotamian Astrology: An Introduction to Babylonian and Assyrian Celestial Divination* (Copenhagen, 1995), 54–73, revising the classic work of A. L. Oppenheim, "Divination and Celestial Observation in the Last Assyrian Empire," *Centaurus* 14 (1969), 97–135.
4. On these points see the splendid synthesis by G. Saliba, "The Role of the Astrologer in Medieval Islamic Society," *Bulletin d'Etudes Orientales* 44 (1992), 45–68.
5. See e.g. Ptolemy *Tetrabiblos* 1.20.
6. See e.g. K. Peutinger, *Briefwechsel*, ed. E. König (Munich, 1932), 390–393; W. Pirckheimer, *Briefwechsel*, ed. E. Reicke et al. (Munich, 1940–1989), III, 276.
7. Oesterreichische Nationalbibliothek MS 6070, fol. 25 recto: "magna enim cupiditate ipsius opera in Germania et Belgio legi."
8. See I. Maclean, "Cardano and His Publishers, 1534–1663," in *Girolamo Cardano: Philosoph, Naturforscher, Arzt*, ed. E. Kessler (Wiesbaden, 1994), 309–338.
9. Cardano, horoscope 67, *Libelli quinque* (1547), 163 ro = *O* V.491.
10. Ibid., geniture 88, 174 vo = *O* V.497.
11. Ibid., geniture 97, 180 ro = *O* V.501.
12. See J. Heilbron's "Introductory Essay" to *John Dee on Astronomy: "Propaedeumata aphoristica" (1558 and 1568)*, ed. and tr. W. Shumaker (Berkeley, 1978), 1–99.

13. British Library 53 b 7 (owned by an unknown reader) = *O* V.40, 41: "132 Pestilentiam regionis unius ex sola stellarum dispositione agnoscere est impossibile. 133 In constitutionibus generalibus etiam cometas et reliqua incidentia observare oportet"; "170 Mercurius in Leone facundos facit, in Ariete autem sermone gratos. 171 Mercurius in Libra vel Aquario ingenium celebre ut nullibi alias praestat, facit et aliquid in Capricorno."
14. UB Leipzig, MS Stadtbibliothek 935, 15 ro: "Quibus Mars est in quarta in loco abiecto, hi infoelices sunt bellatores, ut Fridericus Maximiliani pater et Franciscus Rex Galliae." For the genitures in question, see 16 ro and 20 ro.
15. Ibid., 15 ro: "Venus in XII denotat meretricem."
16. Cardano, geniture 19, *Libelli quinque*, 125 ro = *O* V.471.
17. Cardano, *Aphorismi astrologici, Libelli quinque* (1547), 298 vo–299 ro = *O* V.85–86.
18. J. C. Eade, *The Forgotten Sky: A Guide to Astrology in English Literature* (Oxford, 1984), 90.
19. Ptolemy *Tetrabiblos* 4.9, 1.11.
20. Cardano, *Libri quinque*, 304 vo–305 ro = V.88–89, at 304 vo. For another profession of modesty see geniture 99 (*O* V.502).
21. Cardano, geniture 89, *Libelli quinque* (1547), xx iij ro = *O* V.498.
22. K. H. Burmeister, *Georg Joachim Rhetikus, 1514–1574: Eine Bio-Bibliographie* (Wiesbaden, 1967–1968), III, 121, 123.
23. Ibid., 181, 186; cf. W.-D. Müller-Jahncke, "Zum Prioritätenstreit um die Metoposkopie: Hajek contra Cardano," *Sudhoffs Archiv* 66 (1982), 79–84.
24. Burmeister, III, 160.
25. L. Gaurico, ep. ded. in. J. Peckham, *Perspectiva* (Venice, 1504), ep. ded., [a1 vo] = Title page vo: "Recepi itaque ac mox depravatos supra tercentum locos in suum candorem restituimus, docuimusque non aliter loqui, quam ab ipso olim autore iussi. Et, ut res apertius intelligeretur, in suos capitulatim tractatulos distinximus, figurasque etiam ipsas pene confusas in proprium locum reduximus, omniaque ni fallor in pristinam dignitatem redegimus."
26. With unusual consistency, Cardano describes his grievance in *Libelli duo* (1543), geniture 30, S iv vo = *O* V.477, and in *De propria vita liber*, ed. G. Naudé, 10, 2d ed. (Amsterdam, 1654), 35 = *O* I.9.
27. G. Biondi, "Minima astrologica: Gli astrologi e la guida della vita quotidiana," *Schifanoia* 2 (1986), 41–53; B. Soldati, *La poesia astrologica nel Quattrocento: ricerche e studi* (Florence, 1906).
28. On the reception of Manilius see W. Hübner, "Die Rezeption des astrologischen Lehrgedichts des Manilius in der italienischen Renaissance," *Humanismus und Naturwissenchaften*, ed. R. Schmitz and F. Krafft (Boppard, 1980); A. Maranini, *Filologia fantastica* (Bologna, 1994). See more generally J. Seznec, *The Survival of the Pagan Gods*, tr. B. F. Sessions (New York, 1953); F. Saxl, "The Revival of Late Antique Astrology," *Lectures* (London, 1957), I, 73–84; and the more recent work of K. Lippincott, e.g. "The Iconography of the 'Salone dei

Mesi' and the Study of Latin Grammar in Fifteenth-Century Ferrara," *La Corte di Ferrara e il suo mecenatismo,* ed. M. Pade et al. (Copenhagen, Ferrara, and Modena, 1990), and "Gli dei-decani del Salone dei Mesi di Palazzo Schifanoia," *Alla Corte degli Estensi: Filosofia, arte e cultura a Ferrara nei secoli xv e xvi,* ed. M. Bertozzi (Ferrara, 1994), 181–197; G. Federici Vescovini, "L'astrologia all' Università di Ferrara nel Quattrocento," *La rinascita del sapere: libri e maestri dello studio ferrarese,* ed. P. Castelli (Venice, 1991), 293–306; and A. Field, "Lorenzo Buonincontri and the First Public Lectures on Manilius (Florence, ca. 1475–78)," *Rinascimento* n.s. 36 (1996), 207–225. See also J. Cox-Rearick, *Dynasty and Destiny in Medici Art* (Princeton, 1984).

29. BN Paris MS lat. 7395, 335 ro: "Si qua fides arti quam longo fecerat usu Firmicus in hac genitura eligeret Saturnum datorem vitae et annorum, et tibi adolescens clariss. annos diiudicaret 57"; 337 ro–vo.
30. Cardano, *Libelli duo* (1543), [Kiiij ro] = *O* V.458.
31. Ibid., geniture 49, Zij vo.
32. Cardano, geniture 98, *Libelli quinque* (1547), 180 vo = *O* V.501. For a delicate and insightful study of a later Italian polemic, one also carried on in part by "allusions and deliberate non-citations," see D. B. Meli, "Shadows and Deception: From Borelli's *Theoricae* to the *Saggi* of the Cimento," *British Journal for the History of Science* 31 (1998), 383–402 (quotations at 384).
33. Cardano, *Aphorismi astronomici* III.145, *Libelli quinque* (1547), 240 = *O* V.50.
34. L. Gaurico, *Tractatus astrologicus* (Venice, 1552), 56 ro: "Si Cosmus Medices venit in lucem labente anno Christianae Lyturgiae 1519. Iunio die 12. hora 2. noctis sequentis (diducto quadrante unius horae) Lucas Gauricus vaticinaretur ei annos 72. vel circiter, si forte superaverit annos 52.63. suae aetatis. Quid autem interea portendant Mars in occiduo cardine platice supputatus, et Stilbon ibidem partiliter, Saturnus horoscopi ecodespotes, et Luna in cacodemone, alii diiudicent." On platic and partile aspects and the ruler of the house, see Eade, 78 and 91.
35. Gaurico, *Tractatus,* 54 ro: "Rex Anglorum doctissimus et ditissimus, sed Lutheranus, iussit obtruncari caput uxori, dein concubinae. Ipse ex febre obiit anno 1547, Ianuarii 17. die, aetatis suae anno 55. cum mensibus 5. diebus 6. ex directione horoscopi ad Saturnum."
36. W. Lily, *Christian Astrology Modestly Treated of, in Three Books* (London, 1647; repr. 1985), 656–657; cf. 651: "The *Arte* of *Direction* being onely to find out . . . *When, and at what time, or in what yeer such or such an accident shall come to passe.*" For a brief explanation of the procedures involved, see Eade, 100–102.
37. Gaurico, *Tractatus,* 54 vo: "Plerique Genethliacorum in genitura eius supputabant horoscopum sub tertia Geminorum decuria. Gauricus vero sub tertia Cancri parte: ex qua, tempore Leonis X., publice praedixerat et victoriam contra Elvetios in oppido Marignani prope Mediolanum, ultimo in obsidione Papiae anno 1525. 24. die Februarii, dum esset Venetiis, in vaticinio impresso et divulgato vaticinatus fuit, quatenus ad hostiles Hispanorum militum manus

deduceretur, a suorum militum plerique ductoribus derelictus: quod ita accidisse nemo ibit inficias. Obiit 1547. Aprilis 2"; 51 ro: "Gauricus multo ante in vaticinio quodam publice impresso haec omnia praedixerat."

38. Ibid., 33 ro: "quum primum ex utero matris prodiit, pater astrologus laetus dixit, hodie est mihi natus summus ecclesiae antistes."
39. Ibid., 56 vo.
40. Ibid., 49 vo: "Ipse persuasus a Christophoro Pogio iussit ut Gauricus quater brachiorum torturas experiretur. Dein hora quinta noctis fuit infoelix, tunc vates 25. diebus in carceres atros detrusus. Itaque misello vati veritas nocuit."
41. Ibid., 62 ro: "Ex Venere cum Marte in cacodemone fuit omni libidine flagrans in virginibus et pueris potissimum."
42. Ibid., 58 ro: "Lucas Bellantius Senensis diluit eius argumenta et aniles fabellas, excusans tamen illum fuisse astrologiae ignarum, sed philosophum excellentissimum."
43. Ibid., 7 ro: "Horam qua iaciendus erat primus lapis in fundamento illius edificii circa Ecclesiam sancti Petri et figuram coelestem supputavit Lucas Gauricus Geophonensis episcopus: Vincentius autem Campanatius Bononiensis cum astrolabio inspexit tempus idoneum, clamitans alta voce. Ecce nunc praecise adest hora decima sexta fere completa ab horologio consueto. Et confestim Ennius Verulanus Cardinalis Abanensis Reverendiss. stola candida indutus cum Tyara Cardinea in capite coaptavit in fundamento maximum lapidem marmoreum perbelle expolitum, et cum stegmate Divi Pauli III. Pont. Maximi." On this episode see P. Zambelli, "Many Ends for the World: Luca Gaurico, Instigator of the Debate in Italy and in Germany," *"Astrologi hallucinati": Stars and the End of the World in Luther's Time,* ed. P. Zambelli (Berlin and New York, 1986), 239–263 at 260.
44. Cardano, horoscope 48, *Libelli duo,* Z ro–Z ij ro; Gaurico, *Tractatus,* 17 ro.
45. Cardano, horoscope 13, *Libelli duo,* Oij ro–vo = *O* V.465; Gaurico, *Tractatus,* 73 ro.
46. Gaurico, *Tractatus,* 69 vo: "Martinus fuit imprimis monachus per multos annos: demum expoliavit habitum monialem duxitque in uxorem abbatissam altae staturae Vittimbergensem, et ab illa suscepit duos liberos. Haec mira satisque horrenda 5. planetarum coitio sub Scorpii asterismo in nona coeli statione, quam Arabes religioni deputabant, effecit ipsum sacrilegum hereticum, Christianae religionis hostem acerrimum atque prophanum. Ex horoscopi directione ad Martis coitum irreligiosissimus obiit. Eius anima scelestissima ad inferos navigavit, ab Allecto, Tisiphone et Megera flagellis igneis cruciata perenniter."
47. Lily, 659. Cf. Eade.
48. Cardano, horoscope 11, *Libelli duo,* [Niiij ro–vo at Niiij vo] = *O* V.465.
49. Gaurico, *Tractatus,* 65 vo.
50. Cardano, horoscope 65, ccij vo–cciij ro = *O* V.490; Gaurico, *Tractatus,* 38 ro. For an amusing discussion of the problems connected with house division,

written from the point of view of one who had struggled to master them in his youth, see H. Estienne, *Noctes Parisinae,* in Aulus Gellius, *Noctes Atticae,* ed. H. Estienne (Paris, 1585), 150–151.

51. Gaurico, *Tractatus,* 21 vo: "Lucas vero Gauricus in mille propemodum genituris experientia compertum habuit, fuisse longioris vitae illos, qui habuerunt in eorum genituris omnes planetas sub terra, quam qui supra terram."
52. Cardano, geniture 39, *Libelli duo* (1543), [V iiij] vo = *O* V.480: "Hic publice laceratus est, anno 1506, quo ei praedictum fuerat, periturum acerba morte: nam non erat ei dispositor vitae, praeter ascendens. Erant enim planetae omnes sub terra."
53. Ptolemy, *Quadripartitum,* ed. Cardano (1555), 206 = *O* V.560.
54. Ibid., 199 = *O* V.558.
55. See n. 61 below.
56. British Library MS Sloane 325, fols. 71 vo–77 vo (largely, but not entirely, consisting of genitures from Gaurico, with commentary by Smith). On this manuscript see J. G. Nichols, "Some Additions to the Biographies of Sir John Cheke and Sir Thomas Smith," *Archaeologia* 38 (1859), 98–127 at 103–112, 116–120. A note at 71 ro, not in Smith's hand, reads "Hae geniturae ex Gaurico."
57. Bodleian Library MS Ashm. 157. Smith copied Cardano's horoscope for Luther in MS Sloane 325, 78 ro.
58. On Harvey see *Gabriel Harvey's Marginalia,* ed. G. C. Moore Smith (Stratford-upon-Avon, 1913); V. F. Stern, *Gabriel Harvey: His Life, Marginalia, and Library* (Oxford, 1979); L. A. Jardine and A. T. Grafton, "'Studied for Action': How Gabriel Harvey Read His Livy," *Past & Present* 129 (1990), 30–78. His copy of Gaurico is Bodleian Library 4° Rawl. 61, signed on the title page: "Gh. gabrielharvejus. 1580. Arte, et virtute."
59. Harvey, Bodleian Library 4° Rawl 61, 65 vo: "Garcaeus hunc adhuc modum praecipuè commendat propositione 10. et 11. de erigendis figuris coeli."
60. Ibid., 66 ro: "Paridis, et suiipsius Apologia, in Cardani cap. 11: de motuum restitutione. Item alia breuissima de libris propriis. Quam transcripsi in fine ultimi tractatus, hîc."
61. Ibid., 122 vo: "gabrielisharveij, et amicorum. 1580 . . . In primis etiam Cardani duodecim Illustres Geniturae. Item aliae Centum Cardani Geniturae. Ipsius etiam Christi nativitas admirabilis. De cuius Astrologica Analysi, eccè nominatim s[upra], 65.b. Cardani autem brevissima Apologia, de libris propriis: L. Gauricus de diuisione domorum me arguit, sed non intellexit mentem nostram: pro qua etiam scripsit Antonius Alphasianus senator ad me. Nec vllum amplius verbum."
62. Ibid., 78 vo: "Gaurici antagonista: sed pseudopropheta."
63. Ibid., 77 ro: "De Melanchthone satis honorifice, excepta religione: ut etiam ipse Sadoletus de Erasmo, Melanchthone, Bucero, Sturmio. Humanior, et candidior plaerisq[ue] alijs Pontificijs."

64. Ibid., 69 vo: "Confer cum Cardani Genese 14, in exemplis centu[m] Genituraru[m]: quae est Lutheri. Item cum Genese 46. Quae est Henrici VIII. Angliae regis. In quibus iudicia notatu multò digniora."
65. Ibid., 21 vo: "Certè non contemnenda tanta experientia, et autoritas tantae scientiae coniuncta: idq[ue] in Aula prudentis pontificis."
66. Ibid., 22 ro: "Praecipuè hîc mihi observandum videtur, quod Gauricus suam est ausus Astrologicam Experientiam opponere ipsius Ptolemaei artificiosis observationibus."
67. Ibid., 57 ro.
68. See *Dictionary of National Biography*, s.v. Bruarne, Richard.
69. British Library C 112 c 5, *Libelli quinque* (1547), 114 vo: "L. Gauricus scribit M. Luth. natum anno D. 1484."
70. Eade, 26–30, 47–49.
71. Cardano, "Operis peroratio," *Aphorismi astronomici, Libelli quinque* (1547), 307 ro = *O* V.90.
72. Ibid., 307 vo = *O* V.90.
73. Ibid., 307 vo = *O* V.90–91.
74. Ibid., 307 ro = *O* V.90.
75. Cardano, *Contradicentium medicorum libri duo* (Paris, 1564), pt. ii: *Contradicentium medicorum liber secundus continens contradictiones centum et octo. Addita praeterea eiusdem autoris, De sarza parilia, De Cina radice, Consilium pro Dolore vago, disputationes etiam quaedam aliae non inutiles* (Paris, 1565), "HIERON. CARDANVS MEDICVS AD LECTOREM," 298 recto-verso: "neque nobis, quod sibi plerique nostrorum temporum affuisse gloriantur, Mecoenates ulli unquam fuerunt: utinamque non magis fuissent, qui obessent, ita ut sine auxilio, ita etiam sine impedimento fuisse. Solus Sfondratus Cardinalis, annis ab hinc tribus aut quatuor, non mihi levi fuit auxilio: ita tamen ut ob fortunam meam potius propulsaverit iniuriam (neque tamen id parum fuit) quam evexerit. Fuerunt et qui ad Astrologiam impulerint, non tam, ut reor, quod sperarent, quam irriderent artem quae prorsus vana et habebatur et erat. Nempe in tam absurdo labore nihil contulere, ut neque alius quispiam. Fortuna ne id acciderit mea, an temporum vitio, non sat scio. Verum mihi cum illo non secus ac Herculi cum Euristheo contigit. Quae inaccessa enim sperabat, ad illa mittens mundum a multis incommodis liberavit. Sic nos aliqua spe lactati, dum in incerto vagamur labore, Arithmeticam complevimus, Astrologiam quae futura praedicare docet in lucem eruimus: documimusque nullam aliam artem, nec medicam ipsam, minus esse fallacem. Ex centum enim iudiciis tum temporum, tum singularium hominum, mensibus ab hinc decemocto (nam vix duo anni sunt, quo tantum absolvimus laborem) editis, nullum irritum fuit. Verum privatim ab initio, non tantum quod metueremus infamiam, sed ob indignationem potius ista prosequebantur, suntque huiusce rei in edito anno praeterito libro non pauca experimenta. Dii boni, quantum potest invidia! Olim cum medicus essem, astrologiae vero

ignarus, pro astrologo habebar, pro medico non habebar, nunc defervescente paululum invidia, medicus sum ex toto, non astrologus. Ergo ea de causa, ut essem quod non essem, non essem quod essem, quasi ludibrium de me agente fortuna, liberalitatem Alphonsi Avali Principis expertus sum. Qui quandiu non alieno, sed suo vixit arbitrio, et splendidus, et liberalis, et virtutum amantissimus fuit."

7. The Astrologer as Political Counsellor

1. F. Baron, *Doctor Faustus from History to Legend* (Munich, 1978), 42–44.
2. Cardano, geniture 17, *Libelli duo* (1543), Pij ro–vo at Pij vo = *O* V.467–468 at 468.
3. Cardano, geniture 88, *Libelli quinque* (1547), 174 vo = *O* V.497.
4. Ibid., geniture 77, 169 ro = V.494.
5. Ibid., geniture 82, 171 vo = V.496.
6. F. A. Yates, *The Art of Memory* (Chicago and London, 1966), 134, 136; L. Bolzoni, *Il teatro della memoria* (Padua, 1984).
7. Cardano, *De propria vita liber*, ed. G. Naudé, 10, 2d ed. (Amsterdam, 1654), 50 = *O* I.12.
8. See C. Vianello, "Feste, tornei, congiure nel cinquecento milanese," *Archivio storico lombardo* n.s. 1 (1936), 370–423 at 380–381.
9. Berlin-Dahlem, Geheimes Preussisches Staatsarchiv, HBA A4 214: "Cum autem ex sermone Cels. V. intellexissem, Celsitudinem Vestram expetere aliquarum nativitatum longiorem enarrationem, misi hanc epistolam meae voluntatis declarandae caussa. Offero ea in re meam operam, si Celsitudo Vestra significaverit mihi, quas geneses enarrari velit. Nos in scholis occupati non possumus multas enarrare. Longa est enim computatio. Sed cum Celsitudo Vestra optime sentiat de his artibus et literas magna virtute tueatur, declarandae gratitudinis caussa libenter aliquas geneses Celsitudini Vestrae enarrabo."
10. Ibid., 217: "Proinde cur enarrationes genesium nondum mitto, de quibus nominatim Vestra Celsitudo ad me scripsit."
11. Ibid., 223: "et plurima mea commoda neglexi, quae tum ex iudiciis nativitatum apud reges, principes et alios claros viros, tum etiam aliis honestis viis comparare mihi poteram, ut multi norunt."
12. See E. Kroker, "Nativitäten und Konstellationen aus der Reformationszeit," *Schriften des Vereins für die Geschichte Leipzigs* 6 (1900), 3–33.
13. W. Sherman, *John Dee* (Amherst, 1995).
14. Smith's collection of horoscopes is British Library MS Sloane 325; see N. Clulee, *John Dee's Natural Philosophy: Between Religion and Science* (London and New York, 1988), 246 n. 23 and chap. 5 above.
15. M. Ficino, *De vita coelitus comparanda* (Venice, 1516), fol. 160 ro: "Vidi equidem lapillum Florentiam advectum ex India, ibi e capite draconis erutum, rotundum ad numi figuram, punctis ordine quam plurimis quasi stellis natu-

raliter insignitum, qui aceto perfusus movebatur parumper in rectum, immo obliquum, mox ferebatur in gyrum, donec exhalaret vapor aceti." On the origins and evolution of this passage see B. P. Copenhaver, "Hermes Trismegistus, Proclus, and the Question of a Philosophy of Magic in the Renaissance," *Hermeticism and the Renaissance,* ed. I. Merkel and A. G. Debus (Washington, D.C., London, and Toronto, 1988), 79–110 at 89, 100, esp. 100 n. 64.

16. M. Ficino, *Three Books on Life,* ed. and tr. C. V. Kaske and J. R. Clark (Binghamton, 1989), 316–317. According to Clulee, Dee read Ficino's book a decade after he met Cardano, but the nature of their joint interest in the stone presumably can be connected to what Dee eventually found in the text by which he entered his recollection.
17. Ptolemy, *Quadripartitum,* ed. Cardano (Basel, 1554), 10–11 = *O* V.100.
18. Dee, marginal note in his copy of Ficino (Folger Shakespeare Library BF 1501 J2 copy 2): "Similem ego lapidem vidi et eiusdem qualitatis: anno 1552 vel 1553. Aderant Cardanus Mediolanensis, Ioannes Franciscus, et Monsier Braudaulphin Legatus Regis Gallici in aedibus legati in Sowthwerk." The incident was not unique: Cardano also inspected a stone which resembled a meteorite in the collection of John Hamilton's physician Gulielmus Casanatus. Curiosity, in the sixteenth century, was often closely linked to civility. See L. Daston and K. Park, *Wonders and the Order of Nature, 1150–1750* (New York, 1998), 165.
19. P. Brind'Amour, *Nostradamus astrophile* (Ottawa, 1993), 306–307.
20. Cardano, *Liber xii geniturarum,* in Ptolemy, *Quadripartitum,* ed. Cardano (Lyons, 1555), 49–51 = *O* V.515.
21. N. Siraisi, *The Clock and the Mirror: Girolamo Cardano and Renaissance Medicine* (Princeton, 1997), 33–35.
22. Cardano, *Liber xii geniturarum* (1555), 25 = *O* V.508.
23. Ibid., 26 = *O* V.509.
24. Ibid., 141 = *O* V.541.
25. Ibid., 147 = *O.* V.543.
26. Ibid.
27. Ptolemy *Tetrabiblos* 4.7.
28. UB Leipzig, MS Stadtbibliothek 935, 14 vo: "Septima domus mulieris, si est ascendens viri, significat tranquillam coniunctionem viri et mulieris."
29. Anonymous note on the recto of the last blank in a copy of Cardano, *Libelli duo* (1543), Vienna, Österreichische Nationalbibliothek, 72 X 5: "Huic geniturae Ladislai comparavit Io: de monte regio genituram suam sic ut sequitur: Item ascendens nativitatis mee non differt ab ascendente huius per 12 gradus, igitur amicitie offitia faciet mihi natus iste. Item in loco Iovis in nativitate mea est luna in nativitate eius."
30. Cardano, *Liber xii geniturarum* (1555), 37–38 = *O* V.512.
31. Ibid.
32. Ibid. Cf. Cardano, *De propria vita liber,* 15 (1654), 50 = *O* I.12.
33. Cardano, *Liber xii geniturarum* (1555), 17 = *O* V.506.

34. R. Barnes, *Prophecy and Gnosis* (Stanford, 1988).
35. D. Ruderman, *Kabbalah, Magic, and Science: The Cultural Universe of a Sixteenth-Century Jewish Physician* (Cambridge, Mass., and London, 1988), chap. 6.
36. Cardano, *Liber xii geniturarum,* in Ptolemy, *Quadripartitum,* ed. Cardano (Basel, 1554), 422, previously quoted by F. Secret, "Jérôme Cardan en France," *Studi francesi* 30 (1966), 480–485 at 480. For another account see *De propria vita liber* 13 (1654), 44 = *O* I.11; 32 (1654), 101 = *O* I.24.
37. Cardano, *Liber xii geniturarum* (1555), 41 = *O* V.513.
38. Ibid.
39. Ibid., 30–36 = *O* V.510–511. The end of this text in the 1555 edition reads (36): "Habet autem haec genesis contrarietates mirabiles quasdam, velut morbosus ad senectam, bona temperie, cum uxoris orbus, oboesus et ingeniosus, benefacere et calumniari, ac talia."
40. Ibid., 19 = *O* V.507.
41. Ibid., 5 = *O* V.503.
42. Ibid., 6–10 = *O* V.504.
43. See e.g. Conrad Heingarten's horoscope for Jean II de Bourbon, BN Paris MS lat. 7446, and M. Préaud, *Les astrologues à la fin du Moyen Age* (Paris, 1984).
44. For a full study of one such astrologer and his client see R. Reisinger, *Historische Horoskopie* (Wiesbaden, 1997).
45. R. Castagnola, *I Guicciardini e le scienze occulte* (Florence, 1990), 114–115.
46. W. Pirckheimer, *Briefwechsel,* ed. E. Reicke et al. (Munich, 1940–1989), I, 446, 455, 539, 540–541; II, 20, 44, 104–108, 115, 362–368, 451, 508–512; III, 114, 283.
47. See in general Brind'Amour.
48. Leowitz is best known for his *De coniunctionibus magnis* (London, 1573); see in general Barnes.
49. Nostradamus, *Lettres inédites,* ed. J. Dupèbe (Geneva, 1983), 39.
50. Ibid., 45–46.
51. Ibid., 69–71, 73–75.
52. Ibid., 152–162. One of the horoscopes Nostradamus drew up is in the Österreichische Nationalbibliothek, Vienna.
53. Ibid., 14.
54. Cf. J. Armstrong, "An Italian Astrologer at the Court of Henry VIII," *Italian Renaissance Studies,* ed. E. F. Jacob (London, 1960), 433–454.
55. Cardano, *Liber xii geniturarum* (1555), 148 = *O* V.544.
56. Cf. Ptolemy *Tetrabiblos* 4.8; W. Lilly, *Christian Astrology Modestly Treated of, in Three Books* (London, 1647; repr. 1985), 606–611.
57. Cf. J. Heilbron, "Introductory Essay," *John Dee on Astronomy: "Propaedeumata aphoristica" 1558 and 1568,* ed. and tr. W. Shumaker (Berkeley, 1978), 52–53, followed by Clulee, 73.
58. Cardano, *Liber xii geniturarum* (1555), 21 = *O* V.507 (cf. Ptolemy *Tetrabiblos* 3.10).

59. Ibid.
60. Ibid.
61. Ibid., 21–22 = V.507.
62. Ibid., 22 = V.507.
63. Ibid., 23 = *O* V.508.
64. Ibid.
65. Österreichische Nationalbibliothek MS 7433, e.g. 2 verso–3 recto: "Immo, ni me celestia fallant, procul dubio Marte tuo poteris Rex invictissime Regum Turcharum rabiem mox superare malam, ipsorumque Ducem manibus post terga revinctum duces. Dein Magno Caesare maior eris. Nil profecto blandior tuae Maiestati"; 10 recto (revolution for 1534–35): "et uti reor Constantinopolitanae urbis sceptra et coronam suscipies uti ex illius horoscopo et annuae huius conversionis elicitur." Gaurico suffered a more public catastrophe when the death of Henri II in a tournament prevented him from leading the triumphal career the astrologer had predicted. See g. Minois, *Geschichte der Zukunft,* tr. E. Moldenhauer (Düsseldorf and Zurich, 1998), 409.
66. Cardano, *Liber xii geniturarum* (1555), 22 = *O* V.507–508. Cardano thus both has his cake—shows that his art could have predicted the king's imminent death—and eats it too—by insisting that he is too honest to pretend that he had carried out the prediction properly and concealed the results. For Cardano's later and more optimistic view on this episode see *De propria vita liber* 42 (1654), 155 = *O* I.36.
67. Cf. M. Muccillo, "Luca Gaurico: astrologie e 'prisca theologia,'" *Nouvelles de la République des Lettres,* 2 (1990), 21–44.
68. On the social history of astrology in Rome see the recent studies of M. T. Fögen, *Die Enteignung der Wahrsager* (Frankfurt, 1993); D. Potter, *Prophets and Emperors* (Cambridge, Mass., 1994); and T. S. Barton, *Power and Knowledge* (Ann Arbor, 1994). On the political activities of medieval astrologers see H. M. Carey, *Courting Disaster: Astrology at the English Court and University in the Later Middle Ages* (London, 1992).
69. Firmicus Maternus *Mathesis* 2.30.5; for the original context of this argument—which perhaps reflected Diocletian's insistence on his own control of all earthly powers and events, his refusal to accept, as earlier emperors had, the superiority of the skies to his own will—see Fögen, 276–284.
70. Ptolemy, *Quadripartitum,* ed. Cardano (1555), 76 = *O* V.118. Cf. *Dictionary of Scientific Biography,* s.v. Firmicus Maternus, by D. Pingree.
71. Gaurico, *Tractatus,* 49 verso: "Itaque misello vati veritas nocuit."
72. Cardano, *De interrogationibus liber,* in Ptolemy, *Quadripartitum,* ed. Cardano (1555), 206 = *O* V.560.
73. Cardano, *Liber xii geniturarum* (1555), 42–44; later version in *O* V.513–514; see Secret. Cardano recorded receipt of a letter from Ranconet in *De propria vita liber* 32 (1654), 101 = *O* I.24, and borrowed a book from him (*Quadripartitum,* 1555, 2).

74. Cardano, *Liber xii geniturarum* (1555), 53–55 = *O* V.516.
75. Ibid., 56 = *O* V.516.
76. Ibid., 56 = *O* V.516.

8. Classical Astrology Restored

1. On Cardano's relationship with Alciato see *De propria vita liber*, ed. G. Naudé, 15, 2d ed. (Amsterdam, 1654), 50 = *O* I.12; 48, 198 = *O* I.46.
2. C. Dionisotti, *Europe in Sixteenth-Century Italian Literature* (Oxford, 1971).
3. Cardano, *Libelli duo* (1543), O ij ro–vo = *O* V.466. On Alciato see in general *Dizionario biografico degli italiani*, s.v. Alciato, by R. Abbondanza.
4. See in general W. S. Heckscher, *The Princeton Alciato Companion* (New York, 1989).
5. A. Alciato, *Emblem* 102, "Quae supra nos, nihil ad nos," in *Emblemata*, ed. C. Mignault (Antwerp, 1578), 348–349 at 349:

   roduntur variis prudentum pectora curis
   qui caeli affectant scire deumque vices.

   In his commentary on this emblem, Mignault emphasized that it applies to philosophers who claim to know more than human beings can, but he also recognized that "poterit etiam non incommode torqueri in eos qui astrologi iudiciarii vulgo nuncupantur, quorum animus quantis vagetur erroribus, alii viderint."
6. Ibid., *Emblem* 103, "In astrologos," 353:

   Astrologus caveat quicquam praedicere; praeceps
   Nam cadet impostor dum supra astra volat.

   Mignault, in his commentary on this emblem, thanks his friend Franciscus Juret, who had shown him Pico's *Disputationes* (2.9), which discussed the allegorical interpretation of Icarus as a failed astrologer (Alciato, *Emblemata*, ed. Mignault, 353–355 at 354). Though Mignault did not suggest this explicitly, it seems at least possible that Alciato drew here on astrology's most notorious Renaissance critic. G. Ernst was the first to comment on the relevance of these emblems to Cardano, in "'Veritatis amor dulcissimus': aspetti di astrologia in Cardano," *Religione, ragione e natura* (Milan, 1991), 199. Cf. also C. Ginzburg, *Clues, Myths, and the Historical Method*, tr. J. C. Tedeschi and A. Tedeschi (Baltimore and London, 1989).
7. Cardano, *Libelli duo* (1543), O ii ro = *O* V.466.
8. Ibid., dd iij vo = *O* V.727.
9. Ibid. = *O* V.728.
10. See M. Muccillo, "Luca Gaurico: astrologia e 'prisca teologia,'" *Nouvelles de la République des Lettres* 2 (1990), 21–44; cf. more generally N. Jardine, *The Birth*

of History and Philosophy of Science (Cambridge, 1984; repr. with corrections, 1988), and M. J. B. Allen, *Synoptic Art: Marsilio Ficino on the History of Platonic Interpretation* (Florence, 1998), and, for an insightful study of the conflict between the two historical models available for describing the development of astrology—one ascribing it to an original divine revelation, the other to progressive human effort—see S. Bokdam, "Les mythes de l'origine de l'astrologie à la Renaissance," *Divination et controverse religieuse en France au xvie siècle* (Paris, 1987), 57–72.

11. Cardano, *Libelli duo* (1543), dd iij vo–dd iiij ro = *O* V.728.
12. Ibid., dd iiii ro = *O* V.728.
13. Ibid.
14. See e.g. P. L. Rose, *The Italian Renaissance of Mathematics* (Geneva, 1975); D. Mugnai Carrara, *La biblioteca di Nicolò Leoniceno* (Florence, 1991); A. Borst, *Das Buch der Naturgeschichte* (Heidelberg, 1994); G. Ferrari, *L'esperienza del passato* (Florence, 1996).
15. See V. Nutton's brilliant monograph *John Caius and the Manuscripts of Galen* (Cambridge, 1987).
16. For Pico's historical critique of astrology see his *Disputationes adversus astrologiam divinatricem*, ed. E. Garin (Florence, 1946–1952), esp. bks. 11–12, and A. Grafton, *Commerce with the Classics* (Ann Arbor, 1997), chap. 3.
17. See generally W. Smith, *The Hippocratic Tradition* (Ithaca and London, 1979), and V. Nutton, "'Prisci dissectionum professores': Renaissance Humanists and Anatomy," *The Uses of Greek and Latin: Historical Essays*, ed. A. C. Dionisotti et al. (London, 1988).
18. For an exhaustive and insightful treatment of Cardano's Hippocratism see N. Siraisi, *The Clock and the Mirror: Girolamo Cardano and Renaissance Medicine* (Princeton, 1997), chap. 6.
19. Ibid., 127–128.
20. Cardano, geniture 53, *Libelli duo* (1543) aa i vo = *O* V.486; cf. *De propria vita liber* 40 (1654), 144–146 = *O* I.34.
21. Cardano, *De libris propriis* (1557), *O* I.63.
22. Cardano, "Libellus de libris propriis, cui titulus est, Ephemerus," *De sapientia* (Nuremberg, 1544), 422–423 = *O* I.56–57.
23. Cardano, *Aphorismi astronomici*, IIII.65, *Libelli quinque* (1547), 250 ro = *O* V.56 (a passage underlined by a reader of the copy of the first edition now in the British Library, 53 b 7): "Non male omnino videtur Copernicus existimasse, Lunam solam circa elementa versari, ut centrum, nam vere operationes eius sunt a caeteris planetis diversae multum."
24. Cardano did not wholly approve of *De revolutionibus*, however: see ibid., I.69, 212 vo = *O* V.32, also underlined in the British Library copy: "Copernici autem nondum perspecta est recte sententia: vix enim, quae vellet, dicere visus est" (surely one of the very earliest references to Copernicus' main hypothesis in print).

25. Cardano, *Aphorismi astronomici,* I.1, *Libelli quinque* (1547), 207 vo = *O* V.29: "Vita brevis, ars longa." Cardano's own translation of Hippocrates' *Aphorisms* appeared in the same year, 1547, and from the same publisher as the *Libelli quinque;* Bokdam, 57 and n. 1.
26. Cardano, *Aphorismi astronomici,* I.101, 215 vo = *O* V.35.
27. Ibid., III. 141, 254 vo–255 ro = *O* v. 59.
28. Ibid., IIII.140, 254 vo = *O* V.59.
29. Ibid., V.32, 257 vo = 61.
30. Ibid., III.164, 242 ro = 51.
31. Ibid., I.101, 215 vo = 35.
32. Ibid., 307 vo = 91.
33. For a Protestant and a Catholic sample of such views see respectively R. Goclenius, *Synopsis astrologiae specialis,* in his *Synopsis methodica geometriae, astronomiae, astrologiae, opticae et geographiae* (Frankfurt, 1620), where he tried to distinguish "veram & licitam astrologiam ab ea, quae magicis incantationibus corrupta ac depravata est, ex qua illicitum divinationum genus dependet, ut fatalem horam ad unguem praedicere, quod de Domitiano refert Suetonius c. 16," and M. Del Rio, *Disquisitionum magicarum libri sex* (Cologne, 1679), IV.iii.1, 609: "Quando Astrologi verum dicunt, tum multo diligentius esse cavendos, quia satis clarum hoc signum foret, eos pactum cum daemone inivisse, ut ait D. Augustin. et de Thrasyllo Dion. indicat, cum scribit solitum affirmare, quae nuncia longinquis e regionibus adferrentur."
34. Cardano, *De libris propriis* (1557), *O* I.72.
35. Ptolemy, *Quadripartitum,* ed. Cardano (Basel, 1554), 2 = *O* V.94: "Mirum est autem, quod a tam paucis, tam celebris utilisque liber sit expositus."
36. BN, Paris, MS lat. 7305, 5 vo: "Cum itaque stellarum verificationem ad arcis tue Bellepartici meridianum pro era tua absolvissemus, ultro se nobis obtulit divi Ptholomei quattuor tractatuum liber: in quo et totius iudiciarie astrologie radices et regule quadruviali naturalique ratiocinatione continentur. Cuius tanta erat obscuritas, tum propter succinctam sui brevitatem, tum propter verborum ponderosam gravitatem, ut vix a quocunque intelligi potuerit. Hunc interpretandum suscepimus, clausas eius sententias aperturi, quo studiosorum universitati prodessemus, et Ptholomei nostri lectio familiarior efficeretur. Hic enim (veluti aureo suo splendore luna cuncta minora superat sidera) omnes astronomie scriptores facile antecedit."
37. Ibid.: "Quem ante nos Hali doctissimus philosophus exactissime interpretatus est, cuius commentariis contenti fuissemus, nisi transcriptorum inertia plerique omnes eius loci depravati fuissent." Cf. Ptolemy, *Quadripartitum,* ed. Cardano (1554), 2 = *O* V.94: "Is vero si veram mentem Ptolemaei verborum translatione explicatam habuisset, forsan nos hoc labore liberasset."
38. For example, Giuliano Ristori, whose lectures on the text, given at Pisa, are preserved in Florence, Bibl. Riccardiana, MS 157; see *Firenze e la Toscana dei Medici nell'Europa del Cinquecento* (Florence, 1980), 372. J.-P. Boudet reconstructs

the library—and gives a rich sense of the culture—of one of the most historically minded of Cardano's predecessors in *Lire dans le ciel: La bibliothèque de Simon de Phares, astrologue du xve siècle* (Brussels, 1994).

39. Ptolemy, *Quadripartitum,* ed. Cardano (1554), 1 = *O* V.93.
40. Ibid., 198 = *O* V.242.
41. G. Valla, *Commentationes in Ptolemaei Quadripartitum* (Venice, 1502), ep. ded., A vo: "Ptolemaeus mathematicorum omnium facile princeps ut quidam scripsere Adriani vixit temporibus ad Antoninumque usque pervenit: quo tempore Galenum inclitum medicine auctorem perhibent floruisse."
42. Ptolemy, *Quadripartitum,* ed. Cardano (1554), 26–28 = *O* V.112–113.
43. Ibid., 1 = *O* V.93.
44. Ibid.; cf. 81 = *O* V.154.
45. Ibid., 11 = *O* V.99–100 at 100.
46. Ptolemy *Tetrabiblos* 1.20–21.
47. Ibid., 1.18.
48. Ptolemy, *Quadripartitum,* ed. Cardano (1554), 81 = *O* V.154.
49. Ibid., 53 = *O* V.133.
50. For a more detailed account of the context within which Cardano developed these arguments, see A. Grafton, "From Apotheosis to Analysis: Some Late Renaissance Histories of Classical Astronomy," *History and the Disciplines: The Reclassification of Knowledge in Early Modern Europe,* ed. D. R. Kelley (Rochester, N.Y., 1997), 261–276.
51. Cardano, *De supplemento almanach* 22, *Libelli duo* (1543), F ij vo = *O* V.590.
52. Ptolemy, *Quadripartitum,* ed. Cardano (1555), 33–34 = *O* V.117–118, at 117.
53. Ibid., 34 = *O* V.118.
54. Ibid. Again drawing on medicine, Cardano regretted that unlike Galen and Aetius, good medical writers both, Firmicus had "consistently suppressed the names of his sources; if he had added these it would have been easy to guess how much credibility each of his rules should enjoy" (*O* V.118).
55. Ptolemy, *Quadripartitum,* ed. Cardano (Basel, 1578), 194 = *O* V.158–159, quoting *In Claudii Ptolemaei Quadripartitum enarrator ignoti nominis etc.,* ed. H. Wolf (Basel, 1559), e.g. 194–195: "Meminit et Porphyrius in nulla alia re utilis quam in commemorandis huiusmodi nominibus Trasibuli et Petosiridis, qui ante Ptolemaeum in magna fuerunt existimatione, quos etiam vocat vetustiores, sed et Antigoni et Psnani Aegyptiorum."
56. BN, Paris, MS lat. 7305, fol. 80 ro–vo: "Illi de Egipto fuerunt sapientes magici antiquo tempore. Nam ipsi studio et exercitio maximi viri in scientiis fuerunt et in sapientiis omnibus de quibus homines se iuvant. Et hoc scimus per cronicas sapientum antiquorum et per ea quae de eorum operibus remanserunt a multis mille annis usque ad hodiernum diem . . . Et Caldei sunt illi de Babilonia qui Egiptianos sequuti sunt in scientia astronomie."
57. Ptolemy, *Quadripartitum,* ed. Cardano (1578), 194 = *O* V.159.
58. A. Grafton, *Joseph Scaliger* (Oxford, 1983–1993), I, chap. 7.

59. Ptolemy, *Quadripartitum,* ed. Cardano (1554), 3 = *O* V.94–95.
60. Aulus Gellius *Noctes atticae* 14.1.36.
61. Ptolemy, *Quadripartitum,* ed. Cardano (1554), 7 = *O* V.97.
62. See P. Hadot, *Exercices spirituels et philosophie antique* (Paris, 1981); M. Nussbaum, *The Therapy of Desire* (Princeton, 1994).
63. Nussbaum, 353.
64. Ptolemy, *Quadripartitum,* ed. Cardano (1554), 24 = *O* V.110.
65. Ibid., 16 = *O* V.104.
66. See esp. G. Lloyd, *Magic, Reason, and Experience* (Cambridge, 1979); T. Barton, *Power and Knowledge* (Ann Arbor, 1994); and, for wider discussions of the economic turn in recent work on ancient science, L. Taub, "The Rehabilitation of Wretched Subjects," *Early Science and Medicine* 2 (1997), 74–87, and H. King, "Beyond the Medical Market-Place: New Directions in Ancient Medicine," ibid., 88–97.
67. Ptolemy, *Quadripartitum,* ed. Cardano (1554), 15 = *O* V.103.
68. Ibid., 17–18 = *O* V.105. Cardano refers to *Epidemics* 5.27.
69. Ptolemy, *Tetrabiblos,* ed. and tr. F. E. Robbins (Cambridge, Mass., 1940), 1.2.
70. Cardano, geniture 99, *Libelli quinque* (1547) 182 ro = *O* V.502.
71. Ptolemy, *Quadripartitum,* ed. Cardano (1554), 21 = *O* V.108.
72. Ptolemy *Tetrabiblos* 2.10, tr. Robbins.
73. Ptolemy, *Quadripartitum,* ed. Cardano (1554), 169 = *O* V.223.
74. Ibid., 178 = *O* V.230.
75. Ptolemy *Tetrabiblos* 2.10.
76. Ptolemy, *Quadripartitum,* ed. Cardano (1554), 166–167 = *O* V.221bis.
77. Ibid., 21 = *O* V.108. Cf. A. A. Long, "Astrology: Arguments pro and contra," *Science and Speculation: Studies in Hellenistic Theory and Practice,* ed. J. Barnes et al. (Cambridge and Paris, 1982), 165–192.
78. Ptolemy, *Quadripartitum,* ed. Cardano (1554), 148 = *O* V.206.
79. Ptolemy *Tetrabiblos* 1.13. Cf. J. V. Field, *Kepler's Geometrical Cosmology* (Chicago, 1988).
80. Ptolemy, *Tetrabiblos* 3.8.
81. Ptolemy, *Quadripartitum,* ed. Cardano (1554), 225–226 = *O* V.263. For the place name Middleton Stoney see W. G. Waters, *Jerome Cardan: A Biographical Study* (London, 1898), 258.
82. Cf. J. Céard, *La nature et les prodiges* (Geneva, 1977); *Die Wickiana,* ed. M. Senn (Küsnacht-Zurich, 1975); L. Daston and K. Park, *Wonders and the Order of Nature, 1150–1750* (New York, 1998).
83. Ptolemy, *Quadripartitum,* ed. Cardano (1554), 108 = *O* V.177. For Cardano's interpretation of the causes of cannibalism in the New World, which was quite original, see F. Lestringant, *Le cannibale* (Paris, 1994), chap. 9.
84. Ptolemy, *Tetrabiblos* 2.9, tr. Robbins.
85. Ptolemy, *Quadripartitum,* ed. Cardano (1554), 154 = *O* V.211.
86. Ibid., 150 = *O* V.208. Cardano follows Ptolemy here.

87. Ibid., 104 = *O* V.173.
88. Ibid., 104 = *O* V.173–174.
89. Ibid., 26–31 = *O* V.112–113; ibid. (1578), 216 = *O* V.174. Cf. Ernst, 204–207.
90. Ptolemy, *Quadripartitum,* ed. Cardano (1578), 216 = *O* V.174.
91. Ibid. (1554), 134 = *O* V.195.
92. C. Leowitz, *De coniunctionibus magnis* (Lauingen, 1564). For the context and impact of this work see R. Barnes, *Prophecy and Gnosis* (Stanford, 1988); Grafton, *Scaliger,* II, pt. 1.
93. Ernst, 207–212.
94. Ptolemy, *Tetrabiblos,* ed. Cardano (1555), 369–375 = *O* V.221–222. For an annotated translation, see W. Shumaker, *Renaissance Curiosa* (Binghamton, N.Y., 1982), chap. 2.
95. On the exegetical traditions and debates connected with the star of the Magi see M. Screech, "The Magi and the Star (Matthew 2)," *Histoire de l'exégèse au xvi siècle,* ed. O. Fatio and P. Fraenkel (Geneva, 1978), 385–409.
96. See G. Pico della Mirandola, *Disputationes adversus astrologiam divinatricem,* ed. E. Garin (Florence, 1946–52), I, 604 n. 1.
97. Ibid., 606.
98. T. Rosselli, *Apologeticus contra cucullatos,* in P. Zambelli, *Una reincarnazione di Pico ai tempi di Pomponazzi* (Milan, 1991), 127.
99. Cf. Shumaker.
100. Ptolemy, *Quadripartitum,* ed. Cardano (1554), 196–197 = *O* V.221.
101. Ibid., 222. For a strikingly similar argument, cf. Ficino's effort to determine precisely what methods the Magi used to find their way to Jesus, in his sermon "De stella magorum," *Opera* (Basel, 1576), 489–491.

9. Rival Disciplines Explored

1. Cardano, *Liber de libris propriis* (Lyons, 1557), 78–79 = *O* I.74.
2. For examples of such diagrams, see S. K. Heninger, Jr., *The Cosmographicall Glasse* (San Marino, 1979).
3. Leonardo Dati's account, printed in M. Palmieri, *Libro del Poema chiamato Citta di Vita,* ed. M. Rooke, Smith College Studies in Modern Languages VIII, 1–2; IX, 1–4 (Northampton and Paris, 1926–1928), II, 261–262. For rich parallels from a text much closer to Cardano's own period see A. Yagel, *A Valley of Vision,* tr. and ed. D. B. Ruderman (Philadelphia, 1990).
4. For the earlier background see A. Scott, *Origen and the Life of the Stars* (Oxford, 1991; repr. 1994).
5. G. Steiner, "The Historicity of Dreams," *No Passion Spent: Essays, 1978–1996* (London, 1996), 207–223 at 221.
6. See in general P. Burke, *Varieties of Cultural History* (Ithaca, 1997), and S. F. Price, "The Future of Dreams: From Freud to Artemidorus," *Past & Present* 113 (1986), 3–37. Also helpful for the larger context are G. Guidorizzi, "L'interpretazione

dei sogni nel mondo tardoantico: oralità e scrittura," *I sogni nel Medioevo,* ed. T. Gregory (Rome, 1985), 149–178; S. M. Oberhelman, *The Oneirocriticon of Achmet* (Lubbock, 1991), chaps. 1–3; P. E. Dutton, *The Politics of Dreaming in the Carolingian Empire* (Lincoln and London, 1994;) S. F. Kruger, *Dreaming in the Middle Ages* (Cambridge, 1992); F. Berriot, ed., *Exposicions et significacions des songes et Les songes Daniel* (Geneva, 1989), 12–52. For two other sixteenth-century physicians' use of dreams see R. Cooper, "Deux médecins royaux onirocrites: Jehan Thibault et Auger Ferrier," *Le Songe à la Renaissance,* ed. F. Charpentier (Saint-Etienne, 1990), 53–60. And for a pioneering application of anthropological methods to a rich body of historical material, which avoids the problems of anachronism that have bedeviled previous attempts, see S. Jama, *La nuit de songes de René Descartes* (Paris, 1998).

7. See the fine analysis of A. Browne, "Girolamo Cardano's *Somniorum Synesiorum libri iiii,*" *Bibliothèque de l'Humanisme et Renaisance* 40 (1979), 123–135. For earlier efforts to connect astrology with oneiromancy see T. Gregory, "I sogni e gli astri," *I sogni nel Medioevo,* ed. Gregory, 111–148.
8. Cf. G. Dagron, "Le saint, le savant, l'astrologue: Etude de thèmes hagiographiques à travers quelques recueils de 'Questions et réponses' des Ve-VIIe siècles," *Hagiographie, cultures et sociétés, ive-xiie siècles* (Paris, 1981), 143–156; P. Brown, *Authority and the Sacred* (Cambridge, 1995), 69. I borrow the notion of an "inherited conglomerate" from the classic work of E. R. Dodds, *The Greeks and the Irrational* (Berkeley, 1951), though I use it to different effect.
9. See D. Gentilcore, *From Bishop to Witch* (Manchester and New York, 1992); cf. G. Tomlinson, *Music in Renaissance Magic* (Chicago, 1993). G. Pomata, *La promessa di guarigione: malati e curatori in antico regime Bologna, xvi–xviii secoli* (Bari, 1994) = *Contracting a Cure,* tr. G. Pomata et al. (Baltimore, 1998); B. Duden, *Geschichte unter der Haut: Ein Eisenacher Arzt und seine Patientinnen um 1730* (Stuttgart, 1987) = *The Woman beneath the Skin,* tr. T. Dunlap (Cambridge, Mass., and London, 1991).
10. For a case study in this process of definition and the ensuing conflicts, see J. Céard, "Médicine et démonologie: les enjeux d'un débat," *Diable, diables et diableries au temps de la Renaissance,* ed. M. T. Jones-Davies (Paris, 1988), 97–112.
11. On talismanic magic in the Renaissance see D. P. Walker, *Spiritual and Demonic Magic from Ficino to Campanella* (London, 1958); H. C. Agrippa, *De occulta philosophia libri tres,* ed. V. Perrone Compagni (Leiden, New York, and Cologne, 1992); P. Béhar, *Les langues occultes de la Renaissance* (Paris, 1996).
12. Cardano, *De interrogationibus liber,* in Ptolemy, *Quadripartitum,* ed. Cardano (Lyons, 1555), 181–208, at 203 = *O* V.559 (where Cardano discussed the ticklish question of whether astrology could determine the legitimacy of a child, a question with obvious moral and legal consequences).
13. See N. Siraisi, *The Clock and the Mirror: Girolamo Cardano and Renaissance Medicine* (Princeton, 1997).

14. Cardano, *De propria vita liber,* ed. G. Naudé, 40.12, 2d ed. (Amsterdam, 1654), 139 = *O* 1.33.
15. Ibid..
16. G. Ferrari, "Public Anatomy Lessons and the Carnival: The Anatomy Theatre of Bologna," *Past & Present* 117 (1987), 50–106.
17. Cardano, *De propria vita liber* 42 (1654), 154–155 = *O* I.36.
18. W.-D. Müller-Jahncke, *Astrologisch-magische Theorie und Praxis in der Heilkunde der frühen Neuzeit* (Stuttgart, 1985).
19. See N. Siraisi and A. Grafton, "Between the Election and My Hopes: Girolamo Cardano and Medical Astrology," *Archimedes,* forthcoming.
20. Cardano, *De interrogationibus liber,* in Ptolemy, *Quadripartitum,* ed. Cardano (1555), 207 = *O* V.560.
21. See e.g. J.-C. Margolin's brilliant essay, "Rationalisme et irrationalisme dans la pensée de Jérôme Cardan," *Revue de l'Université de Bruxelles* nos. 2–3 (February-March 1969), 1–40, and the just critique of it by Browne, 123–124.
22. Cardano, *De rerum varietate libri xvii* (Avignon, 1558), VIII.44, 435 = *O* III.170.
23. E. E. Evans-Pritchard, *Witchcraft, Oracles, and Magic among the Azande* (Oxford, 1937); cf. G. E. R. Lloyd, *Magic, Reason, and Experience* (Cambridge, 1979), 17–18.
24. H. C. Agrippa, *De occulta philosophia libri tres,* 1.51; ed. Perrone Compagni, 183, quoting Pliny *Naturalis historia* 28.7.36–37.
25. See Cardano, *De rerum varietate* (1558), XVI.90, 785 = *O* III.311. As is evident, Cardano did not take up the question of why, according to Pliny, saliva could also intensify a blow. On the difficulty of recalling sensations see also Cardano, *De propria vita liber* 43, (1654), 164–166 = *O* I.39., Cf. also Cardano, *De subtilitate libri XXI* (Lyons, 1554), XII, 448 = *O* III.558: "Imaginatio etiam doloris alieni, in aliquibus suscitat Venerem, adeo quod, ut refert Ioannes Mirandula, quidam non arrigebat nisi vapularet, multi nisi verberarent." Here he refers to a famous passage in Pico's *Disputationes adversus astrologiam divinatricem* (3.27).
26. Cardano, *De subtilitate* (Nuremberg, 1550), title page (this blurb also appears on the verso of the title page in the Paris editions of 1550 and 1551): "Habes hoc in libro, candide Lector, plus quam sesquimille variarum, non vulgarium, sed difficilium, occultarum et pulcherrimarum rerum causas, vires, et proprietates, ab authore hinc inde experimento observatas: quae non solum propter cognitionem delectabiles, sed etiam ad varios usus, tum privatos, tum publicos, multo utiliores, quam hactenus plurimorum scripta, quae etsi ex philosophia sint, minoris tamen momenti esse, legens haec et illa, haud mecum dissentiet: uti singula in adiecto indice perspicue licet cernere."
27. Ibid., 291 = *O* III.583–584.
28. Cardano, *De subtilitate* (Paris, 1551), bk. 2, 56 vo–57 ro; bk. 6, 123 vo–124 ro; bk. 7, 160 ro.
29. Cardano, ep. ded., *De subtilitate* (Basel, 1554), α3 ro: "multi enim legent: pauci,

imo vix ulli, omnia quae hic scripta sunt, assequi poterunt: cum etiam plurima sub cortice lateant praestantiora his quae explicantur."

30. See in general the erudite works of W. Eamon, *Science and the Secrets of Nature* (Princeton, 1994), and L. Daston and K. Park, *Wonders and the Order of Nature, 1150–1750* (New York, 1998).
31. Cardano, *De subtilitate* (1554), "auctor lectori," α4 ro: "En lector candide absolutum opus de Subtilitate, cuius umbram solam prioribus editionibus habuisti . . . cum duorum millium ac ducentarum pulcherrimarum rerum, praeter infinitas alias, quas indice comprehendere immensi fuisset laboris, vires atque proprietates varias, et non vulgares, sed occultas atque difficiles, ab ipso autore experimento confirmatas, causas quoque illarum ac demonstrationes explicet."
32. See e.g. J. J. Berns, *Die Herkunft des Automobils aus Himmelstrionfo und Höllenmaschine* (Berlin, 1996).
33. Cardano, *De subtilitate* (Paris, 1551), bk. 6, 133 ro.
34. Ibid., bk. 2, 52 ro.
35. See L. B. Campbell, *Scenes and Machines on the English Stage during the Renaissance* (Cambridge, 1923; repr. New York, 1960) N. Clulee, *John Dee's Natural Philosophy: Between Science and Religion* (London and New York, 1988); D. Ruderman, *Kabbalah, Magic, and Science: The Cultural Universe of a Sixteenth-Century Jewish Physician* (Cambridge, Mass., 1988); Yagel.
36. Cardano, "Libellus de libris propriis, cui titulus est Ephemerus," *De sapientia libri quinque* (Nuremberg, 1544), 426 = *O* I.58.
37. Ibid. = *O* I.58: "ut illius imago etiam nunc me torqueat."
38. Ibid., 429.
39. Ibid.
40. See Price.
41. See Browne.
42. Cardano, *Somniorum Synesiorum libri iiii* (Basel, 1562), I.1, 1: "Neminem puduit, se fateri somniorum interpretem, cum alia genera divinandi aspernarentur, ac etiam irriserint plurimi. Verum ne miscendo falsa veris et inania utilibus, atque e re praedicendo, tanquam nulla arte opus sit ad interpretationem, aut etiam falsis vatibus credendo plura admitterentur in populo flagitia: Moses vulgarem usum, ut et plerumque aliarum periculosarum rerum interdixit. Itaque ut non nisi medicis medendi facultas est, et sacerdotibus divina tractandi, et legum peritis iudicandi: ita non nisi sapientibus licere debet somnia interpretari."
43. P. Pomponazzi, *De naturalium effectuum causis sive de Incantationibus* (Basel, 1567; repr. Hildesheim and New York, 1970), 122–123: "Verum et corpora coelestia non solum sic dirigunt homines, verum etiam manifesta indicia futurorum eventuum dant hominibus, modo in somniis, modo in vigiliis secundum apparitionem diversarum figurarum, ut infinita exempla de somniis adducere possem ex Plutarcho et infinitis aliis authoribus, quae omnia praetermitto."

See in general 120–155. Cf. F. Graiff, "I prodigi e l'astrologia nei commenti di Pietro Pomponazzi al *De caelo,* alla *Meteora e al De generatione,*" *Medioevo* 2 (1976), 331–361.

44. C. Peucer, *Commentarius de praecipuis divinationum generibus* (Wittenberg, 1553), 182 vo–203 ro, esp. 200 vo: "Diabolici generis sunt omnia illa, quae Diabolus olim offudit aethnicis, ubi ad delubra idolorum captandarum talium praestigiarum causa involuti victimarum pellibus cubabant: quaeque nunc Anabaptistis et similibus fanaticis in abdito ad novas patefactiones velut hiantibus, aut magis et veneficis, et promiscue omnibus non conversis ad Deum."
45. Cardano, *De rerum varietate libri XVII* (Basel, 1557), 8.40, 294–295.
46. Cardano, *De propria vita liber* 37 (1654), 118 = *O* I.28.
47. Cardano, *De subtilitate libri XXI,* (Paris, 1551), bk. 19, 305 vo = *O* III.656.
48. Ibid., 305 vo–306 ro: = *O* III.656.
49. Ibid., 306 ro = *O* III.656. Cf. Cardano, *De propria vita liber* 3 (1654), 000 = *O* I.2.
50. S. Clark, *Thinking with Demons: The Idea of Witchcraft in Early Modern Europe* (Oxford, 1997).
51. Cardano, *De rerum varietate,* 8.43, 314–315 = *O* III.161.
52. Ibid., 16.93, 658 = *O* III.334.
53. Ibid.
54. See also G. Zanier, *Ricerche sulla diffusione e fortuna del "De incantationibus" di Pomponazzi* (Florence, 1975), 50–55, and Cardano, *De vita propria* 42, *O* I.36–37.
55. See Cardano, *De propria vita liber* 39 (1654), 130 = *O* I.31, where he rejects chiromancy as an evil discipline like the study of poison, and explains that he never attempted to study physiognomics "nam longa res est, difficillima, et quae multa memoria indiget, et sensibus acutis, quae mihi adesse haud credo"; 45 (1654), 178 = *O* I.42, where he describes his work on metoposcopy, the analysis of faces, as belonging to physiognomics, though he still emphasizes the difficulty of verifying the art.
56. Ibid., 43 (1654), 162 = *O* I.38: "de contumacia horologii, quae in causas facile naturales referri potest."
57. Ibid., 41 (1654), 151 = *O* I.36.
58. See esp. J.-M. Sallmann, *Naples et ses saints à l'âge baroque (1540–1750)* (Paris, 1994), 182, 194, 274–277, 303–310.
59. Cardano, *De propria vita liber* 38, (1654), 127–128 = *O* I.30; cf. G. Zarri, *Le sante vive: cultura e religiosità femminile nella prima età moderna* (Turin, 1990), 116 and 155 n. 232. In the terms of formal argumentation, Cardano's *splendor* was a version of the trope of *enargeia,* for which see M. Wintroub, "The Looking Glass of Facts: Collecting, Rhetoric, and Citing the Self in the Experimental Natural Philosophy of Robert Boyle," *History of Science* 35 (1997), 189–217.
60. See the "vita anonyma" of Alberti, now thought to have been written by Alberti himself, in R. Fubini and A. Nenci Gallorini, "L'autobiografia di Leon Battista Alberti. Studio e edizione," *Rinascimento,* 2d ser. 12 (1972), 21–78, at 76.

61. Peucer, 291 recto: "Sed fortasse obiecerit quispiam, cur portentosa faciam deliquia, et singulares casus eventaque tristia praeire affirmem, cum nec contra observatum, notum, et usitatum naturae cursum, nec secundum insuetiorem minusque ordinariam rationem accidere ea luminibus constet, sed ex lege et consequutione motuum necessaria."
62. R. Goclenius, *Uranoscopiae, chiroscopiae, metoposcopiae, et ophthalmoscopiae contemplatio* (Frankfurt, 1608), 159–160, where Goclenius rejects "diabolic" forms of divination "ut sunt, qui hodie nescio quid monstri in crystallo monstrantes futura praesagiunt imperitioribus. Impia enim omnia superstitiosa et *anaitiologeta* praesagia atque vaticinia serio detestor, nec quicquam huic meae Chiroscopiae cum illis erit commune."
63. Ibid., 272: "Septem in experimentis habeo, et inter hos duos magnos viros, quibus Martia in fronte divulsa, intercisa et cruciformis conspecta est: quinque ex iis decollati sunt, reliqui in violentia grassatorum transfossi."
64. Cf. the highly instructive work of R. J. Smith, *Fortune-Tellers and Philosophers: Divination in Traditional Chinese Society* (Boulder, San Francisco, and Oxford, 1991).
65. Peucer, 291 verso–292 recto, esp. 291 verso. On the tensions in Peucer's thought see R. Barnes, *Prophecy and Gnosis* (Stanford, 1988), 99, 107–108, 148. Barnes also offers a wealth of information about the larger context within which Peucer worked, the luxuriant jungle of different forms of prophecy that flourished in Lutheran Germany throughout the sixteenth century. For a more general discussion, see D. Cantimori, "Umanesimo e luteranesimo di fronte alla scolastica: Caspar Peucer," *Rivista di studi germanici* 2 (1937) 417–438 = *Umanesimo e religione nel Rinascimento,* 2d ed. (Turin, 1975), 88–111.
66. J. Bodin, *Methodus ad facilem historiarum cognitionem* (Paris, 1566); *De re publica* (Paris, 1576). See M. J. Tooley, "Bodin and the Medieval Theory of Climate," *Speculum* 28 (1953), 64–83; C. Glacken, *Traces on the Rhodian Shore* (Berkeley, 1967); M.-D. Couzinet, *Histoire et méthode à la Renaissance: Une lecture de la Methodus ad facilem historiarum cognitionem de Jean Bodin* (Paris, 1996), 277, 303–308.
67. J. Bodin, *De la démonomanie des sorciers* (Paris, 1587; repr. Paris, 1979), I.ii, 12 ro.
68. See F. von Bezold, "Jean Bodin als Okkultist und seine Démonomanie," *Historische Zeitschrift* 105 (1910), 1–64, and C. Baxter, "Jean Bodin's Daemon and His Conversion to Judaism," *Jean Bodin: Verhandlungen der internationalen Bodin-Tagung in München,* ed. H. Denzer (Munich, 1973), 1–21.
69. Zanier, 9 n. 36; P. Pomponazzi, *De naturalium effectuum causis, Opera* (Basel, 1567; repr. New York and Hildesheim, 1970), 139–141. For the interaction of different forms of prophecy in the ancient world, see D. Potter, *Prophets and Emperors* (Cambridge, Mass., 1994) and cf. Manilius 1.25–112. For the continued juxtaposition of radically varied forms of prediction long after Cardano's time, see A. Geneva, *Astrology and the Seventeenth-Century Mind: William Lilly and the Language of the Stars* (Manchester and New York, 1995), chap. 4.

70. Gaurico, *Tractatus astrologicus* (Venice, 1552), fol. 19 recto-verso.
71. Simon Forman's astrological autobiography was published long ago as *The Autobiography and Personal Diary of Dr. Simon Forman,* ed. J. O. Halliwell (London, 1849). The original, MS Ashmole 208, contains a detailed horoscope with yearly revolutions. On the versos of the revolutions, Forman entered autobiographical comments full of curious detail on his practice of prophecy (32 vo), necromancy (43 vo, 45 vo), and calling angels and spirits (43 vo). In another work in the same manuscript, he wrote "Of Visions that the said S. had being yet a childe" (137 ro). See also the rich biography of Melanchthon by Camerarius, which records many instances of the reformer's divinatory prowess: J. Camerarius, *De vita Philippi Melanchthonis narratio,* ed. G. Th. Strobelius (Halle, 1777), e.g. 76–79, 95–96, 99, 195, 248–250, 322. For a later example of eclectic use of astrology and many other disciplines of prediction, also from England, see the fine edition of *An Astrological Diary of the Seventeenth Century* by M. Hunter and A. Gregory (Oxford, 1988).
72. M. Ficino, *De vita coelitus comparanda* (Venice, 1516), Folger Shakespeare Library BF 1501 J 2 copy 2, 44 recto (on a text by Synesius of Cyrene): "Si autem per omnia significantur omnia, quippe cum omnia in uno animali mundo sint germana, atque sunt hae veluti *omniformes literae,* sicut in libro, sic in universo *signatae,* partim quidem phoeniciae, partim vero aegyptiae, partim assyriae. has autem sapiens ipse legit"; "Cabala nostra τοῦ ὄντος."
73. Censorinus *De die natali* 17.15, 21.4–6.
74. Marinus' *Vita Procli*—a text that became readily available in Latin in 1568, when it appeared along with Guilelmus Xylander's edition of Marcus Aurelius.
75. See generally Potter. Junius' edition of Eunapius, *De vitis philosophorum et sophistarum* (Antwerp, 1568), rested on a copy of the Farnese manuscript made available by the great collector Joannes Sambucus (ibid., II, 199)—the text of which, Junius complained, was so corrupt that it had forced him "hariolarum more divinare" in filling gaps and emending errors (ibid., 199–200). John Dee owned, and entered a few notes in, a copy of this work (Bodleian Library 80 E 8 Art. Seld.).
76. Aelius Aristides, *Orationum tomi tres,* tr. W. Canter (Basel, 1566), ad lect., +4ro-vo: "Veruntamen Aesculapius, quem religiose colebat, eum tandem infinitis pharmacis, lotionibus, inediis, vomitibus, venae sectionibus, cursibus, declamationibus, peregrinationibus, ac similibus aliis secundum quietem imperatis, praeter omnem spem ac prope naturam sanavit." Cf. for a very different reaction E. R. Dodds, *Pagan and Christian in an Age of Anxiety: Some Aspects of Religious Experience from Marcus Aurelius to Constantine* (Cambridge, 1965; repr. 1991). Not surprisingly, Dorat read and cited Cardano in his turn. See P. Ford, "Jean Dorat and the Reception of Homer in Renaissance France," *International Journal of the Classical Tradition* 2 (1995), 265–274.
77. F. A. Yates, *The French Academies of the Sixteenth Century* (London, 1947; 2d ed., London and New York, 1988); P. Brind'Amour, "Introduction," in Nos-

tradamus, *Les premières centuries ou propheties,* ed. Brind'Amour (Geneva, 1996), lii–lxviii.

78. Gabriel Harvey, note in his copy of Luca Gaurico, *Tractatus astrologicus* (Venice, 1552), Bodleian Library 4to Rawl. 61, fol. 19 verso: "Sed quanto adhuc verior certiorque Sosipatrae divinatio, e Chaldaeorum ut videtur Astrologia et Physiognomia: Cabalisticis nescio quibus principiis et experimentis mirabiliter expedita."
79. G. Naudé, "De Cardano iudicium," in Cardano, *De propria vita liber* (1654), sig. *6 verso–*7 recto = *O* I.i 2 ro-vo.
80. Cardano, *De varietate rerum,* 634 = *O* III.322; cf. 682 = *O* III.345.
81. Cf. T. Barton, *Power and Knowledge* (Ann Arbor, 1994).
82. See Ptolemy, *Quadripartitum,* ed. Cardano (Basel, 1554), 18 (*O* V.105).
83. See the translation of and commentary on *De ludo aleae liber,* in O. Ore, *Cardano: The Gambling Scholar* (Princeton, 1953). Cf. T. Krisher, "Interpretationen zum *Liber de ludo aleae,*" in *Girolamo Cardano: Philosoph, Naturforscher, Arzt,* ed. E. Kessler (Wiesbaden, 1994), 207–217. There was classical precedent for treating the fall of dice as impossible for an astrologer to predict: Gellius *Noctes Atticae* 14.1. Cf. also *De propria vita liber* 30 (1654), 78–91 = *O* I.18–22.
84. Cardano, *Arcana aeternitatis,* 14, *O* X.29.
85. F. Lestringant, *Le cannibale* (Paris, 1994), chap. 9.
86. Cardano, *Arcana politica* (Amsterdam, 1635), chap. 128, "De geniis, fato, astrologia et fortuna," 581: "Dicebat mihi prorex Gallus apud Scotos: Rex noster cognovit Fortunam esse feminam: baculo debere domari: verberatam tamdiu venturam in partes nostras." The whole paragraph makes clear how hard Cardano found it to define his position on which forces did most to shape an individual's life or larger historical events.
87. Cardano, *De propria vita liber* 49 (1654), 201–202 = *O* I.47–48. In the *Proxeneta,* however, Cardano treats the same episode as an instance of the providential care he has enjoyed: *Arcana politica* 1.4, 28–29 at 28: "Dicam autem quid mihi contigeret nuper, ut intelligas quam minimis Deus servet aut perdat quem velit." For similar ruminations on near disasters, with attempts to specify their astrological causes and the role of providence, see *An Astrological Diary,* ed. Hunter and Gregory, 176–177, 188–189, 226–227, 230–231, 236–237, 240–241, 245 (30 August 1694): "About 9h 8′ A.M. A Tile from the Eves of my woodhouse, fell down just clear of my head: so near that the dust of the Mortar that came down with it, flew upon my Hat. But the merciful Providence of God preserved me . . . [a figure of the heavens follows] Note that Mars was just then risen; &c."
88. Cardano, *De propria vita liber* 40 (1654), 140 = *O* I.33; cf. J. Sturrock, *The Language of Autobiography: Studies in the First Person Singular* (Cambridge, 1993), 80–81.
89. Ptolemy, *Quadripartitum,* ed. Cardano (Lyons, 1555), A*3 ro: "Divinitus occasionem oblatam credidi, quam effugere non possem."

90. Kepler to an unknown correspondent, 3 April 1611; *Gesammelte Werke,* ed. M. Caspar et al. (Munich, 1937–), XVI, 373–375; see B. Bauer, "Die Rolle des Hofastrologen und Hofmathematicus als fürstlicher Berater," *Höfischer Humanismus,* ed. A. Buck (Weinheim, 1989), 93–117.
91. M. Foucault, *Les mots et les choses* (Paris, 1966), chap. 2.
92. Cf. Zanier, 54 n. 20 and 91–93.

10. Cardano on Cardano

1. Cardano, *De propria vita liber,* ed. G. Naudé, 37, 2d ed. (Amsterdam, 1654), 121–122 = *O* 1.29. Here as elsewhere I borrow occasional phrases from the useful translation by J. Stoner, *The Book of My Life* (London and Toronto, 1931).
2. For Dante and other parallels see F. Cardini, "Sognare a Firenze fra Trecento e Quattrocento," *Le mura di Firenze inargentate* (Palermo, 1993), 29–57.
3. The terrifying character of the ascent is reminiscent of one of the dreams described in the *Passio Perpetuae,* a text not published until the middle of the seventeenth century, when Lucas Holstenius equipped it with a remarkable commentary. Cf. E. R. Dodds, *Pagan and Christian in an Age of Anxiety: Some Aspects of Religious Experience from Marcus Aurelius to Constantine* (Cambridge, 1965), for a psychological reading of Perpetua's ascent.
4. Cardano, *De libris propriis* (Lyons, 1557), 23–24 = *O* I.64.
5. Cardano, *De libris propriis, Somniorum Synesiorum libri iiii* (Basel, 1562), 11 = *O* I.100–101.
6. Cardano, *De libris propriis* (1557), 25 = *O* I.64.
7. Ibid., 26 = *O* I.64: "Casa illa et puer quid ostendat, nondum intelligo."
8. Cardano, *De libris propriis* (1562), 12 = *O* I.101.
9. Cardano, *De propria vita liber* 40 (1654), 123 = *O* I.29.
10. G. Cardano, *De propria vita liber, ex bibliotheca G. Naudaei* (Paris, 1643; 2d ed., Amsterdam, 1654).
11. Misch's account remains the fullest and one of the most perceptive: *Geschichte der Autobiographie,* IV, pt. 2 (Frankfurt, 1969), 696–732. For Goethe see 697; for Cellini, 696. See also the sensitive essay by H. Pfeiffer, "Girolamo Cardano and the Melancholy of Writing," *Materialities of Communication,* ed. H. U. Gumbrecht and K. L. Pfeiffer, tr. W. Whobrey (Stanford, 1994), 227–241, and the rich treatments of the autobiographical tradition in the West, including Cardano, by A. Robeson Burr, *The Autobiography: A Critical and Comparative Study* (Boston and New York, 1909), esp. chap. 7, 86–128; K. J. Weintraub, *The Value of the Individual* (Chicago, 1978); and J. Sturrock, *The Language of Autobiography: Studies in the First Person Singular* (Cambridge, 1993), 74–83.
12. For some specimens of this innovative brand of scholarship see *Ego-Dokumente: Annäherung an den Menschen in der Geschichte,* ed. W. Schulze (Berlin 1996), esp. R. Dekker, "Ego-Dokumente in den Niederlanden vom 16. bis zum 17. Jahrhundert," 33–57; J. S. Amelang, "Spanish Autobiography in the Early

Modern Era," 59–71; K. von Greyerz, "Spuren eines vormodernen Individualismus in englischen Selbstzeugnissen des 16. und 17. Jahrhunderts," 131–145.

13. J. Goldberg, "Cellini's *Vita* and the Conventions of Early Autobiography," *Modern Language Notes* 89 (1974), 71–83; cf. more generally M. Mascuch, *Origins of the Individualist Self: Autobiography and Self-Identity in England, 1591–1791* (Cambridge, 1997).
14. See T. F. Mayer and D. R. Woolf, "Introduction," in *The Rhetorics of Life-Writing in Early Modern Europe,* ed. T. F. Mayer and D. R. Woolf (Ann Arbor, 1995), 1–37. The fullest and richest analysis of the forms of autobiography in Renaissance Italy remains the clasic work of M. Guglielminetti, *Memoria e scrittura* (Turin, 1977).
15. Mayer and Woolf, 12–19; T. C. Price Zimmermann, "Paolo Giovio and the Rhetoric of Individuality," ibid., 39–62.
16. Cardano, *De libris propriis* (1562), 28 = *O* I.108.
17. Cardano, "De libris propriis," in *De sapientia libri quinque* (Nuremberg, 1544), 418; 1562, 23 = *O* I.55, 106: "Imitatus sum in hoc scribendi genere Galenum et Erasmum, qui ambo catalogum librorum suorum scripserunt." For Galen's *De libris propriis* (19.8–48K) see his *Selected Works,* ed. and tr. P. N. Singer (Oxford, 1997), 3–22; for Erasmus' *Compendium vitae* see *Opus epistolarum Des. Erasmi Roterodami,* ed. P. S. Allen et al. (Oxford, 1906–1958), I. On Galen see V. Nutton, "Galen and Medical Autobiography," *From Democedes to Harvey: Studies in the History of Medicine* (London, 1988); on Erasmus see A. Flitner, *Erasmus im Urteil seiner nachwelt* (Tübingen, 1952), and B. Mansfield, *Phoenix of His Age* (Toronto and Buffalo, 1979).
18. Cardano, *De libris propriis* (1562), 4–6 = *O* I.97.
19. Cardano, *De propria vita liber* 6 (1654), 19–20 = *O* I.5.
20. Ibid., 8 (1654), 27 = *O* I.7.
21. Ibid.
22. N. Siraisi, "Cardano and the Art of Medical Narrative," *Journal of the History of Ideas* 51 (1991), 581–602; Siraisi, *The Clock and the Mirror: Girolamo Cardano and Renaissance Medicine* (Princeton, 1997).
23. Misch, 717.
24. Cf. Sturrock, 77, who treats these sums of days as "mathematical." For a similar effort at detailed correlation by another astrologer, see the interesting remark of R. Goclenius, *Uranoscopiae, chiroscopiae, metoposcopiae, et ophthalmoscopiae contemplatio,* (Frankfurt, 1608), 57–58: "Ipse ego Lunam tempore geniturae meae deprehendi in cardine Occidentis in signo aquarii ab altero malefico partili quadrato sauciatam, quanto fuerim in periculo aquae, cum in finibus Sueciae navis Lubecensis, in qua tunc una cum aliis eram, ad scopulum latentem plenis velis agitata, submergeretur, nobis in cymbam prosilientibus, testantur etiamnunc mecum eodem navigio utentes cum Sueci, tum Lubecenses anno 1597. mens. Mart."
25. Sturrock, 75–76, 78–81.

26. See in general M. Ficino, *Three Books on Life,* ed. and tr. C. V. Kaske and J. Clark (Binghamton, N.Y., 1988), and D. P. Walker, *Spiritual and Demonic Magic from Ficino to Campanella* (London, 1958). Ficino's recommendations for sucking milk and blood, though rarely mentioned by historians, were taken quite seriously by two early readers of copies of *De vita* now in the Houghton Library, Harvard, who summarized them neatly in marginal notes.
27. See *The Body in Parts,* ed. D. Hillman and C. Mazzio (London, 1997), esp. the essays by D. Hillman and M. Schoenfeldt.
28. Cardano, *Libelli quinque* (Nuremberg, 1547), fol. 124 ro: "Et fuit anno 1538, et timui ne morerer, et non apparuit aegritudo qua decumberem, sed sola copia urinae, quae excedebat generaliter xxx. uncias singula nocte, et cogebar quater surgere ad mingendum, et erat sine ardore, et ego intelligens causam auxiliatus sum cum calidis, et protinus cessavit multitudo, ut nullo modo cogar surgere de nocte. Attamen remansit semper maior quantitas urinae quam prius solerem emittere, et quamvis propter trinum Veneris, qui succedit corpori Saturni, res semper cesserit in melius, nunquam tamen ex toto liberabor."
29. Ibid., 122 vo: "Elegissem certe libentius alienam, cum difficillimum sit de seipso recte loqui posse. Sed cum haec solum mihi vere cognita sit, laboraverimque in ea annis plusquam triginta, ob id malui periculo meo etiam, ut soleo, studiosis satisfacere. Disponam igitur primo horas decem significatorum hoc modo."
30. British Library MS Sloane 325, 2 ro, published by J. G. Nichols, "Some Additions to the Biographies of Sir John Cheke and Sir Thomas Smith," *Archaeologia* 38 (1859), 98–127 at 116–119.
31. For Cardano's final analysis of his horoscope see *De propria vita liber* 2 (1654), 5–7 = *O* I.2.
32. Cardano, *De libris propriis* (1562), 3 = *O* I.97: "Alium quoque de pituita, et alium de re Venerea: quos ambos nondum absolutos, felis urina corrupit: unde illos abieci. Conscripsi et alium de Chiromantia, quem in libros de rerum varietate transtuli: ita toto illo sexennio, quo in eo oppido artem exercui, magnis cum laboribus, parum mihi, multo minus aliis profui. Detinebar inconditis cogitationibus et studiis irritis, non satis prospera et foelice Minerva." On the guides to proper living that flourished in this period see in general R. Bell, *How to Do It: Guides to Good Living for Renaissance Italians* (Chicago and London, 1999); for diet see B. Platina, *On Right Pleasure and Good Health,* ed. M. E. Milham (Tempe, Ariz., 1998).
33. Cardano, *De propria vita liber* 13 (1654), 42–44 = *O* I.10–11. Cf. ibid., (1654), 60–61 = *O* I.14–15.
34. See ibid., 11 (1654), 36–37 = *O* I.9.
35. A. Jacobson Schutte, *Autobiography of an Aspiring Saint* (Chicago and London, 1996).
36. See A. Vauchez, "Les stigmates de Saint François et leurs détracteurs dans les derniers siècles du moyen âge," *Mélanges d'Archéologie et d'Histoire* 80 (1968),

596–625; R. Goffen, *Spirituality in Conflict: Saint Francis and Giotto's Bardi Chapel* (College Park, 1988), chap. 2; A. Davidson, "Miracles of Bodily Transformation, or, How St. Francis Received the Stigmata," *Picturing Science, Producing Art,* ed. C. A. Jones and P. Galison (New York and London, 1998), 101–124; K. Park, "Impressed Images: Reproducing Wonders," ibid., 254–271; J.-M. Sallmann, *Naples et ses saints à l'âge baroque (1540–1750)* (Paris, 1994), 283; P. Dinzelbacher, *Heilige oder Hexen? Schicksale auffäliger Frauen in Mittelalter und Frühneuzeit* (Zurich, 1995; repr. Reinbek bei Hamburg, 1997), esp. 249–285.

37. See Chapter 9 above.
38. Cardano, *De propria vita liber* 30 (1654), 84–85 = *O* I.20.
39. Cf. Hunter, "Introduction," *An Astrological Diary,* ed. Hunter and Gregory, 26, emphasizing that Samuel Jeake—like Cardano—wrote with his audience very much in mind.
40. Cf. Ptolemy, *Quadripartitum,* ed. Cardano (Lyons, 1555), 69–78 with the final version in *O* V.520–522. Cardano's suppressed prediction (1555, 78) reads: "Exacto igitur 68. si potero, in annis 74. pervenit ascendens ad quadratum Veneris et Mercurii. Et quia Mercurius est in forma Saturni et finis Veneris, significat morbum varium et multiplicem, qui cum incidat in decrepitam aetatem, facile occidit. De hoc autem si evasero 56. et 68. diligentius considerabo."
41. Cardano, *Liber xii geniturarum,* in Ptolemy, *Quadripartitum,* ed. Cardano (Lyons, 1555), 67 (*O* V.520): "Et quia est mulier non amplius me extendo, nisi quod fuit ingeniosa, sapiens, liberalis, proba et amans filiorum." In the final edition, Cardano excised the words "et amans filiorum."
42. Cf. D. E. Harkness, "Managing an Experimental Household: The Dees of Mortlake and the Practice of Natural Philosophy," *Isis* 88 (1997), 247–262.
43. Some contemporaries—e.g. the young Jacques-Auguste de Thou—also remarked on the bizarre conduct that Cardano described, and took it as evidence of his lack of mental balance. See H. Morley, *Jerome Cardan: The Life of Girolamo Cardano of Milan, Physician* (London, 1854), II, 294.
44. G. Cardano, *Arcana politica* (Amsterdam, 1635), chap. 31, "Silentii laus," 96–100, e.g. 98: "In universum, scite tacere, ut philosophus ille regi innuit, non minus est, quam scire loqui."
45. G. Naudé, "De Cardano iudicium," in Cardano, *De propria vita liber* (1654), sigs. *5 verso–*6 recto. Cf. e.g. R. Villari, *Elogio della dissimulazione* (Rome, 1987); P. Zagorin, *Ways of Lying* (Cambridge, Mass., 1990); P. Burke, *The Fortunes of the Courtier* (Cambridge, 1995); and, above all, H. Lethen, *Verhaltenslehren der Kälte* (Frankfurt, 1994).
46. Cardano, *De propria vita liber* 21 (1654), 42–44 = *O* I.11.
47. For the later Middle Ages see M. Préaud, *Les astrologues à la fin du Moyen Age* (Paris, 1984).
48. Bartholomew Reisacher, horoscope for Anna, archduchess of Austria, Österreichische Nationalbibliothek MS 10754, fol. 40 recto: "Prae se feret igitur

virilem quandam severitatem ac authoritatem, erit ad iram proclivis et vindictae cupida. Erit idonea gubernationi ac administrationi alicuius."

49. Bodleian Library MS Ashmole 176, fol. 36 recto: "Cum luna in signo masculino et sol in feminino reperiantur, faciunt mutatis vicibus nunc virilem, nunc mollem in venereis, eoque deterius quod venus est masculina et mars foemininus ex natura signi: et pollutiones hi naturales, non tamen contra naturam indicant, praesertim in boreali viro, sicuti in Astrologicis docuimus."

50. Cf. Goclenius' remark on p. 70 about some of the qualities he had observed in genitures, few of which could have made happy news for their subjects or their subjects' parents: "Morum vehementiam et crudelitatem significavit Mars in ascendente, solus morum significator in signo Librae: cuius rei vidi plura exempla: mortem autem violentam ex ferro denotavit Luna in occidente ad oppositionem eiusdem, et Saturni coniunctionem festinans: et hae rationes sunt evidentissimae, iuxta aphorismum astrologicum. Luminaria in angulis ab alterutro maleficorum vel utroque sauciata, mortem violentam portendunt."

51. Cardano *De propria vita liber* 10 (1654), 32 = *O* I.8.

52. Cardano, *Libelli quinque* (1547), 122 ro-vo: "profundam cogitationem, studium, diligentiam, summamque laboris patientiam praestat: obscuros tamen effectus, qui ab his proveniunt, efficit, quod in sexto loco sit, ingeniumque turbidum propter lacteam viam, falsamque memoriam, quamvis magnam, infirmumque corpus: et reliqua, quae et si bona non sint, hucusque tamen non queant improbari." Cf. Misch, 706.

53. Cardano, *Liber xii geniturarum,* in Ptolemy, *Quadripartitum,* ed. Cardano (Lyons, 1555), 84–85 = *O* V.523. Cf. Misch for a fine discussion of this text. Though Cardano worked for a long time on his own horoscope, the paratactic style of explication which he adopted may have owed something to another astrologer. In his *Libelli quinque* (1547), 180 recto, Cardano gave his geniture 97, that of Emperor Maximilian I, remarking: "Hanc genituram ego posui, quia est exemplum Schonerij, qui nuper aedidit librum in hac arte." J. Schöner had in fact published this geniture and discussed it intensively in his *De iudiciis nativitatum libri tres* (Nuremberg, 1545). This text includes a presentation by Melanchthon; the copy Schöner gave Melanchthon, or one of them, inscribed, is Herzog August Bibliothek, Wolfenbüttel, 117 Quodl. 2 (4). Schöner's long and probing analyses of Maximilian's character closely resemble Cardano's readings of his own chart in form. See e.g. I.7, xxxix recto: "Conclusio secunda. Significatur itaque ratione Martis, natum futurum audacem, potentem, fortem, iracundum, armorum cupidum, bellorum autorem, animosum, sine pavore mortis pericula aggredientem, neminem sibi praeferet nec cuiquam se unquam submittet."

54. Cardano, *Liber xii geniturarum* (1555), 83 = *O* V.523

55. Ibid., 84 = *O* V.523: "Et quamvis mores nostri sint (alia non nobis propria) ut nec laudare citra iactantiam, nec vituperare citra amentiam posse videamur,

nos hic non de moribus philosophia et educatione acquisitis sermonem habemus, verum de naturalibus ac talibus quorum non puduerit Socratem dici stupidum, imperitum et intemperantem esse. Alia enim est naturalis affectio, alia studiorum et disciplinae, qua mores uniuscuiusque instituuntur."

56. UB Leipzig, MS Stadtbibliothek 935. 1 ro: "Cum videmus ad quae vitia proni simus propter stellas aut temperamenta, maiore vigilantia regendi sunt mores, ne malae inclinationes vincant."

57. British Library MS Sloane 325, 37 ro: "Ineptum ad disciplinas, tardum ingenio, credulum, mobilem, inconstantem, facile per errorem peccantem, vafrum, infidum, impetuosum, temerarium, obliviosum, mendacem facit haec constitutio. Et nisi multa bona aeducatione corrigatur, qui propter delicta sua magnam aliquando poenam merebitur." For yet another, similar moralizing interpretation of a geniture, see the anonymous "Farrago Thematum genethlialogicorum collecta per A. R. G. L. Witebergae" bound with L. Gaurico, *Tractatus astrologicus* (Venice, 1552), in Herzog August Bibliothek, Wolfenbüttel, 35.2 Astron., fol. 259 recto (geniture of Ambrosius Glandorpius, born 1542): "D.O.M. Significatur magna vis ingenii et calliditas excellens et multum consilii et audaciae sed adversationes et impedimenta non mediocria. DEVS gubernet et flectat tantam naturae vim ad negotia salutaria. Aliquid et paterna institutio proficere poterit, si initio rectis opinionib. tenerum pectus imbuet. Nihil humile aut sordidum cogitabit haec natura et favetur magis ad honesta propter loca solis, lunae et Iovis. Sed Saturni et Martis coniunctio accendet pravos aliquos impetus. Ideo primum assuefaciendus est ad intellectum et amorem honestarum rerum. Erit et consiliarius magnorum principum &c." Glandorpius did produce one *Epicedion* (Wittenberg, 1564), a work three leaves long.

58. L. A. Jardine and A. Grafton, "'Studied for Action': How Gabriel Harvey Read His Livy," *Past & Present* 129 (1990), 30–78.

59. Cardano, *De propria vita liber* 2 (1654), 6 = *O* I.2.

60. In ibid., 26 (1654), 68–69 = *O* I.16–17, Cardano ascribed the end of his sufferings to a dream about his future wife.

61. Cf. S. Schade, *Schadenzauber und die Magie des Körpers* (Worms, 1983), and J. L. Koerner, *The Moment of Self-Portraiture in German Renaissance Art* (Chicago and London, 1993). On the role played by spells even in medical explanations of impotence, see D. Jacquart and C. Thomasset, *Sexuality and Medicine in the Middle Ages*, tr. M. Adamson (Princeton, 1988), 169–173.

62. For the persistence of such beliefs, drawn bodily from the *Malleus maleficarum*, in the Romagna, see G. Menghi, *Compendio dell'arte essorcistica* (Bologna, 1576; repr. Genoa, 1987), II.5, 114–120; III.4, 250. For Menghi's use of the *Malleus*—as well as local, oral traditions—see O. Franceschini, "Postfazione" to the 1987 Genoa reprint. Similar views, and an even more systematic treatment of the forms the problem took, appear in F. M. Guazzo's *Compendium maleficarum* of 1608, tr. E. A. Ashwin (London, 1929; repr. New York, 1988), II.4, 91–95.

63. S. Clark, *Thinking with Demons: The Idea of Witchcraft in Early Modern Europe* (Oxford, 1997).
64. Cardano, *De propria vita liber* 33 (1654), 104 = *O* I.25.
65. See Cardano, *De libris propriis* (1562), 4 = *O* I.97: "Ego tamen, qui tot puellarum pulchrarum atque nobilium et divitum amore nunquam succendi potueram: quique mihi conscius eram veneficii aut naturalis impotentiae . . ."
66. See Siraisi.
67. Cf. M. Dewar, *Sir Thomas Smith* (London 1964). Dewar treats the rise of Smith's interest in astrology as an irrational or despairing effort to compensate for his fall, with Somerset, the first of the great men appointed to "Protect" England for young Edward, in 1549 (65)—even though Smith himself made clear that his interest revived long after the crisis of the Protector's regime, in 1555; see British Library, MS Sloane 325, 4 ro: "Ao 1555o Circa Menses Octob. No et December vehementissimus ardor et desiderium me incessit astrologiam discendi ut vix noctu propter illud studium conquiescerem: cuiusmodi etiam cupiditas anno ut coniectabam 20 aut 21o meae aetatis me invasit." Such attitudes are typical of most works on Cardano before those of A. Ingegno, G. Ernst, and N. Siraisi.
68. C. Peucer, *Commentarius de praecipuis divinationum generibus* (Wittenberg, 1553), 34 ro: "Norunt exactissime coelestium corporum naturas, vires, atque effectiones, et in eum finem condita esse sciunt, ut naturam elementarem unaquaeque pars, alia alio modo, moveat immutetque, et varie efficiat ac temperet primis qualitatibus diversimode iunctis ac mixtis inter se. Ab his qualitatibus et alia occulta vi stellarum, hominum temperamenta mirabiliter affici intelligunt et experiuntur, et quid quaevis stellae, quovis loco aut constitutione vel designent, vel gignant atque efficiant, perspiciunt integerrime."
69. See *Aubrey's Brief Lifes,* ed. O. L. Dick (London, 1949; repr. Ann Arbor, 1957), liv–lv, c; cf. M. Hunter, *John Aubrey and the Realm of Learning* (London, 1975).
70. See Zimmermann.
71. Cardano, *De propria vita liber* 23 (1654), 63 = *O* I.15.
72. Ibid., 32 (1654), 95–96 = *O*, I.23. See also the intensely misanthropic chapter 53 (1654), 223–226 = *O* I.53.
73. Ibid., 9 (1654), 31 = *O* I.8: "cuperem notum esse quod sim, non opto ut sciatur qualis sim"; Thomas Browne, *Hydriotaphia, or Urne-Burial,* V, *Works,* ed. G. Keynes (London, 1928; repr. London, Toronto and Chicago, 1967), I, 167, quoted by Stoner, 302. Browne noted that Cardano, in saying this, was "disparaging his horoscopal inclination and judgement of himself."
74. Cardano, *De propria vita liber* 31 (1654), 91–95 = *O* I.22.
75. Ibid., prooemium (1654), 1 = *O* I.1.
76. Marcus Aurelius Antoninus *De seipso seu vita sua libri xii,* ed. and tr. G. Xylander (Zurich, 1569).
77. Ibid., 20 (bk. 1).
78. Ibid., 20–24 (bk. 1).

79. Ibid., ep. ded., 5[misnumbered 21]–6: "Enimvero ANTONINVM ego iudico (neque aliter sentire doctos existimo) non id modo his voluisse in commentariis explicare, quibus ipse in rebus animum suum occupasset, quibusque praeceptis, exemplis, et rationibus sese ad hominis, civis, imperatoris, adeoque philosophi nomen cum dignitate tuendum informavisset: sed una demonstrasse, quae esset vera atque expedita ad tranquillitatem animi, et eam quae homini in hac vita contingere potest felicitatem consequendam via." For a full discussion of Marcus' views on time see P. Hadot, *La citadelle intérieure* (Paris, 1992), chap. 7; for an interesting discussion of Xylander's scholarly limitations, see ibid., 39–42.
80. See the beautiful study of J. Papy, "Lipsius and Marcus Welser: The Antiquarian's Life as *via media*," *Bulletin de l'Institut Historique Belge de Rome* 68 (1998), 173–190 at 184–190.
81. For Cardano's unquenchable desire for expensive pens, glass spheres, and other material goods of the sort despised by Marcus, see *De propria vita liber* 18 (1654), 57 = *O* I.14; cf. Pfeiffer.
82. Cardano, *De propria vita liber,* prooemium (1654), 2 = *O* I.1.
83. Ibid., 37 (1654), 113–114 = *O* I.27. Cf. Simon Forman's description "Of Visions that the said S. had being yet a childe," Bodleian Library MS Ashmole 208, 137 ro. Forman, loved by his father but not by his brothers or his mother, slept in a "lyttle bed" by that of his father, "and so sone as he was alwaies lad downe to slepe he should see in visions alwaies many mighti mountaines and hills com rowling againste him, as though they wold overron him and falle on him and brust him. yet he gote upp allwais to the top of them and with moch adoe wente over them. Then should he see many grete waters like to drowne him boilinge and raginge against him as thoughe they wold swallowe him up, yet he thought he did overpasse them. And thes dremes and visions he had every nighte continually for 3. or 4. yers space."
84. Cardano, *De propria vita liber* 31 (1654), 91–92 = *O* I.22. Cf. chap. 46 (1654), 184–186 = *O* I.43–44.
85. Ibid., 41 (1654), 146–147 = *O* I.34–35.
86. Ibid., 33 (1654), 104 = *O* I.25: "afferebant quoque nativitatum fasciculos, ut de his pronunciarem, tanquam ariolus et vates, non ut medicinae professor." Cf. 39 (1654), 129–133 = *O* I.31.
87. Cardano, *Liber xii geniturarum* (1555), 78.

11. The Astrologer as Empiricist

1. Oxford, Bodleian Library, MS Aubrey 6, fol. 12 vo; J. Aubrey, *Brief Lives,* ed. A. Clark, 2 vols. (Oxford, 1898), I, 9. This appears above William Petty's horoscope, of which Aubrey remarked, ibid., 12 vo = *Brief Lives,* ed. Clark, II, 139: "This was donne, and a Judgement upon it, by Charles Snell Esq. of Alderholt, neer Fordingbridge in Hampshire."

2. Oxford, Bodleian Library, MS Aubrey 23 (Aubrey's *Collectio geniturarum;* see M. Hunter, *John Aubrey and the Realm of Learning* [London, 1975], 129 and n. 3 for the date), 12 ro-vo.
3. For some typical critical remarks, any of which Cardano might have made, see e.g. Oxford, Bodleian Library, MS Aubrey 23, 52 vo, on Hobbes's nativity: "I had the yeare and day and houre from his owne mouth"; 53 vo, on Walter Charleton: "borne at Shepton Malet in Com. Somst. Febr. 2d 1619 about 6 h P.M. his mother being then at supper. q day of ye weeke [last sentence crossed out]"; 55 vo, a note in another hand, on William Count of Pembroke: "His Nativity was calculated by old Mr Th. Allen. His death was foretold, wch happened true at the time foretold. being well in health he made a feast ate and dranke plentifully, went to bed and found dead in the morning."
4. Anthony Wood to Aubrey, 23 March 1672, Oxford, Bodleian Library, MS Aubrey 23, 62 vo.
5. Oxford, Bodleian Library, MS Aubrey 23, 77 ro, on a criminal (note in margin): "This is ye Copie of his Mothers owne handwriting": "Charles Pamphlin was borne the last day of August before day, the howre I did justly know, but I guesse it might be about 3. or 4 a clock in the morning being fryday the August after the King was beheaded, wch I thinke was 29 yeares since last August. He was hanged in Convent-Garden on a Gibbet, for stealing his Msts Chapelle plate, May 22. 1678."
6. Oxford, Bodleian Library, MS Aubrey 23, 29 vo. On Browne's propensity for introspection see V. Woolf, *The Common Reader* (London, 1925).
7. P. Brind'Amour, *Nostradamus astrophile* (Paris and Ottawa, 1993), 467–470.
8. C. Ginzburg, *Occhiacci di legno: Nove riflessioni sulla distanza* (Milan, 1998), 15–39.
9. Cf. R. Reisinger, *Historische Horoskopie* (Wiesbaden, 1997).
10. G. B. Della Porta, *Coelestis physiognomia,* ed. A. Paolella (Naples, 1996).

BIBLIOGRAPHY

Manuscripts and Annotated Books

Berlin-Dahlem
  Geheimes Preussisches Staatsarchiv
    HBA A4 214
    HBA A4 217
    HBA A4 223
Cambridge, Mass.
  Houghton Library
    *GC5.C7906.540a. Cardano, *Libelli duo,* 1543, owned by Fridericus Staphylus
    *IC5.C1782.543l. Cardano, *Libelli duo,* 1543, owned by Janus Cornarius
Hamburg
  Staats- und Universitätsbibliothek Carl von Ossietzky
    Supellex Epistolica 45 (folio)
    Supellex Epistolica 59 (folio)
Leipzig
  Universitätsbibliothek
    Stadtbibliothek 935
London
  British Library
    C 112 c 5, Cardano, *Libelli quinque,* 1547, owned by Richard Bruarne
    53 b 7, Cardano, *Libelli quinque,* 1547, owner anonymous
    Sloane 325
Munich
  Bayerische Staatsbibliothek
    clm 27003
    4° Astr. U 35a, Cardano, *Libelli quinque,* 1547, owned by an unknown reader

Oxford
Bodleian Library
4° Rawl. 61, Gaurico, *Tractatus astrologicus,* 1552, owned by Gabriel Harvey
8° E 8 Art. Seld., Eunapius, *Vitae sophistarum,* 1568, owned by John Dee
Ashmole D 50, Cardano, *Somniorum Synesiorum libri IIII,* 1562, owned by John Aubrey
Ashmole 157, Cardano, *Libelli quinque,* 1547, owned by Thomas Smith and William Lilly
Ashmole 165, Gaurico, *Tractatus astrologicus,* 1552, owned by William Lilly
Ashmole 497, F. Giuntini, *Speculum astrologiae,* 1573, owned by William Lilly
Ashmole 570, Ptolemy, *Quadripartitum,* ed. Cardano, 1578, owned by Elias Ashmole
Ashmole 176
Ashmole 208
Aubrey 6
Aubrey 23

Paris
Bibliothèque Nationale
lat. 7305
lat. 7395
lat. 7446

Princeton, N.J.
Private collection.
J. Stoeffler and J. Flaum, *Almanach nova plurimis annis venturis inservientia* Venice, 1522, owned by an anonymous student of astrology

Vatican City
Biblioteca Apostolica Vaticana
Vat. lat. 1794

Vienna
Österreichische Nationalbibliothek
72 J 35, Cardano, *Libelli duo,* 1543, owned by Philipp Melanchthon
72 X 5 Cardano, *Libelli duo,* 1543, owner anonymous
MS 6070
MS 10754

Washington, D.C.
Folger Shakespeare Library
BF 1501 J2 copy 2 Ficino, *De vita coelitus comparanda,* 1516, owned by John Dee

Wolfenbüttel

Herzog August Bibliothek

35.2 Astron. "Farrago thematum genethlialogicorum collecta per A.R.G.L. Witebergae," bound with Luca Gaurico, *Tractatus astrologicus,* 1552

117 Quodl. 2 (4), J. Schöner, *De iudiciis nativitatum libri tres,* 1545, presented by Schöner to Melanchthon

Primary Sources

Aelius Aristides, *Orationum tomi tres,* tr. W. Canter. Basel, 1566.

Agrippa, H. C. *De occulta philosophia libri tres,* ed. V. Perrone Compagni. Leiden, New York, and Cologne, 1992.

Alberti, L. B. *Opere volgari,* ed. C. Grayson. 3 vols. Bari, 1960–1973.

Alciato, A. *Emblemata,* ed. C. Mignault. Antwerp, 1578.

Amboise, F d'. *Discours ou traité des devises.* Paris, 1620.

Ashmole, E. *Elias Ashmole (1617–1692): His Autobiographical and Historical Notes, His Correspondence, and Other Contemporary Sources Relating to His Life and Work,* ed. C. H. Josten. 5 vols. Oxford, 1966.

Aubrey, J. *Aubrey's Brief Lives,* ed. O. L. Dick. London, 1949; repr. Ann Arbor, 1957.

——— *Brief Lives,* ed. A. Clark. 2 vols. Oxford, 1898.

Bellanti, L. *Defensio astrologiae.* Venice, 1502.

Benatius, J. *Prognosticon anni MCCCCCII.* Bologna, 1502.

Berriot, F., ed. *Exposicions et significacions des songes et Les songes Daniel.* Geneva, 1989.

Bodin, J. *De la démonomanie des sorciers.* Paris, 1587; repr. Paris, 1979.

——— *De republica,* Paris, 1576.

——— *Methodus ad facilem historiarum cognitionem.* Paris, 1566.

Brahe, T. *Opera omnia,* ed. J. L. E. Dreyer. Copenhagen, 1913; repr. Amsterdam, 1972.

Browne, T. *Works,* ed. G. Keynes. 4 vols. London, 1928; repr. London, Chicago, and Toronto, 1964.

Camerarius, J. *De vita Philippi Melanchthonis narratio,* ed. G. Th. Strobelius. Halle, 1777.

Campanella, T. *Articuli prophetales,* ed. G. Ernst. Florence, 1977.

Cane, O. *Pronostico del Anno M.D.XL.* N.p., 1540.

Cardano, G. *Arcana politica.* Amsterdam, 1635.

——— *The Book of My Life,* tr. J. Stoner. London and Toronto, 1931.

——— *De malo recentiorum medicorum medendi usu libellus.* Venice, 1536.

——— *De propria vita liber,* ed. G. Naudé. 2d ed. Amsterdam, 1654.

——— *De rerum varietate libri xvii.* Basel, 1557.

——— *De rerum varietate libri xvii.* Avignon, 1558.

——— *De subtilitate.* Nuremberg, 1550.

——— *De subtilitate.* Paris, 1551.

——— *De subtilitate.* Lyons, 1554.

——— *Encomium Neronis: Edition, Übersetzung und Kommentar.* ed. N. Eberl. Frankfurt, Berlin, Bern, New York, Paris and Vienna, 1994.

——— *Libelli duo.* Nuremberg, 1543.

——— *Libelli quinque.* Nuremberg, 1547.

——— "Libellus de libris propriis, cui titulus est Ephemerus." *De sapientia libri quinque.* Nuremberg, 1544.

——— *Libellus qui dicitur Supplementum almanach. Libellus alius de restitutione temporum et motuum coelestium, quinque principum geniture cum expositione, quinque eruditorum virorum geniture cum expositione.* Milan, 1538.

——— *Liber de libris propriis.* Lyons, 1557.

——— *Liber de libris propriis.* Basel, 1562. In Cardano, *Somniorum Synesiorum libri iiii.* Basel, 1562.

——— *Opera,* ed. C. Spon. 10 vols. Lyons, 1663; repr. Stuttgart-Bad Canstatt, 1966.

——— *Pronostico o vero iudicio generale composto per lo eccelente Messer Hieronymo Cardano phisico Milanese, dal 1534 insino al 1550. Con molti capitoli eccellenti.* Venice, 1534/1535.

——— *Pronostico generale,* ed. G. Ernst. In *Girolamo Cardano: Le opere, le fonti, la vita,* ed. M. Baldi and G. Canziani. Milan, 1999.

——— *Somniorum Synesiorum, omnis generis insomnia explicantes, libri iiii.* Basel, 1562.

——— ed. Ptolemy, *Quadripartitum.* Basel, 1554.

——— ed. Ptolemy, *Quadripartitum.* Lyons, 1555.

——— ed. Ptolemy, *Quadripartitum.* Basel, 1578.

Castagnola, R., ed. *I Guicciardini e le scienze occulte.* Florence, 1990.

Castiglione, B. *Gallorum Insubrum antiquae sedes.* Milan, 1541.

Coopland, G. W., ed. *Nicole Oresme and the Astrologers.* Liverpool, 1952.

Corpus reformatorum, ed. C. G. Bretschneider et al. Halle, 1834–.

Dee, J. *John Dee on Asronomy = Propaedeumata aphoristica (1558 and 1568),* ed. and tr. W. Shumaker, int. J. Heilbron. Berkeley, 1978.

Della Porta, G. B. *Coelestis physiognomia,* ed. A. Paolella. Naples, 1996.

Erasmus, D. *Opus epistolarum D. Erasmi Roterodami,* ed. P. S. Allen et al. Oxford, 1906–1958.

Eunapius, *De vitis philosophorum et sophistarum,* ed. H. Junius. Antwerp, 1568.

Estienne, H. *Noctes Parisinae.* In Aulus Gellius, *Noctes Atticae,* ed. H. Estienne. Paris, 1585.

Ficino, M. *De vita coelitus comparanda.* Venice, 1516.

——— *Opera omnia.* Basel, 1576; repr. ed. P. O. Kristeller, Turin, 1959.

——— *Three Books on Life,* ed. and tr. C. V. Kaske and J. R. Clark. Binghamton, N.Y., 1989.

Fontana, D. M. *Ad Illustrissimum Dominum D. Iohannem Benti. de Aragonia etc. . . . Prognosticon in annum 1501.* Bologna, 1501.

Forman, S. *The Autobiography and Personal Diary of Dr. Simon Forman,* ed. J. O. Halliwell. London, 1849.

Fuchs, C. H., ed. *Die ältesten Schriftsteller über die Lustseuche in Deutschland, von 1493 bis 1510.* Göttingen, 1843.

Galen. *Selected Works,* tr. and ed. P. N. Singer. Oxford, 1997.

Garin, E., et al., ed. *Testi umanistici su l'Ermetismo.* Rome, 1955.

Gasser, A. P. *Prognosticum astrologicum ad annum Christi MDXLIIII.* Nuremberg, 1543.

Gaurico, L. *Tractatus astrologicus.* Venice, 1552.

Goclenius, R. *Synopsis astrologiae specialis.* In Goclenius, *Synopsis methodica geometriae, astronomiae, astrologiae, opticae et geographiae.* Frankfurt, 1620.

——— *Uranoscopiae, chiroscopiae, metoposcopiae, et ophthalmoscopiae contemplatio.* Frankfurt, 1608.

Grünpeck, J. *Pronosticon anni MDXXXII usque ad annos MDXXXX.* Regensburg, 1532; repr. Milan, 1532.

Guazzo, F. M. *Compendium maleficarum,* tr. E. A. Ashwin. London, 1929; repr. New York, 1988.

Gudius, M., et al. *Marquardi Gudii et doctorum virorum ad eum epistolae.* Utrecht, 1697.

Guicciardini, F. *Opere,* ed. V. de Caprariis. Milan and Naples, 1953.

Harvey, G. *Gabriel Harvey's Marginalia,* ed. G. C. Moore Smith. Stratford-upon-Avon, 1913.

Jeake, S. *An Astrological Diary of the Seventeenth century: Samuel Jeake of Rye, 1652–1699,* ed. M. Hunter and A. Gregory. Oxford, 1988.

Jones, A., ed. *The Astrological Papyri from Oxyrhynchus.* Philadelphia, forthcoming.

Kepler, J. *Gesammelte Werke,* ed. M. Caspar et al. Munich, 1937—

Leowitz, C. *De coniunctionibus magnis.* Lauingen, 1564.

Lilly, W. *Christian Astrology Modestly Treated of, in Three Books.* London, 1647; repr. 1985.

Marcus Aurelius Antoninus. *De seipso seu vita sua libri xii,* ed. and tr. G. Xylander. Zurich, 1569.

Menghi, G. *Compendio dell'arte essorcistica.* Bologna, 1576; repr. ed. O. Franceschini, Genoa, 1987.

Mizauld, A. *Ephemerides aeris perpetuae, seu popularis et rusica tempestatum astrologia, ubique terrarum et vera et certa.* Antwerp, 1555.

Montaigne, Michel de. *Journal de voyage,* ed. F. Rigolot. Paris, 1992.

Montulmo, A. de. *De iudiciis nativitatum liber praeclarissimus.* Nuremberg, 1540.

Morhof, D. G. *Polyhistor, literarius, philosophicus et practicus,* 3d ed. 2 vols. Lübeck, 1732.

Nifo, A. *Ad Apotelesmata Ptolemaei eruditiones.* Naples, 1513.

——— *De falsa diluvii prognosticatione.* Florence, 1520.

——— *De nostrarum calamitatum causis liber.* Venice, 1505.

Nostradamus, M. de. *Les premières centuries ou propheties,* ed. P. Brind'Amour. Geneva, 1996.

——— *Lettres inédites,* ed. J. Dupèbe. Geneva, 1983.

Palmieri, M. *Libro del Poema chiamato Citta di Vita,* ed. M. Rooke. Smith College Studies in Modern Languages, VIII, 1–2; IX, 1–4. Northampton and Paris, 1926–1928.

Peckham, J. *Perspectiva,* ed. L. Gaurico. Venice, 1504.

——— *Perspectiva communis,* ed. F. Cardano. Milan, 1482/83?

Peucer, C. *Commentarius de praecipuis divinationum generibus.* Wittenberg, 1553.

Peutinger, K. *Briefwechsel,* ed. E. König. Munich, 1923.

Pico della Mirandola, G. *Disputationes adversus astrologiam divinatricem,* ed. E. Garin. 2 vols. Florence, 1946–1952.

Pighius, A. *Adversus prognosticatorum vulgus, qui annuas praedictiones edunt, et se astrologos mentiuntur, astrologiae defensio.* Paris, 1518.

Pirckheimer, W. *Briefwechsel,* ed. E. Reicke et al. 3 vols. Munich, 1940–1989.

Platina, B. *On Right Pleasure and Good Health,* ed. M. E. Milham. Tempe, Ariz., 1998.

Pomponazzi, P. *De naturalium effectuum causis sive de Incantationibus.* Basel, 1567; repr. Hildesheim and New York, 1970.

Pontano, G. G. *De rebus coelestibus libri XIV.* Basel, 1530.

Ptolemy. *Tetrabiblos,* ed. and tr. F. E. Robbins. Cambridge, Mass., 1940.

Rheticus, G. J. *Narratio prima,* ed. H. Hugonnard-Roche et al. Wrocław, 1982.

Rogeriis, Ioannes de. *Ad Christianissimum Gallorum regem Prognosticon anni 1537.* Rome, 1537.

Salutati, C. *De fato et fortuna,* ed. C. Bianca. Rome, 1985.

Schöner, J. *De iudiciis nativitatum libri tres.* Nuremberg, 1545.

Shumaker, W. *Renaissance Curiosa.* Binghamton, N.Y., 1982.

Stoeffler, J. *Ephemerides,* ed. P. Pitatus. Tübingen, 1548.

Stoeffler, J., and J. Flaum. *Almanach nova plurimis annis venturis inservientia.* Venice, 1506.

Valla, G. *Commentationes in Ptolemaei Quadripartitum.* Venice, 1502.

Wolf, H., ed. *In Claudii Ptolemaei Quadripartitum enarrator ignoti nominis.* Basel, 1559.

Yagel, A. *A Valley of Vision,* tr. and ed. D. B. Ruderman. Philadelphia, 1990.

Secondary Sources

Abbondanza, R. *Dizionario biografico degli italiani,* s.v. Andrea Alciato.

Adorno, T. W. *The Stars Down to Earth and Other Essays on the Irrational in Culture,* ed. S. Crook. London and New York, 1994.

Alberigo, G. *Dizionario biografico degli italiani,* s.v. Archinto, Filippo.

Albonico, S. *Il ruginoso stile.* Milan, 1990.

Allen, M. J. B. *Synoptic Art: Marsilio Ficino on the History of Platonic Interpretation.* Florence, 1998.

Amelang, J. "Spanish Autobiography in the Early Modern Era." *Ego-Dokumente:*

Annäherung an den Menschen in der Geschichte, ed. W. Schulze. Berlin, 1996. Pp. 59–71.

Armstrong, J. "An Italian Astrologer at the Court of Henry VIII." *Italian Renaissance Studies,* ed. E. F. Jacob. London, 1960. Pp. 433–454.

Arrizabalaga, J., J. Henderson, and R. French. *The Great Pox.* New Haven and London, 1997.

Barnes, R. *Prophecy and Gnosis.* Stanford, 1988.

Baron. F. *Doctor Faustus from History to Legend.* Munich, 1978.

——— "Who Was the Historical Faustus? Interpreting an Overlooked Source." *Daphnis* 18 (1989), 297–302.

Barton, T. *Ancient Astrology.* London, 1994

——— *Power and Knowledge.* Ann Arbor, 1994.

Bauer, B. "Die Rolle des Hofastrologen und Hofmathematicus als fürstlicher Berater." *Höfischer Humanismus,* ed. A. Buck. Weinheim, 1989. Pp. 93–117.

Baxter, C. "Jean Bodin's Daemon and His Conversion to Judaism." *Jean Bodin: Verhandlungen der internationalen Bodin Tagung in München,* ed. H. Denzer. Munich, 1973. Pp. 1–21.

Béhar, P. *Les langues occultes de la Renaissance.* Paris, 1996.

Bell, R. *How to Do It: Guides to Good Living for Renaissance Italians.* Chicago and London, 1999.

Berns, J. J. *Die Herkunft des Automobils aus Himmelstrionfo und Höllenmaschine.* Berlin, 1996.

Bezold, F. von. "Jean Bodin als Okkultist und seine Démonomanie." *Historische Zeitschrift* 105 (1910), 1–64.

Biondi, G. "Minima astrologica. Gli astrologi e la guida della vita quotidiana." *Schifanoia* 2 (1986), 41–48.

Blair, A. *The Theater of Nature: Jean Bodin and Renaissance Science.* Princeton, 1997.

Bock, G. *Thomas Campanella.* Tübingen, 1974.

Bokdam, S, "Les mythes de l'origine de l'astrologie à la Renaissance." *Divination et controverse religieuse en France au xvie siècle.* Paris, 1987. Pp. 57–72.

Bolzoni, L. *Il teatro della memoria.* Padua, 1984.

Borst, A. *Das Buch der Naturgeschichte: Plinius und seine Leser im Zeitalter des Pergaments.* Heidelberg, 1994.

Boudet, J.-P. *Live dans le ciel. La bibliothèque de Simon de Phares, astrologue du xve siècle.* Brussels, 1994.

——— "Simon de Phares et les rapports entre astrologie et prophétie à la fin du Moyen Age," *Les textes prophétiques et la prophétie en occident (XII–XVI siècle),* ed. A. Vauchez. Rome, 1990. Pp. 327–358.

Bowden, M. E. "The Scientific Revolution in Astrology." Diss. Yale, 1974.

Bremmer, J. "Prophets, Seers, and Politics in Greece, Israel, and Early Modern Europe." *Numen* 40 (1993), 150–183.

Brind'Amour, P. *Nostradamus astrophile.* Ottawa and Paris, 1993.

Brown, P. *Authority and the Sacred.* Cambridge, 1995.

Browne, A. "Girolamo Cardano's *Somniorum Synesiorum libri iiii.*" *Bibliothèque d'Humanisme et Renaissance* 40 (1979), 123–135.

Burckhardt, J. *Die Kultur der Renaissance in Italien: Ein Versuch.* Darmstadt, 1955.

Burke, P. *The Fortunes of the Courtier.* Cambridge, 1995.

——— *Varieties of Cultural History* (Ithaca, 1997).

Burmeister, K. H. *Achilles Pirmin Gasser, 1505–1577.* 3 vols. Wiesbaden, 1970–1975.

——— *Georg Joachim Rhetikus, 1514–1574: Eine Bio-Bibliographie.* 3 vols. Wiesbaden, 1967–1968.

Campbell, L. B. *Scenes and Machines on the English Stage during the Renaissance.* Cambridge, 1923; repr. New York, 1960.

Cantimori, D. *Eretici italiani del Cinquecento.* Florence, 1939.

——— "Note su alcuni aspetti della propaganda religiosa nell'Europa del Cinquecento." *Aspects de la propagande religieuse.* Geneva, 1957. = *Umanesimo e religione nel Rinascimento,* 2d ed. Turin, 1975. Pp. 164–181.

——— "Umanesimo e luteranesimo di fronte alla scolastica: Caspar Peucer." *Rivista di studi germanici* 2 (1937) 417–438. = *Umanesimo e religione nel Rinascimento,* 2d ed. Turin, 1975. Pp. 88–111.

Cardini, F. "Sognare a Firenze fra Trecento e Quattrocento." *Le mure di Firenze inargentate.* Palermo, 1993. Pp. 29–57.

Carey, H. M. *Courting Disaster: Astrology at the English Court and University in the Later Middle Ages.* New York, 1992.

Casanova, E. "L'astrologia e la consegna del bastone al capitano generale della repubblica fiorentina." *Archivio storico italiano* 5th ser. 7 (1891), 134–144.

Cassirer, E. *The Individual and the Cosmos in Renaissance Philosophy,* tr. M. Domandi. New York, 1963.

Céard, J. "Médicine et démonologie: les enjeux d'un débat." *Diable, diables et diableries au temps de la Renaissance,* ed. M. T. Jones-Davies. Paris, 1988. Pp. 97–112.

——— *La nature et les prodiges.* Geneva, 1977.

Chabod, F. *Storia di Milano nell'epoca di Carlo V.* Turin, 1971.

Christian, W., Jr. *Apparitions in Late Medieval and Renaissance Spain.* Princeton, 1981.

Clark, S. *Thinking with Demons: The Idea of Witchcraft in Early Modern Europe.* Oxford, 1997.

Clulee, N. *John Dee's Natural Philosophy: Between Science and Religion.* London and New York, 1988.

Cooper, R. "Deux médecins royaux onirocrites: Jehan Thibault et Auger Ferrier." *Le songe à la Renaissance,* ed. F. Charpentier. Saint-Etienne, 1990. Pp. 53–60.

Copenhaver, B. "Hermes Trismegistus, Proclus, and the Question of a Philosophy of Magic in the Renaissance." *Hermeticism and the Renaissance,* ed. I. Merkel and A. G. Debus. Washington, D.C., London, and Toronto, 1988. Pp. 79–110.

Couzinet, M.-D. *Histoire et méthode à la Renaissance: Une lecture de la Methodus ad facilem historiarum cognitionem de Jean Bodin.* Paris, 1996.

Cox-Rearick, J. *Dynasty and Destiny in Medici Art.* Princeton, 1984.

Cumont, F. *L'Egypte des astrologues.* Brussels, 1937.

Curry, P. *Prophecy and Power.* Princeton, 1989.

Dagron, G. "Le saint, le savant, l'astrologue: Etude de thèmes hagiographiques à travers quelques recueils de 'Questions et réponses' des Ve-VIIe siècles." *Hagiographie, cultures et sociétés, ive-xiie siècles.* Paris, 1981. Pp. 143–156.

Daston, L., and K. Park. *Wonders and the Order of Nature, 1150–1750,* New York, 1998.

Davidson, A. "Miracles of Bodily Transformation, or, How St. Francis Received the Stigmata." *Picturing Science, Producing Art,* ed. C. A. Jones and P. Galison. New York and London, 1998. Pp. 101–124.

Dekker, R. "Ego-Dokumente in den Niederlanden vom 16. bis zum 17. Jahrhundert." *Ego-Dokumente: Annäherung an den Menschen in der Geschichte,* ed. W. Schulze. Berlin, 1996. Pp. 33–57.

Demandt, A. *Der Fall Roms.* Munich, 1984.

Dewar, M. *Sir Thomas Smith.* London, 1964.

Dilg, P. "Der Kosmas-und-Damian-Hymnus des Theodoricus Ulsenius (um 1460–nach 1508)." *Orbis pictus,* ed. W. Dressendörfer and W.-D. Müller-Jahncke. Frankfurt, 1985. Pp. 65–72.

Dinzelbacher, P. *Heilige oder Hexen? Schicksale auffäliger Frauen in Mittelalter und Frühneuzeit.* Zurich, 1995; repr. Reinbek bei Hamburg, 1997.

Dionisotti, C. *Europe in Sixteenth-Century Italian Literature.* Oxford, 1971.

Dobin, H. *Merlin's Disciples.* Stanford, 1990.

Dodds, E. R. *The Greeks and the Irrational.* Berkeley, 1951.

——— *Pagan and Christian in an Age of Anxiety: Some Aspects of Religious Experience from Marcus Aurelius to Constantine.* Cambridge, 1965; repr. 1991.

Dohrn-van Rossum, G. *History of the Hour: Clocks and Modern Temporal Orders,* tr. T. Dunlap. Chicago, 1996.

Duden, B. *Geschichte unter der Haut: Ein Eisenacher Arzt und seine Patientinnen um 1730.* Stuttgart, 1987. = *The Woman Beneath the Skin,* tr. T. Dunlap. Cambridge, Mass., and London, 1991.

Dutton, P. E. *The Politics of Dreaming in the Carolingian Empire.* Lincoln and London, 1994.

Eade, J. C. *The Forgotten Sky: A Guide to Astrology in English Literature.* Oxford, 1984.

Eamon, W. *Science and the Secrets of Nature.* Princeton, 1994.

Ernst, G. *Religione, ragione e natura.* Milan, 1991.

Evans-Pritchard, E. E. *Witchcraft, Oracles, and Magic among the Azande.* Oxford, 1937.

Federici Vescovini, G. *Astrologia e scienza. La crisi dell'aristotelismo sul cadere del Trecento e Biagio Pelacani da Parma.* Florence 1979.

——— "L'astrologia all'Università di Ferrara nel Quattrocento." *La rinascita del sapere: libri e maestri dello studio ferrarese,* ed. P. Castelli. Venice, 1991. Pp. 293–306.

Ferrari, G. *L'esperienza del passato: Alessandro Benedetti filologo e medico umanista.* Florence, 1996.

——— "Public Anatomy Lessons and the Carnival: The Anatomy Theatre of Bologna." *Past & Present* 117 (1987), 50–106.

Festinger, L., et al. *When Prophecy Fails.* Minneapolis, 1956.

Field, A. "Lorenzo Buonincontri and the First Public Lectures on Manilius (Florence, ca. 1475–78)." *Rinascimento* n.s. 36 (1996), 207–225.

Field, J. V. *Kepler's Geometrical Cosmology.* Chicago, 1988.

——— "A Lutheran Astrologer: Johannes Kepler." *Archive for History of Exact Science* 31 (1984), 225–268.

Findlen, P. *Possessing Nature.* Berkeley and Los Angeles, 1994.

Firenze e la Toscana dei Medici nell'Europa del Cinquecento. Florence, 1980.

Flint, V. *The Rise of Magic in Early Medieval Europe.* Princeton, 1991.

Flitner, A. *Erasmus im Urteil seiner Nachwelt.* Tübingen, 1952.

Fögen, M. T. *Die Enteignung der Wahrsager.* Frankfurt, 1993.

Ford, P. "Jean Dorat and the Reception of Homer in Renaissance France." *International Journal of the Classical Tradition* 2 (1995), 265–274.

Foucault, M. *The History of Sexuality,* III: *The Care of the Self,* tr. R. Hurley. New York, 1986.

——— *Les mots et les choses.* Paris, 1966.

Garin, E. "Magic and Astrology." *Science and Civic Life in the Italian Renaissance,* tr. P. Munz. Gloucester, Mass., 1978.

——— *Lo zodiaco della vita.* Rome and Bari, 1982.

Geneva, A. *Astrology and the Seventeenth-Century Mind: William Lilly and the Language of the Stars.* Manchester and New York, 1995.

Gentilcore, D. *From Bishop to Witch.* Manchester and New York, 1992.

Gerl, A. *Trigonometrisch-Astronomisches Rechnen kurz vor Copernicus: Der Briefwechsel Regiomontanus-Bianchini.* Stuttgart, 1989.

Ginzburg, C. *Clues, Myths, and the Historical Method,* tr. J. C. Tedeschi and A. Tedeschi. Baltimore and London, 1989.

——— *Occhiacci di legno: Nove riflessioni sulla distanza.* Milan, 1998.

Glacken, C. *Traces on the Rhodian Shore.* Berkeley, 1967.

Glasser, R. *Time in French Life and Thought,* tr. C. G. Pearson. Manchester, 1972.

Gliozzi, M. *Dictionary of Scientific Biography,* s.v. Cardano, Girolamo.

Goffen, R. *Spirituality in Conflict: Saint Francis and Giotto's Bardi Chapel.* College Park, 1988.

Goldberg, J. "Cellini's *Vita* and the Conventions of Early Autobiography." *Modern Language Notes* 89 (1974), 71–83.

Gombrich, E. H. *Symbolic Images.* Oxford, 1972; repr. 1978.

Goody, J. *The Culture of Flowers.* Cambridge, 1993.

Grafton, A. "The Ancient City Restored: Archaeology, Ecclesiastical History, and Egyptology." *Rome Reborn,* ed. A. Grafton. Vatican City, Washington, D.C., New Haven, and London, 1993. Pp. 87–123.

——— *Commerce with the Classics.* Ann Arbor, 1997.

——— "From Apotheosis to Analysis: Some Late Renaissance Histories of Classical Astronomy." *History and the Disciplines: The Reclassification of Knowledge in Early Modern Europe,* ed. D. R. Kelley. Rochester, N.Y., 1997. Pp. 261–276.

——— "Girolamo Cardano and the Tradition of Classical Astrology," *Proceedings of the American Philosophical Society* 142 (1998), 323–354.

——— "Girolamo Cardano und die Tradition der klassischen Astrologie," *Scientia poetica* 2 (1998), 1–26.

——— *Joseph Scaliger.* Oxford, 1983–1993.

Graiff, F. "I prodigie l'astrologia nei commenti di Pietro Pomponazzi al *De caelo,* alla *Meteora* e al *De Generatione.*" *Medievo* 2 (1976), 331–361.

Gregori, C. "Rappresentazione e difesa: Osservazioni sul *De vita propria* di Gerolamo Cardano." *Quaderni storici* 73 (1990), 225–234.

Gregory, T. "I sogni e gli astri." *I sogni nel Medioevo,* ed. T. Gregory. Rome, 1985. Pp. 111–148.

Grenzmann, L. *Traumbuch Artemidori.* Baden-Baden, 1980.

Greyerz, K. von. "Spuren eines vormodernen Individualismus in englischen Selbstzeugnissen des 16. und 17. Jahrhunderts." *Ego-Dokumente: Annäherung an den Menschen in der Geschichte,* ed. W. Schulze. Berlin, 1996. Pp. 131–145.

Guglielminetti, M. *Memoria e scrittura.* Turin, 1977.

Guidorizzi, G. "L'interpretazione dei sogni nel mondo tardoantico: oralità e scrittura." *I sogni nel Medioevo,* ed. T. Gregory. Rome, 1985. Pp. 149–178.

Hadot, P. *La citadelle intérieure: Introduction aux "Pensées" de Marc-Aurèle.* Paris, 1992. = *The Inner Citadel: The Meditations of Marcus Aurelius,* tr. Michael Chase. Cambridge, Mass., 1998.

——— *Exercices spirituels et philosophie antique.* Paris, 1981.

Harkness, D. E. "Managing an Experimental Household: The Dees of Mortlake and the Practice of Natural Philosophy." *Isis,* 88 (1997), 247–262.

Headley, J. *Tommaso Campanella and the Transformation of the World.* Princeton, 1997.

Heckscher, W. *The Princeton Alciati Companion,* New York, 1989.

Hellmann, G. *Beiträge zur Geschichte der Meteorologie.* Berlin, 1904–1922.

Heninger, S. K., Jr. *The Cosmographical Glass.* San Marino, 1979.

——— *Touches of Sweet Harmony.* San Marino, 1974.

Hieronymus, F. *1448 Petri/Schwabe 1988. Eine traditionsreiche Basler Offizin im Spiegel ihrer frühen Drucke.* Basel, 1997.

Hillman, D., and C. Mazzio, ed. *The Body in Parts.* London, 1997.

Hollander, A. *Sex and Suits.* New York, 1994.

Hübner, W. "Die Rezeption des astrologischen Lehrgedichts des Manilius in der italienischen Renaissance." *Humanismus und Naturwissenschaften,* ed. R. Schmitz and F. Krafft. Boppard, 1980. Pp. 39–67.

Hunter, M. *John Aubrey and the Realm of Learning.* London, 1975.

Hutton, J. *The Greek Anthology in France and in the Latin Writers of the Netherlands to the Year 1800.* Ithaca, 1946; repr. with corrections, New York, 1967.

Ingegno, A. *Saggio sulla filosofia di Cardano.* Florence, 1980.

Jacquart, D., and C. Thomasset. *Sexuality and Medicine in the Middle Ages,* tr. M. Adamson. Princeton, 1988.

Jama, S. *La nuit de songes de René Descartes.* Paris, 1998.

Jardine, L. A., and A. T. Grafton. "'Studied for Action': How Gabriel Harvey Read His Livy." *Past & Present* 129 (1990), 30–78.

Jardine, N. *The Birth of History and Philosophy of Science.* Cambridge, 1984; repr. with corrections, 1988.

Kennedy, E. S., and D. Pingree. *The Astrological History of Masha'allah.* Cambridge, Mass., 1971.

Kessler, E., ed. *Girolamo Cardano: Philosoph, Naturforscher, Arzt.* Wiesbaden, 1994.

King, H. "Beyond the Medical Market-Place: New Directions in Ancient Medicine." *Early Science and Medicine* 2 (1997), 88–97.

Koch-Westenholz, U. *Mesopotamian Astrology: An Introduction to Babylonian and Assyrian Celestial Divination.* Copenhagen, 1995.

Koerner, J. L. *The Moment of Self-Portraiture in German Renaissance Art.* Chicago and London, 1993.

Krisher, T. "Interpretationen zum *Liber de ludo aleae,*" in *Girolamo Cardano: Philosoph, Naturforscher, Arzt,* ed. E. Kessler. Wiesbaden, 1994. Pp. 207–217.

Kristeller, P. O. *Studies in Renaissance Thought and Letters.* Rome, 1956.

Krois, J. *Cassirer, Symbolic Form, and History.* New Haven, 1987.

Kroker, E. "Nativitäten und Konstellationen aus der Reformationszeit." *Schriften des Vereins für die Geschichte Leipzigs* 6 (1900), 3–33.

Kruger, F. *Dreaming in the Middle Ages.* Cambridge, 1992.

Kurze, D. "Prophecy and History: Lichtenberger's Forecasts of Events to Come," *Journal of the Warburg and Courtauld Institutes* 21 (1958), 63–85.

Kusukawa, S. *The Transformation of Natural Philosophy: The Case of Philipp Melanchthon.* Cambridge, 1995.

Langermann, Y. "Some Astrological Themes in the Thought of Abraham Ibn Ezra." *Rabbi Abraham Ibn Ezra: Studies in the Writings of a Twelfth-Century Jewish Polymath,* ed. I. Twersky and J. M. Harris. Cambridge, Mass., and London, 1993. Pp. 28–85.

Lawn, B. *The Salernitan Questions.* Oxford, 1963.

Le Goff, J. *Time, Work, and Culture in the Middle Ages,* tr. A. Goldhammer. Chicago, 1980.

Lestringant, F. *Le cannibale.* Paris, 1994.

Lethen, H. *Verhaltenslehren der Kälte.* Frankfurt, 1994.

Lippincott, C. "Gli dei-decani del Salone dei Mesi di Palazzo Schifanoia." *Alla Corte degli estensi: Filosofia, arte e cultura a Ferrara nei secoli xv e xvi,* ed. M. Bertozzi. Ferrara, 1994. Pp. 181–197.

——— "The Iconography of the 'Salone dei Mesi' and the Study of Latin Grammar in Fifteenth-Century Ferrara." *La Corte di Ferrara e il suo mecenatismo,* ed. M. Pade et al. Copenhagen, Ferrara, and Modena, 1990.

Lloyd, G. *Magic, Reason, and Experience.* Cambridge, 1979.

Long, A. A. "Astrology: Arguments For and Against." *Science and Speculation,* ed. J. Barnes et al. Cambridge and Paris, 1982. Pp. 165–193.

Louthan, H. *The Quest for Compromise: Peacemakers in Counter-Reformation Vienna.* Cambridge, 1997.

Love, H. *Scribal Publication in Seventeenth-Century England.* Oxford, 1993.

Lubkin, G. *A Renaissance Court: Milan under Galeazzo Maria Sforza.* Berkeley, 1994.

Macdonald, M. *Mystical Bedlam.* Cambridge, 1981.

Macey, D. *The Lives of Michel Foucault.* London, 1993; repr. 1994.

Maclean, I. "Cardano and His Publishers." *Girolamo Cardano: Philosoph, Naturforscher, Arzt,* ed. E. Kessler. Wiesbaden, 1994.

——— "Foucault's Renaissance Episteme Reconsidered: An Aristotelian Counterblast." *Journal of the History of Ideas* 59 (1998), 149–166.

——— "The Interpretation of Natural Signs: Cardano's *De subtilitate* versus Scaliger's *Exercitationes.*" *Occult and Scientific Mentalities in the Renaissance,* ed. B. Vickers. Cambridge, 1984. Pp. 231–252.

Mansfield, B. *Phoenix of His Age.* Toronto and Buffalo, 1979.

Maranini, A. *Filologia fantastica.* Bologna, 1994.

Margolin, J.-C. "Rationalisme et irrationalisme dans la pensée de Jérôme Cardan." *Revue de l'Université de Bruxelles* nos. 2–3 (February-March 1969), 1–40.

Marotti, A. *Manuscript, Print, and the English Renaissance Lyric.* Ithaca, 1995.

Mascuch, M. *Origins of the Individualist Self: Autobiography and Self-Identity in England, 1591–1791.* Cambridge, 1997.

Massing, J. M. "Dürer's Dreams." *Journal of the Warburg and Courtauld Institutes* 49 (1986), 238–244.

Mayer, T. F., and D. R. Woolf. "Introduction." *The Rhetorics of Life-Writing in Early Modern Europe,* ed. T. F. Mayer and D. R. Woolf. Ann Arbor, 1995. Pp. 1–37.

McCluskey, S. C. *Astronomies and Cultures in Early Medieval Europe.* Cambridge, 1998.

McNair, P. "Poliziano's Horoscope." *Cultural Aspects of the Italian Renaissance: Essays in Honour of Paul Oskar Kristeller,* ed. C. H. Clough. Manchester and New York, 1976. Pp. 262–275.

Meli, D. B. "Shadows and Deception: From Borelli's *Theoricae* to the *Saggi* of the Cimento." *British Journal for the History of Science* 31 (1998), 383–402.

Midelfort, H. E. *Mad Princes of Renaissance Germany.* Charlottesville and London, 1994.

Milani, M. *Gerolamo Cardano.* Milan, 1990.

Millas Vallicroza, J. M. *Estudios sobre Azarquiel.* Madrid, 1950.

Minois, G. *Geschichte der Zukunft,* tr. E. Moldenhauer. Düsseldorf and Zurich, 1998. (*Histoire de l'avenir,* Paris, 1996.)

Misch, G. *Geschichte der Autobiographie.* 3d ed. 8 vols. in 4. Frankfurt, 1949–1969.

Morley, H. *Jerome Cardan: The Life of Girolamo Cardano of Milan, Physician.* 2 vols. London, 1854.

Muccillo, M. "Luca Gaurico: Astrologia e 'prisca theologia.'" *Nouvelles de la République des Lettres* 2 (1990), 21–44.

Mugnai Carrara, D. *La biblioteca di Nicolò Leoniceno.* Florence, 1991.

Müller-Jahncke, W.-D. *Astrologisch-magische Theorie und Praxis in der Heilkunde der frühen Neuzeit. Sudhoffs Archiv,* Supplement. Stuttgart, 1985.

——— "Zum Prioritätenstreit um die Metoposkopie: Hajek contra Cardano." *Sudhoffs Archiv* 66 (1982), 79–84.

Mülsow, M. *Frühneuzeitliche Selbsterhaltung. Telesio und die Naturphilosophie der Renaissance.* Tübingen, 1998.

Murray, O. Review of R. MacMullen, *Enemies of the Roman Order. Journal of Roman Studies* 59 (1969), 261–265.

Naudé, G. "De Cardano iudicium." G. Cardano, *De propria vita liber,* 2d ed. Amsterdam, 1654.

Neugebauer, O. *The Exact Sciences in Antiquity.* Providence, 1957; repr. New York, 1969.

——— "The Study of Wretched Subjects." *Isis* 42 (1951), repr. in Neugebauer, *Astronomy and History.* New York, Berlin, Heidelberg, and Tokyo, 1983. P. 3.

——— and N. Swerdlow. *Mathematical Astronomy in Copernicus's De Revolutionibus.* 2 vols. New York, Berlin, Heidelberg, and Tokyo, 1984.

——— and H. B. Van Hoesen. *Greek Horoscopes.* Philadelphia, 1959.

Niccoli, O. *Prophecy and People in Renaissance Italy,* tr. L. G. Cochrane. Princeton, 1990.

Nichols, J. G. "Some Additions to the Biographies of Sir John Cheke and Sir Thomas Smith." *Archaeologia* 38 (1859), 98–127.

North, J. "Astrology and the Fortunes of Churches." *Centaurus* 24 (1980), 181–211.

——— *Chaucer's Universe.* Oxford, 1988; repr. with corrections, 1990.

——— *Horoscopes and History.* London, 1986.

Nussbaum, M. *The Therapy of Desire.* Princeton, 1994.

Nutton, V. "Galen and Medical Autobiography." *From Democedes to Harvey: Studies in the History of Medicine.* London, 1988.

——— *John Caius and the Manuscripts of Galen.* Cambridge, 1987.

——— "'Prisci dissectionum professores': Renaissance Humanists and Anatomy." *The Uses of Greek and Latin: Historical Essays,* ed. A. C. Dionisotti et al. London, 1988.

Oberhelman, S. M. *The Oneirocriticon of Achmet.* Lubbock, Tex., 1991.

Olmi, G. *L'inventario del mondo.* Bologna, 1992.

Oppenheim, A. L. "Divination and Celestial Observation in the Last Assyrian Empire." *Centaurus* 14 (1969), 97–135.

Pagden, A., ed. *The Languages of Political Theory in Early Modern Europe.* Cambridge, 1987.

Papy, J. "Lipsius and Marcus Welser: The Antiquarian's Life as *via media.*" *Bulletin de l'Institut Historique Belge de Rome* 68 (1998), 173–190.

Parel, A. J. *The Machiavellian Cosmos.* New Haven and London, 1992.

Park, K. "Impressed Images: Reproducing Wonders." *Picturing Science, Producing Art,* ed. C. A. Jones and P. Galison. New York and London, 1998. Pp. 254–271.

Pfeiffer, H. "Girolamo Cardano and the Melancholy of Writing." *Materialities of Communication,* ed. H. U. Gumbrecht and K. L. Pfeiffer, tr. W. Whobrey. Stanford, 1994. Pp. 227–241.

Pine, M. *Pietro Pomponazzi: Radical Philosopher of the Renaissance.* Padua, 1986.

Pingree, D. *Dictionary of Scientific Biography,* s.v. Firmicus Maternus.

——— *From Astral Omens to Astrology: From Babylon to Bīkāner.* Rome, 1997.

——— *The Thousands of Abu Ma'Shar.* London, 1968.

——— ed. *Vettii Valentis Anthologiarum libri novem.* Leipzig, 1986.

——— and B. Goldstein. *Levi ben Gerson's Prognostication for the Conjunction of 1345.* Philadelphia, 1990.

Pomata, G. *La promessa di guarigione: malati e curatori in antico regime Bologna, xvi–xviii secoli.* Bari, 1994. = *Contracting a Cure,* tr. G. Pomata et al. Baltimore, 1998.

Potter, D. *Prophets and Emperors.* Cambridge, Mass., 1994.

Préaud, M. *Les astrologues à la fin du Moyen Age.* Paris, 1984.

Price, D. J. *The Equatorie of the Planetis.* Cambridge, 1955.

Price, S. F. "The Future of Dreams: From Freud to Artemidorus." *Past & Present* 113 (1986), 3–37.

Pruckner, N. *Studien zu den astrologischen Schriften von Heinrich von Langenstein.* Leipzig and Berlin, 1933.

Pyle, C. M. *Milan and Lombardy in the Renaissance: Essays in Cultural History.* Rome, 1997.

Quinlan-McGrath, M. "The Villa Farnesina, Time-telling, and Renaissance Astrological Practice." *Journal of the Warburg and Courtauld Institutes* 58 (1995), 52–71.

Reeves, M., *The Influence of Prophecy in the Later Middle Ages.* Oxford, 1969.

——— ed. *Prophetic Rome in the High Renaissance Period.* Oxford, 1992.

Reisinger, R. *Historische Horoskopie. Das Iudicium magnum des Johannes Carion für Albrecht Dürers Patenkind.* Wiesbaden, 1997.

Rochberg-Halton, F. "Babylonian Horoscopes and their Sources." *Orientalia* 58 (1989), 102–123.

——— "Elements of the Babylonian Contribution to Hellenistic Astrology." *Journal of the American Oriental Society* 108 (1988), 51–62.

——— "New Evidence for the History of Astrology." *Journal of Near Eastern Studies* 43 (1984), 115–140.

Roper, R. "Stealing Manhood: Capitalism and Magic in Early Modern Germany." *Oedipus and the Devil.* London and New York, 1994. Pp. 125–144.

Rose, P. L. *The Italian Renaissance of Mathematics.* Geneva, 1975.

Ruderman, D. B. "Giovanni Mercurio da Correggio's Appearance as Seen through the Eyes of an Italian Jew." *Renaissance Quarterly* 28 (1975), 309–322.

——— *Jewish Thought and Scientific Discovery in Early Modern Europe.* New Haven and London, 1995.

——— *Kabbalah, Magic, and Science: The Cultural Universe of a Sixteenth-Century Jewish Physician.* Cambridge, Mass., and London, 1988.

Rusconi, R. *L'attesa della fine. Crisi della società, profezia ed Apocalisse in Italia al tempo del grande scisma d'Occidente (1378–1417).* Rome, 1979.

Russell, P. A. "Astrology as Popular Propaganda: Expections of the End in the German Pamphlets of Joseph Grünpeck (d. 1533?)." *Forme e destinazione del messaggio religioso,* ed. A. Rotondò. Florence, 1991. Pp. 165–195.

Sachs, A. "Babylonian Horoscopes." *Journal of Cuneiform Studies* 6 (1952), 49–75.

Saliba, G. "The Role of the Astrologer in Medieval Islamic Society." *Bulletin d'Etudes Orientales* 44 (1992), 45–68.

Sallmann, J.-M. *Naples et ses saints à l'âge baroque (1540–1750).* Paris, 1994.

——— Review of O. Niccoli, *Prophecy and People in Renaissance Italy. Annales: Economies, Sociétés, Civilisations* 47 (1992), 144–146.

Saxl, F. "The Revival of Late Antique Astrology." *Lectures.* 2 vols. London, 1957. I, 73–84.

Schade, S. *Schadenzauber und die Magie des Körpers.* Worms, 1983.

Schottenloher, K., and J. Binkowski. *Flugblatt und Zeitung.* 2 vols. Munich, 1985.

Schuster, G. and F. Wagner. *Die Jugend und Erziehung der Kurfürsten von Brandenburg und Könige von Preussen,* vol. I. Berlin, 1906.

Schutte, A. Jacobson. *Autobiography of an Aspiring Saint.* Chicago and London, 1996.

Scott, A. *Origen and the Life of the Stars.* Oxford, 1991; repr. 1994.

Schulze, W., ed. *Ego-Dokumente: Annäherung an den Menschen in der Geschichte.* Berlin, 1996.

Screech, M. "The Magi and the Star (Matthew 2)." *Histoire de l'exégèse au xvi siècle,* ed. O. Fatio and P. Fraenkel. Geneva, 1978. Pp. 385–409.

Secret, F. "Filippo Archinto, Cardano et Guillaume Postel." *Studi francesi* 29 (1965), 173–176.

——— "Jérôme Cardan en France." *Studi francesi* 30 (1966), 480–485.

Seifert, A. *Der Rückzug der biblischen Prophetie von der neueren Geschichte: Studien zur Geschichte der Reichstheologie des frühneuzeitlichen deutschen Protestantismus.* Cologne and Vienna, 1990.

Senn, M., ed. *Die Wickiana.* Küsnacht-Zurich, 1975.

Seznec, J. *The Survival of the Pagan Gods,* tr. B. F. Sessions. New York, 1953.

Sherman, W. *John Dee.* Amherst, 1995.

Simon, G. *Kepler astronome astrologue.* Paris, 1979.

Siraisi, N. "Girolamo Cardano and the Art of Medical Narrative." *Journal of the History of Ideas* 52 (1991), 581–602.

——— *The Clock and the Mirror: Girolamo Cardano and Renaissance Medicine.* Princeton, 1997.

——— *Medieval and Early Renaissance Medicine.* Chicago and London, 1990.

——— and A. Grafton. "Between the Election and My Hopes: Girolamo Cardano and Medical Astrology." *Archimedes,* forthcoming.

Smith, R. J. *Fortune-Tellers and Philosophers: Divination in Traditional Chinese Society.* Boulder, San Francisco, and Oxford, 1991.

Smith, W. *The Hippocratic Tradition.* Ithaca and London, 1979.

Smoller, L. "The Alphonsine Tables and the End of the World: Astrology and Apocalyptic Calculation in the Later Middle Ages." *The Devil, Heresy, and Witchcraft in the Middle Ages: Essays in Honor of Jeffrey B. Russell,* ed. A. Ferreiro. Leiden, Boston, and Cologne, 1998. Pp. 211–239.

——— *History, Prophecy, and the Stars.* Princeton, 1994.

Soldati, B. *La poesia astrologica nel Quattrocento: Ricerche e studi.* Florence, 1906.

Staats, R. "Luthers Geburtsjahr 1484 und das Geburtsjahr der evangelischen Kirche 1519." *Bibliothek und Wissenschaft* 18 (1984), 61–84.

Steiner, G. "The Historicity of Dreams." *No Passion Spent: Essays, 1978–1996.* London, 1996. Pp. 207–223.

Stern, V. F. *Gabriel Harvey: His Life, Marginalia, and Library.* Oxford, 1979.

Sturrock, J. *The Language of Autobiography: Studies in the First Person Singular.* Cambridge, 1993.

Swerdlow, N. "Annals of Scientific Publishing: Johannes Petreius's Letter to Rheticus." *Isis* 83 (1992), 270–274.

——— "The Recovery of the Exact Sciences of Antiquity." *Rome Reborn,* ed. A. Grafton. Vatican City, Washington, D.C., New Haven, and London, 1993. Pp. 125–167.

Talkenberg, H. *Sintflut: Prophetie und Zeitgeschehen in Texten und Holzschnitten astrologischer Flugschriften, 1488–1528.* Tübingen, 1990.

Tateo, F. *Astrologia e moralità in Giovanni Pontano.* Bari, 1960.

Taub, L. "The Rehabilitation of Wretched Subjects." *Early Science and Medicine* 2 (1997), 74–87.

Teramoto, M. *Die Psalmmottetendrucke des Johannes Petreius in Nürnberg (gedruckt 1538–1542).* Tutzing, 1983.

Tester, S. J. *A History of Western Astrology.* Woodbridge and Wolfeboro, 1987.

Thomas, K. V. *Religion and the Decline of Magic.* New York, 1971.

Thorndike, L. *History of Magic and Experimental Science.* 8 vols. New York, 1923–1958.

Tomlinson, G. *Music in Renaissance Magic.* Chicago, 1993.

Tooley, M. J. "Bodin and the Medieval Theory of Climate." *Speculum* 28 (1953), 64–83.

Trinkaus, C. "The Astrological Cosmos and Rhetorical Culture of Giovanni Gioviano Pontano." *Renaissance Quarterly* 38 (1985), 446–472.

Vasoli, C. *I miti e gli astri.* Naples, 1977.

Vauchez, A. "Les stigmates de Saint François et leurs détracteurs dans les derniers siècles du moyen âge." *Mélanges d'Archéologie et d'Histoire* 80 (1968), 595–625.

Vianello, C. "Feste, tornei, congiure nel cinquecento milanese." *Archivio storico lombardo* n.s. 1 (1936), 370–423.

Villari, R. *Elogio della dissimulazione.* Rome, 1987.

——— *The Revolt of Naples,* tr. J. Newell with J. A. Marino. Cambridge, 1993.

Walker, D. P. *Spiritual and Demonic Magic from Ficino to Campanella.* London, 1958.

Warburg, A. *Heidnisch-Antike Weissagung in Wort und Bild zu Luthers Zeiten,* SB Akad. Heidelberg, 1919. Heidelberg, 1920; repr. in Warburg, *Gesammelte Schriften: Studienausgabe,* ed. H. Bredekamp et al. (Berlin, 1998). I, 1.2.

——— *Images from the Region of the Pueblo Indians of North America,* tr. M. Steinberg. Ithaca, 1995.

Waters, W. G. *Jerome Cardan: A Biographical Study.* London, 1898.

Webster, C. *From Paracelsus to Newton.* Cambridge, 1982; repr. 1984.

Weinstein, D. *Savonarola and Florence.* Princeton, 1970.

Weintraub, K. J. *The Value of the Individual.* Chicago, 1978.

Westman, R. "Copernicus and the Prognosticators: The Bologna Period, 1496–1500." *Universitas: Newsletter of the International Centre for the History of Universities and Science, University of Bologna,* December 1993, 1–5.

Wiesendanger, H. *Zwischen Wissenschaft und Aberglaube.* Frankfurt, 1989.

Winkler, J. *The Constraints of Desire.* New York and London, 1990.

Wintroub, M. "The Looking Glass of Facts: Collecting, Rhetoric, and Citing the Self in the Experimental Natural Philosophy of Robert Boyle." *History of Science* 35 (1997), 189–217.

Woolf, Virginia. *The Common Reader.* London, 1925.

Woudhuysen, H. R. *Sir Philip Sidney and the Circulation of Manuscripts, 1558–1640.* Oxford, 1996.

Yates, F. A. *The Art of Memory.* Chicago and London, 1966.

——— *The French Academies of the Sixteenth Century.* London, 1947; 2d ed., London and New York, 1988.

——— *Giordano Bruno and the Hermetic Tradition.* London, 1964.

Zagorin, P. *Ways of Lying.* Cambridge, Mass., 1990.

Zambelli, P. "Astrologi consiglieri del principe a Wittenberg." *Annali dell'Istituto Storico Italo-Germanico in Trento* 19 (1992), 497–543.

——— "Aut diabolus aut Achillinus. Fisionomia, astrologia e demonologia nel metodo di un aristotelico." *Rinascimento* n.s. 18 (1978), 59–86.

——— "Da Giulio II a Paolo III. Come l'astrologo provocatore Luca Gaurico divenne vescovo." *La città dei segreti,* ed. F. Troncarelli. Milan, 1985. Pp. 299–323.

——— "Der Himmel über Wittenberg: Luther, Melanchthon und andere Beobachter von Kometen." *Annali dell'Istituto Storico Italo-Germanico in Trento* 20 (1994), 39–62.

——— "Eine Gustav-Hellmann-Renaissance? Untersuchungen und Kompilationen zur Debatte über die Konjunktion von 1524 und das Ende der Welt auf deutschem Sprachgebiet." *Annali dell'Istituto Storico Italo-Germanico in Trento* 18 (1992), 413–455.

——— *L'ambigua natura della magia.* Milan, 1991; 2d ed., Venice, 1996.

——— "Many Ends for the World: Luca Gaurico, Instigator of the Debate in Italy and in Germany." *"Astrologi hallucinati": Stars and the End of the World in Luther's Time,* ed. P. Zambelli. Berlin and New York, 1986. Pp. 239–263.

——— *Una reincarnazione di Pico ai tempi di Pomponazzi.* Milan, 1994.

——— ed. *"Astrologi hallucinati": Stars and the End of the World in Luther's Time.* Berlin and New York, 1986.

Zanier, G. *Ricerche sulla diffusione e fortuna del "De incantationibus" di Pomponazzi.* Florence, 1975.

Zarri, G. *Le sante vive: cultura e religiosità femminile nella prima età moderna.* Turin, 1990.

Zimmermann, T. C. Price. "Paolo Giovio and the Rhetoric of Individuality." *The Rhetorics of Life-Writing in Early Modern Europe,* ed. T. F. Mayer and D. R. Woolf. Ann Arbor, 1995. Pp. 39–62.

Addendum

Several informative studies on Cardano—above all the collection of articles cited below—appeared too late to be taken into account in this book, but eminently deserve mention. On Cardano's autobiographical writings see now the previously unpublished recension of the *De libris propriis* edited by M. Baldi and G. Canziani, "Una quarta redazione del *De libris propriis,*" *Rivista di storia della filosofia* 53 (1998), 767–798, and the important essay by I. Maclean, "Interpreting the *De libris propriis,*" *Girolamo Cardano: le opere, le fonti, la vita,* ed. M. Baldi and G. Canziani (Milan, 1999), 13–33. For the rich material now being unearthed on Cardano's relations with the Inquisition and the Index, see U. Baldini, "Cardano negli archivi dell'Inquisizione e dell'Indice: Note su una ricerca," *Rivista di storia della filosofia* 53 (1998), 761–766. Finally, it should be noted that an English translation of G. Ernst's classic article on Cardano as an astrologer will appear in a forthcoming volume of *Archimedes.*

INDEX

Rheterus 56